EQUITY ASSET VALUATION

CFA Institute is the premier association for investment professionals around the world, with over 85,000 members in 129 countries. Since 1963 the organization has developed and administered the renowned Chartered Financial Analyst® Program. With a rich history of leading the investment profession, CFA Institute has set the highest standards in ethics, education, and professional excellence within the global investment community, and is the foremost authority on investment profession conduct and practice.

Each book in the CFA Institute Investment Series is geared toward industry practitioners along with graduate-level finance students and covers the most important topics in the industry. The authors of these cutting-edge books are themselves industry professionals and academics and bring their wealth of knowledge and expertise to this series.

EQUITY ASSET VALUATION

John D. Stowe, CFA

Thomas R. Robinson, CFA

Jerald E. Pinto, CFA

Dennis W. McLeavey, CFA

BICENTENNIAL
BICENTENNIAL
1807
WILEY
2007
BICENTENNIAL
BICENTENNIAL

John Wiley & Sons, Inc.

Library of Congress Cataloging-in-Publication Data:

Equity asset valuation / John D. Stowe . . . [et al.].
    p. cm.—(CFA Institute investment series)
  ISBN-13 978-0-470-05282-2 (cloth)
  ISBN-10 0-470-05282-1 (cloth)
 1. Investment analysis. 2. Securities—Valuation. 3. Investments—
Valuation. I. Stowe, John D.
  HG4529.E63 2006
  332.63'221—dc22

                                      2006052563

Printed in the United States of America.

10 9 8 7 6 5 4

To our friends and colleagues, brothers and sisters,
lost on 11 September 2001.

And to Adette, Doug, David, Jason, and Laura.
J.D.S.

To Linda.
T.R.R.

To the Morris Pinto family of Potsdam, New York.
J.E.P.

To my sister, Pam, and her family.
D.W.M.

CONTENTS

CHAPTER 4
Market-Based Valuation: Price Multiples   165

CHAPTER 5
Residual Income Valuation   243

FOREWORD

I was delighted when asked to write the Foreword for this important finance textbook. The title, *Equity Asset Valuation*, is clear and direct. So, too, is the content of this volume. The emphasis is on rigorous, but commonsense, approaches to investment decision making.

The writers are recognized experts in their fields of accounting, financial analysis, and investment theory. They have not written a book filled with cute catch phrases or simplistic rules of thumb. The authors have avoided histrionics and emphasized clear reasoning. Indeed, students and interested professionals will find discussions that are thorough and theoretically sound, and will help form the basis of their own education as a thoughtful investor.

I strongly believe that valuation is the most critical element of successful investment. Too often, market participants overemphasize the near-term flow of news and fail to consider whether that information, be it favorable or unfavorable, is already priced into the security. The daily commotion of the trading floor, or instant analysis based on fragmentary information, may be of interest to some. But history shows that market noise and volatility are usually distractions which impede good decision making. At their worst, they can encourage decisions that are simply wrong.

The long-term performance of financial assets is inextricably linked to their underlying value. This, in turn, is driven by the fundamental factors discussed within this book. Will the macroeconomic backdrop be supportive? Is the company well managed? What are the revenues and earnings generated by the company? How strong are the balance sheet and cash flows? Students enrolled in graduate and undergraduate courses in finance, as well as interested readers, will be taken step by step through the process of professional-level analysis.

This volume was initially conceived as a series of readings for candidates for the designation of Chartered Financial Analyst (CFA). The CFA program is administered by CFA Institute based in Charlottesville, Virginia, and with offices in Europe and Asia. Those who sit for the series of three comprehensive examinations are typically professional investors, such as analysts and portfolio managers, who have opted to hone their skills. Many already have advanced degrees and experience in the industry, yet they come to these materials seeking to improve their understanding and competence. I was one of those candidates, and am proud to hold the CFA designation. I had the pleasure of serving on the board of governors of the organization, including as chairman of the board, during the 1990s.

You might wonder why these readings should appeal to a broader audience. Why should an individual investor be interested in the nuts and bolts of security analysis? Simply stated, the responsibility for good investment decision making has increasingly shifted toward the individual. There are many factors involved, including the rising wealth of some households, and the desire to ensure that the financial assets are properly managed. But the most compelling element has been the ongoing structural change in the approach to retirement funding.

In recent years, many employers have limited the defined-benefit (DB) pension programs that had become the standard in the United States and other developed economies. Under these DB programs, employers have the obligation to provide a defined level of benefits to their retired workers, and the employers assumed the fiduciary responsibility of managing the pension funds to generate good returns on the plans' financial assets. These employers run the gamut, from major corporations to government agencies to small entities.

There has been a seismic shift away from defined benefits programs to defined contribution (DC) plans in which employers contribute to each worker's retirement account but do not manage the funds. Today, individual workers are increasingly encouraged to invest for their own future through DC programs such as those dubbed 401(k), named after a section of the U.S. federal tax code, and Individual Retirement Accounts (IRAs). In these plans, the individual has the ultimate responsibility to manage those funds. Unhappily, early data on this do not bode well. Annual returns are below those achieved by DB plans, and many workers do not maximize their own contributions to their own accounts. It would appear that many workers are not well prepared to make the decisions that will allow for a comfortable retirement in the years ahead.

A major challenge lies ahead. Individuals must prepare to make suitable decisions regarding their savings and investments. The financial literacy of Americans, and individuals in other developed economies, has improved in recent years but still falls short of what will be needed. Much of the media coverage emphasizes the short-term movements and news flow in financial markets, not the basics of investment analysis.

Consumers of this book, students, and lay readers alike will develop a keen appreciation for the various ways in which companies and their securities can be analyzed. By the end of the first chapter, readers will gain useful insight into the role of professional analysts, the challenges and limitations of their work, and most importantly, the critical role played by the performance of the underlying companies in the ultimate performance of stocks and related securities.

The subsequent chapters delve further into the details. You will find well-constructed descriptions of several approaches to valuation, including those based on earnings, dividends, revenues, and cash flows. Sophisticated methodologies based on enterprise value, residual income, and internal returns, are also presented as part of the continuum of possible approaches.

Of particular importance for the classroom setting, there are comprehensive discussions, and numerous examples to work through. These exercises will help ensure that students of finance understand more than the mechanics of the calculations. They also illustrate situations in which different techniques are best used or, alternatively, may have serious limitations. This latter aspect, understanding the potential shortcomings of an approach to investing, is essential.

Too many investors, both professional and individual, fail to recognize when the simple arithmetic of investing may be misleading. For example, a price-to-earnings (P/E) ratio of a stock may be interpreted quite differently depending on whether prevailing inflation and interest rates are high or low. Similarly, the industry in which the underlying company does most of its business, or the volatility of its earnings flow, can also affect whether the P/E ratio is signaling attractive valuation or an overpriced security.

The authors offer useful guidelines to the most appropriate methodologies to use under differing circumstances. After all, investing options now include several categories of financial assets, and the globalization of capital flows means that there is literally a world of possible investments.

The lessons contained in the textbook apply to far more than publicly traded equities. In the past decade, there has been a surge of financial flows into less traditional asset categories. These include private equity, venture capital, derivatives, structured fixed income, and a host of other alternatives all of which still pose the central question to investors: How should this investment opportunity be priced? The authors provide appropriate techniques and the concepts behind them, within these covers.

But this is not to suggest that this text can be followed, like a cookbook, without thought or adjustment. With many timely insights, the authors have endeavored to explain what adjustments might be necessary, and what pitfalls might be found in each methodology. A common concern is the quality of accounting data provided on a company's performance. Another concern is accuracy of economic data provided by government agencies. Even when there has been no attempt to deceive, data can be misleading or subject to revision, calling into question the conclusions which were originally derived.

There are no certainties in investing. I strongly suggest, however, that a disciplined approach can dramatically improve the likelihood of long-term success. History has borne this out repeatedly. This textbook, along with others in this series, offers a sturdy foundation for increasing the likelihood of making good investment decisions on a consistent basis.

ABBY JOSEPH COHEN, CFA
New York City

ACKNOWLEDGMENTS

We would like to acknowledge the assistance of many individuals who played a role in producing this book.

Robert R. Johnson, CFA, Managing Director of CFA and CIPM Programs at CFA Institute, saw the need for specialized curriculum materials and initiated this project. Jan R. Squires, CFA, contributed an orientation stressing motivation and testability. His ideas, suggestions, and chapter reviews have helped to shape the project. Philip J. Young, CFA, provided a great deal of assistance with learning outcome statements. Mary K. Erickson, CFA, provided chapter reviews with a concentration in accounting. Donald L. Tuttle, CFA, oversaw the entire job analysis project and provided invaluable guidance on what the generalist needs to know.

The Executive Advisory Board of the Candidate Curriculum Committee provided invaluable input: Chair, Peter B. Mackey, CFA, and members James W. Bronson, CFA, Alan M. Meder, CFA, and Matthew H. Scanlan, CFA, as well as the Candidate Curriculum Committee Working Body.

Detailed manuscript reviews were provided by Michelle R. Clayman, CFA, John H. Crockett, Jr., CFA, Thomas J. Franckowiak, CFA, Richard D. Frizell, CFA, Jacques R. Gagne, CFA, Mark E. Henning, CFA, Bradley J. Herndon, CFA, Joanne L. Infantino, CFA, Muhammad J. Iqbal, CFA, Robert N. MacGovern, CFA, Farhan Mahmood, CFA, Richard K. C. Mak, CFA, Edgar A. Norton, CFA, William L. Randolph, CFA, Raymond D. Rath, CFA, Teoh Kok Lin, CFA, Lisa R. Weiss, CFA, and Yap Teong Keat, CFA.

Detailed proofreading was performed by Dorothy C. Kelly, CFA, and Gregory M. Noronha, CFA. Copy editing was done by Fiona Russell.

Wanda Lauziere, of CFA Institute, served as project manager and guided the book through production.

INTRODUCTION

CFA Institute is pleased to provide you with this Investment Series covering major areas in the field of investments. These texts are thoroughly grounded in the highly regarded CFA Program Candidate Body of Knowledge (CBOK®) that draws upon hundreds of practicing investment professionals and serves as the anchor for the three levels of the CFA Examinations. In the year this series is being launched, more than 120,000 aspiring investment professionals will each devote over 250 hours of study to master this material as well as other elements of the Candidate Body of Knowledge in order to obtain the coveted CFA charter. We provide these materials for the same reason we have been chartering investment professionals for over 40 years: to improve the competency and ethical character of those serving the capital markets.

PARENTAGE

One of the valuable attributes of this series derives from its parentage. In the 1940s, a handful of societies had risen to form communities that revolved around common interests and work in what we now think of as the investment industry.

Understand that the idea of purchasing common stock as an investment—as opposed to casino speculation—was only a couple of decades old at most. We were only 10 years past the creation of the U.S. Securities and Exchange Commission and laws that attempted to level the playing field after robber baron and stock market panic episodes.

In January 1945, in what is today CFA Institute *Financial Analysts Journal*, a fundamentally driven professor and practitioner from Columbia University and Graham-Newman Corporation wrote an article making the case that people who research and manage portfolios should have some sort of credential to demonstrate competence and ethical behavior. This person was none other than Benjamin Graham, the father of security analysis and future mentor to a well-known modern investor, Warren Buffett.

The idea of creating a credential took a mere 16 years to drive to execution but by 1963, 284 brave souls, all over the age of 45, took an exam and launched the CFA credential. What many do not fully understand was that this effort had at its root a desire to create a profession where its practitioners were professionals who provided investing services to individuals in need. In so doing, a fairer and more productive capital market would result.

A profession—whether it be medicine, law, or other—has certain hallmark characteristics. These characteristics are part of what attracts serious individuals to devote the energy of their life's work to the investment endeavor. First, and tightly connected to this Series, there must be a body of knowledge. Second, there needs to be some entry requirements such as those required to achieve the CFA credential. Third, there must be a commitment to education at many levels. Fourth, a profession must serve a purpose beyond one's direct selfish interest. In this case, by properly conducting one's affairs and putting client interests first, the investment professional can work as a fair-minded cog in the wheel of the incredibly productive global capital markets. This encourages the citizenry to part with their hard-earned savings to be redeployed in fair and productive pursuit.

As C. Stewart Sheppard, founding executive director of the Institute of Chartered Financial Analysts said, "Society demands more from a profession and its members than it does from a professional craftsman in trade, arts, or business. In return for status, prestige, and autonomy, a profession extends a public warranty that it has established and maintains conditions of entry, standards of fair practice, disciplinary procedures, and continuing education for its particular constituency. Much is expected from members of a profession, but over time, more is given."

"The Standards for Educational and Psychological Testing," put forth by the American Psychological Association, the American Educational Research Association, and the National Council on Measurement in Education, state that the validity of professional credentialing examinations should be demonstrated primarily by verifying that the content of the examination accurately represents professional practice. In addition, a practice analysis study, which confirms the knowledge and skills required for the competent professional, should be the basis for establishing content validity.

For more than 40 years, hundreds upon hundreds of practitioners and academics have served on CFA Institute curriculum committees sifting through and winnowing all the many investment concepts and ideas to create a body of knowledge and the CFA curriculum. One of the hallmarks of curriculum development at CFA Institute is its extensive use of practitioners in all phases of the process.

CFA Institute has followed a formal practice analysis process since 1995. The effort involves special practice analysis forums held, most recently, at 20 locations around the world. Results of the forums were put forth to 70,000 CFA charterholders for verification and confirmation of the body of knowledge so derived.

What this means for the reader is that the concepts contained in these texts were driven by practicing professionals in the field who understand the responsibilities and knowledge that practitioners in the industry need to be successful. We are pleased to put this extensive effort to work for the benefit of the readers of the Investment Series.

BENEFITS

This series will prove useful both to the undergraduate student of capital markets, who is seriously contemplating entry into the extremely competitive field of investment management, and to the more seasoned professional who is looking for a user-friendly way to keep one's knowledge current. All chapters include extensive references for those who would like to dig deeper into a given concept, and this particular book includes end of chapter questions for students. The other titles in the series include workbooks that provide a summary of each chapter's key points to help organize your thoughts, as well as sample questions and answers to test yourself on your progress.

For the new student, the essential concepts that any investment professional needs to master are presented in a time-tested fashion. This material, in addition to ongoing university study and reading the financial press, will help future professionals better understand the investment field. I believe that the general public seriously underestimates the disciplined processes needed for the best investment firms and individuals to prosper. These texts lay the basic groundwork for many of the processes that successful firms use. Without this base level of understanding and an appreciation for how the capital markets work to properly price securities, you may not find competitive success. Furthermore, the concepts herein give a genuine sense of the kind of work that is to be found day to day managing portfolios, doing research, or related endeavors.

The investment profession, despite its relatively lucrative compensation, is not for everyone. It takes a special kind of individual to fundamentally understand and absorb the teachings from this body of work and then convert that into application in the practitioner world. In fact, most individuals who enter the field do not survive in the longer run. The aspiring professional should think long and hard about whether this is the field for him or herself. There is no better way to make such a critical decision than to be prepared by reading and evaluating the gospel of the profession.

The more experienced professional understands that the nature of the capital markets requires a commitment to continuous learning. Markets evolve as quickly as smart minds can find new ways to create an exposure, to attract capital, or to manage risk. A number of the concepts in these pages were not present a decade or two ago when many of us were starting out in the business. Hedge funds, derivatives, alternative investment concepts, and behavioral finance are examples of new applications and concepts that have altered the capital markets in recent years. As markets invent and reinvent themselves, a best-in-class foundation investment series is of great value.

Those of us who have been at this business for a while know that we must continuously hone our skills and knowledge if we are to compete with the young talent that constantly emerges. In fact, as we talk to major employers about their training needs, we are often told that one of the biggest challenges they face is how to help the experienced professional, laboring under heavy time pressure, keep up with the state of the art and the more recently educated associates. This series can be part of that answer.

CONVENTIONAL WISDOM

It doesn't take long for the astute investment professional to realize two common characteristics of markets. First, prices are set by conventional wisdom, or a function of the many variables in the market. Truth in markets is, at its essence, what the market believes it is and how it assesses pricing credits or debits on those beliefs. Second, as conventional wisdom is a product of the evolution of general theory and learning, by definition conventional wisdom is often wrong or at the least subject to material change.

When I first entered this industry in the mid-1970s, conventional wisdom held that the concepts examined in these texts were a bit too academic to be heavily employed in the competitive marketplace. Many of those considered to be the best investment firms at the time were led by men who had an eclectic style, an intuitive sense of markets, and a great track record. In the rough-and-tumble world of the practitioner, some of these concepts were considered to be of no use. Could conventional wisdom have been more wrong? If so, I'm not sure when.

During the years of my tenure in the profession, the practitioner investment management firms that evolved successfully were full of determined, intelligent, intellectually curious investment professionals who endeavored to apply these concepts in a serious and disciplined manner. Today, the best firms are run by those who carefully form investment hypotheses and test them rigorously in the marketplace, whether it be in a quant strategy, in comparative shopping for stocks within an industry, or in many hedge fund strategies. Their goal is to create investment processes that can be replicated with some statistical reliability. I believe those who embraced the so-called academic side of the learning equation have been much more successful as real-world investment managers.

THE TEXTS

Approximately 35 percent of the Candidate Body of Knowledge is represented in the initial four texts of the series. Additional texts on corporate finance and international financial statement analysis are in development, and more topics may be forthcoming.

One of the most prominent texts over the years in the investment management industry has been Maginn and Tuttle's *Managing Investment Portfolios: A Dynamic Process*. The third edition updates key concepts from the 1990 second edition. Some of the more experienced members of our community, like myself, own the prior two editions and will add this to our library. Not only does this tome take the concepts from the other readings and put them in a portfolio context, it also updates the concepts of alternative investments, performance presentation standards, portfolio execution and, very importantly, managing individual investor portfolios. To direct attention, long focused on institutional portfolios, toward the individual will make this edition an important improvement over the past.

Quantitative Investment Analysis focuses on offering students some key tools that are needed for today's professional investor. In addition to presenting the classic concepts of time value of money, discounted cash flow applications, and probability material, there are two aspects that can be of value over traditional thinking.

First are the chapters dealing with correlation and regression that ultimately figure into the formation of hypotheses for purposes of testing. This gets to a critical skill that many professionals are challenged by: the ability to sift out the wheat from the chaff. For most investment researchers and managers, their analysis is not solely the result of newly created data and tests that they perform. Rather, they synthesize and analyze primary research done by others. Without a rigorous manner by which to understand quality research, not only can you not understand good research, you really have no basis by which to evaluate less rigorous research. What is often put forth in the applied world as good quantitative research lacks rigor and validity.

Second, the last chapter on portfolio concepts moves the reader beyond the traditional capital asset pricing model (CAPM) type of tools and into the more practical world of multifactor models and to arbitrage pricing theory. Many have felt that there has been a CAPM bias to the work put forth in the past, and this chapter helps move beyond that point.

Equity Asset Valuation is a particularly cogent and important read for anyone involved in estimating the value of securities and understanding security pricing. A well-informed professional would know that the common forms of equity valuation—dividend discount modeling, free cash flow modeling, price/earnings models, and residual income models (often known by trade names)—can all be reconciled to one another under certain assumptions. With a deep understanding of the underlying assumptions, the professional investor can better understand what other investors assume when calculating their valuation estimates. In my prior life as the head of an equity investment team, this knowledge would give us an edge over other investors.

Fixed Income Analysis has been at the frontier of new concepts in recent years, greatly expanding horizons over the past. This text is probably the one with the most new material for the seasoned professional who is not a fixed-income specialist. The application of option and derivative technology to the once staid province of fixed income has helped contribute to an explosion of thought in this area. And not only does that challenge the professional to stay up to speed with credit derivatives, swaptions, collateralized mortgage securities, mortgage backs, and others, but it also puts a strain on the world's central banks to provide oversight and the risk of a correlated event. Armed with a thorough grasp of the new exposures, the professional investor is much better able to anticipate and understand the challenges our central bankers and markets face.

I hope you find this new series helpful in your efforts to grow your investment knowledge, whether you are a relatively new entrant or a grizzled veteran ethically bound to keep up to date in the ever-changing market environment. CFA Institute, as a long-term committed participant of the investment profession and a not-for-profit association, is pleased to give you this opportunity.

JEFF DIERMEIER, CFA
President and Chief Executive Officer
CFA Institute
September 2006

EQUITY ASSET VALUATION

CHAPTER 1

THE EQUITY VALUATION PROCESS

LEARNING OUTCOMES

After completing this chapter, you will be able to do the following:

- Define valuation.
- Discuss the uses of valuation models.
- Discuss the importance of expectations in the use of valuation models.
- Explain the role of valuation in portfolio management.
- Discuss the steps in the valuation process, and the objectives and tasks within each step.
- Discuss the elements of a competitive analysis for a company.
- Contrast top-down and bottom-up approaches to economic forecasting.
- Contrast quantitative and qualitative factors in valuation.
- Discuss the importance of quality of earnings analysis in financial forecasting and identify the sources of information for such analysis.
- Describe quality of earnings indicators and risk factors.
- Define intrinsic value.
- Define and calculate alpha.
- Explain the relationship between alpha and perceived mispricing.
- Discuss the use of valuation models within the context of traditional and modern concepts of market efficiency.
- Contrast the going-concern concept of value to the concept of liquidation value.
- Define fair value.
- Contrast absolute and relative valuation models, and describe examples of each type of model.
- Explain the broad criteria for choosing an appropriate approach for valuing a particular company.
- Discuss the role of ownership perspective in valuation.
- Explain the role of analysts in capital markets.
- Discuss the contents and format of an effective research report.
- Explain the responsibilities of analysts in performing valuations and communicating valuation results.

1. INTRODUCTION

Every day thousands of participants in the investment profession—investors, portfolio managers, regulators, researchers—face a common and often perplexing question: What is the value of a particular asset? The answers to this question usually determine success or failure in achieving investment objectives. For one group of those participants—equity analysts—the question and its potential answers are particularly critical, for determining the value of an ownership stake is at the heart of their professional activities and decisions. To determine value received for money paid, to determine relative value—the prospective differences in risk-adjusted return offered by different stocks at current market prices—the analyst must engage in valuation. **Valuation** is the estimation of an asset's value based either on variables perceived to be related to future investment returns or on comparisons with similar assets. Skill in valuation is one very important element of success in investing.

Benjamin Graham and David L. Dodd's *Security Analysis* (1934) represented the first major attempt to organize knowledge in this area for the investment profession. Its first sentence reads: "This book is intended for all those who have a serious interest in security values." *Equity Asset Valuation* addresses candidates in the Chartered Financial Analyst (CFA®) Program of CFA Institute; all readers, however, with a "serious interest in security values" should find the book useful. Drawing on knowledge of current professional practice as well as both academic and investment industry research in finance and accounting, this book presents the major concepts and tools that analysts use in conducting valuations and communicating the results of their analysis to clients.

In this introductory chapter we address some basic questions: "What is equity valuation?" "Who performs equity valuation?" "What is the importance of industry knowledge?" and "How can the analyst effectively communicate his analysis?" This chapter answers these and other questions and lays a foundation for the remaining four chapters of the book. In Chapter 2, we examine the fundamentals of models that view a common stock's value as the present value of its expected future cash flows or returns. We then present in detail the simplest group of such models, dividend discount models. In Chapter 3, we focus entirely on free cash flow models, a popular group of models that define cash flows differently than dividend discount models. In Chapter 4, we turn to a very important group of valuation tools, price multiples, which relate stock price to some measure of value per share such as earnings. The final chapter of the book returns to a present value approach using a third major definition of return, residual income.[1]

The balance of this chapter is organized as follows: Section 2 surveys the scope of equity valuation within the overall context of the portfolio management process. In various places in this book, we will discuss how to select an appropriate valuation approach given a security's characteristics. In Section 3, we address valuation concepts and models and examine the first three steps in the valuation process—understanding the company, forecasting company performance, and selecting the appropriate valuation model. Section 4 discusses the analyst's role and responsibilities in researching and recommending a security for purchase or sale. Section 5 discusses the content and format of an effective research report—the analyst's work in valuation is generally not complete until he communicates the results of his analysis—and

---

[1]We will define all of these terms in subsequent chapters.

highlights the analyst's responsibilities in preparing research reports. Section 6 summarizes the chapter.

2. THE SCOPE OF EQUITY VALUATION

Investment analysts work in a wide variety of organizations and positions; as a result, they find themselves applying the tools of equity valuation to address a range of practical problems. In particular, analysts use valuation concepts and models to accomplish the following:

- **Selecting stocks.** Stock selection is the primary use of the tools presented in this book. Equity analysts must continually address the same question for every common stock[2] that is either a current or prospective portfolio holding, or for every stock that he or she is professionally assigned to analyze: Is this a security my clients should purchase, sell, or continue to own? Equity analysts attempt to identify securities as fairly valued, overvalued, or undervalued, relative to either their own market price or the prices of comparable securities.
- **Inferring (extracting) market expectations.** Market prices reflect the expectations of investors about the future prospects of companies. Analysts may ask, what expectations about a company's future performance are consistent with the current market price for that company's stock? This question may concern the analyst for several reasons:
  - There are historical and economic reasons that certain values for earnings growth rates and other company fundamentals may or may not be reasonable. (**Fundamentals** are characteristics of a company related to profitability, financial strength, or risk.)
  - The extracted expectation for a fundamental characteristic may be useful as a benchmark or comparison value of the same characteristic for another company.[3]
- **Evaluating corporate events.** Investment bankers, corporate analysts, and investment analysts use valuation tools to assess the impact of corporate events such as mergers, acquisitions, divestitures, spin-offs, management buyouts (MBOs), and leveraged recapitalizations.[4] Each of these events may affect a company's future cash flows and so the value of equity. Furthermore, in mergers and acquisitions, the company's own common stock is

---

[2]In the United Kingdom, *ordinary share* is the term corresponding to *common stock* (for short, *share* or *stock*)—the ownership interest in a corporation that represents the residual claim on the corporation's assets and earnings.

[3]To extract or reverse-engineer a market expectation, the analyst must specify a model that relates market price to expectations about fundamentals, and calculate or assume values for all fundamentals except the one of interest. Then the analyst calculates the value of the remaining fundamental that calibrates the model value to market price (makes the model value equal market price)—this value is the extracted market expectation for the variable. Of course, the model that the analyst uses must be appropriate for the characteristics of the stock.

[4]A **merger** is the combination of two corporations. An **acquisition** is also a combination of two corporations, usually with the connotation that the combination is not one of equals. In a **divestiture**, a corporation sells some major component of its business. In a **spin-off**, the corporation separates off and separately capitalizes a component business, which is then transferred to the corporation's common stockholders. In an **MBO**, management repurchases all outstanding stock, usually using the proceeds of debt issuance; in a **leveraged recapitalization**, some stock remains in the hands of the public.

often used as currency for the purchase; investors then want to know whether the stock is fairly valued.

- **Rendering fairness opinions**. The parties to a merger may be required to seek a fairness opinion on the terms of the merger from a third party such as an investment bank. Valuation is at the center of such opinions.
- **Evaluating business strategies and models**. Companies concerned with maximizing shareholder value must evaluate the impact of alternative strategies on share value.
- **Communicating with analysts and shareholders**. Valuation concepts facilitate communication and discussion among company management, shareholders, and analysts on a range of corporate issues affecting company value.
- **Appraising private businesses**. Although this book focuses on publicly traded companies, another important use of the tools we present is to value the common stock of private companies. The stock of private companies by definition does not trade publicly; consequently, we cannot compare an estimate of the stock's value with a market price. For this and other reasons, the valuation of private companies has special characteristics. The analyst encounters these challenges in evaluating initial public offerings (IPOs), for example.[5]

EXAMPLE 1-1   Inferring Market Expectations

On September 21, 2000, Intel Corporation (Nasdaq NMS: INTC)[6] issued a press release containing information about its expected revenue growth for the third quarter of 2000. The announced growth fell short of the company's own prior prediction by 2 to 4 percentage points and short of analysts' projections by 3 to 7 percentage points. In response to the announcement, Intel's stock price fell nearly 30 percent during the following five days.

Was the information in Intel's announcement sufficient to explain a loss of value of that magnitude? Cornell (2001) examined this question using a valuation approach that models the value of a company's equity as the present value of expected future cash flows from operations minus the expenditures needed to maintain the company's growth. (We will discuss such *free cash flow models* in detail in Chapter 3.) What future revenue growth rates were consistent with Intel's stock price of $61.50 just prior to the press release, and $43.31 only five days later?

---

[5]An **initial public offering** is the initial issuance of common stock registered for public trading by a formerly private corporation. Later in this chapter, we mention one issue related to valuing private companies, marketability discounts.

[6]In this book, the shares of real companies are identified by an abbreviation for the stock exchange or electronic marketplace where the shares of the company are traded, followed by a ticker symbol or formal acronym for the shares. For example, Nasdaq NMS stands for "Nasdaq National Market System," an electronic marketplace in the United States managed by the National Association of Securities Dealers, Inc., and INTC is the ticker symbol for Intel Corporation on the Nasdaq NMS. (Many stocks are traded on a number of exchanges worldwide, and some stocks may have more than one formal acronym; we usually state just one marketplace and one ticker symbol.) For fictional companies we do not give the marketplace, but we often give the stock an acronym by which we can refer to it.

Using a conservatively low discount rate, Cornell estimated that the price of $61.50 was consistent with a growth rate of 20 percent a year for the subsequent 10 years (and then 6 percent per year thereafter). The price of $43.31 was consistent with a decline of the 10-year growth rate to well under 15 percent per year. In the final year of the forecast horizon (2009), projected revenues with the lower growth rate would be $50 billion below the projected revenues based on the pre-announcement price. Because the press release did not obviously point to any changes in Intel's fundamental long-run business conditions (Intel attributed the quarterly revenue growth shortfall to a cyclical slowing of demand in Europe), Cornell's detailed analysis left him skeptical that the stock market's reaction could be explained in terms of fundamentals.

Was investors' reaction to the press release therefore irrational? That was one possible interpretation. Cornell also concluded, however, that Intel's stock was overvalued prior to the press release. For example, the 20 percent revenue growth rate consistent with the pre-announcement stock price was much higher than Intel's growth rate averaged over the previous five years when the company was much smaller. Cornell viewed the press release as "a kind of catalyst which caused movement toward a more rational price, even though the release itself did not contain sufficient long-run valuation information to justify that movement."[7] Analysts can perform the same type of analysis as Cornell did. Exercises of this type are very useful for forming a judgment on the reasonableness of market prices. It is also noteworthy that Cornell found much lacking in the valuation discussions in the 28 contemporaneous analysts' reports on Intel that he examined. Although all reports made buy or sell recommendations, he characterized their discussions of fundamental value as "typically vague and nebulous."[8] To the extent Cornell's assessment was accurate, the reports would not meet the criteria for an effective research report that we present later in this chapter.

2.1. Valuation and Portfolio Management

Although valuation can take place without reference to a portfolio, the analysis of equity investments is conducted within the context of managing a portfolio. We can better appreciate the scope of valuation when we recognize valuation as a part of the overall portfolio management process. An investor's most basic concern is generally not the characteristics of a single security but the risk and return prospects of his or her total investment position. How does valuation, focused on a single security, fit into this process?

From a portfolio perspective, the investment process has three steps: *planning, execution*, and *feedback* (which includes *evaluating* whether objectives have been achieved, and *monitoring and rebalancing* of positions). Valuation, including equity valuation, is most closely associated with the planning and execution steps.

- **Planning**. In the planning step, the investor identifies and specifies **investment objectives** (desired investment outcomes relating to both risk and return) and **constraints** (internal or external limitations on investment actions). An important part of planning is the concrete

---

[7] Cornell (2001, p. 134).
[8] Cornell (2001, p. 131).

elaboration of an **investment strategy**, or approach to investment analysis and security selection, with the goal of organizing and clarifying investment decisions.

Not all investment strategies involve making valuation judgments about individual securities. For example, in indexing strategies, the investor seeks only to replicate the returns of an externally specified index—such as the Financial Times Stock Exchange (FTSE) Eurotop 300, which is an index of Europe's 300 largest companies. Such an investor could simply buy and hold those 300 stocks in index proportions, without the need to analyze individual stocks.

Valuation, however, is relevant, and critical, to active investment strategies. To understand active management, it is useful to introduce the concept of a **benchmark**—the comparison portfolio used to evaluate performance—which for an index manager is the index itself. **Active investment managers** hold portfolios that differ from the benchmark in an attempt to produce superior risk-adjusted returns. Securities held in different-from-benchmark weights reflect expectations that differ from consensus expectations (**differential expectations**). The manager must also translate expectations into value estimates, so that securities can be ranked from relatively most attractive to relatively least attractive. This step requires valuation models. In the planning phase, the active investor may specify quite narrowly the kinds of active strategies to be used and also specify in detail valuation models and/or criteria.

- **Execution.** In the execution step, the manager integrates investment strategies with expectations to select a portfolio (the **portfolio selection/composition decision**), and portfolio decisions are implemented by trading desks (the **portfolio implementation decision**).

3. VALUATION CONCEPTS AND MODELS

In Section 3, we turn our attention to the valuation process. This process includes understanding the company to be valued, forecasting the company's performance, and selecting the appropriate valuation model for a given valuation task.

3.1. The Valuation Process

We have seen that the valuation of a particular company is a task within the context of the portfolio management process. Each individual valuation that an analyst undertakes can be viewed as a process with the following five steps:

1. *Understanding the business.* This involves evaluating industry prospects, competitive position, and corporate strategies. Analysts use this information together with financial statement analysis to forecast performance.
2. *Forecasting company performance.* Forecasts of sales, earnings, and financial position (pro forma analysis) are the immediate inputs to estimating value.
3. *Selecting the appropriate valuation model.*
4. *Converting forecasts to a valuation.*
5. *Making the investment decision (recommendation).*

The fourth and fifth steps are addressed in detail in the succeeding chapters of this book. Here we focus on the first three steps. Because common stock represents the ownership interest in a company, analysts must carefully research the company before making a recommendation about the company's stock.

An in-depth understanding of the business and an ability to forecast the performance of a company help determine the quality of an analyst's valuation efforts.

3.2. Understanding the Business

Understanding a company's economic and industry context and management's strategic responses are the first tasks in understanding that company. Because similar economic and technological factors typically affect all companies in an industry, industry knowledge helps analysts understand the basic characteristics of the markets served by a company and the economics of the company. An airline industry analyst will know that jet fuel costs are the second biggest expense for airlines behind labor expenses, and that in many markets airlines have difficulty passing through higher fuel prices by raising ticket prices. Using this knowledge, the analyst may inquire about the degree to which different airlines hedge the commodity price risk inherent in jet fuel costs. With such information in hand, the analyst is better able to evaluate risk and forecast future cash flows. Hooke (1998) discussed a broad framework for industry analysis.

An analyst conducting an industry analysis must also judge management's strategic choices to better understand a company's prospects for success in competition with other companies in the industry or industries in which that company operates. Porter (1998) may lead analysts to focus on the following questions:

1. *How attractive are the industries in which the company operates, in terms of offering prospects for sustained profitability?* Inherent industry profitability is one important factor in determining a company's profitability. Analysts should try to understand **industry structure**—the industry's underlying economic and technical characteristics—and the trends affecting that structure. Analysts must also stay current on facts and news concerning all the industries in which the company operates, including the following:

   - industry size and growth over time,
   - recent developments (management, technological, financial) in the industry,
   - overall supply and demand balance,
   - subsector strength/softness in the demand–supply balance, and
   - qualitative factors, including the legal and regulatory environment.

2. *What is the company's relative competitive position within its industry?* Among factors to consider are the level and trend of the company's market share in the markets in which it operates.

3. *What is the company's competitive strategy?* Three general corporate strategies for achieving above-average performance are

   - **cost leadership**—being the lowest cost producer while offering products comparable to those of other companies, so that products can be priced at or near the industry average;

- **differentiation**—offering unique products or services along some dimensions that are widely valued by buyers so that the company can command premium prices; and
- **focus**—seeking a competitive advantage within a target segment or segments of the industry, based on either cost leadership (**cost focus**) or differentiation (**differentiation focus**).

The analyst can assess whether a company's apparent strategy is logical or faulty only in the context of thorough knowledge of the company's industry or industries.

4. *How well is the company executing its strategy?* Competitive success requires not only appropriate strategic choices, but also competent execution.

One perspective on the above issues often comes from the companies themselves in regulatory filings, which analysts can compare with their own independent research.[9]

EXAMPLE 1-2   Competitive Analysis

Veritas DGC Inc. (NYSE: VTS) is a provider of seismic data—two- or three-dimensional views of the earth's subsurface—and related geophysical services to the natural gas and crude oil (petroleum) industry. Oil and gas drillers purchase such information to increase drilling success rates and so lower overall exploration costs.

According to Standard & Poor's Corporation, VTS's peer group is "Oil & Gas—Geophysical Data Technologies" in Oil & Gas Equipment and Services. Competitors include WesternGeco, a joint venture of Schlumberger Ltd. (NYSE: SLB) and Baker Hughes Inc. (NYSE: BHI); Petroleum Geo-Services (NYSE: PGO), which in late 2001 announced plans to merge with VTS; Dawson Geophysical (Nasdaq NMS: DWSN); Compagnie Générale de Géophysique (NYSE: GGY); and Seitel, Inc. (NYSE: SEI).

1. Discuss the economic factors that may affect demand for the services provided by VTS and its competitors, and explain a logical framework for analyzing and forecasting revenue for these companies.
2. Explain how comparing the level and trend in profit margin (net income/sales) and revenue per employee for the above companies may help in evaluating whether one of these companies is the cost leader in the peer group.

Solution to 1: Because VTS provides services related to oil and gas exploration, the level of exploration activities by oil and gas producers is probably the major factor determining the demand for VTS's services. In turn, the prices of natural gas and crude oil are critical in determining the level of exploration activities. Therefore, among other economic factors, an analyst should research those relating to supply and demand for natural gas and crude oil.

---

[9]For example, companies filing Form 10-Ks with the U.S. Securities and Exchange Commission identify legal and regulatory issues and competitive factors and risks.

- **Supply factors in natural gas.** Factors include natural gas inventory levels. Energy analysts should be familiar with sources for researching this information, such as the American Gas Association (AGA) for gas inventory levels in the United States.
- **Demand factors in natural gas.** These factors include household and commercial use of natural gas and the amount of new power generation equipment being fired by natural gas.
- **Supply factors in crude oil.** Factors include capacity constraints and production levels in OPEC and other oil-producing countries. Analysts should be familiar with sources such as the American Petroleum Institute for researching these factors.
- **Demand factors in crude oil.** Factors include household and commercial use of oil and the amount of new power generation equipment using oil products as its primary fuel.

For both crude oil and natural gas, projected economic growth rates could be examined as a demand factor and depletion rates as a supply side factor.

Solution to 2:   Profit margin reflects cost structure; in interpreting profit margin, however, analysts should evaluate any differences in companies' abilities to affect profit margin through power over price. A successfully executed cost leadership strategy will lower costs and raise profit margins. All else equal, we would also expect a cost leader to have relatively high sales per employee, reflecting efficient use of human resources.

3.3. Forecasting Company Performance

The second step in the valuation process—forecasting company performance—can be viewed from two perspectives: the economic environment in which the company operates and the company's own financial characteristics.

3.3.1. Economic Forecasting

Industry analysis and competitive analysis take place within the larger context of macroeconomic analysis. As an approach to forecasting, moving from the international and national macroeconomic forecasts to industry forecasts and then to individual company and asset forecasts is known as a **top-down forecasting approach**. For example, Benninga and Sarig (1997) illustrated how, starting with forecasts of the level of macroeconomic activity, an analyst might project overall industry sales and the market share of a company within the industry to arrive at revenue forecasts for the company.[10] It is also possible to aggregate individual company forecasts of analysts (possibly arrived at using various methodologies) into industry forecasts, and finally into macroeconomic forecasts; doing so is called a **bottom-up forecasting approach**. Figure 1-1 illustrates the two approaches.

A bottom-up forecasting approach is subject to the problem of inconsistent assumptions. For example, different analysts may assume different inflationary environments,

---

[10]Benninga and Sarig (1997, Chapter 5). See also Chapter 19 of Reilly and Brown (2000).

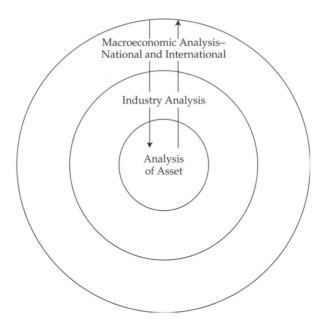

FIGURE 1-1   The Top-Down and Bottom-Up Approaches to Equity Analysis

and this may compromise the comparability of resulting individual stock valuations. In a top-down approach, an organization can ensure that all analysts use the same inflation assumption.[11]

3.3.2. Financial Forecasting

The analyst integrates the analysis of industry prospects and competitive and corporate strategy with financial statement analysis to formulate specific numerical forecasts of such items as sales and earnings. Techniques of financial forecasting are presented in detail in later chapters of this book, and also in White, Sondhi, and Fried (1998), Higgins (2001), Reilly and Brown (2000), and Benninga and Sarig (1997), which are useful complementary readings.

Analysts may consider qualitative as well as quantitative factors in financial forecasting and valuation. For example, some analysts may modify their overall valuation judgments and

---

[11]A related but distinct concept is **top-down investing** versus **bottom-up investing** as one broad description of types of active investment styles. For example, a top-down investor, based on a forecast that an economy is about to transition out of an economic recession, might increase exposure to shares in the Basic Materials sector, because profits in that economic sector are typically sensitive to changes in macroeconomic growth rates; at the same time exposure to recession-resistant sectors such as Consumer Non-Durables might be reduced. (The preceding would describe a **sector rotation strategy**, an investment strategy that overweights economic sectors that are anticipated to outperform or lead the overall market.) In contrast, an investor following a bottom-up approach might decide that a security is undervalued based on some valuation indicator, for example, without making an explicit judgment on the overall economy or the relative value of different sectors. Note that some forecasting and investing approaches mix top-down and bottom-up elements.

recommendations based on qualitative factors. These may include the analyst's viewpoint on the business acumen and integrity of management as well as the transparency and quality of a company's accounting practices. Although analysts may attempt to reflect the expected direction of such considerations in their financial forecasts or to otherwise quantify such factors, no formal valuation expression can fully capture these factors.[12] We caution that qualitative adjustments to valuation opinions are necessarily subjective.

3.3.2.1. Using Accounting Information   In working with quantitative forecasting tools, the analyst must attempt to use the most appropriate and reliable information available. A key source of such information is a company's accounting information and financial disclosures. Equity analysts study financial results and disclosures for information bearing on the company's current and future ability to create economic value. Reports to shareholders can differ substantially, however, with respect to the *accuracy* of reported accounting results as reflections of economic performance and the *detail* in which results are disclosed.

The investigation of issues relating to accuracy is often broadly referred to as **quality of earnings analysis**. The term broadly includes the scrutiny of *all* financial statements, including the balance sheet; that is, quality of earnings analysis includes scrutiny of balance sheet management as well as earnings management. With respect to detail, more detail is almost always superior to less, particularly in those areas of accounting practice (e.g., pensions, mergers and acquisitions, currency translation) where cursory examination seldom proves useful.

Equity analysts will generally benefit by developing their ability to assess a company's quality of earnings. An analyst who can skillfully analyze a company's financial statements can more accurately value a security than peer analysts with only a superficial understanding of the numbers. Also, extensive research suggests that analysts can generally expect stock prices to reflect quality of earnings considerations.[13] Skill in quality of earnings analysis, however, comes only with a thorough knowledge of financial statement analysis as well as practical experience.[14] Careful scrutiny and interpretation of footnotes to accounting statements, and of all other relevant disclosures, is essential to a quality of earnings analysis. Examples of only a few of the many available indicators of possible problems with a company's quality of earnings are provided in Table 1-1.

Various examples throughout this book will touch on analyst adjustments to reported financial results. Both the importance of accounting practices in influencing reported financial results and the judgment that analysts need to exercise in using those results in any valuation model are illustrated in Example 1-3.

---

[12] For example, management will react to future opportunities and risks that the analyst cannot anticipate at the time of the valuation.

[13] The literature is vast, but see in particular Fairfield and Whisanant (2000) and the references therein. Studies have also documented the *Briloff effect* showing that when a company's accounting games are exposed in *Barron's*, its stock price declines rapidly (Abraham Briloff is an accounting professor at Baruch College, City University of New York, who has explored the subject extensively). Other literature shows that bond market participants see through attempts at smoothing earnings and in some cases (the institutional bond market) penalize it (see Robinson and Grant 1997 and Robinson, Grant, Kauer, and Woodlock 1998).

[14] Sources for our discussion on quality of earnings analysis and accounting risk factors include Hawkins (1998), Levitt (1998), Schilit (2002), and White, Sondhi, and Fried (1998), as well as American Institute of Certified Public Accountants *Consideration of Fraud in a Financial Statement Audit* (28 February 2002) and International Federation of Accountants, International Standards on Auditing 240, *The Auditor's Responsibility to Consider Fraud and Error in an Audit of Financial Statements* (March 2001).

TABLE 1-1   Selected Quality of Earnings Indicators

Category	Observation	Potential Interpretation
Revenues and gains	Recognizing revenue early, for example: • Bill-and-hold sales • Lessor use of capital lease classification • Recording sales of equipment or software prior to installation and acceptance by customer	Acceleration in the recognition of revenue boosts reported income masking a decline in operating performance.
	Classification of nonoperating income or gains as part of operations.	Income or gains may be nonrecurring and may not relate to true operating performance, in fact, perhaps masking a decline in operating performance.
Expenses and losses	Deferral of expenses by capitalizing expenditures as an asset. For example: • Customer acquisition costs • Product development costs	May boost current income at the expense of future income. May mask problems with underlying business performance.
	Use of nonconservative estimates and assumptions, such as • Long depreciable lives • Long periods of amortization • High pension discount rate • Low assumed rate of compensation growth for pensions • High expected return on assets for pension	Nonconservative estimates may indicate actions taken to boost current reported income. Changes in assumptions may indicate an attempt to mask problems with underlying performance in the current period.
Balance sheet issues (may also affect earnings)	Use of special purpose entities (SPEs).[15]	Assets and/or liabilities may not be properly reflected on the balance sheet. Income may also be overstated by sales to the special purpose entity or a decline in the value of assets transferred to the SPE.

---

[15] A **special purpose entity** is a nonoperating entity created to carry out a specified purpose, such as leasing assets or securitizing receivables. The use of SPEs is frequently related to off-balance-sheet financing (financing that does not currently appear on the balance sheet).

EXAMPLE 1-3   Quality of Earnings Warning Signs

Livent, Inc., was a publicly traded theatrical production company that staged a number of smash hits such as Tony-award winning productions of *Showboat* and *Fosse*. Livent capitalized preproduction costs including expenses for pre-opening advertising, publicity and promotion, set construction, props, costumes, and salaries and fees paid to the cast and crew musicians during rehearsals. The company then amortized these capitalized costs over the expected life of the theatrical production based on anticipated revenues.

1. State the effect of Livent's accounting for preproduction costs on its reported earnings per share.

In Chapter 3 and elsewhere we will encounter the popular concept of EBITDA: earnings before interest, taxes, depreciation, and amortization (interest, taxes, depreciation, and amortization are added back to earnings). Some analysts use ratios such as EBITDA/interest expense and debt/EBITDA to assess one aspect of a company's financial strength, debt-paying ability.

2. If an analyst calculated EBITDA/interest expense and debt/EBITDA based on Livent's accounting for preproduction costs without adjustment, how might the analyst be misled in assessing Livent's financial strength?

Solution to 1: Livent's accounting for preproduction costs immediately increased reported earnings per share because it deferred expenses. Instead of immediately expensing costs, Livent reported them on its balance sheet as an asset. The warning signal—the deferral of expenses—indicates very aggressive accounting; preproduction costs should have been expensed immediately because of the tremendous uncertainty about revenues from theatrical productions. There was no assurance that there would be revenues against which expenses could be matched.

Solution to 2: Livent did not deduct preproduction costs from earnings as expenses. If the amortization of capitalized preproduction costs were then added back to earnings, the EBITDA/interest and debt/EBITDA ratios would not reflect in any way the cash outflows associated with items such as paying pre-opening salaries; but cash outflows reduce funds available to meet debt obligations. The analyst who mechanically added back amortization of preproduction costs to calculate EBITDA would be misled into overestimating Livent's financial strength. Based on a closer look at the company's accounting, we would properly not add back amortization of preproduction expenses in computing EBITDA. If preproduction expenses are not added back, a very different picture of Livent's financial health would emerge. In 1996, Livent's reported debt/EBITDA ratio was 1.7, but the ratio without adding back amortization for preproduction costs was 5.5. In 1997, debt/EBITDA was 3.7 based on positive EBITDA of $58.3 million, but EBITDA without the add-back was *negative* $52.6 million.[16] In November 1998, Livent declared bankruptcy and it is now defunct.

---

[16] Moody's Investor Services (2000). The discussion of this example is indebted to that report.

Analysts recognize a variety of risk factors that may signal possible future negative surprises. A working selection of these risk factors would include the following (AICPA 2002):

- Poor quality of accounting disclosures, such as segment information, acquisitions, accounting policies and assumptions, and a lack of discussion of negative factors.
- Existence of related-party transactions.
- Existence of excessive officer, employee, or director loans.
- High management or director turnover.
- Excessive pressure on company personnel to make revenue or earnings targets, particularly when combined with a dominant, aggressive management team or individual.
- Material non-audit services performed by audit firm.
- Reported (via regulatory filings) disputes with and/or changes in auditors.
- Management and/or directors' compensation tied to profitability or stock price (through ownership or compensation plans). Although such arrangements are desirable, they can indicate a risk of aggressive reporting as well.
- Economic, industry, or company-specific pressures on profitability, such as loss of market share or declining margins.
- Management pressure to meet debt covenants or earnings expectations.
- A history of securities law violations, reporting violations, or persistent late filings.

EXAMPLE 1-4   Benjamin Graham on Accounting

In a manuscript from 1936 (reprinted in Ellis 1991), Benjamin Graham pictures the chair of a major corporation outlining how his company will return to profitability in the middle of the Great Depression of the 20th century:

"Contrary to expectations, no changes will be made in the company's manufacturing or selling policies. Instead, the bookkeeping system is to be entirely revamped. By adopting and further improving a number of modern accounting and financial devices the corporation's earning power will be amazingly transformed."

The top item on the chair's list gives a flavor of the progress that will be made: "Accordingly, the Board has decided to extend the write-down policy initiated in the 1935 report, and to mark down the Fixed Assets from $1,338,552,858.96 to a round *Minus* $1,000,000,000 . . . As the plant wears out, the liability becomes correspondingly reduced. Hence, instead of the present depreciation charge of some $47,000,000 yearly there will be an annual *appreciation credit* of 5 percent, or $50,000,000. This will increase earnings by no less than $97,000,000 per annum." Summing up, the chair shares the foresight of the Board: ". . . [T]he Board is not unmindful of the possibility that some of our competitors may seek to offset our new advantages by adopting similar accounting improvements . . . Should necessity arise, moreover, we believe we shall be able to maintain our deserved superiority by introducing still more advanced bookkeeping methods, which are even now under development in our Experimental Accounting Laboratory."

3.4. Selecting the Appropriate Valuation Model

Skill in selecting, applying, and interpreting valuation models is important in investment analysis and valuation.[17] In this section, we discuss the third step in the valuation process—selecting the appropriate model for the valuation task at hand. First we address alternative value perspectives, then we present absolute and relative valuation models, and we close with a discussion of issues in model selection.

3.4.1. Value Perspectives

Several value perspectives serve as the foundation for the variety of valuation models available to the equity analyst; intrinsic value is the necessary starting point, but other concepts of value—going-concern value, liquidation value, and fair value—are also important.

3.4.1.1. Intrinsic Value   The quality of the analyst's forecasts, in particular the expectational inputs used in valuation models, is a key element in determining investment success. *For an active strategy to be consistently successful, the manager's expectations must differ from consensus expectations and be, on average, correct as well.* Only when accurate forecasts are combined with an appropriate valuation model will the analyst obtain a useful estimate of intrinsic value. The **intrinsic value** of an asset is the value of the asset given a hypothetically complete understanding of the asset's investment characteristics.

Valuation is an inherent part of the active manager's attempt to produce positive excess risk-adjusted return. An excess risk-adjusted return is also called an **abnormal return** or **alpha**. The manager hopes to capture a positive alpha as a result of his efforts to estimate intrinsic value. Any departure of market price from the manager's estimate of intrinsic value is a perceived **mispricing** (calculated as the difference between the estimated intrinsic value and the market price of an asset). Any perceived mispricing becomes part of the manager's expected holding-period return estimate, which is the manager's forecast of the total return on the asset for some holding period.[18] An expected holding-period return is the sum of expected capital appreciation and investment income, both stated as a proportion of purchase price. Naturally, expected capital appreciation incorporates the investor's perspective on the convergence of market price to intrinsic value. In a forward-looking (*ex ante*) sense, an asset's alpha is the manager's expected holding-period return minus the fair (or equilibrium) return on the asset given its risk, using some model relating an asset's average returns to its risk characteristics. The fair return on an asset given its risk is also known as its required rate of return (we will define and explain this concept further in Chapter 2).

$$\text{\textit{Ex ante} alpha} = \text{Expected holding-period return} - \text{Required return} \qquad (1\text{-}1)$$

In a backward-looking (*ex post*) sense, alpha is actual return minus the contemporaneous required return. Contemporaneous required return is what investments of similar risk actually earned during the same period.

$$\text{\textit{Ex post} alpha} = \text{Actual holding-period return} - \text{Contemporaneous required return} \qquad (1\text{-}2)$$

---

[17]The remaining chapters of this book will discuss these issues in detail for the valuation approaches presented.

[18]For brevity, we sometimes use *return* for *rate of return* in this discussion.

To illustrate these concepts, assume that an investor's expected holding-period return for a stock for the next 12 months is 12 percent, and the stock's required return, given its risk, is 10 percent. The *ex ante* alpha is $12 - 10 = 2$ percent. Assume that a year passes, and the stock has a return of -5 percent. The *ex post* alpha depends on the contemporaneous required return. If the contemporaneous required return was -8 percent, the stock would have an *ex post* alpha of $-5 - (-8) = 3$ percent.

EXAMPLE 1-5   Intrinsic Value and Return Concepts (1)

As an automotive industry analyst, you are researching Fiat S.p.A. (Milan Stock Exchange: FIA.MI), a leading Italian-headquartered automobile manufacturer. You have assembled the following information and assumptions as of late March 2002:

- The current share price of FIA.MI is €15.895 (based on the closing price on 22 March 2002).
- Your estimate of FIA.MI's intrinsic value is €17.26.
- Over the course of one year, you expect the mispricing of FIA.MI shares, equal to €17.26 − €15.895 = €1.365, to be fully corrected. In addition to the correction of mispricing, you forecast additional price appreciation of €1.22 per share over the course of the year as well as the payment of a cash dividend of €0.61.
- You estimate that the required rate of return on FIA.MI shares is 10.6 percent a year.

Using the above information:
1. State whether FIA.MI shares are overvalued, fairly valued, or undervalued, based on your forecasts.
2. Calculate the expected one-year holding-period return on FIA.MI stock.
3. Determine the expected alpha for FIA.MI stock.

Solution to 1: Because FIA.MI's intrinsic value of €17.26 is greater than its current market price €15.895, FIA.MI appears to be undervalued, based on your forecasts.

Solution to 2: The expected holding-period return is the sum of expected price appreciation plus the expected return from dividends. To calculate the expected price appreciation, we add €1.365 (from the convergence of price to intrinsic value) plus €1.22 (from the additional forecasted price appreciation) and obtain €2.585. The expected dividend is €0.61. The sum of expected price appreciation plus expected dividends is €3.195. The expected holding-period return for one year is €3.195/€15.895 = 0.201 or 20.1 percent.

Solution to 3: The expected holding-period return of 20.1 percent minus the required rate of return of 10.6 percent gives a positive expected excess risk-adjusted return or positive expected alpha of 9.5 percent.

The equity analyst recognizes that, no matter how hard he or she works to identify mispriced securities, uncertainty is associated with realizing a positive expected alpha, however accurate the forecasts and whatever the valuation approach used. Even if the analyst is highly confident about the accuracy of forecasts and risk adjustments, there is no means of ensuring the ability to capture the benefits of any perceived mispricing without risk. Convergence of the market price to perceived intrinsic value may not happen within the investor's investment horizon, if at all.[19] One uncertainty in applying any valuation methodology concerns whether the analyst has accounted for all sources of risk reflected in an asset's price. Because competing equity risk models will always exist, there is no possible final resolution to this dilemma. Differences in valuation judgments resulting from applying alternative models of equity risk are illustrated in Example 1-6.

EXAMPLE 1-6   Intrinsic Value and Return Concepts (2)

As an active investor, you have developed forecasts of returns for three securities and translated those forecasts into expected rate of return estimates. You have also estimated the securities' required rates of return using two models that we will discuss in Chapter 2: the capital asset pricing model (CAPM) and the Fama–French (FF) three-factor model. As a next step, you intend to rank the securities by alpha.

TABLE 1-2   Rates of Return

	Expected Rate of Return	CAPM Required Rate of Return	FF Required Rate of Return
Security 1	0.15	0.10	0.12
Security 2	0.07	0.12	0.07
Security 3	0.09	0.10	0.10

Based on the information in Table 1-2:
1. Calculate the *ex ante* alphas of each security.
2. Rank the securities by relative attractiveness using the CAPM, and state whether each security is overvalued, fairly valued, or undervalued.

Solution to 1:   The analyst can develop two sets of estimates of alpha, because the securities have different required rates of return depending on whether risk is modeled using the CAPM or FF model.

CAPM

$$\text{Alpha of Security } 1 = 0.15 - 0.10 = 0.05 \text{ or 5 percent}$$

$$\text{Alpha of Security } 2 = 0.07 - 0.12 = -0.05 \text{ or } -5 \text{ percent}$$

$$\text{Alpha of Security } 3 = 0.09 - 0.10 = -0.01 \text{ or } -1 \text{ percent}$$

---

[19] Related to this uncertainty is the concept of a catalyst. Besides evidence of mispricing, some active investors look for the presence of a particular market or corporate event (**catalyst**) that will cause the marketplace to re-evaluate a company's prospects.

Fama–French

Alpha of Security 1 = 0.15 − 0.12 = 0.03 or 3 percent

Alpha of Security 2 = 0.07 − 0.07 = 0.00 or 0 percent

Alpha of Security 3 = 0.09 − 0.10 = −0.01 or −1 percent

Solution to 2: With an alpha of 5 percent, using the CAPM, Security 1 is the only security with a positive expected risk-adjusted return and is relatively most attractive. Security 3 ranks second with an alpha of −1 percent, and Security 2 is last with an alpha of −5 percent. Both Security 3 and 2 appear to be overvalued, however, because they have negative alphas.

Throughout this book, we distinguish between market price, P, and intrinsic value (value for short), V. We accept the possibility of mispricing, which raises the question of the relationship between the analyst's efforts and the concept of market efficiency. **Market efficiency** is a finance perspective on capital markets that asserts, in the **traditional efficient markets formulation**, that an asset's market price is the best available estimate of its intrinsic value. A more modern formulation, the **rational efficient markets formulation** (Grossman and Stiglitz 1980), recognizes that no investor will rationally incur the expenses of gathering information unless he or she expects to be rewarded by higher gross returns compared with the free alternative of accepting the market price. Furthermore, modern theorists recognize that when intrinsic value is hard to ascertain (as is the case for common stock) and when trading costs exist, there is even further room for price to diverge from value.[20]

Thus the perspective of this book is consistent with some concepts of market efficiency. Many analysts often view market prices both with respect and with skepticism. They seek to identify mispricing. At the same time, they often rely on price eventually converging to intrinsic value. They also recognize distinctions between the levels of market efficiency in different markets or tiers of markets (for example, stocks heavily followed by analysts and stocks neglected by analysts).

3.4.1.2. Other Value Measures   A company generally has one value if it is immediately dissolved and another value if it continues in operation. The **going-concern assumption** is the assumption that the company will maintain its business activities into the foreseeable future. The **going-concern value** of a company is its value under a going-concern assumption. Once established as publicly traded, most companies have relatively long lives. Models of going-concern value are the focus of this book.

In addition to going-concern value, however, the marketplace considers other values. A company's **liquidation value** is its value if it were dissolved and its assets sold individually.[21]

---

[20] See Lee, Myers, and Swaminathan (1999).

[21] Liquidation value should be distinguished from what is sometimes called the **breakup value** or **private market value** of a company, which is the sum of the expected value of the company's parts if the parts were independent entities. In contrast to liquidation value, breakup value is a going-concern concept of value because in estimating a company's breakup value, the company's parts are usually valued individually as going concerns.

For many companies, the value added by assets working together and by human capital applied to managing those assets makes estimated going-concern value greater than liquidation value. A persistently unprofitable business, however, may be worth more "dead" than "alive." The higher of going-concern value or liquidation value is the company's fair value. If the marketplace has confidence that the company's management is acting in the owners' best interests, market prices should on average reflect fair value. **Fair value** is the price at which an asset (or liability) would change hands between a willing buyer and a willing seller when the former is not under any compulsion to buy and the latter is not under any compulsion to sell.

3.4.2. Absolute Valuation Models

The two broad types of going-concern models of valuation are absolute valuation models and relative valuation models. An **absolute valuation model** is a model that specifies an asset's intrinsic value. Such models can supply a point estimate of value that can be compared with the asset's market price. Present value models, the most important type of absolute equity valuation model, are regarded in academic finance theory as the fundamental approach to equity valuation. The logic of such models is that the value of an asset to an investor must be related to the returns that an investor expects to receive from holding that asset. Loosely speaking, we can refer to those returns as the asset's cash flows, and such models are also referred to as discounted cash flow models.

A **present value model** or **discounted cash flow model** of equity valuation views the value of common stock as being the present or discounted value of its expected future cash flows. For common stock, one familiar type of cash flow is dividends, which are discretionary distributions to shareholders authorized by a corporation's board of directors. Dividends represent cash flows at the shareholder level in the sense that they are paid directly to shareholders. Present value models based on dividends, the subject of Chapter 2, are called **dividend discount models**. Rather than defining cash flows as dividends, analysts frequently define cash flows at the company level. Common shareholders in principle have an equity ownership claim on the balance of the cash flows generated by a company after payments have been made to claimants senior to common equity, such as bondholders and preferred stockholders (and the government as well, which takes taxes), whether or not such flows are distributed in the form of dividends.

The two main company-level definitions of cash flow in current use are free cash flow and residual income.[22] Free cash flow is based on cash flow from operations but takes into account the reinvestment in fixed assets and working capital necessary for a going concern; we will define free cash flow with more precision in later chapters. Present value models based on a free cash flow concept include models known as the **free cash flow to equity model** and the **free cash flow to the firm model**, presented in Chapter 3. We also explore **residual income models** in Chapter 5. These are present value models of equity valuation based on accrual accounting earnings in excess of the opportunity cost of generating those earnings.

As discussed, an important group of equity valuation models is present value models. The present value approach is the familiar technique for valuing bonds, and models such as the dividend discount model are often presented as straightforward applications of the bond valuation model to common stock. In practice, however, the application of present value models to common stock typically involves greater uncertainty than is the case with bonds; that uncertainty centers on two critical inputs for present value models—the cash

---

[22]To reiterate, we are using *cash flow* in a broad rather than technical accounting sense in this discussion.

flows and the discount rate(s). Bond valuation addresses a stream of cash payments specified in number and amount in a legal contract (the **bond indenture**). In contrast, in valuing a stock, an analyst must define the specific cash flow stream to be valued—dividends or free cash flow, for example. No cash flow stream is contractually owed to common stockholders. Evaluating business, financial, technological, and other risks, the analyst must then forecast the amounts of the chosen flows without reference to contractual targets. Substantial uncertainty often surrounds such forecasts. Furthermore, the forecasts must extend into the indefinite future because common stock has no maturity date. Establishing the appropriate discount rate or rates in equity valuation is also subject to greater uncertainty for a stock than for an option-free bond of an issuer with no credit risk (e.g., a U.S. government security) or a corporate issuer of high investment grade quality. The widespread availability, use, and acceptance of bond ratings—coupled with the more certain nature of cash flows described above for such bonds—mean that appropriate discount rates for different levels of risk can be at least inferred if not observed directly from yields in the bond market. No such ratings or certain cash flows exist for stocks, so the analyst is faced with a much more subjective and uncertain assessment of the appropriate discount rate for a given stock. (For some bonds, however, such as mortgage-backed securities, asset-backed securities, and structured notes, the appropriate discount rate as well as the bond's cash flows can pose challenges in estimation comparable to those for equity.) Finally, in addition to the uncertainty associated with cash flows and discount rates, the equity analyst may need to address other issues, such as the value of corporate control or the value of unutilized assets.

The present value approach applied to stock valuation, therefore, presents a high order of complexity. Present value models are ambitious in what they attempt—an estimate of intrinsic value—and offer concomitant challenges. Graham and Dodd (1934) suggested that the analyst consider stating a range of intrinsic values. To that end, in later chapters we discuss the usefulness of sensitivity analysis in discounted cash flow valuation.

Although this book presents many of the equity valuation tools in wide professional use today, it cannot explore every specialist valuation tool the analyst may encounter. For example, a company may be valued on the basis of the market value of the assets or resources it controls. This approach is sometimes called **asset-based valuation** and also qualifies as a type of absolute valuation model. For appropriate companies, asset-based valuation can provide an independent estimate of value, and experienced analysts are always interested in alternative, independent estimates of value.

EXAMPLE 1-7   Asset-Based Valuation

Analysts often apply asset-based valuation to natural resource companies. For example, a crude oil producer such as Petrobras (NYSE: PBR) might be valued on the basis of the market value of its current proven reserves in barrels of oil, minus a discount for estimated extraction costs. A forest industry company such as Weyerhauser (NYSE: WY) might be valued on the basis of the board meters (or board feet) of timber it controls. Today, however, fewer companies than in the past are involved only in natural resources extraction or production. For example, Occidental Petroleum (NYSE: OXY) features petroleum in its name but also has substantial chemical manufacturing operations. For such cases, the total company might be valued as the sum of its divisions, with the natural resource division valued on the basis of its proven resources.

3.4.3. Relative Valuation Models

Relative valuation models constitute the second chief type of going-concern valuation models. **Relative valuation models** specify an asset's value relative to that of another asset. The idea underlying relative valuation is that similar assets should sell at similar prices, and relative valuation is typically implemented using price multiples.

Perhaps the most familiar price multiple, reported in most newspaper stock quotation listings, is the price–earnings multiple (P/E), which is the ratio of a stock's market price to the company's earnings per share. A stock selling at a P/E that is low relative to the P/E of another closely comparable stock (in terms of anticipated earnings growth rates and risk, for example) is *relatively undervalued* (a good buy) relative to the comparison stock. For brevity, we might state simply *undervalued*, but we must realize that if the comparison stock is overvalued (in an absolute sense, in relation to intrinsic value), so might be the stock we are calling undervalued. Therefore, it is useful to maintain the verbal distinction between *undervalued* and *relatively undervalued*.[23] Frequently, relative valuation involves a group of comparison assets, such as an industry group, rather than a single comparison asset, and the comparison value of the P/E might be the mean or median value of the P/E for the group of assets. The approach of relative valuation as applied to equity valuation is often called the method of comparables (or just comparables) and will be the subject of Chapter 4.

EXAMPLE 1-8   Relative Valuation Models

While researching Smithson Genomics, Inc., (STHI)[24] in the Healthcare Information Services industry, you encounter a difference of opinions. One analyst's report claims that STHI is at least 15 percent *overvalued*, based on a comparison of its P/E with the median P/E of peer companies in the Healthcare Information Services industry and taking account of company and peer group fundamentals. A second analyst asserts that Smithson is *undervalued* by 10 percent, based on a comparison of STHI's P/E with the median P/E of the Russell 3000 Index, a broad-based U.S. equity index. Both analyses appear to be carefully executed and reported. Can both analysts be right?

Yes. The assertions of both analysts concern *relative* valuations. The first analyst claims that STHI is *relatively* overvalued compared with its peers (in the sense of the purchase cost of a unit of earnings, P/E). Suppose that the entire Healthcare Information Services industry is substantially undervalued in relation to the overall market as represented by the Russell 3000. STHI could then also be relatively undervalued relative to the Russell 3000. Both analysts can be right because they are making relative valuations. Analysts ultimately care about the investment implications of their

---

[23] Only **expectational arbitrage**—investing on the basis of differential expectations—is possible whether a stock is absolutely or relatively mispriced. When two stocks are relatively mispriced, an investor might use the expectational arbitrage strategy known as pairs arbitrage to attempt to exploit the mispricing. **Pairs arbitrage** is a trade in two closely related stocks that involves buying the relatively undervalued stock and selling short the relatively overvalued stock.

[24] This company is fictional; as such, we do not identify a stock exchange or other marketplace before stating the (fictional) ticker symbol or acronym.

information. If the second analyst believes that the market price of the Russell 3000 fairly represents that index's intrinsic value, then she might expect a positive alpha from investing in STHI, even if some other peer group companies possibly command higher expected alphas. In practice, the analyst may consider other factors such as market liquidity in relation to the intended position size. On the other hand, if the analyst thought that the overall market valuation was high, the analyst might anticipate a negative alpha from investing in STHI. Relative valuation is tied to relative performance. The analyst in many cases may want to supplement such information with estimates of intrinsic value.

The method of comparables is characterized by a wide range of possible implementation choices—Chapter 4 discusses six different price multiples and some variations of them. Practitioners will often examine a number of price multiples for the complementary information they may provide. In summary, the method of comparables does not specify intrinsic value without making the further assumption that the comparison asset is fairly valued. The method of comparables has the advantages of being simple, related to market prices, and grounded in a sound economic principle (that similar assets should sell at similar prices). Price multiples are widely recognized by investors; and, as we will illustrate in Chapter 4, analysts can restate an absolute valuation in terms of a price multiple to communicate their analysis in a way that will be widely understood.

3.4.4. Issues in Model Selection and Interpretation

How do we select a valuation model? The later chapters discussing present value models and price multiples offer specific guidance on model selection. The broad criteria for model selection are that the valuation model be

- consistent with the characteristics of the company being valued;
- appropriate given the availability and quality of data; and
- consistent with the purpose of valuation, including the analyst's ownership perspective.

We have argued that understanding the business is the first step in the valuation process. When we understand the company, we understand the nature of its assets and also how it uses those assets to create value. For example, a bank is composed largely of marketable or potentially marketable assets and securities, and a relative valuation based on assets (as recognized in accounting) has more relevance than a similar exercise for a service company with few marketable assets.

The availability and quality of data are limiting factors in making forecasts and sometimes in using specific financial performance measures. As a result, data availability and quality also bear on our choice of valuation model. Discounted cash flow models make intensive use of forecasts. As we shall see, the dividend discount model is the simplest such model, but if we do not have a record of dividends or other information to accurately assess a company's dividend policy, we may have more confidence applying an apparently more complex present value model. Similar considerations also apply in selecting a specific relative valuation approach. As an example, meaningful comparisons using P/E ratios may be hard to make for a company with highly volatile or persistently negative earnings.

The purpose or perspective of the analyst—for example, the ownership perspective—can also influence the choice of valuation approach. This point will become more apparent as we study concepts such as free cash flow and enterprise value later in this book. Related to purpose, the analyst is frequently a consumer as well as a producer of valuations and research reports. Analysts must consider potential biases when reading reports prepared by others: Why was this particular valuation method chosen? Are the valuation model and its inputs reasonable? Does the adopted approach make the security look better (or worse) than another standard valuation approach?

In addition to the preceding broad considerations in model selection, three other specific issues may affect the analyst's use and interpretation of valuation models: control premiums, marketability discounts, and liquidity discounts. A controlling ownership position in a company (e.g., more than 50 percent of outstanding shares) carries with it control of the board of directors and the valuable option of redeploying the company's assets. When control is at issue, the price of that company's stock will generally reflect a **control premium**. Most quantitative valuation expressions do not explicitly model such premiums. As we shall discuss later, however, certain models are more likely than others to yield valuations consistent with a control position. A second consideration generally not explicitly modeled is that investors require an extra return to compensate for lack of a public market or lack of marketability. The price of non-publicly traded stocks then generally reflects a **marketability discount**. There is also evidence that among publicly traded stocks, the price of shares with less depth to their markets (less liquidity) reflects a **liquidity discount**.[25]

As a final note to this introduction of model selection, it is important to recognize that professionals frequently use multiple valuation models or factors in common stock selection. According to the *Merrill Lynch Institutional Factor Survey* (2001), respondent institutional investors report using an average of approximately eight valuation factors in selecting stocks.[26] There are a variety of ways in which multiple factors can be used in stock selection. One prominent way, stock screens, will be discussed in Chapter 4. As another example, analysts may rank each security in a given investment universe by relative attractiveness according to a particular valuation factor. They could then combine the rankings for a security into a single composite ranking by assigning weights to the individual factors. Analysts may use a quantitative model to assign those weights.

4. PERFORMING VALUATIONS: THE ANALYST'S ROLE AND RESPONSIBILITIES

Whatever the setting in which they work, investment analysts are involved either directly or indirectly in valuation. Their activities are varied:

- Although sometimes focusing on organizing and analyzing corporate information, the publicly distributed research reports and services of independent vendors of financial information almost invariably offer valuation information and opinions.

---

[25] See, for example, Amihud and Mendelson (1986).

[26] *Factors* include valuation models as well as variables such as return on equity; these surveys included 23 such factors and covered the period 1989–2001.

- In investment management firms, trusts and bank trust departments, and similar institutions, an analyst may report valuation judgments to a portfolio manager or to an investment committee.[27] The analyst's valuation expertise is important not only in investment disciplines involving security selection based on detailed company analysis, but also in highly quantitative investment disciplines; quantitative analysts work in developing, testing, and updating security selection methodologies.[28]
- Analysts at corporations may perform some valuation tasks similar to those of analysts at money management firms (e.g., when the corporation manages in-house a sponsored pension plan). Both corporate analysts and investment bank analysts may also identify and value companies that could become acquisition targets.
- Analysts associated with investment firms' brokerage operations are perhaps the most visible group of analysts offering valuation judgments—their research reports are widely distributed to current and prospective retail and institutional brokerage clients.

In conducting their valuation activities, investment analysts play a critical role in collecting, organizing, analyzing, and communicating corporate information, and in recommending appropriate investment actions based on sound analysis. When they do those tasks well, analysts

- help their clients achieve their investment objectives by enabling those clients to make better buy and sell decisions;
- contribute to the efficient functioning of capital markets (in providing analysis that leads to informed buy and sell decisions, analysts help make asset prices better reflections of underlying values; when asset prices accurately reflect underlying values, capital flows more easily to its highest-value uses); and
- benefit the suppliers of capital, including shareholders, by monitoring management's performance. Monitoring managers may inhibit those managers from exploiting corporate resources for their own benefit.[29]

EXAMPLE 1-9   What Are Analysts Expected to Do?

When analysts at brokerage firms recommend a stock to the public that later performs very poorly, or when they fail to uncover negative corporate activities, they can sometimes come under public scrutiny. Industry leaders may then be asked to respond to such criticism and to comment on expectations about the role and responsibilities of analysts. One such instance occurred in the United States as a consequence of the late 2001 collapse of Enron Corporation, an energy trading company. In testimony before the

---

[27] Such analysts are widely known as **buy-side analysts**, in contrast to analysts who work at brokerages, who are known as **sell-side analysts**. Brokerages provide or sell services to institutions such as investment management firms, explaining this terminology. **Brokerage** is the business of acting as agents for buyers or sellers, usually in return for commissions.

[28] Ranking stocks by some measure(s) of relative attractiveness (subject to a risk control discipline), as we will discuss in more detail later, forms one key part of quantitative equity investment disciplines.

[29] See Jensen and Meckling (1976) for a classic analysis of the costs of stockholder–manager conflicts.

U. S. Senate (excerpted below), the President and CEO of CFA Institute offered a summary of the working conditions and responsibilities of brokerage analysts. In the following passage, **due diligence** refers to investigation and analysis in support of a recommendation; the failure to exercise due diligence may sometimes result in liability according to various securities laws. "Wall Street analysts" refers to analysts working in the U.S. brokerage industry (sell-side analysts).

> What are Wall Street analysts expected to do? These analysts are assigned companies and industries to follow, are expected to research fully these companies and the industries in which they operate, and to forecast their future prospects. Based on this analysis, and using appropriate valuation models, they must then determine an appropriate fair price for the company's securities. After comparing this fair price to the current market price, the analyst is able to make a recommendation. If the analyst's "fair price" is significantly above the current market price, it would be expected that the stock be rated a "buy" or "market outperform."
>
> How do Wall Street analysts get their information? Through hard work and due diligence. They must study and try to comprehend the information in numerous public disclosure documents, such as the annual report to shareholders and regulatory filings . . . and gather the necessary quantitative and qualitative inputs to their valuation models.
>
> This due diligence isn't simply reading and analyzing annual reports. It also involves talking to company management, other company employees, competitors, and others, to get answers to questions that arise from their review of public documents. Talking to management must go beyond participation in regular conference calls. Not all questions can be voiced in those calls because of time constraints, for example, and because analysts, like journalists, rightly might not wish to "show their cards," and reveal the insights they have gotten through their hard work, by asking a particularly probing question in the presence of their competitors.
>
> Wall Street analysts are also expected to understand the dynamics of the industry and general economic conditions before finalizing a research report and making a recommendation. Therefore, in order for their firm to justify their continued employment, Wall Street analysts must issue research reports on their assigned companies and must make recommendations based on their reports to clients who purchase their firm's research.[30]

From the beginnings of the movement to organize financial analysis as a profession rather than as a commercial trade, one guiding principle has been that the analyst must hold himself accountable to both standards of competence and standards of conduct.[31]

---

[30]Thomas A. Bowman, CFA. Testimony to the Committee on Governmental Affairs (excerpted) U.S. Senate, 27 February 2002.
[31]See the Articles of Incorporation (1959) of the Institute of Chartered Financial Analysts, a predecessor organization of AIMR and CFA Institute, as well as Hayes (1962) and Graham (1963).

Competence in investment analysis requires a high degree of training, experience, and discipline.[32] Additionally, the investment professional is in a position of trust, requiring ethical conduct towards the public, clients, prospects, employers, employees, and fellow analysts. For CFA Institute members, this position of trust is reflected in the Code of Ethics and Standards of Professional Conduct to which members subscribe, as well as in the Professional Conduct Statement that they submit annually. The Code and Standards guide the analyst to independent, well-researched, and well-documented analysis. Valuation is closely associated with analyst recommendations that often form the basis for investment action; ensuring that work product is consistent with the Code and Standards is therefore an overriding priority.

5. COMMUNICATING VALUATION RESULTS: THE RESEARCH REPORT

Writing is an important part of an analyst's job. Whether a research report is for review by an investment committee or a portfolio manager in an investment management firm, or for distribution to the retail or institutional clients of a brokerage firm, research reports share several common elements. In this section we discuss the content of an effective research report, one adaptable format for writing such a report, and the analyst's responsibilities in preparing a research report.

5.1. Contents of a Research Report

To understand what a research report should include, we need to ask what readers seek to gain from reading the report. One key focus is the investment recommendation. In evaluating how much attention and weight to give to a recommendation, the reader will look for persuasive supporting arguments. The relevance to this book, of course, is that a key element supporting a recommendation is the valuation of the security. Understanding the business is the first step in valuation. Therefore, the reader will want to understand the prospects for both the industry and the company. The quality of this industry and company analysis bears heavily on the quality of the valuation and recommendation. Some readers of research reports are also interested in background information, and some reports contain detailed historical descriptive statistics about the industry and company. To summarize, most research reports cover the following three broad areas:

- description (presentation of facts; this brings the reader up to date on the company's sales, earnings, new products, and the macroeconomic and industry contexts in which the company operates);
- analysis and forecasts for the industry and company; and
- valuation and recommendation.

How well the analyst executes the above tasks determines the usefulness of the report. Writing an effective research report is a challenging task. An effective research report:

- contains timely information;
- is written in clear, incisive language;

---

[32]Competence in this sense is reflected in the examination and work experience requirements that are prerequisites for obtaining the CFA designation.

- is unbiased, objective, and well researched;
- contains analysis, forecasts, valuation, and a recommendation that are internally consistent;
- presents sufficient information that the reader can critique the valuation;
- states the risk factors present for an investment in the company; and
- discloses any potential conflicts of interests faced by the analyst.

Analysts, whose goal is to produce research of distinguished quality and usefulness, should keep the above points in mind when writing a research report.

Because the subject of this book is valuation, we focus our remaining comments on the valuation information in research reports. Observers have sometimes criticized the valuation analysis in many research reports.[33] The analyst needs to maintain a conceptual distinction between a *good company* and a *good investment*. The expected alpha on a common stock purchase depends on the price paid for the stock, whatever the business prospects of the issuing company. The analyst who is overly enthusiastic about a company's prospects sometimes may be tempted to state a positive recommendation without substantial effort at valuation. Such a report might offer interesting background industry information, but the analysis would not be thorough.

The analyst can state his or her specific forecasts, convert those forecasts into an estimate of intrinsic value (describing the model), and compare intrinsic value with market price (or make a similarly careful relative valuation). Qualitative factors and other considerations may affect a recommendation and merit discussion. Superior research reports also contain a section on risk factors that objectively addresses the uncertainty associated with investing in the security. Research reports often state a target price for a stock. Readers can make little use of a target price for a stock unless the report describes the basis for computing the target, supplies a time frame for reaching the target, and conveys information on the uncertainty of reaching the target.

EXAMPLE 1-10   Research Reports

The following two passages are closely based on the valuation discussions of actual companies in two short research notes (for Passage A, a two-page report dated March 2002; for B, a single-page report issued July 2001). The company names used in the passages, however, are fictional.

(A) At a recent multiple of 6.5, our earnings per share multiple for 2002, the shares were at a discount to our projection of 14 percent growth for the period ... MXI has two operating segments ... In valuing the segments separately, employing relative acquisition multiples and peer mean values, we found fair value to be above recent market value. In addition, the shares trade at a discount to book value (0.76). Based on the value indicated by these two valuation metrics, we view the shares as worth holding. However, in light of a weaker economy over the near term, dampening demand for MXI's services, our enthusiasm is tempered.

---

[33]Cornell (2001) is one example, and comments in the financial press have appeared from time to time.

> *[Elsewhere in the report, MXI receives the firm's highest numerical quantitative outlook evaluation.]*
>
> (B) Although TXI outperformed the overall stock market by 20 percent since the start of the year, it definitely looks undervalued as shown by its low multiples … *[the values of the P/E and another multiple are stated]*. According to our dividend discount model valuation, we get to a valuation of €3.08 implying an upside potential of 36.8 percent based on current prices. The market outperform recommendation is reiterated. *[In a parenthetical expression, the current dividend, assumed dividend growth rates, and their time horizons are given. The analyst also briefly explains and calculates the discount rate. Elsewhere in the report the current price of TXI is given as €2.25.]*

Although some of the concepts mentioned in the two passages may not yet be familiar, we can begin to assess the above two reporting efforts.

Passage A communicates the analysis awkwardly. The meaning of "the shares were at a discount to our projection of 14 percent growth for the period" is not completely clear. Presumably the analyst is projecting the earnings growth rate for 2002 and stating that the P/E is low in relation to that expected growth rate. The analyst next discusses valuing MXI as the sum of its divisions. In describing the method as "employing relative acquisition multiples and peer mean values," the analyst does not convey a clear picture of what was done. It is probable that companies similar to each of MXI's divisions were identified; then the mean or average value of some unidentified multiple for those comparison companies was calculated and used as the basis for valuing MXI. The writer is vague, however, on the extent of MXI's undervaluation. The analyst states that MXI's price is below its book value (an accounting measure of shareholders' investment) but draws no comparison with the average price-to-book value ratio for stocks similar to MXI, for example.[34] Finally, the verbal summation is feeble and hedged. Although filled with technical verbiage, Passage A does not communicate a coherent valuation of MXI.

In the second sentence of Passage B, by contrast, the analyst gives an explicit valuation of TXI and the information needed to critique it. The reader can also see that €3.08, which is elsewhere stated in the research note as the target price for TXI, implies the stated price appreciation potential for TXI (€3.08/€2.25 − 1, approximately 37 percent). In the first sentence in Passage B, the analyst gives information that might support the conclusion that TXI is undervalued, although the statement lacks strength because the analyst does not explain why the P/E is "low." The verbal summary is clear. Using much less space than the analyst in Passage A, the analyst in Passage B has done a superior job of communicating the results of his valuation.

5.2. Format of a Research Report

Equity research reports may be logically presented in several ways. The firm in which the analyst works sometimes specifies a fixed format for consistency and quality control purposes. Without claiming superiority to other ways to organize a report, we offer Table 1-3 as an

---

[34] We will discuss the price-to-book value ratio in Chapter 4.

TABLE 1-3   A Format for Research Reports

Section	Purpose	Content	Comments
Table of Contents	• Shows report's organization	• Consistent with narrative in sequence and language	This is typically used in very long research reports only.
Summary and Investment Conclusion	• Communicate the large picture • Communicate major specific conclusions of the analysis • Recommend an investment course of action	• Capsule description of the company • Major recent developments • Earnings projections • Other major conclusions • Valuation summary • Investment action	An executive summary; may be called simply "Summary."
Business Summary	• Present the company in more detail • Communicate a detailed understanding of the company's economics and current situation • Provide and explain specific forecasts	• Company description to the divisional level • Industry analysis • Competitive analysis • Historical performance • Financial forecasts	Reflects the first and second steps of the valuation process. Financial forecasts should be explained adequately and reflect quality of earnings analysis.
Risks	• Alert readers to the risk factors in investing in the security	• Possible negative industry developments • Possible negative regulatory and legal developments • Possible negative company developments • Risks in the forecasts • Other risks	Readers should have enough information to determine how the analyst is defining and assessing the risks specific to investing in the security.

TABLE 1-3   *Continued*

Section	Purpose	Content	Comments
Valuation	• Communicate a clear and careful valuation	• Description of model(s) used • Recapitulation of inputs • Statement of conclusions	Readers should have enough information to critique the analysis.
Historical and Pro Forma Tables	• Organize and present data to support the analysis in the Business Summary		This is generally a separate section in longer research reports only. Many reports fold all or some of this information into the Business Summary section.

adaptable format by which the analyst can communicate research and valuation findings in detail. (Shorter research reports and research notes obviously may employ a more compact format.)

5.3. Research Reporting Responsibilities

All analysts have an obligation to provide substantive and meaningful content in a clear and comprehensive report format. Analysts who are CFA Institute members, however, have an additional and overriding responsibility to adhere to the Code of Ethics and the Standards of Professional Conduct in all activities pertaining to their research reports. The CFA Institute Code of Ethics states:

> *Members of CFA Institute must ... use reasonable care and exercise independent professional judgment when conducting investment analysis, making investment recommendations, taking investment actions, and engaging in other professional activities.*

Going beyond this general statement of responsibility, some specific Standards of Professional Conduct particularly relevant to an analyst writing a research report are shown in Table 1-4.

6. SUMMARY

In this chapter, we have discussed the scope of equity valuation, outlined the valuation process, introduced valuation concepts and models, discussed the analyst's role and responsibilities in conducting valuation, and described the elements of an effective research report in which analysts communicate their valuation analysis.

- Valuation is the estimation of an asset's value based on variables perceived to be related to future investment returns, or based on comparisons with closely similar assets.
- Valuation is used for

TABLE 1-4   Selected CFA Institute Standards of Professional Conduct Pertaining to Research Reports*

Standard of Professional Conduct	Responsibility
I(C)	Members and Candidates must not knowingly make any misrepresentations relating to investment analysis, recommendations, actions, or other professional activities.
V(A)1	Members and Candidates must exercise diligence, independence, and thoroughness in analyzing investments, making investment recommendations, and taking investment actions.
V(A)2	Members and Candidates must have a reasonable and adequate basis, supported by appropriate research and investigation, for any investment analysis, recommendation, or action.
V(C)	Members and Candidates must develop and maintain appropriate records to support their investment analysis, recommendations, actions, and other investment-related communications with clients and prospective clients.
V(B)2	Members and Candidates must use reasonable judgment in identifying which factors are important to their investment analyses, recommendations, or actions and include those factors in communications with clients and prospective clients.
V(B)3	Members and Candidates must distinguish between fact and opinion in the presentation of investment analysis and recommendations.
V(B)1	Members and Candidates must disclose to clients and prospective clients the basic format and general principles of the investment processes used to analyze investments, select securities, and construct portfolios and must promptly disclose any changes that might materially affect those processes.
I(B)	Members and Candidates must not knowingly make any misrepresentations relating to investment analysis, recommendations, actions, or other professional activities.

*The most recent edition of the CFA Institute *Standards of Practice Handbook* can be found on the CFA web site (www.cfainstitute.org).

- stock selection,
- inferring (extracting) market expectations,
- evaluating corporate events,
- fairness opinions,
- evaluating business strategies and models,
- communication among management, shareholders, and analysts, and
- appraisal of private businesses.

- The three steps in the portfolio management process are planning, execution, and feedback. Valuation is most closely associated with the planning and execution steps.

  - For active investment managers, plans concerning valuation models and criteria are part of the elaboration of an investment strategy.
  - Skill in valuation plays a key role in the execution step (in selecting a portfolio, in particular).

- The valuation process has five steps:

    1. Understanding the business.
    2. Forecasting company performance.
    3. Selecting the appropriate valuation model.
    4. Converting forecasts to a valuation.
    5. Making the investment decision (recommendation).

- The tasks within "understanding the business" include evaluating industry prospects, competitive position, and corporate strategies. Because similar economic and technological factors typically affect all companies in an industry, and because companies compete with each other for sales, both industry knowledge and competitive analysis help analysts understand a company's economics and its environment. The analyst can then make more accurate forecasts.

- Two approaches to economic forecasting are top-down forecasting and bottom-up forecasting. In top-down forecasting, analysts use macroeconomic forecasts to develop industry forecasts and then make individual company and asset forecasts consistent with the industry forecasts. In bottom-up forecasting, individual company forecasts are aggregated to industry forecasts, which in turn may be aggregated to macroeconomic forecasts.

- Careful scrutiny and interpretation of financial statements, footnotes to financial statements, and other accounting disclosures are essential to a quality of earnings analysis. Quality of earnings analysis concerns the scrutiny of possible earnings management and balance sheet management.

- The intrinsic value of an asset is its value given a hypothetically complete understanding of the asset's investment characteristics.

- Alpha is an asset's excess risk-adjusted return. *Ex ante* alpha is expected holding-period return minus required return given risk. Historical alpha is actual holding-period return minus the contemporaneous required return.

- Active investing is consistent with rational efficient markets and the existence of trading costs and assets whose intrinsic value is difficult to determine.

- The going-concern assumption is the assumption that a company will continue operating for the foreseeable future. A company's going-concern value is its value under the going-concern assumption and is the general objective of most valuation models. In contrast, liquidation value is the company's value if it were dissolved and its assets sold individually.

- Fair value is the price at which an asset would change hands if neither buyer nor seller were under compulsion to buy/sell.

- Absolute valuation models specify an asset's intrinsic value, supplying a point estimate of value that can be compared with market price. Present value models of common stock (also called discounted cash flow models) are the most important type of absolute valuation model.

- Relative valuation models specify an asset's value relative to the value of another asset. As applied to equity valuation, relative valuation is known as the method of comparables: In applying the method of comparables, analysts compare a stock's price multiple to the price multiple of a similar stock or the average or median price multiple of some group of stocks.

- Relative equity valuation models do not address intrinsic value without the further assumption that the price of the comparison value accurately reflects its intrinsic value.

- The broad criteria for selecting a valuation approach are that the valuation approach be

    - consistent with the characteristics of the company being valued;
    - appropriate given the availability and quality of the data; and
    - consistent with the analyst's valuation purpose and perspective.

- Valuation may be affected by control premiums (premiums for a controlling interest in the company), marketability discounts (discounts reflecting the lack of a public market for the company's shares), and liquidity discounts (discounts reflecting the lack of a liquid market for the company's shares).
- Investment analysts play a critical role in collecting, organizing, analyzing, and communicating corporate information, as well as in recommending appropriate investment actions based on their analysis. In fulfilling this role, they help clients achieve their investment objectives and contribute to the efficient functioning of capital markets. Analysts can contribute to the welfare of shareholders through monitoring the actions of management.
- In performing valuations, analysts need to hold themselves accountable to both standards of competence and standards of conduct.
- An effective research report
  - contains timely information;
  - is written in clear, incisive language;
  - is unbiased, objective, and well researched;
  - contains analysis, forecasts, valuation, and a recommendation that are internally consistent;
  - presents sufficient information that the reader can critique the valuation;
  - states the risk factors for an investment in the company; and
  - discloses any potential conflicts of interests faced by the analyst.

- Analysts have an obligation to provide substantive and meaningful content. CFA Institute members have an additional overriding responsibility to adhere to the CFA Institute Code of Ethics and relevant specific Standards of Professional Conduct.

PROBLEMS

1. A. State four uses or purposes of valuation models.
   B. Which use of valuation models may be the most important to a working equity portfolio manager?
   C. Which uses would be particularly relevant to a corporate officer?
2. In Example 1-1 based on Cornell's (2001) study of Intel Corporation, in which Cornell valued Intel using a present value model of stock value, we wrote:
   "What future revenue growth rates were consistent with Intel's stock price of $61.50 just prior to the release, and $43.31 only five days later? Using a conservatively low discount rate, Cornell estimated that the price of $61.50 was consistent with a growth rate of 20 percent a year for the subsequent 10 years (and then 6 percent per year thereafter)."

   A. If Cornell had assumed a higher discount rate, would the resulting revenue growth rate estimate consistent with a price of $61.50 be higher or lower than 20 percent a year?
   B. Explain your answer to Part A.

3. A. Explain the role of valuation in the planning step of the portfolio management process.
   B. Explain the role of valuation in the execution step of the portfolio management process.
4. Explain why valuation models are important to active investors but not to investors trying to replicate a stock market index.

5. An analyst has been following Kerr-McGee Corporation (NYSE: KMG) for several years. He has consistently felt that the stock is undervalued and has always recommended a strong buy. Another analyst who has been following Nucor Corporation (NYSE: NUE) has been similarly bullish. The tables below summarize the prices, dividends, total returns, and estimates of the contemporaneous required returns for KMG and NUE from 1998 to 2001.

Data for KMG

Year	Price at Year-End	Dividends	Total Annual Return	Contemporaneous Required Return
1997	$54.22			
1998	33.97	$1.80	−34.0%	26.6%
1999	54.38	1.80	65.4	19.6
2000	63.96	1.80	20.9	−8.5
2001	53.93	1.80	−12.9	−11.0

Data for NUE

Year	Price at Year-End	Dividends	Total Annual Return	Contemporaneous Required Return
1997	$45.66			
1998	41.31	$0.48	−8.5%	29.2%
1999	52.93	0.52	29.4	21.5
2000	38.96	0.60	−25.3	−9.3
2001	52.80	0.68	37.3	−12.1

The total return is the price appreciation and dividends for the year divided by the price at the end of the previous year. The contemporaneous required return is the average actual return for the year realized by stocks that were of the same risk as KMG or NUE, respectively.

A. Without reference to any numerical data, what can be said about each analyst's *ex ante* alpha for KMG and NUE, respectively?

B. Calculate the *ex post* alphas for each year 1998 through 2001 for KMG and for NUE.

6. On the last trading day of 2000 (29 December 2000), an analyst is reviewing his valuation of Wal-Mart Stores (NYSE: WMT). The analyst has the following information and assumptions:

• The current price is $53.12.
• The analyst's estimate of WMT's intrinsic value is $56.00.
• In addition to the full correction of the difference between WMT's current price and its intrinsic value, the analyst forecasts additional price appreciation of $4.87 and a cash dividend of $0.28 over the next year.
• The required rate of return for Wal-Mart is 9.2 percent.

    A. What is the analyst's expected holding-period return on WMT?

    B. What is WMT's *ex ante* alpha?

    C. Calculate *ex post* alpha, given the following additional information:

> - Over the next year, 29 December 2000 through 31 December 2001, Wal-Mart's actual rate of return was 8.9 percent.
> - In 2001, the realized rate of return for stocks of similar risk was −10.4 percent.

7. The table below gives information on the expected and required rates of return based on the CAPM for three securities an analyst is valuing:

	Expected Rate	CAPM Required Rate
Security 1	0.20	0.21
Security 2	0.18	0.08
Security 3	0.11	0.10

    A. Define *ex ante* alpha.

    B. Calculate the expected alpha of Securities 1, 2, and 3 and rank them from most attractive to least attractive.

    C. Based on your answer to Part B, what risks attach to selecting among Securities 1, 2, and 3?

8. Benjamin Graham (1963) wrote that "[t]here is . . . a double function of the Financial Analyst, related in part to securities and in part to people."

    A. Explain the analyst's function related to people.

    B. How does the analyst's work contribute to the functioning of capital markets?

9. In a research note on the ordinary shares of the Mariella Burani Fashion Group (Milan Stock Exchange: MBFG.MI) dated early July 2001 when a recent price was €7.73 and projected annual dividends were €0.05, an analyst stated a target price of €9.20. The research note did not discuss how the target price was obtained or how it should be interpreted. Assume the target price represents the expected price of MBFG.MI. What further specific pieces of information would you need to form an opinion on whether MBFG.MI was fairly valued, overvalued, or undervalued?

10. You are researching XMI Corporation (XMI). XMI has shown steady earnings per share growth (18 percent a year during the last seven years) and trades at a very high multiple to earnings (its P/E ratio is currently 40 percent above the average P/E ratio for a group of the most comparable stocks). XMI has generally grown through acquisition, by using XMI stock to purchase other companies. These companies usually trade at lower P/E ratios than XMI.

    In investigating the financial disclosures of these acquired companies and in talking to industry contacts, you conclude that XMI has been forcing the companies it acquires to accelerate the payment of expenses before the acquisition deals are closed. Such acceleration drives down the acquired companies' last reported cash flow and earnings per share numbers. As one example, XMI asks acquired companies to immediately pay all pending accounts payable, whether or not they are due. Subsequent to the acquisition, XMI reinstitutes normal expense payment patterns. After it acquires a company, XMI appears to have a pattern of speeding up revenue recognition as well. For example, one overseas telecommunications subsidiary changed its accounting to recognize up front the expected revenue from sales of network capacity that spanned decades. The above policies and accounting facts do not appear to be have been adequately disclosed in XMI's shareholder communications.

A. Characterize the effect of the XMI expensing policies with respect to acquisitions on XMI's post-acquisition earnings per share growth rate.

B. Characterize the quality of XMI earnings based on its expensing and revenue-recognition policies with respect to acquisitions.

C. In discussing the current price of XMI, the question states that XMI's "P/E ratio is currently 40 percent above the average P/E ratio for a group of the most comparable stocks." Characterize the type of valuation model implicit in such a statement.

D. State two *risk factors* in investing in XMI, in the sense in which that term was used in the discussion of quality of earnings.

CHAPTER 2

DISCOUNTED DIVIDEND VALUATION

LEARNING OUTCOMES

After completing this chapter, you will be able to do the following:

- Explain the economic rationale for discounted cash flow (DCF) valuation.
- Give three definitions of expected cash flow that can be used in discounted cash flow valuation, discuss the advantages and disadvantages of each, and identify the investment situations in which each is suitable.
- Determine whether a dividend discount model (DDM) is appropriate for valuing a stock.
- Explain the components of the required rate of return on equity used to discount expected future cash flows.
- Discuss the capital asset pricing model (CAPM), arbitrage pricing theory (APT), and bond yield plus risk premium approaches to determining the required rate of return for an equity investment.
- Calculate the required rate of return for an equity investment using each major approach.
- Calculate the Gordon growth model (GGM) equity risk premium estimate.
- State three limitations to the CAPM and APT approaches to determining the required return on equity.
- Describe and give an example of the build-up approach to determining the required return on equity.
- Calculate the expected holding-period return on a stock given its current price, expected next-period price, and expected next-period dividend.
- Contrast the expected holding-period return with the required rate of return.
- Discuss the effect on expected return of the convergence of price to value, given that price does not equal value.
- Calculate the value of a common stock using the DDM for one-, two-, and multiple-period holding periods.
- State the equation and explain the general form of the DDM.
- Discuss the two major approaches to the dividend-forecasting problem.
- Explain the assumptions of the Gordon growth model.
- Calculate the value of a common stock using the Gordon growth model.
- Discuss the choice of growth rate in the Gordon growth model in relation to the growth rate of the economy.
- Calculate the expected rate of return or implied dividend growth rate in the Gordon growth model, given the market price.

- Explain and calculate the justified leading and trailing price to earnings ratios (P/Es) based on fundamentals, using the Gordon growth model.
- Calculate the value of fixed-rate perpetual preferred stock given the stock's annual dividend and the discount rate.
- Explain and calculate the present value of growth opportunities (PVGO) given current earnings per share, the required rate of return, and the market price of the stock (or value of the stock).
- Explain the strengths and limitations of the Gordon growth model.
- Justify the selection of the Gordon growth model to value a company, given the characteristics of the company being valued.
- Explain the assumptions and justify the selection of the two-stage DDM, the H-model, the three-stage DDM, and spreadsheet modeling.
- Explain the concepts of the growth phase, transitional phase, and maturity phase of a business.
- Explain the concept of terminal value and discuss alternative approaches to determining the terminal value in a discounted dividend model.
- Calculate the value of common stock using the two-stage DDM, the H-model, and the three-stage DDM.
- Justify the selection of a particular multistage dividend discount model given the characteristics of the company being valued.
- Explain how to estimate the implied expected rate of return for any DDM, including the two-stage DDM, the H-model, the three-stage DDM, and the spreadsheet model.
- Calculate the implied expected rate of return for the H-model and a general two-stage model.
- Explain the strengths and limitations of the two-stage DDM, the H-model, the three-stage DDM, and the spreadsheet model.
- Define the concept of sustainable growth rate and explain the underlying assumptions.
- Calculate the sustainable growth rate for a company.
- Explain how the DuPont model can be used to forecast the return on equity for use in estimating the sustainable growth rate.
- Discuss how dividend discount models are used as a discipline for portfolio selection, and explain two risk control methodologies.

1. INTRODUCTION

Common stock represents an ownership interest in a business. A business in its operations generates a stream of cash flows, and as owners of the business, common stockholders have an equity ownership claim on those future cash flows. Beginning with John Burr Williams (1938), analysts have developed this insight into a group of valuation models known as discounted cash flow (DCF) valuation models. DCF models—which view the intrinsic value of common stock as the present value of its expected future cash flows—are a fundamental tool in both investment management and investment research. This chapter is the first of three chapters that describe DCF models and address how to apply those models in practice.

What tasks do we face in approaching common stock valuation as a present value problem? We can distinguish two broad challenges.

The first challenge is to define exactly what we mean by *future cash flows* and, what is practically the heart of valuation, forecast what they will be in the future. In this chapter, we take the perspective that dividends—distributions to shareholders authorized by a corporation's board of directors—are an appropriate definition of cash flows. The class of models based on this idea is called dividend discount models, or DDMs. The basic objective of using a DDM is to value a stock. Among the questions we will address in this chapter that will help us apply DDMs are

- What implementation of the dividend discount model is suitable for a specific company?
- How do we forecast dividends?
- How can we use a dividend discount model to infer the market's estimate of the earnings growth rate or to infer a stock's expected rate of return?
- How are dividend discount models used in security selection?

Our second challenge is to estimate the appropriate rate of return to use for discounting cash flows back to the present, the discount rate. Our definitions of discount rate and cash flow must be coordinated, but the main alternative approaches to estimating discount rates are common to all present value models, so we shall also discuss discount rates in this chapter.

The chapter is organized as follows: Section 2 provides an overview of present value models. A general statement of the dividend discount model follows in Section 3. Forecasting dividends, individually and in detail, into the indefinite future is not generally practicable, so we usually simplify the dividend-forecasting problem. One approach is to assign dividends to a stylized growth pattern. The simplest pattern—dividends growing at a constant rate forever—is the constant growth (or Gordon growth) model, discussed in Section 4. For some companies, it is more appropriate to view earnings and dividends as having multiple stages of growth; we present multistage dividend discount models in Section 5. An alternative approach is to forecast dividends individually up to some date and then apply a simplifying assumption to estimate the terminal stock price. This approach is conveniently handled with the use of spreadsheets. We present spreadsheet modeling in Section 5 as well. Finally, Section 6 lays out the determinants of dividend growth rates and the use of DDMs in investment management.

2. PRESENT VALUE MODELS

The end product of the equity analysis process for individual securities is an investment recommendation. In the valuation part of the process, we estimate whether an asset is fairly valued, overvalued, or undervalued in the marketplace. Present value models are important tools for reaching such judgments. In this section, we discuss the economic rationale for valuing an asset as the present value of its expected future cash flows. We also discuss alternative definitions of cash flows and present the major alternative methods for estimating the discount rate.

2.1. Valuation Based on the Present Value of Future Cash Flows

The value of an asset must be related to the benefits or returns we expect to receive from holding it. We call those returns the asset's future cash flows (we will define *cash flow* more concretely and technically later). We also need to recognize that a given amount of money received in the future is worth less than the same amount of money received today. Money received today gives us the option of immediately spending and consuming it. So money has a time value. When valuing an asset, before adding up the estimated future cash flows, we must

discount each cash flow back to the present: We reduce the cash flow's value with respect to how far away it is in time. The two elements of discounted cash flow valuation—estimating the cash flows, and discounting the cash flows to account for the time value of money—provide the economic rationale for discounted cash flow valuation. Additional intuition comes from the observation that in the baseline case, in which the timing and amounts of future cash flows are known with certainty, if we invest an amount equal to the present value of future cash flows at the given discount rate, that investment will replicate all of the asset's cash flows (with no money left over).

For some assets, such as government debt, cash flows may be essentially known with certainty—that is, they are risk-free. The appropriate discount rate for a risk-free cash flow is a risk-free rate of interest. For example, if an asset has a single, certain cash flow of $100 to be received in two years, and the risk-free interest rate is 5 percent a year, the value of the asset is the present value of $100 discounted at the risk-free rate, $100/(1.05)^2 = 90.70.

In contrast to risk-free debt, future cash flows for equity investments are not known with certainty—they are risky. Introducing risk makes applying the present value approach much more challenging. The most common approach to dealing with risky cash flows involves two adjustments relative to the risk-free case. First, we discount the *expected* value of the cash flows, viewing the cash flows as random variables.[1] Second, we adjust the discount rate to reflect the risk of the cash flows.

The following equation expresses the concept that an asset's value is the present value of its (expected) future cash flows:

$$V_0 = \sum_{t=1}^{\infty} \frac{CF_t}{(1+r)^t} \qquad (2\text{-}1)$$

where

V_0 = the value of the asset at time $t = 0$ (today)
CF_t = the cash flow (or the expected cash flow, for risky cash flows) at time t
r = the discount rate or required rate of return

For simplicity, we represent the discount rate in Equation 2-1 as the same for all time periods, a flat term structure of discount rates. The analyst has the latitude in this model, however, to apply different discount rates to different cash flows.[2]

Equation 2-1 gives an asset's value from the perspective of today ($t = 0$). Likewise, an asset's value at some point in the future equals the value of all subsequent cash flows discounted back to that point in time. Example 2-1 illustrates these points.

---

[1] The expected value of a random quantity is the mean or average value of its possible outcomes, in which each outcome's weight in the average is its probability of occurrence. See DeFusco, McLeavey, Pinto, and Runkle (2001) for all statistical concepts used in this book.

[2] Different discount rates could reflect different degrees of cash flow riskiness or different risk-free rates at different time horizons. Differences in cash flow riskiness may be caused by differences in business risk, operating risk (use of fixed assets in production), or financial risk or leverage (use of debt in the capital structure). The simple expression given is adequate for the discussion, however.

EXAMPLE 2-1   Value as the Present Value of Future Cash Flows

We expect an asset to generate cash flows of $100 in one year, $150 in two years, and $200 in three years. The value of this asset today, using a 10 percent discount rate, is

$$V_0 = \frac{100}{(1.10)^1} + \frac{150}{(1.10)^2} + \frac{200}{(1.10)^3}$$

$$= 90.909 + 123.967 + 150.263 = \$365.14$$

The value at $t = 0$ is $365.14. We use this same logic to value an asset at a future date. The value of the asset at $t = 1$ is the present value, discounted back to $t = 1$, of all cash flows after this point. This value, V_1, is

$$V_1 = \frac{150}{(1.10)^1} + \frac{200}{(1.10)^2}$$

$$= 136.364 + 165.289 = \$301.65$$

At any point in time, the asset's value is the value of future cash flows (CF) discounted back to that point. Because V_1 represents the value of CF_2 and CF_3 at $t = 1$, the value of the asset at $t = 0$ is also the present value of CF_1 and V_1:

$$V_0 = \frac{100}{(1.10)^1} + \frac{301.653}{(1.10)^1}$$

$$= 90.909 + 274.23 = \$365.14$$

Finding V_0 as the present value of CF_1, CF_2, and CF_3 is logically equivalent to finding V_0 as the present value of CF_1 and V_1.

Although the principles behind discounted cash flow valuation are simple, applying the theory to equity valuation can be challenging. Four broad steps in applying DCF analysis to equity valuation are

- choosing the class of DCF model—equivalently, selecting a specific definition of cash flow;
- forecasting the cash flows;
- choosing a discount rate methodology; and
- estimating the discount rate.

In the next section, we present an overview of three alternative definitions of cash flow. The selected cash flow concept defines the type of DCF model we can use: the dividend discount model, the free cash flow model, or the residual income model. The next section also broadly characterizes the types of valuation problems for which analysts often choose a particular model. (We supply further details when each model is discussed individually.) Then, in Section 2.3, we discuss choosing a discount rate methodology and estimating the discount rate. We leave the discussion of cash flow forecasting to the chapters on each alternative DCF model.

2.2. Streams of Expected Cash Flows

In present value models of stock valuation, the three most widely used definitions of returns are dividends, free cash flow, and residual income. We discuss each definition in turn.

The dividend discount model defines cash flows as dividends. The basic argument for using this definition of cash flow is that an investor who buys and holds a share of stock generally receives cash returns only in the form of dividends.[3] In practice, analysts usually view investment value as driven by earnings. Does the definition of cash flow as dividends ignore earnings not distributed to shareholders as dividends? Reinvested earnings should provide the basis for increased future dividends. Therefore, the DDM accounts for reinvested earnings when it takes all future dividends into account. Because dividends are less volatile than earnings and other return concepts, the relative stability of dividends may make DDM values less sensitive to short-run fluctuations in underlying value than alternative DCF models. Analysts often view DDM values as reflecting long-run intrinsic value.

A stock either pays dividends or does not pay dividends. A company might not pay dividends on its stock because the company is not profitable and has no cash to distribute. Also, a company might not pay dividends for the opposite reason: because it is very profitable. For example, a company may reinvest all earnings—paying no dividends—to take advantage of profitable growth opportunities. As that company matures and faces fewer attractive investment opportunities, it may initiate dividends.

There are international differences in dividend policy. As one contrast, more than 90 percent of the FTSE Eurotop 300 stocks pay dividends, compared with approximately 70 percent of the stocks in the S&P 500 as of the beginning of 2002.[4] Nevertheless, in the United States, the majority of all companies with publicly traded shares do not pay dividends, and the fraction of dividend-paying companies has been declining. According to Fama and French (2001), 20.8 percent of U.S. stocks paid dividends in 1999, compared with 66.5 percent in 1978. This decline was caused by a reduced propensity to pay dividends over time as well as an increase in the population of smaller publicly traded companies with low profitability and large growth opportunities.[5] Can we apply the DDM to non-dividend-paying companies? In theory we can, as we will illustrate later, but in practice we generally do not.

Predicting the timing of dividend initiation and the magnitude of future dividends without any prior dividend data or specifics about dividend policy to guide the analysis is generally not practical. For a non-dividend-paying company, analysts usually prefer a model that defines returns at the company level (as free cash flow or residual income—we define these concepts shortly), rather than at the stockholder level (as dividends). Another consideration in the choice of models relates to ownership perspective. An investor purchasing a small ownership share does not have the ability to meaningfully influence the timing or magnitude of the distribution of the company's cash to shareholders. That perspective is the one taken in applying a dividend discount model. The only access to the company's value is through

---

[3]Corporations can also effectively distribute cash to stockholders through stock repurchases (also called buybacks). This fact does not affect the argument, however.

[4]*Financial Times of London*, January 28, 2002.

[5]Even controlling for profitability and growth opportunities, the propensity of companies to pay dividends has been declining in the U.S. markets, according to Fama and French (2001).

the receipt of dividends, and dividend policy is taken as a given. If dividends do not bear an understandable relation to value creation in the company, applying the DDM to value the stock is prone to error.

Generally, the definition of returns as dividends, and the DDM, is most suitable when

- the company is dividend-paying (i.e., the analyst has a dividend record to analyze);
- the board of directors has established a dividend policy that bears an understandable and consistent relationship to the company's profitability; and
- the investor takes a non-control perspective.

Often, companies with established dividends are seasoned companies, profitable but operating outside the economy's fastest-growing subsectors. Professional analysts often apply a dividend discount model to value the common stock of such companies.

EXAMPLE 2-2 Occidental Petroleum and Hormel Foods: Is the DDM an Appropriate Choice?

As director of equity research at a brokerage, you have final responsibility in the choice of valuation models. Two analysts have approached you on the use of a dividend discount model: an oil industry analyst examining Occidental Petroleum Corporation (NYSE: OXY) and a food industry analyst examining Hormel Foods (NYSE: HRL). Table 2-1 gives the most recent 10 years of data. (In the table, EPS is earnings per share, DPS is dividends per share, and payout ratio is DPS divided by EPS. "E$4.92" means that $4.92 is an estimated value.)

TABLE 2-1   OXY and HRL: The Earnings and Dividends Record

	1992	1993	1994	1995	1996	1997	1998	1999	2000	2001
OXY										
EPS	$0.41	$0.12	−$0.36	$1.31	$1.86	$0.39	$0.88	$1.58	$4.26	E$4.92
DPS	$1.00	$1.00	$1.00	$1.00	$1.00	$1.00	$1.00	$1.00	$1.00	$1.00
Payout Ratio	244%	833%	NM*	76%	54%	256%	114%	63%	23%	E20%
HRL										
EPS	$0.62	$0.66	$0.77	$0.79	$0.52	$0.72	$0.93	$1.11	$1.20	$1.30
DPS	$0.18	$0.22	$0.25	$0.29	$0.30	$0.39	$0.32	$0.33	$0.35	$0.37
Payout Ratio	29%	33%	32%	37%	58%	54%	34%	30%	29%	28%

*NM = Not meaningful
Source: Standard & Poor's Stock Reports.

Answer the following questions based on the information in Table 2-1:

1. State whether a dividend discount model is an appropriate choice for valuing OXY. Explain your answer.

2. State whether a dividend discount model is an appropriate choice for valuing HRL. Explain your answer.

Solution to 1: Based only on the data given in Table 2-1, a DDM does not appear to be an appropriate choice for OXY. Although OXY is dividend-paying, OXY's dividends do not bear an understandable and consistent relationship to earnings. Dividend payout ratios have varied from 833 percent to 20 percent when earnings have been positive. Dividends have been constant at $1.00 a share throughout the period, and earnings have been very volatile. If the volatility reflected only random, transitory effects on profitability, the analyst might consider a DDM. However, earnings since 1998 appear to be at a consistently higher level than in 1992–94. Expected EPS of $4.92 in 2001 represents a 12-fold increase from $0.41 in 1992. Because dividends do not appear to adjust to reflect changes in value, applying a DDM to OXY is probably inappropriate. Valuing OXY on another basis, such as company-level definition of cash flows, is more appropriate.

Solution to 2: The historical earnings of HRL show a long-term upward trend, with the exception of 1996 and 1997. Although you might want to research those divergent payout ratios, HRL's dividends have generally followed its growth in earnings. Dividends per share of $0.37 in 2001 were roughly twice the level of $0.18 in 1992, and earnings per share have also doubled over that period. In summary, because HRL is dividend-paying and dividends bear an understandable and consistent relationship to earnings, using a DDM to value HRL is appropriate.

Valuation is a forward-looking exercise. In practice, the analyst would check for public disclosures concerning changes in dividend policy going forward. We will return to discuss the valuation of Hormel stock in Example 2-22.

A second definition of returns is free cash flow. The term *cash flow* has been given many meanings in different contexts. Above, we have used the term informally, referring to returns to ownership (equity). We now want to give it a more technical meaning, related to accounting usage. Over a given period of time, a company can add to cash (or use up cash) by selling goods and services. This money is cash flow from operations (for that time period). Cash flow from operations is the critical cash flow concept addressing a business's underlying economics. Companies can also generate (or use up) cash in two other ways. First, a company affects cash through buying and selling assets, including investment and disinvestment in plant and equipment. Second, a company can add to or reduce cash through its financing activities. Financing includes debt and equity. For example, issuing bonds increases cash, and buying back stock decreases cash (all else equal).[6]

---

[6]Internationally, accounting definitions may not be fully consistent with the above concepts in distinguishing between types of sources and uses of cash. Although the implementation details are not the focus here, an example can be given. U.S. generally accepted accounting principles (GAAP) include a financing item, net interest payments, in *cash flow from operating activities*, so careful analysts working with U.S. accounting data often add back after-tax net interest payments to cash flow from operating activities when calculating cash flow from operations. Under International Accounting Standards, companies may or may not include interest expense as an operating cash flow.

Assets supporting current sales may need replacement because of obsolescence or wear and tear, and the company may need new assets to take advantage of profitable growth opportunities. The concept of free cash flow responds to the reality that, for a going concern, some of the cash flow from operations is not "free" but rather needs to be committed to reinvestment and new investment in assets. **Free cash flow to the firm** (FCFF) is cash flow from operations minus capital expenditures. Capital expenditures—reinvestment in new assets, including working capital—are needed to maintain the company as a going concern, so only that part of cash flow from operations remaining after such reinvestment is "free." (This definition is conceptual; Chapter 3 defines free cash flow concepts in detail.) FCFF is the part of the cash flow generated by the company's operations that can be withdrawn by bondholders and stockholders without economically impairing the company. Conceptually, the value of common equity is the present value of expected future FCFF—the total value of the company—minus the market value of outstanding debt.

Another approach to valuing equity works with free cash flow to equity. **Free cash flow to equity** (FCFE) is cash flow from operations minus capital expenditures, or FCFF, from which we net all payments to debtholders (interest and principal repayments net of new debt issues). Debt has a claim on the cash of the company that must be satisfied before any money can be paid to stockholders, so money paid on debt is not available to common stockholders. Conceptually, common equity can be valued as the present value of expected FCFE. FCFF is a pre-debt free cash flow concept; FCFE is a post-debt free cash flow concept. The FCFE model is the baseline free cash flow valuation model for equity, but the FCFF model may be easier to apply in several cases, such as when the company's leverage (debt in its capital structure) is expected to change significantly over time, as we will discuss in more detail in the chapter on free cash flow valuation.

Valuation using a free cash flow concept is popular in current investment practice. We can calculate free cash flow (FCFF or FCFE) for any company. We can always examine the record of free cash flows, in contrast to dividends. FCFE can be viewed as measuring what a company can afford to pay out in dividends. Even for dividend-paying companies, a free cash flow model valuation may be preferred when dividends exceed or fall short of FCFE by significant amounts.[7] FCFE also represents cash flow that can be redeployed outside the company without affecting the company's capital investments. A controlling equity interest can effect such a redeployment. As a result, free cash flow valuation is appropriate for investors who want to take a control perspective. (Even a small shareholder may want to take such a perspective when there is potential for the company to be acquired, because stock price should reflect the price an acquirer would pay.)

Just as there are cases in which an analyst would find it impractical to apply the DDM, applying the free cash flow approach is a problem in some cases. Some companies have intense capital demands and, as a result, have negative expected free cash flows far into the future. As one example, a retailer may be constantly constructing new outlets and be far from saturating even its domestic market. Even if the retailer is currently very profitable, free cash flow may be negative indefinitely because of the level of capital expenditures. The present value of a series of negative free cash flows is a negative number: The use of a free cash flow model may entail a long forecast horizon to capture the point at which expected free cash flow turns positive. The

---

[7]In theory, when period-by-period dividends equal FCFE, the DDM and FCFE models should value stock identically, if all other assumptions are consistent. See Miller and Modigliani (1961), a classic reference for the mathematics and theory of present value models of stock value.

uncertainty associated with distant forecasts may be considerable. In such cases, the analyst may have more confidence using another approach, such as residual income valuation.

Generally, defining returns as free cash flow and using the FCFE (and FCFF) models are most suitable when

- the company is not dividend-paying;
- the company is dividend-paying but dividends significantly exceed or fall short of free cash flow to equity;
- the company's free cash flows align with the company's profitability within a forecast horizon with which the analyst is comfortable; and
- the investor takes a control perspective.

The third and final definition of returns that we will discuss in this overview is residual income. Conceptually, **residual income** for a given time period is the earnings for that period in excess of the investors' required return on beginning-of-period investment (common stockholders' equity). Suppose shareholders' initial investment is $200 million, and the required rate of return on the stock is 8 percent. The required rate of return is investors' **opportunity cost** for investing in the stock: the alternative return that investors forgo when investing in the stock. The company earns $18 million in the course of a year. How much value has the company added for shareholders? A return of 0.08 × $200 million = $16 million just meets the amount investors could have earned in an equivalent-risk investment (by the definition of opportunity cost). Only the residual or excess amount of $18 million − $16 million = $2 million represents value added, or an economic gain, to shareholders. So, $2 million is the company's residual income for the period. The residual income approach attempts to match profits to the time period in which they are earned (but not necessarily realized as cash); in contrast to accounting net income (which has the same goal in principle), however, residual income attempts to measure the value added in excess of opportunity costs.

The residual income model states that a stock's value is book value per share plus the present value of expected future residual earnings. (Book value per share is common stockholders' equity divided by the number of common shares outstanding.) In contrast to the dividend and free cash flow models, the residual income model introduces a stock concept, book value per share, into the present value expression. Nevertheless, the residual income model can be viewed as a restatement of the dividend discount model, using a company-level return concept. Dividends are paid out of earnings and are related to earnings and book value through a simple expression.[8] The residual income model is a useful addition to an analyst's toolbox. Because we can always calculate the record of residual income, we may use a residual income model for both dividend-paying and non-dividend-paying stocks. Analysts may choose a residual income approach for companies with negative expected free cash flows within their comfortable forecast horizon. In such cases, a residual income valuation often

---

[8] Book value of equity at t = (Book value of equity at $t - 1$) + (Earnings over $t - 1$ to t)−(Dividends paid at t), so long as anything that goes through the balance sheet (affecting book value) first goes through the income statement (reflected in earnings), apart from ownership transactions. The condition that all changes in the book value of equity other than transactions with owners are reflected in income is known as **clean surplus accounting**. U.S. and international accounting standards do not always follow clean surplus accounting; the analyst, therefore, in using this expression, must critically evaluate whether accounting-based results conform to clean surplus accounting and, if they do not, adjust them appropriately.

brings the recognition of value closer to the present as compared with a free cash flow valuation, producing higher value estimates.

The residual income model has an attractive focus on profitability in relation to opportunity costs.[9] Knowledgeable application of the residual income model requires a detailed knowledge of accrual accounting; consequently, in cases for which the dividend discount model is suitable, analysts may prefer it as the simpler choice. Management sometimes exercises its discretion within allowable accounting practices to distort the accuracy of its financials as a reflection of economic performance. If the quality of accounting disclosure is good, the analyst may be able to calculate residual income by making appropriate adjustments (to reported net income and book value, in particular). In some cases, the degree of distortion and the quality of accounting disclosure can be such that the application of the residual income model is error-prone.

Generally, the definition of returns as residual income, and the residual income model, is most suitable when

- the company is not dividend-paying, as an alternative to a free cash flow model; or
- the company's expected free cash flows are negative within the analyst's comfortable forecast horizon.

In summary, the three most widely used definitions of returns to investors are dividends, free cash flow, and residual income. Although claims are often made that one cash flow definition is inherently superior to the rest—often following changing fashions in investment practice—a more flexible viewpoint is practical. The analyst may find that one model is more suitable to a particular valuation problem. The analyst may also develop more expertise in applying one type of model. In practice, skill in application—in particular, the quality of forecasts—is frequently decisive for the usefulness of the analyst's work.

In the next section, we discuss a task that we face no matter which DCF model we apply: the determination of the discount rate. We will then present the dividend discount model in detail.

2.3. Discount Rate Determination

In a previous section, we stated that two of the tasks in applying DCF analysis to equity valuation are choosing a discount rate methodology and estimating the discount rate. In this section, we present and illustrate the major alternative methods available for determining the discount rate. (**Discount rate** is a general term for any rate used in finding the present value of a future cash flow.)

In choosing a discount rate, we want it to reflect both the time value of money and the riskiness of the stock. The risk-free rate represents the time value of money. A **risk premium** represents compensation for risk, measured relative to the risk-free rate. The risk premium is an expected return in excess of the risk-free rate that is related to risk. When we decide on a discount rate that reflects both the time value of money and an asset's risk, as we perceive it, we have determined our required rate of return. A **required rate of return** is the minimum rate of return required by an investor to invest in an asset, given the asset's riskiness. Sometimes we refer to *the* required rate of return for an asset. This is a required rate of return on an asset

---

[9]Executive compensation schemes are sometimes based on a residual income concept, including branded variations such as Economic Value Added (EVA®) from Stern Stewart & Co.

that we infer using market data, which should represent a type of consensus perspective on the asset's risk. Generally, we use such required rates of return in DCF valuation. In this book, we use the notation r for the required rate of return on the asset we are discussing. The required rate of return on common stock is also known as the **cost of equity**.

Whether we define cash flow as dividends, free cash flow to equity, or residual income, we use a cost-of-equity concept of the required rate of return, because each of those return concepts is a post-debt flow to equity. If we use a FCFF valuation model, we are defining cash flows as the cash flows available to bondholders, common stockholders, and preferred stockholders, if any. Consequently, in FCFF valuation, we use the cost of capital (taking into account all sources of financing) as the required rate of return. To use the precise term, we use the **weighted-average cost of capital**—the weighted average of the cost of equity, the after-tax cost of debt,[10] and the cost of preferred stock. The weight on each cost component is the fraction of total long-term financing (common stock, debt, preferred stock) that each financing source represents, at market values, in the company's desired or target capital structure. No matter what cash flow concept we use, we need to calculate the cost of equity. The cost of equity is the most challenging element in discount-rate determination and will be our focus in this discussion.

We present two major approaches to determining the cost of equity:

- an equilibrium model method, based on either the capital asset pricing model (CAPM) or arbitrage pricing theory (APT), and
- the bond yield plus risk premium method.

Equilibrium methods are based on formal economic models. (**Equilibrium** describes a condition in which supply equals demand.) These models address in particular the structure of the risk premium that we add to the risk-free rate. The bond yield plus risk premium method is based on empirical relationships.

The CAPM states that the expected return on an asset is related to its risk as measured by beta:

$$E(R_i) = R_F + \beta_i[E(R_M) - R_F] \qquad (2\text{-}2)$$

where

$$\begin{aligned}
E(R_i) &= \text{the expected return on asset } i \text{ given its beta} \\
R_F &= \text{the risk-free rate of return} \\
E(R_M) &= \text{the expected return on the market portfolio} \\
\beta_i &= \text{the asset's sensitivity to returns on the market portfolio, equal to } \mathrm{Cov}(R_i, R_M)/ \\
& \quad\; \mathrm{Var}(R_M)
\end{aligned}$$

The term in square brackets is the **market risk premium**, the expected return on the market minus the risk-free rate. The CAPM thus states that the expected return on an asset, given its beta, is the risk-free rate plus a risk premium equal to beta times the market risk premium. In practice, we always estimate beta with respect to an equity market index when using the

---

[10]In some countries, including the United States, interest on debt is tax deductible, which reduces its cost. Common and preferred stock dividends are not tax deductible, so an after-tax/before-tax distinction is not made for those components of the cost of capital.

CAPM to estimate the cost of equity. So in practice, discussing equity, we are concerned specifically with the **equity risk premium** (defining the market as the equity market).

We can use the CAPM-based expected rate of return for a common stock as the cost of equity in a DCF valuation. That rate is $E(R_i) = r$, the required rate of return on equity. Given that the CAPM describes equilibrium, so that all risk is captured by beta, investors make risk adjustments based on beta. We must clearly distinguish between the expected return given by a model, which is an equilibrium expected return (an estimate of the fair return) based on a model, and an individual's expected return on an asset based on current market prices (which may differ from intrinsic value). The CAPM can be used in any national market.

EXAMPLE 2-3   Calculating the Cost of Equity Using the CAPM

You are valuing J.C. Penney Company (NYSE: JCP), a major consumer goods retailer, as of the end of 2001. As one step, you need to estimate the required rate of return on JCP stock. Based on its beta of 0.55, a historical risk premium of 5.7 percent, and a risk-free rate of 5.7 percent, the required rate of return on JCP according to the CAPM is $R_F + \beta_i[E(R_M) - R_F] = 0.057 + (0.55 \times 0.057) = 0.08835$, or 8.8 percent. (In this case, the risk-free rate and the risk premium happen to be the same.)

To use the CAPM, we need to answer two questions:

- What proxy for risk-free rate of return do we adopt?[11]
- How do we define and estimate the equity risk premium?

The definition of the risk-free rate should be coordinated with how the equity risk premium is calculated.

The choices for the risk-free rate are a short-term government debt rate, such as a 30-day T-bill rate, or a long-term government bond yield to maturity. Common stock has no maturity date. As a consequence, common stock is a long-duration asset (Fabozzi [2000] discusses duration as a measure of the futurity of an asset's cash flows). Because it is logical to match the duration of the risk-free measure to the duration of the asset being valued, this book uses the current yield to maturity on a liquid long-term government bond as the risk-free rate. The available maturities of government bonds change over time and differ among national markets. If a 20-year maturity is available and trades in a liquid market, however, its yield is a reasonable choice as an estimate of the risk-free rate for equity valuation.[12] In many international markets, only bonds of shorter maturity are available or have a liquid market. A 10-year government bond yield is another common choice.

---

[11] In this context, a proxy is something used to represent a concept.
[12] The Ibbotson U.S. long-term government bond yield is based on a portfolio of 20-year average maturity T-bonds. We use that series in the suggested historical estimate of the U.S. equity risk premium.

TABLE 2-2   U.S. Annual Total Returns: 1926–2000

Series	Geometric Mean (%)	Arithmetic Mean (%)	Standard Deviation (%)
Common stocks	11.0	13.0	20.2
Small company stocks	12.4	17.3	33.4
Long-term corporate bonds	5.7	6.0	8.7
Long-term government bonds	5.3	5.7	9.4
Intermediate-term government bonds	5.3	5.5	5.8
Treasury bills	3.8	3.9	3.2
Inflation	3.1	3.2	4.4

Source: Ibbotson Associates.

We need to address estimation of the equity risk premium to have a workable method. Clearly, to be consistent, the equity risk premium should be relative to a long-term government bond yield. So we define the equity risk premium as the expected return on a broad equity index in excess of the long-term government bond yield to maturity (or yield). The CAPM estimate of the cost of equity is then

$$
\begin{aligned}
\text{CAPM cost of equity} = \ & \text{Current long-term government bond yield} \\
& + \text{Stock's beta} \\
& \times \text{Estimated equity risk premium relative} \\
& \text{to the long-term yield}
\end{aligned}
\tag{2-3}
$$

Two broad approaches exist for estimating the equity risk premium, one based on historical average differences between equity market returns and government debt returns, the other based on expectational data (for example, expected earnings on the equity index). When reliable, long-term records of equity return are available, the historical method is the most familiar and popular choice. An expectational method is consistent with the forward-looking nature of valuation; it may be the only available alternative for an emerging stock market.

In taking a historical approach, we face a choice between using the arithmetic mean return (typically, the average of one-year rates of return) and using the geometric mean return (the compound rate of growth of the index over the study period). The arithmetic mean more accurately measures average one-period returns; the geometric mean more accurately measures multiperiod growth. The dilemma is that the CAPM (as well as the APT) is a single-period model, suggesting the use of the arithmetic mean; but common stock investment often has a long time horizon, and valuation involves discounting cash flows over many periods, suggesting the use of the geometric mean. Estimates of risk premiums using geometric means are consistently smaller than estimates using arithmetic means, and the differences can be significant. We can illustrate this concept for U.S. markets using data from *Stocks, Bonds, Bills, and Inflation*, published annually by Ibbotson Associates, given in Table 2-2.

Using long-term government bond returns as a proxy for the risk-free rate of return and geometric means, the historical estimate of the U.S. equity risk premium is 5.7 percent (11.0 percent minus 5.3 percent).[13] Using arithmetic means, we arrive at an estimate of

---

[13]Calculating the geometric mean of the difference of two series as the difference in geometric means involves an approximation with a negligible error.

TABLE 2-3   Historical Equity Risk Premiums around the World: 1900–2000

Country	Equity Risk Premium (based on long bond rate)	Equity Risk Premium (based on T-bill rate)
Australia	5.9%	7.1%
Canada	4.6	4.6
Denmark (from 1915)	2.5	2.8
France	5.0	7.7
Germany (98 years ex-1923/4)	6.9	5.1
Italy	5.0	7.1
Japan	6.4	7.5
Netherlands	4.8	5.2
Sweden	5.8	6.1
Switzerland (from 1911)	2.8	4.3
United Kingdom	5.3	4.9
United States	4.6	5.8
Average	5.0	5.7

Source: Dimson, Marsh, and Staunton (2000).

7.3 percent (13.0 percent minus 5.7 percent). Although the debate is inconclusive, this book uses geometric means, not only for the previously given reasons but also because geometric means produce estimates of the equity risk premium that are more consistent with the predictions of economic theory.[14] To summarize, we can calculate the historical estimate of the market risk premium as the historical geometric mean return on a representative equity index minus the historical geometric mean return on long-term government bonds in the same country's markets.

Table 2-3 shows historical estimates of the equity risk premium for 12 major markets over the period 1900–2000.

Historical estimates of the equity premiums have limitations. **Survivorship bias**, which results when poorly performing companies are removed from membership in an index, tends to inflate historical estimates of the equity risk premium (the data in Table 2-3 reflect a correction for survivorship bias, however).[15] Because of the great volatility in equity returns, a long data series is needed to estimate the premium with any precision, even assuming the target (the underlying value) is fixed. However, there is evidence from a number of markets that the equity risk premium varies over time. Data from distant periods may be questionably relevant for the future, our concern in valuation. To address this concern, we can use an estimator of the equity risk premium based explicitly on expectational data. Probably the most frequently encountered estimate of this type (that is, based on expectational data) is the Gordon growth model (GGM) equity risk premium estimate:[16]

---

[14]See Mehra and Prescott (1985). The relatively large size of the historical U.S. equity premium relative to that predicted by theory, given estimates of investors' risk aversion, is known as the "equity premium puzzle." The geometric mean was also the choice of Dimson, Marsh, and Staunton (2000) in their authoritative survey of world equity markets.

[15]Copeland, Koller, and Murrin (2000) recommend a downward adjustment of 1.5 percent to 2.0 percent for survivorship bias in the S&P 500 Index, using arithmetic mean estimates. In their development of the Millennium Book series, Dimson et al. took great care to correct for survivorship data.

GGM equity risk premium estimate

= (Dividend yield on the index based on year-ahead forecasted dividends

+ Consensus long-term earnings growth rate)

− Current long-term government bond yield   (2-4)

As of the end of 2001, the consensus future five-year earnings growth rate on the S&P 500 Index was 7.0 percent, according to First Call/Thomson Financial (compared with a 12.15 percent earnings growth rate over the previous five years). Based on consensus forecasts of the next year's earnings and an S&P 500 level of 1145, the forecasted dividend yield was 1.2 percent. The 20-year U.S. government bond yield was 5.8 percent. Therefore, according to Equation 2-4, the Gordon growth model estimate of the U.S. equity risk premium was $0.012 + 0.070 − 0.058 = 0.024$, or 2.4 percent. As with any approach to estimating the risk premium, the Gordon growth model has possible limitations. The fact that different approaches may lead to different premium estimates and possibly different actions is part of the challenge of valuation.[17]

The CAPM is an established method of estimating the cost of equity. Its strengths are simplicity and familiarity. Beta is easily obtained from a variety of sources. The balance of evidence, however, shows that the CAPM beta describes risk incompletely. In practice, coefficients of determination (R-squared) for individual stocks' beta regressions may range from 2 percent to 40 percent, with many under 10 percent. For many markets, evidence suggests that multiple factors drive returns. At the cost of greater complexity and expense, the analyst can consider using an equilibrium model based on multiple factors. Such models are known as arbitrage pricing theory (APT) models. Whereas the CAPM adds a single risk premium to the risk-free rate, APT models add a set of risk premiums. APT models have the form

$$E(R_i) = R_F + (\text{Risk premium})_1 + (\text{Risk premium})_2 + \cdots + (\text{Risk premium})_K \qquad (2\text{-}5)$$

where $(\text{Risk premium})_i = (\text{Factor sensitivity})_i \times (\text{Factor risk premium})_i$. **Factor sensitivity** is the asset's sensitivity to a particular factor (holding all other factors constant). The **factor risk premium** is the factor's expected return in excess of the risk-free rate.[18]

One type of APT model incorporates company-specific attributes. An example of such models is the Fama–French (1993) three-factor model. This model's factors are

---

[16]Recent examples of the application of this model (to U.S. markets) are Jagannathan, McGrattan, and Scherbina (2000) and Fama and French (2001). The Gordon growth model estimate has also been used in institutional research for international markets (Stux 1994). Most analysts forecast the earnings growth rate rather than the dividend growth rate, which is technically specified in theory, so we use the earnings growth rate in the above expression. Given a constant dividend payout ratio, a reasonable approximation for broad equity indexes, the two growth rates should be equal. We present the Gordon growth model later in this chapter.

[17]Fama and French (2001) found that prior to 1950, the historical and Gordon growth model estimates for the U.S. equity risk premium agree, but from 1950–99, the Gordon growth model estimate averages less than half the historical estimate. They attribute the difference to the effect of positive earnings surprises relative to expectations on realized returns.

[18]For a slightly more technical statement of the APT, see Chapter 11 of DeFusco, McLeavey, Pinto, and Runkle (2001).

- RMRF, the return on a value-weighted equity index in excess of the one-month T-bill rate.
- SMB (small minus big), a size (market capitalization) factor. SMB is the average return on three small-cap portfolios minus the average return on three large-cap portfolios.
- HML (high minus low), the average return on two high book-to-market portfolios minus the average return on two low book-to-market portfolios.[19]

A second type of APT model employs macroeconomic factors. For example, the Burmeister, Roll, and Ross (1994) or BIRR model is based on five macroeconomic factors that affect the average returns of U.S. stocks. The five factors are the following:

- Confidence risk, the unanticipated change in the return difference between 20-year corporate and 20-year government bonds. (When investors' confidence is high, investors should be willing to accept a smaller reward for bearing this risk, hence the name.)
- Time horizon risk, the unanticipated change in the return difference between 20-year government bonds and 30-day Treasury bills. This factor reflects willingness to invest for the long term.
- Inflation risk, the unexpected change in the inflation rate. Nearly all stocks have negative sensitivity to this factor, as their returns decline with positive surprises in inflation.
- Business-cycle risk, the unexpected change in the level of real business activity.
- Market-timing risk, the portion of the S&P 500 total return that is not explained by the first four risk factors. Almost all stocks have positive sensitivity to this factor.

Each of the five BIRR factors can be interpreted as affecting the numerator or the denominator of Equation 2-1, the DCF valuation equation. Equation 2-6 is the equation for the BIRR model for the United States, using factor risk premium values in Burmeister et al; that study estimated risk premiums relative to the T-bill rate.

$$E(R_i) = \text{T-bill rate} + (\text{Sensitivity to confidence risk} \times 2.59\%)$$
$$- (\text{Sensitivity to time horizon risk} \times 0.66\%)$$
$$- (\text{Sensitivity to inflation risk} \times 4.32\%)$$
$$+ (\text{Sensitivity to business-cycle risk} \times 1.49\%)$$
$$+ (\text{Sensitivity to market-timing risk} \times 3.61\%) \qquad (2\text{-}6)$$

EXAMPLE 2-4   Calculating the Cost of Equity Using an APT Model

You have estimated the factor sensitivities of Johnson & Johnson, Inc., common stock (NYSE: JNJ) on BIRR factors. These are given in Table 2-4, with the factor sensitivities of the S&P 500 for comparison.

---

[19]See http://mba.tuck.dartmouth.edu/pages/faculty/ken.french/ for more information on the Fama–French model and factor data information.

TABLE 2-4   Factor Sensitivities in the BIRR Model

Risk Factor	JNJ Factor Sensitivity	S&P 500 Factor Sensitivities
Confidence risk	0.17	0.27
Time horizon risk	0.74	0.56
Inflation risk	−0.15	−0.37
Business-cycle risk	1.16	1.71
Market-timing risk	0.72	1.00

Using the factor risk premiums estimated by Burmeister et al. and with a T-bill rate of 5 percent, calculate the required rate of return for JNJ using the multifactor model.

The required rate of return for JNJ is

$$r = 5.00\% + (0.17 \times 2.59\%) - (0.74 \times 0.66\%) - (-0.15 \times 4.32\%)$$
$$+ (1.16 \times 1.49\%) + (0.72 \times 3.61\%)$$
$$= 9.93\%$$

Using the CAPM or APT, at least three possible sources of error exist in our cost-of-equity estimates: model uncertainty (concerning whether the model is correct), input uncertainty (for example, are the equity risk premium and risk-free rate used in the CAPM correct?), and uncertainty about the true current value of the stock's beta or factor sensitivity or sensitivities. (When we obtain beta by conducting the needed regression of stock returns on an equity index's returns ourselves, we should check the t-statistic of beta and note the regression's R-squared as indicators of the usefulness of CAPM for explaining returns on the stock.)[20] Having an alternative to the CAPM and APT is useful. For companies with publicly traded debt, the **bond yield plus risk premium method** (BYPRP) provides a quick estimate of the cost of equity.[21] The estimate is

BYPRP cost of equity = YTM on the company's long-term debt + Risk premium   (2-7)

The yield to maturity (YTM) on the company's long-term debt incorporates the time value of money and default risk, which is related to the business's profitability and leverage. The risk premium compensates for the additional risk of equity compared with debt (debt has a prior claim on the cash flows of the company). In U.S. markets, the typical risk premium added is 3–4 percent, based on experience.

---

[20] See DeFusco et al. (2001) for definitions of these terms and a discussion of issues surrounding estimating beta.

[21] Although simple, the method has been used in serious contexts. For example, the Board of Regents of the University of California in a retirement plan asset/liability study (July 2000) used the 20-year T-bond rate plus 3.3 percent as the single estimate of the equity risk premium.

EXAMPLE 2-5   The Cost of Equity of IBM from
Two Perspectives
___

You are valuing the stock of International Business Machines Corporation (NYSE:
IBM) as of December 21, 2001, and you have gathered the following information:

> 20-year T-bond yield to maturity: 5.8%
> IBM 8.375s of 2019 yield to maturity: 6.238%

The IBM bonds, you note, are investment grade (rated A1 by Standard & Poor's and
A+ by Moody's Investors Service). The beta on IBM stock is 1.24.

1. Calculate the cost of equity using the CAPM. Assume that the equity risk
    premium is 5.7 percent.
2. Calculate the cost of equity using the bond yield plus risk premium approach,
    with a risk premium of 3 percent.
3. Suppose you found that IBM stock, which closed at 121.45 on December 21,
    2001, was slightly undervalued based on a DCF valuation using the CAPM cost
    of equity from Question 1. Does the alternative estimate of the cost of equity
    from Question 2 support the conclusion based on Question 1?

Solution to 1: $E(R_i) = 0.058 + 0.057\beta_i = 0.058 + 0.057 \times 1.24 = 0.058 + 0.0706$
$= 0.1286$, or 12.9%.

Solution to 2: We add 3 percent to the IBM bond YTM: 6.238% + 3% = 9.238%, or
9.2%. Note that the difference between the IBM and T-bond YTM is 0.438 percent, or
44 basis points. This amount plus 3 percent is the total risk premium versus Treasury
debt.

Solution to 3: *Undervalued* means that the value of a security is greater than market
price. All else equal, the smaller the discount rate, the higher the estimate of value.
The inverse relationship between discount rate and value, holding all else constant, is a
basic relationship in valuation. If IBM appears to be undervalued using the CAPM cost
of equity estimate of 12.9 percent, it will appear to be even more undervalued using a
9.2 percent cost of equity based on the bond yield plus risk premium method.

How can we estimate the cost of equity for a privately held company? In contrast to publicly
traded shares, we will not have a record of market prices for a private company's stock and
cannot calculate beta or factor sensitivities of the shares directly. The cost of equity using either
the CAPM or APT is the sum of the risk-free rate and one or more risk premiums. Business
valuators of privately held businesses often determine a discount rate by a **build-up method**.
The cost of equity using a build-up method is the sum of risk premiums, in which one or
more of the risk premiums is typically subjective rather than grounded in a formal model such
as the CAPM or APT. For example, the cost of equity may be calculated as the sum of the

current risk-free rate and an equity risk premium, plus or minus a subjective company-specific risk adjustment.[22]

The bond yield plus risk premium method is, in fact, a build-up method applying to companies with publicly traded debt. A build-up method other than the bond yield plus risk premium method can sometimes be useful when valuing publicly traded stock as well (as Example 2-10 later will show). The CAPM's reliability for estimating the cost of equity, as judged by R-squared or beta's t-statistic, may be suspect in a particular case. The company may have no publicly traded debt so that the bond yield plus risk premium method is not feasible. Using an APT estimate of the cost of equity is one alternative; using an estimate that is the sum of the risk-free rate, an equity risk premium, and a company-specific risk adjustment is another.

In the next section, we present the general form of the dividend discount model as a prelude to discussing the particular implementations of the model that are suitable for different sets of attributes of the company being valued.

3. THE DIVIDEND DISCOUNT MODEL

Investment analysts use a wide range of models and techniques to estimate the value of common stock, including present value models. In Section 2.2, we discussed three common definitions of returns for use in present value analysis: dividends, free cash flow, and residual income. In this section, we develop the most general form of the dividend discount model.

The DDM is the simplest and oldest present value approach to valuing stock. In a survey by Block (1999), 42 percent of respondents viewed the DDM as "very important" or "moderately important" for determining the value of individual stocks. Beginning in 1989, the *Merrill Lynch Institutional Factor Survey* has assessed the popularity of 23 valuation factors and methods among a group of institutional investors. From 1989 to 2000, the DDM has ranked as high as fifth in popularity. Besides its continuing significant position in practice, the DDM has an important place in both academic and practitioner equity research. The DDM is, for all these reasons, a basic tool in equity valuation.

3.1. The Expression for a Single Holding Period

From the perspective of a shareholder who buys and holds a share of stock, the cash flows he or she will obtain are the dividends paid on it and the market price of the share when he or she sells it. The future selling price should in turn reflect expectations about dividends subsequent to the sale. In this section, we will see how this argument leads to the most general form of the dividend discount model. In addition, the general expression we develop for a finite holding period corresponds to one practical approach to DDM valuation; in that approach, the analyst forecasts dividends over a finite horizon, as well as the terminal sales price.

If an investor wishes to buy a share of stock and hold it for one year, the value of that share of stock today is the present value of the expected dividend to be received on the stock plus the present value of the expected selling price in one year:

$$V_0 = \frac{D_1}{(1+r)^1} + \frac{P_1}{(1+r)^1} = \frac{D_1 + P_1}{(1+r)^1} \qquad (2\text{-}8)$$

---

[22] See Hawkins and Paschall (2000) for more information on private company valuation, including the determination of the discount rate in private market valuations.

where

V_0 = the value of a share of stock today, at $t = 0$

P_1 = the expected price per share at $t = 1$

D_1 = the expected dividend per share for Year 1, assumed to be paid at the end of the year at $t = 1$

r = the required rate of return on the stock

Equation 2-8 applies to a single holding period the principle that an asset's value is the present value of its future cash flows. In this case, the expected cash flows are the dividend in one year (for simplicity, assumed to be received as one payment at the end of the year)[23] and the price of the stock in one year.

EXAMPLE 2-6   DDM Value with a Single Holding Period

Suppose that you expect General Motors Corporation (NYSE: GM) to pay a $2.00 dividend next year and that you expect the price of GM stock to be $58.00 in one year. The required rate of return for GM stock is 10 percent. What is your estimate of the value of GM stock?

Discounting the expected dividend of $2.00 and the expected sales price of $58.00 at the cost of equity of 0.10, we obtain

$$V_0 = \frac{D_1 + P_1}{(1 + r)^1} = \frac{\$2.00 + \$58.00}{(1 + 0.10)^1} = \frac{\$60.00}{1.10} = \$54.55$$

Using Equation 2-8, we can explore an important point concerning return concepts. Supposing V_0 is equal to today's market price, P_0, solve Equation 2-8 for r:

$$r = \frac{D_1 + P_1}{P_0} - 1 = \frac{D_1}{P_0} + \frac{P_1 - P_0}{P_0} \tag{2-9}$$

This sum of the expected dividend yield (D_1/P_0) and the expected price appreciation ($[P_1 - P_0]/P_0$) is the **expected holding-period return**, or simply expected return, on the stock. We must clarify that we have equated value to price in Equation 2-9; however, we typically use the DDM to try to identify securities for which price differs from value. We use some method independent of the DDM to obtain the required rate of return for use in a DDM valuation. Although *expected return* and *required rate of return* are often used interchangeably on an informal basis, the two are different concepts that should not be confused. Specifically, an expected return based on a calculation such as Equation 2-9 and the required rate of return (whether based on the CAPM or another model) differ when price does not exactly reflect

---

[23]Throughout the discussion of the DDM, we assume that dividends for a period are paid in one sum at the end of the period.

value.[24] When current price equals value, we can interpret the required rate of return as an expected holding-period return.

The difference between the expected rate of return based on market prices and the required rate of return is the expected abnormal return or alpha. As active investors, we seek positive alphas: returns in excess of returns that simply compensate for risk. Only with efficient prices (prices equal to intrinsic values) does expected return equal required return (and the difference between expected return and required return, alpha, equals zero).

EXAMPLE 2-7   The Expected Holding-Period Return on DaimlerChrysler Stock

The current stock price of DaimlerChrysler AG ADR (NYSE: DCX) is $44.70. You expect a dividend of $2.08 in one year. You forecast the stock price to be $49.00 in one year. If you purchase DCX at the current market price, what return do you expect to earn over one year?

You use Equation 2-9 to find that the expected one-year return on DCX is

$$r = \frac{D_1 + P_1}{P_0} - 1 = \frac{2.08 + 49.00}{44.70} - 1$$

$$= \frac{51.08}{44.70} - 1$$

$$= 1.1427 - 1$$

$$= 0.1427 = 14.27\%$$

The expected return of 14.27 percent is the sum of the expected dividend yield of $D_1/P_0 = 2.08/44.70 = 4.65$ percent and the expected capital appreciation of $(P_1 - P_0)/P_0 = (49.00 - 44.70)/44.70 = 9.62$ percent.

3.2. The Expression for Multiple Holding Periods

If an investor plans to hold a stock for two years, the value of the stock is the present value of the expected dividend in Year 1, plus the present value of the expect dividend in Year 2, plus the present value of the expected selling price at the end of Year 2.

$$V_0 = \frac{D_1}{(1+r)^1} + \frac{D_2}{(1+r)^2} + \frac{P_2}{(1+r)^2} = \frac{D_1}{(1+r)^1} + \frac{D_2 + P_2}{(1+r)^2} \tag{2-10}$$

The expression for the DDM value of a share of stock for any finite holding period is a straightforward extension of the expressions for one-year and two-year holding periods. For

---

[24]The expected return based on the CAPM is a distinct concept from the expected (holding-period) return.

an *n*-period model, the value of a stock is the present value of the expected dividends for the *n* periods plus the present value of the expected price in *n* periods (at $t = n$).

$$V_0 = \frac{D_1}{(1+r)^1} + \cdots + \frac{D_n}{(1+r)^n} + \frac{P_n}{(1+r)^n} \qquad (2\text{-}11)$$

If we use summation notation to represent the present value of the first *n* expected dividends, the general expression for an *n*-period holding period or investment horizon can be written as

$$V_0 = \sum_{t=1}^{n} \frac{D_t}{(1+r)^t} + \frac{P_n}{(1+r)^n} \qquad (2\text{-}12)$$

Equation 2-12 is significant in DDM application, because analysts may make individual forecasts of dividends over some finite horizon (often two to five years), then estimate the terminal price, P_n, based on one of a number of approaches. We will discuss valuation using a finite forecasting horizon later, under the heading of spreadsheet modeling. Example 2-8 reviews the mechanics of this calculation.

EXAMPLE 2-8   Finding the Stock Price for a Five-Year Forecast Horizon

For the next five years, the annual dividends of a stock are expected to be $2.00, $2.10, $2.20, $3.50, and $3.75. In addition, the stock price is expected to be $40.00 in five years. If the cost of equity is 10 percent, what is the value of this stock?

The present values of the expected future cash flows can be written out as

$$V_0 = \frac{2.00}{(1.10)^1} + \frac{2.10}{(1.10)^2} + \frac{2.20}{(1.10)^3} + \frac{3.50}{(1.10)^4} + \frac{3.75}{(1.10)^5} + \frac{40.00}{(1.10)^5}$$

Calculating and summing these present values gives a stock value of $V_0 = 1.818 + 1.736 + 1.653 + 2.391 + 2.328 + 24.837 = \$34.76$.

The five dividends have a total present value of $9.926 and the terminal stock value has a present value of $24.837, for a total stock value of $34.76.

With a finite holding period, whether one, two, five, or some other number of years, the dividend discount model finds the value of stock as the sum of (1) the present values of the expected dividends over the holding period, and (2) the present value of the expected stock price at the end of the holding period. As we increase the holding period by one year, we have an extra expected dividend term. In the limit (i.e., if we let the holding period extend into the indefinite future), the stock's value is the present value of all expected future dividends.

$$V_0 = \frac{D_1}{(1+r)^1} + \cdots + \frac{D_n}{(1+r)^n} + \cdots \qquad (2\text{-}13)$$

This value can be expressed with summation notation as

$$V_0 = \sum_{t=1}^{\infty} \frac{D_t}{(1+r)^t} \tag{2-14}$$

Equation 2-14 is the general form of the dividend discount model, first presented by John Burr Williams (1938). Even from the perspective of an investor with a finite investment horizon, the value of stock depends on all future dividends. For that investor, stock value today depends *directly* on the dividends the investor expects to receive before the stock is sold and *indirectly* on the expected dividends after the stock is sold, because those future dividends determine the expected selling price.

Equation 2-14, expressing the value of stock as the present value of expected dividends into the indefinite future, presents a daunting forecasting challenge. In practice, of course, we cannot make detailed, individual forecasts of an infinite number of dividends. To use the DDM, we must simplify the forecasting problem. There are two broad approaches, each of which has several variations:

1. We can forecast future dividends by assigning the stream of future dividends to one of several stylized growth patterns. The most commonly used patterns are

   - constant growth forever (the Gordon growth model),
   - two distinct stages of growth (the two-stage growth model and the H-model), and
   - three distinct stages of growth (the three-stage growth model).

The DDM value of the stock is then found by discounting the dividend streams back to the present. We present the Gordon growth model in Section 4. We present the two-stage, H-model, and three-stage growth models in Section 5.

2. We can forecast a finite number of dividends individually up to a terminal point, using pro forma financial statement analysis, for example. The horizon selected reflects the **visibility** of the companies' operations—the extent to which they are predictable with substantial confidence—and will differ for different companies; analysts' detailed forecasts often extend two to five years into the future. We can then forecast either

   - the remaining dividends from the terminal point forward by assigning those dividends to a stylized growth pattern, or
   - the share price at the terminal point of our dividend forecasts (**terminal share price**), using some method (such as taking a multiple of forecasted book value or earnings per share as of that point, based on one of several methods for estimating such multiples).

The stock's DDM value is then found by discounting the dividends (and forecasted price, if any) back to the present. Because a spreadsheet is a convenient way to implement this approach, we call this method **spreadsheet modeling**. We address spreadsheet modeling in Section 5.

Whether we are using dividends or some other definition of cash flow, we generally use one of the above forecasting approaches when we value stock. The challenge in practice is to choose an appropriate model for a stock's future dividends and to develop quality inputs to that model.

4. THE GORDON GROWTH MODEL

The Gordon growth model, developed by Gordon and Shapiro (1956) and Gordon (1962), assumes that dividends grow indefinitely at a constant rate. This assumption, applied to the general dividend discount model (Equation 2-14), leads to a simple and elegant valuation formula that has been influential in investment practice. This section explores the development of the GGM, illustrates its uses, and discusses its strengths and limitations.

4.1. The Gordon Growth Model Equation

The simplest pattern we can assume in forecasting future dividends is growth at a constant rate. In mathematical terms, we can state this assumption as

$$D_t = D_{t-1}(1+g)$$

where g is the expected constant growth rate in dividends and D_t is the expected dividend payable at time t. Suppose, for example, that the most recent dividend, D_0, was €10. Then, if we forecast a 5 percent dividend growth rate, we have for the expected dividend at $t = 1$, $D_1 = D_0(1+g) = $ €10 $\times 1.05 = $ €10.5. For any time t, D_t also equals the $t = 0$ dividend, compounded at g for t periods:

$$D_t = D_0(1+g)^t \qquad (2\text{-}15)$$

To continue the example, at the end of five years the expected dividend is $D_5 = D_0(1+g)^5 = $ €10 $\times (1.05)^5 = $ €10 $\times 1.276282 = $ €12.76. If $D_0(1+g)^t$ is substituted into Equation 2-14 for D_t, we obtain the Gordon growth model. If all of the terms are written out, they are

$$V_0 = \frac{D_0(1+g)}{(1+r)} + \frac{D_0(1+g)^2}{(1+r)^2} + \cdots + \frac{D_0(1+g)^n}{(1+r)^n} + \cdots \qquad (2\text{-}16)$$

Equation 2-16 is a geometric series; that is, each term in the expression is equal to the previous term times a constant, which in this case is $(1+g)/(1+r)$. This equation has a large number of terms that can be simplified algebraically into a much more compact equation:

$$V_0 = \frac{D_0(1+g)}{r-g}, \quad \text{or} \quad V_0 = \frac{D_1}{r-g} \qquad (2\text{-}17)$$

Both equations are equivalent because $D_1 = D_0(1+g)$. In Equation 2-17 we must specify that the cost of equity must be greater than the expected growth rate: $r > g$. If $r = g$ or $r < g$, Equation 2-17 as a compact formula for value assuming constant growth is not valid. If $r = g$, dividends grow at the same rate at which they are discounted, so the value of the stock (as the undiscounted sum of all expected future dividends) is infinite. If $r < g$, dividends grow faster than they are discounted, so the value of the stock is infinite. Of course, infinite values do not make economic sense; so constant growth with $r = g$ or $r < g$ does not make sense.

To illustrate the calculation, suppose that an annual dividend of €5 has just been paid ($D_0 = $ €5). The expected long-term growth rate is 5 percent and the cost of equity is 8 percent. The Gordon growth model value per share is $D_0(1+g)/(r-g) = ($ €5 $\times$

$1.05)/(0.08 - 0.05) = €5.25/0.03 = €175$. When calculating the model value, be careful to use D_1 and not D_0 in the numerator.

The Gordon growth model (Equation 2-17) is one of the most widely recognized equations in the field of security analysis. Because the model is based on indefinitely extending future dividends, the model's required rate of return and growth rate should reflect long-term expectations. Further, model values are very sensitive to both the required rate of return, r, and the expected dividend growth rate, g. In this and other valuation models, it is helpful to perform a sensitivity analysis on the inputs, particularly when we are not confident about the proper values.

Earlier we stated that analysts typically apply DDMs to dividend-paying stocks when dividends bear an understandable and consistent relation to the company's profitability. The same qualifications hold for the Gordon growth model. In addition, the Gordon growth model form of the DDM is most appropriate for companies with earnings expected to grow at a rate comparable to or lower than the economy's nominal growth rate. Businesses growing at much higher rates than the economy often grow at lower rates in maturity, and our horizon in using the Gordon growth model is the entire future stream of dividends.

To determine whether the company's growth rate qualifies it as a candidate for the Gordon growth model, we need an estimate of the economy's nominal growth rate. We can estimate this rate as the sum of the estimated real **gross domestic product** (GDP) growth rate plus the expected long-run inflation rate. (GDP is a money measure of the goods and services produced within a country's borders.) National government agencies as well as the World Bank (www.worldbank.org) publish GDP data. Table 2-5 shows the recent real GDP growth record for the countries listed in Table 2-3. For example, an estimate of the underlying real growth rate of the Canadian economy is 3 percent as of late 2001. With expected inflation of 3 percent, an estimate of the Canadian economy's nominal annual growth rate is 6 percent. When forecasting an earnings growth rate far above the economy's nominal growth rate, analysts should use a multistage DDM in which the final-stage growth rate reflects a growth

TABLE 2-5   Average Annual Real GDP Growth Rates: 1980–2000 (in percent)

	Real GDP Growth Rate	
Country	1980–1990	1990–2000
Australia	3.5%	4.1%
Canada	3.3	2.9
Denmark	2.0	2.4
France	2.4	1.7
Germany	N/A	1.5
Italy	2.4	1.5
Japan	4.0	1.3
Netherlands	2.3	2.9
Sweden	2.3	1.8
Switzerland	2.0	0.7
United Kingdom	3.2	2.5
United States	3.6	3.4

N/A = not available
Source: World Bank.

rate that is more plausible relative to the economy's nominal growth rate, rather than using the Gordon growth model.

EXAMPLE 2-9   Valuation Using the Gordon Growth Model (1)

In Example 2-3, you estimated a required rate of return on J.C. Penney (NYSE: JCP) stock as 8.8 percent using the CAPM. On examination, you believe stable growth at a rate of 6 percent is a good description of the long-term prospects of JCP. JCP's current dividend is $0.50.

1. Calculate the Gordon growth model value for JCP stock.
2. The current market price of JCP stock is $25. Using your answer to Question 1, state whether JCP stock is fairly valued, undervalued, or overvalued.

Solution to 1:   Using Equation 2-17, $V_0 = \dfrac{D_0(1+g)}{r-g} = \dfrac{\$0.50 \times 1.06}{0.088 - 0.06} = \dfrac{\$0.53}{0.028} = \$18.93$.

Solution to 2:   Because the Gordon growth model indicates an intrinsic value for JCP ($18.93) that is less than its market price ($25), you conclude that JCP stock is overvalued according to the Gordon growth model.

The next example illustrates a Gordon growth model valuation introducing some problems the analyst might face in practice.

EXAMPLE 2-10   Valuation Using the Gordon Growth Model (2)

As an analyst for a U.S. domestic equity–income mutual fund, you are evaluating Connecticut Water Service, Inc. (Nasdaq NMS: CTWS), for possible inclusion in the approved list of investments.

Not all countries have traded water utility stocks. In the United States, about 85 percent of the population gets its water from government entities. A group of investor-owned water utilities, however, also supplies water to the public. CTWS is the parent company of three regulated water utility companies serving Connecticut and Massachusetts.

Because CTWS operates in a regulated industry providing an important staple to a stable population, you are confident that its future earnings growth should follow its stable historical growth record. CTWS's return on equity has consistently come in close to the historical median ROE for U.S. businesses of 12.2 percent, reflecting the regulated prices for its product.

Estimated FY2001 and FY2002 EPS are $1.27 and $1.33 according to First Call/Thomson Financial, reflecting 4.7 percent growth. CTWS has a current dividend rate of $0.81. Although CTWS's dividend payout ratio has been relatively stable (73 percent in 2000, 77 percent in 1999, 75 percent in 1998, 77 percent in 1997, and 78 percent in 1996), you conclude that CTWS has not followed an exact fixed-payout dividend policy. CTWS has been conservative in reflecting earnings growth in increased dividends. Your forecast of dividends for FY2002 is $0.83. Your nominal annual GDP growth estimate is 4 percent.

Compared with a mean dividend payout ratio of 76 percent from 1996–2000, you expect a long-term average dividend payout ratio of 70 percent going forward. You anticipate a 3.7 percent long-term dividend growth rate. A recent price for CTWS is $30.00. You estimate CTWS's cost of equity at 6.2 percent.

1. Calculate the Gordon growth model estimate of value for CTWS stock.
2. State whether CTWS appears to be overvalued, fairly valued, or undervalued based on the Gordon growth model estimate of value.
3. Justify the selection of the Gordon growth model for valuing CTWS.
4. CTWS's beta is −0.16. Calculate the CAPM estimate of the cost of equity for CTWS. (Assume an equity risk premium of 5.7 percent. The risk-free rate based on the long-term T-bond was also 5.7 percent as of the price quotation date.)
5. Calculate the Gordon growth estimate of value using the cost of equity from your answer to Question 4. Assuming that a price–earnings ratio (P/E) of 24 based on estimated FY2002 EPS is an approximate guide to value, evaluate whether this Gordon growth estimate is plausible.
6. How does uncertainty in CTWS's cost of equity affect your confidence in your answer to Question 2?

Solution to 1: From Equation 2-17, $V_0 = \dfrac{D_1}{r-g} = \dfrac{\$0.83}{0.062 - 0.037} = \dfrac{\$0.83}{0.025} = \$33.20.$

Solution to 2: Because the Gordon growth model estimate of $33.20 is $3.20 higher than the market price of $30.00, CTWS appears to be slightly undervalued.

Solution to 3: Stable dividend growth is a realistic model for CTWS for the following reasons:

- CTWS profitability is stable as reflected in its return on equity. This reflects predictable demand and regulated prices for its product, water.
- Dividends bear an understandable and consistent relationship to earnings, as evidenced here by a stable dividend payout ratio.
- Earnings growth, at 3.7 percent a year, is less than nominal annual GDP growth for the United States and is plausibly sustainable long term.

Solution to 4:   The cost of equity as given by the CAPM is $R_F + \beta_i[E(R_M) - R_F] =$ $0.057 + (-0.16 \times 0.057) = 0.04788$, or 4.8 percent. As noted above, both R_F and $[E(R_M) - R_F]$ equal the same rate, here 5.7 percent.

Solution to 5:   The Gordon growth value of CTWS using a cost of equity of 4.8 percent is

$$V_0 = \frac{D_1}{r - g} = \frac{\$0.83}{0.048 - 0.037} = \frac{\$0.83}{0.011} = \$75.45$$

$75.45 is an implausible estimate for the value of CTWS judged by a P/E of 24. The $75.45 estimated value represents a P/E of 57 on FY2002 earnings, calculated as $75.45/$1.33 = 56.7 or 57. (The number 24 is taken from peer-group comparisons.) The CAPM estimate of the cost of equity does not appear to be reliable for this stock. In fact, the R-squared for the regression for beta for CTWS is about 2 percent, and the CAPM does not do a good job of explaining the returns on this stock.

Note that Problem 1 used a more plausible cost of equity figure, given as 6.2 percent. CTWS does not have publicly traded debt, so the bond yield plus risk premium method was not available. The cost of equity estimate of 0.062 stated in the problem comes from a build-up approximation. As of year-end 2001, based on the Gordon growth model applied to the S&P 500, the cost of equity for an average U.S. stock was estimated as 8.2 percent. (An average stock has a beta of 1 and should earn the S&P 500 return, on average.) Because CTWS has below-average risk (its earnings have above-average stability and its beta is less than 1.0), we subtracted a subjective company-specific risk adjustment of 2 percent. We should note that an APT estimate of the cost of equity is another possibility to consider.

Solution to 6:   Because of the uncertainty in the cost-of-equity estimate, one has less confidence that CTWS is undervalued. In particular, the analyst may view CTWS as approximately fairly valued.

As mentioned earlier, we need to be aware that Gordon growth model values can be very sensitive to small changes in the values of the required rate of return and expected dividend growth rate. Example 2-11 illustrates a format for a sensitivity analysis.

EXAMPLE 2-11   Valuation Using the Gordon Growth Model (3)

In Example 2-10, the Gordon growth model value for CTWS was estimated as $33.20 based on an expected dividend growth rate of 3.7 percent, a cost of equity of 6.2 percent, and an expected year-ahead dividend of $0.83. What if our estimates of r and g can each vary by 25 basis points? How sensitive is the model value to perturbations in our estimates of r and g? Table 2.6 provides information on this sensitivity.

TABLE 2-6   Estimated Price Given Uncertain Inputs

	$g = 3.45\%$	$g = 3.70\%$	$g = 3.95\%$
$r = 5.95\%$	$33.20	$36.89	$41.50
$r = 6.20\%$	$30.18	**$33.20**	$36.89
$r = 6.45\%$	$27.67	$30.18	$33.20

A point of interest following from the mathematics of the Gordon growth model is that when the spread between r and g is widest ($r = 6.45$ percent and $g = 3.45$ percent) the Gordon growth model value is smallest ($27.67), and when the spread is narrowest ($r = 5.95$ percent and $g = 3.95$ percent) the model value is largest ($41.50). As the spread goes to zero, in fact, the model value increases without bound. The largest value in Table 2.6, $41.50, is 50 percent larger than the smallest value, $27.67. The range of values includes one entry, $27.67, which implies that CTWS is overvalued at its current market price of $30. In summary, our best estimate of the value of CTWS given our assumptions is $33.20, bolded in Table 2.6, but the estimate is quite sensitive to rather small changes in inputs.

Examples 2-10 and 2-11 illustrate the application of the Gordon growth model to a utility, a traditional source for such illustrations. Before applying any valuation model, however, we need to know much more about a company than industry membership. Many utility holding companies in the U.S., for example, now have major, non-regulated business subsidiaries that have fundamentally changed their business characteristics.

In addition to individual stocks, analysts have often used the Gordon growth model to value broad equity market indexes, particularly in developed markets. Such indexes by their nature reflect average economic growth rates.

We can also use the Gordon growth model to value a traditional form of preferred stock, **fixed-rate perpetual preferred stock** (stock with a specified dividend rate that has a claim on earnings senior to the claim of common stock, and no maturity date).[25] If the dividend on the preferred stock is D and payments extend into the indefinite future, we have a **perpetuity** (a stream of level payments extending to infinity) in the constant amount of D. With $g = 0$, which is true because dividends are fixed for such preferred stock, the Gordon growth model becomes

$$V_0 = \frac{D}{r} \tag{2-18}$$

The discount rate, r, capitalizes the amount D, and for that reason is often called a **capitalization rate** in this and any other expression for the value of a perpetuity.

---

[25] With respect to tenor or maturity, perpetual preferred stock has no fixed maturity date; term or retractable preferred stock has a fixed maturity date set at issue.

EXAMPLE 2-12   Valuing Perpetual Preferred Stock

The Royal Bank of Scotland Preferred J (NYSE: RBS-J) stock pays an annual dividend of $2.36 and has a required return of 9.06 percent. What is the value of this preferred stock?

According to the model in Equation 2-18, RBS-J preferred stock is worth $D/r = 2.36/0.0906 = \$26.05$.

A perpetual preferred stock has a level dividend. Another case is a declining dividend (a negative growth rate). The Gordon growth model also accommodates this possibility, as illustrated in Example 2-13.

EXAMPLE 2-13   Gordon Growth Model with Negative Growth

Afton Mines is a profitable company that is expected to pay a $4.25 dividend next year. Because it is depleting its mining properties, the best estimate is that dividends will decline forever at a 10 percent rate. The required rate of return on Afton stock is 12 percent. What is the value of Afton shares?

For Afton, the value of the stock is

$$V_0 = \frac{4.25}{0.12 - (-0.10)}$$

$$= \frac{4.25}{0.22} = \$19.32$$

The negative growth results in a $19.32 valuation for the stock.

4.2. The Implied Dividend Growth Rate

Because the dividend growth rate affects the estimated value of a stock using the Gordon growth model, differences between estimated values of a stock and its actual market value might be explained by different growth rate assumptions. Given price, the expected next-period dividend, and an estimate of the required rate of return, we can infer the dividend growth rate reflected in price assuming the Gordon growth model. (Actually, it is possible to infer the market-price-implied dividend growth based on other DDMs as well.) An analyst can then judge whether the implied dividend growth rate is reasonable, high, or low, based on what he or she knows about the company. In effect, the calculation of the implied dividend growth rate provides an alternative perspective on the valuation of the stock (fairly valued, overvalued, or undervalued). Example 2-14 shows how the Gordon growth model can be used to infer the market's implied growth rate for a stock.

EXAMPLE 2-14   The Growth Rate Implied by the Current Stock Price

Suppose a company has a beta of 1.1. The risk-free rate is 5.6 percent and the market risk premium is 6 percent. The current dividend of $2.00 is expected to grow at 5 percent indefinitely. What is the value of the company's stock? The price of the stock is $40; what dividend growth rate would be required to justify a $40 price?

The required rate of return is $r = R_F + \beta_i[E(R_M) - R_F] = 0.056 + (1.1 \times 0.06) = 0.122$ or 12.2%. The value of one share, using the Gordon growth model, is

$$V_0 = \frac{D_1}{r - g}$$

$$= \frac{2.00(1.05)}{0.122 - 0.05}$$

$$= \frac{2.10}{0.072} = \$29.17$$

The valuation estimate of the model ($29.17) is less than the market value of $40.00. Assuming that the model and the other assumptions ($D_0 = \$2.00$ and $r = 12.2$ percent) are reasonable, the growth rate in dividends required to justify the $40 stock price can be calculated by substituting all known values into the Gordon growth model equation except for g:

$$40 = \frac{2.00(1 + g)}{0.122 - g} \text{ which simplifies to } 4.88 - 40g = 2 + 2g$$

$$42g = 2.88$$

$$g = 0.0686, \text{ or } g = 6.86\%.$$

An expected dividend growth rate of 6.86 percent is required for the stock price to be properly valued at $40.

4.3. Estimating the Expected Rate of Return with the Gordon Growth Model

Under the assumption of efficient prices, the Gordon growth model is frequently used to estimate a stock's expected rate of return given the stock's price and expected growth rate. When the Gordon growth model is solved for r, the expected rate of return is

$$r = \frac{D_0(1 + g)}{P_0} + g = \frac{D_1}{P_0} + g \tag{2-19}$$

The expected rate of return is composed of two parts, the dividend yield (D_1/P_0) and the capital gains (or appreciation) yield (g).

This expected rate of return is similar to the internal rate of return in capital budgeting: The IRR is the discount rate that makes the present value of an investment project's future cash flows equal the investment in the project. Likewise, it is the same concept as the yield to maturity on a bond: The yield to maturity is the discount rate that makes the present value of the bond's coupons and principal repayment equal the bond's market price. The discount rate that makes the present value of future dividends equal the current stock price is the stock's required rate of return.

EXAMPLE 2-15   Finding the Expected Rate of Return with the Gordon Growth Model

Bob Inguigiatto, CFA, has been given the task of developing mean return estimates for a list of stocks as preparation for a portfolio optimization. On his list is FPL Group, Inc. (NYSE: FPL). On analysis, he decides that it is appropriate to model FPL using the Gordon growth model, and he takes prices as reflecting value. The company paid dividends of $2.24 during the past year, and the current stock price is $56.60. The growth rates of dividends and earnings per share have been 4.01 percent and 5.30 percent, respectively, for the past five years. Analysts' consensus estimate of the five-year earnings growth rate is 7.0 percent. Based on his own analysis, Inguigiatto has decided to use 5.50 percent as his best estimate of the long-term earnings and dividend growth rate. Next year's projected dividend, D_1, should be $2.24(1.055) = $2.363. Using the Gordon growth model, FPL's expected rate of return should be

$$r = \frac{D_1}{P_0} + g$$

$$= \frac{2.363}{56.60} + 0.055$$

$$= 0.0417 + 0.055$$

$$= 0.0967 = 9.67\%$$

FPL's expected rate of return is 9.67 percent. The total return can be broken into two components, the dividend yield ($D_1/P_0 = 4.17$ percent) and the capital gains yield ($g = 5.50$ percent).

The Gordon growth model implies a set of relationships about the growth rates of dividends, earnings, and stock value. Stock value will also grow at constant rate g. The current stock price is $V_0 = D_1/(r - g)$. Multiplying both sides by $(1 + g)$, we have $V_0(1 + g) = D_1(1 + g)/(r - g)$, which is $V_1 = D_2/(r - g)$: Both dividends and value have grown at a rate of g (holding r constant). Given a constant payout ratio—a constant, proportional relationship between earnings and dividends—dividends and earnings grow at g.

To summarize, g in the Gordon growth model is the rate of value or capital appreciation (sometimes also called the capital gains yield). Some textbooks state that g is the rate of price appreciation. If prices are efficient (price equals value), price will indeed grow at a rate of g. If there is mispricing, however (i.e., price is different from value), the actual rate of capital appreciation depends on the nature of the mispricing and how fast it is corrected, if at all. For example, if a stock's current price (P_0) is \$50 and intrinsic value (V_0) is \$50.50, the stock is undervalued by \$0.50. Suppose that g is 5 percent and we expect the mispricing to correct in one year. We expect additional capital appreciation of \$0.50/\$50 = 0.01 = 1 percent over and above 5 percent, for total capital gains of 6 percent. As another example, if we expected the mispricing to correct gradually over five years, we would expect an additional capital appreciation of (\$0.50/5)/\$50 = 0.002, or 20 basis points a year over and above 5 percent, for total capital gains of 5.2 percent.[26]

Another characteristic of the model is that the components of total return (dividend yield and capital gains yield) will also stay constant over time, given that price tracks value exactly. The dividend yield, which is D_1/P_0 at $t = 0$, will stay unchanged because both the dividend and the price grow at the same rate, leaving the dividend yield unchanged over time. The capital gains yield, $(V_{t+1} - V_t)/V_t$, will stay constant at g.[27] In the FPL Group example above, the current stock price of \$56.60 will grow at 5.50 percent annually. The dividend yield of 4.17 percent, the capital gains yield of 5.50 percent, and the total return of 9.67 percent will be the same at $t = 0$ and at any time in the future.

4.4. The Present Value of Growth Opportunities

The **present value of growth opportunities** is the part of a stock's total value that comes from profitable future growth opportunities, in contrast to the stock's value associated with assets already in place. In this section, we present an expression for analyzing the total value of a stock into these two components.

Earnings growth can occur under several scenarios, including when a company retains earnings (increasing its capital base) and earns a constant positive return on equity, even if that return is low. Increases in shareholder wealth, however, occur only when reinvested earnings are directed to investments that earn more than the opportunity cost of the funds needed to undertake them (positive net present value projects).[28] Thus, investors actively assess whether and to what degree companies will have the opportunity to invest in profitable projects in the

---

[26] Another issue related to using a DDM to estimate expected return concerns the effects of common stock repurchases. Companies can distribute free cash flow to shareholders in the form of stock repurchases as well as dividends. Dividends and stock repurchases together may better reflect value creation in the company than dividends alone, as a consequence. The DDM can be adapted to explicitly include both dividends and share repurchases. Value and expected return estimates from a DDM should be consistent with such estimates from a discounted dividends and repurchases model.

[27] The fact that the capital gains yield is equal to g is easy to demonstrate:

$$\frac{V_{t+1} - V_t}{V_t} = \frac{D_{t+2}/(r-g) - D_{t+1}/(r-g)}{D_{t+1}/(r-g)} = \frac{D_{t+2} - D_{t+1}}{D_{t+1}} = 1 + g - 1 = g$$

[28] We can interpret this condition of profitability as ROE $> r$ with ROE calculated with the *market* value of equity (rather than the book value of equity) in the denominator. Book value based on historical cost accounting can present a distorted picture of the value of shareholders' investment in the company.

future. In principle, companies without any positive NPV projects should distribute most or all of earnings to shareholders as dividends so the shareholders can redirect capital to more attractive areas. (If earnings are defined as earnings in excess of expenditures needed to preserve the economic value as assets depreciate, theoretically all earnings should be distributed as dividends for such companies.)

We define a company without positive expected NPV projects as a **no-growth company**. When a company distributes all its earnings in dividends (appropriate for a no-growth company), earnings (E) will be flat in perpetuity, assuming a constant return on equity. This flatness occurs because $E = \text{ROE} \times \text{Equity}$, and equity is constant because retained earnings are not added to it. The present value of a perpetuity of E is E/r. We define the **no-growth value per share** as E/r. For any company, the difference between the actual value per share and the no-growth value per share must be the present value of growth opportunities (PVGO)—also known as the **value of growth**.

$$V_0 = \frac{E}{r} + \text{PVGO} \tag{2-20}$$

If prices reflect value ($P_0 = V_0$), PVGO gives the market's estimate of the value of the company's growth. In Example 2-10, for instance, with current earnings of $1.27 for CTWS and a current price of $30, we have $30 = (\$1.27/0.062) + \text{PVGO}$, $30 = \$20.48 + \text{PVGO}$, so PVGO $= \$30 - \$20.48 = \$9.52$. The market assigns 32 percent of the company's value to the value of growth ($\$9.52/\$30 = 0.317$). As analysts, we may be interested in this assignment because the value of growth and the value in hand (no-growth value, based on existing assets) may have different risk characteristics. Whenever we calculate a stock's value, V_0, whether using the Gordon growth or any other valuation model, we can calculate the value of growth, based on the value estimate, using the above equation.

4.5. Gordon Growth Model and the Price–Earnings Ratio

The price–earnings ratio (P/E), which we discuss in detail in Chapter 4, is perhaps the most widely recognized valuation indicator, familiar to readers of both newspaper financial tables and institutional research reports. Using the Gordon growth model, we can develop an expression for P/E in terms of the fundamentals. This expression has two uses:

- When used with forecasts of the inputs to the model, the analyst obtains a **justified** (**fundamental**) P/E—the P/E that is fair, warranted, or justified on the basis of fundamentals (given that the valuation model is appropriate). The analyst can then state his or her view of value in terms not of the Gordon growth model value but of the justified P/E. Because P/E is so widely recognized, this method may be an effective way to communicate the analysis.
- The analyst may also use the expression for P/E to weigh whether the forecasts of earnings growth built into the current stock price are reasonable. What expected earnings growth rate is implied by the actual market P/E? Is that growth rate plausible?

We can state the expression for P/E in terms of the current (or trailing) P/E (today's market price per share divided by trailing 12 months' earnings per share) or in terms of the leading (or forward) P/E (today's market price per share divided by a forecast of the next 12 months' earnings per share, or sometimes the next fiscal year's earnings per share).

Leading and trailing justified P/E expressions can be developed from the Gordon growth model. Assuming that the model can be applied for a particular stock's valuation, the dividend payout ratio is considered fixed. Define b as the retention rate, the fraction of earnings reinvested in the company rather than paid out in dividends. The dividend payout ratio is then, by definition, $(1 - b) =$ Dividend per share/Earnings per share $= D_t/E_t$. If we divide $P_0 = D_1/(r - g)$ by next year's earnings per share, E_1, we have

$$\frac{P_0}{E_1} = \frac{D_1/E_1}{r - g} = \frac{1 - b}{r - g} \qquad (2\text{-}21)$$

This represents a leading P/E, current price divided by next year's earnings. Alternatively, if we divide $P_0 = D_0(1 + g)/(r - g)$ by the current year's earnings per share, E_0, we have

$$\frac{P_0}{E_0} = \frac{D_0(1 + g)/E_0}{r - g} = \frac{(1 - b)(1 + g)}{r - g} \qquad (2\text{-}22)$$

This is a trailing P/E, current price divided by trailing (current-year) earnings.

EXAMPLE 2-16   The Expected P/E Found with the Gordon Growth Model

Harry Trice wants to use the Gordon growth model to find a justified P/E for the French company Carrefour SA (Euronext: CA), a global food retailer specializing in hypermarkets and supermarkets. Trice has assembled the following information:

- Current stock price = €56.94
- Estimated earnings per share for the current year = €1.837
- Dividends for the current year = €0.575
- Dividend growth rate = 8.18%
- Risk-free rate = 5.34%
- Equity risk premium = 5.32%
- Beta versus the CAC index = 0.83

1. What are the justified trailing and leading P/Es based on the Gordon growth model?
2. Based on the justified trailing P/E and the actual P/E, is CA fairly valued, overvalued, or undervalued?

Solution to 1: For CA, the required rate of return using the CAPM is

$$E(R_i) = R_F + \beta_i[E(R_M) - R_F]$$

$$= 5.34\% + 0.83(5.32\%)$$

$$= 9.76\%$$

The dividend payout ratio is

$$(1 - b) = D_0/E_0$$

$$= 0.575/1.837$$

$$= 0.313$$

The justified leading P/E (based on next year's earnings) is

$$\frac{P_0}{E_1} = \frac{1 - b}{r - g} = \frac{0.313}{0.0976 - 0.0818} = 19.8$$

The justified trailing P/E (based on current-year earnings) is

$$\frac{P_0}{E_0} = \frac{(1 - b)(1 + g)}{r - g} = \frac{0.313(1.0818)}{0.0976 - 0.0818} = 21.4$$

Solution to 2: Based on a current price of €56.94 and trailing earnings of €1.837, the trailing P/E is €56.94/€1.837 = 31.0. Because the actual P/E of 31.0 is greater than the justified trailing P/E of 21.4, we conclude that CA appears to be overvalued. We can also express the apparent mispricing in terms of the Gordon growth model. Using Trice's assumptions, the Gordon growth model assigns a value of 0.575(1.0818)/(0.0976 − 0.0818) = €39.37, which is below the current market value of €56.94. The Gordon growth model approach gives a lower stock value than the market price and a lower P/E than the current market P/E.

Later in the chapter, we will present multistage DDMs. We can also develop expressions for the P/E in terms of the variables of multistage DDMs, but the usefulness of these expressions is not commensurate with their complexity. For multistage models, the simple way to calculate a justified leading P/E is to divide the model value directly by the first year's expected earnings. In all cases, the P/E is explained in terms of the cost of equity, expected dividend growth rate(s), and the dividend payout ratio(s). All else equal, higher prices are associated with higher anticipated dividend growth rates.

4.6. Strengths and Weaknesses of the Gordon Growth Model

In Section 2, we presented general characteristics of companies for which dividend discount models are appropriate. For the Gordon growth model implementation to be appropriate, as stated earlier, additional qualifications should be met. The basic question is always whether a model is suitable for the company being valued. Each model has some characteristic strengths and weaknesses. Here we list those of the Gordon growth model, recapping comments on suitability.

Strengths

- The Gordon growth model is often useful for valuing stable-growth, dividend-paying companies.
- It is often useful for valuing broad-based equity indexes.

- The model features simplicity and clarity; it is useful for understanding the relationships among value and growth, required rate of return, and payout ratio.
- It provides an approach to estimating the expected rate of return given efficient prices (for stable-growth, dividend-paying companies). As we show in the next section, the Gordon growth model can readily be used as a component of more-complex DDMs, particularly to model the final stage of growth.

Weaknesses

- Calculated values are very sensitive to the assumed growth rate and required rate of return.
- The model is not applicable, in a practical sense, to non-dividend-paying stocks.
- The model is also inapplicable to unstable-growth, dividend-paying stocks.

5. MULTISTAGE DIVIDEND DISCOUNT MODELS

Earlier, we noted that the basic expression for the DDM (Equation 2-14) is too general for investment analysts to use in practice, as one cannot forecast individually more than a relatively small number of dividends. The strongest simplifying assumption—a stable dividend growth rate from now into the indefinite future, leading to the Gordon growth model—is not realistic for many or even most companies. For many publicly traded companies, practitioners assume growth falls into three stages (see Sharpe, Alexander, and Bailey 1999):

- **Growth phase.** A company in its growth phase typically enjoys rapidly expanding markets, high profit margins, and an abnormally high growth rate in earnings per share (**supernormal growth**). Companies in this phase often have negative free cash flow to equity, because the company invests heavily in expanding operations. Given high prospective returns on equity, the dividend payout ratios of growth-phase companies are often low, or even zero. As the company's markets mature or as unusual growth opportunities attract competitors, earnings growth rates eventually decline.
- **Transition phase.** In this phase, which is a transition to maturity, earnings growth slows as competition puts pressure on prices and profit margins, or as sales growth slows because of market saturation. In this phase, earnings growth rates may be above average but declining towards the growth rate for the overall economy. Capital requirements typically decline in this phase, often resulting in positive free cash flow and increasing dividend payout ratios (or the initiation of dividends).
- **Mature phase.** In maturity, the company reaches an equilibrium in which investment opportunities on average just earn their opportunity cost of capital. Return on equity approaches the cost of equity; and earnings growth, the dividend payout ratio, and the return on equity stabilize at levels that can be sustained long term. We call the dividend and earnings growth rate of this phase the **mature growth rate**. This phase, in fact, reflects the stage in which a company can properly be valued using the Gordon growth model, and that model is one tool for valuing this phase of a currently high-growth company's future.

A company may attempt to restart the growth phase by changing its strategic focuses and business mix. Technological advances may alter a company's growth prospects for better or worse with surprising rapidity. Nevertheless, this growth-phase picture of a company is a useful approximation. The growth-phase concept provides the intuition for multistage DCF models of all types, including multistage dividend discount models. Multistage models are a staple valuation discipline of investment management companies using DCF valuation models. In this section, we present three popular multistage DDMs: the two-stage DDM, the H-model (a type of two-stage model), and the three-stage DDM. Keep in mind that all these models represent stylized patterns of growth; we are attempting to identify the pattern that most accurately approximates our view of the company's future growth.

5.1. Two-Stage Dividend Discount Model

Two common versions of the two-stage DDM exist. The first model assumes a constant growth rate in each stage, such as 15 percent in Stage 1 and 7 percent in Stage 2. The second model assumes a declining dividend growth rate in Stage 1 followed by a fixed growth rate in Stage 2. For example, the growth rate could begin at 15 percent and decline continuously in Stage 1 until it reaches 7 percent. Then it grows forever at 7 percent in Stage 2. This second model, called the H-model, will be presented after the model with fixed growth rates in each stage.

   The first two-stage DDM provides for two dividend growth rates: a high growth rate for the initial period, followed by a sustainable and usually lower growth rate thereafter. The two-stage DDM is based on the multiple-period model

$$V_0 = \sum_{t=1}^{n} \frac{D_t}{(1+r)^t} + \frac{V_n}{(1+r)^n} \tag{2-23}$$

where we use V_n as an estimate of P_n. The two-stage model assumes that the first n dividends grow at an extraordinary short-term rate, g_S:

$$D_t = D_0(1+g_S)^t \tag{2-24}$$

After time n, the annual dividend growth rate changes to a normal long-term rate, g_L. The dividend at time $n+1$ is $D_{n+1} = D_n(1+g_L) = D_0(1+g_S)^n(1+g_L)$, and this dividend continues to grow at g_L. Using D_{n+1}, we can use the Gordon growth model to find V_n:

$$V_n = \frac{D_0(1+g_S)^n(1+g_L)}{r-g_L} \tag{2-25}$$

To find the value at $t = 0$, V_0, we simply find the present value of the first n dividends and the present value of the projected value at time n :

$$V_0 = \sum_{t=1}^{n} \frac{D_0(1+g_S)^t}{(1+r)^t} + \frac{D_0(1+g_S)^n(1+g_L)}{(1+r)^n(r-g_L)} \tag{2-26}$$

EXAMPLE 2-17   Valuing a Stock Using the Two-Stage Dividend Discount Model

General Mills (NYSE: GIS) is a large manufacturer and distributor of packaged consumer food products. Benoit Gagnon, a buy-side analyst covering General Mills, has studied the historical growth rates in sales, earnings, and dividends for GIS, and also has made projections of future growth rates. Gagnon expects the current dividend of $1.10 to grow at 11 percent for the next five years, and that the growth rate will decline to 8 percent and remain at that level thereafter.

Gagnon feels that his estimate of GIS's beta is unreliable, so he is using the bond yield plus risk premium method to estimate the required rate of return on the stock. The yield to maturity of GIS's long-term bond (6.27s of 2019) is 6.67 percent. Adding a 4.0 percent risk premium to the yield-to-maturity gives a required return of 10.67 percent, which Gagnon rounds to 10.7 percent.

Table 2.7 shows the calculations of the first five dividends and their present values discounted at 10.7 percent. The terminal stock value at $t = 5$ is

$$V_5 = \frac{D_0(1 + g_S)^n(1 + g_L)}{r - g_L}$$

$$= \frac{1.10(1.11)^5(1.08)}{0.107 - 0.08}$$

$$= 74.143$$

The terminal stock value and its present value are also given in the table.

TABLE 2-7   General Mills Dividend Calculation

Time	Value	Calculation	D_t or V_t	Present Values $D_t/(1.107)^t$ or $V_t/(1.107)^t$
1	D_1	$1.10(1.11)$	1.221	1.103
2	D_2	$1.10(1.11)^2$	1.355	1.106
3	D_3	$1.10(1.11)^3$	1.504	1.109
4	D_4	$1.10(1.11)^4$	1.670	1.112
5	D_5	$1.10(1.11)^5$	1.854	1.115
5	V_5	$1.10(1.11)^5(1.08)/(0.107-0.08)$	74.143	44.5997
Total				50.1447

In this two-stage model, we are forecasting the five individual dividends during the first stage and then calculating their present values. We use the Gordon growth model to derive the terminal value (the value of the dividends in the second stage at the beginning of Stage 2). As shown above, the terminal value is $V_5 = D_6/(r - g_L)$. The Period 6 dividend is $2.002 (= D_5 \times 1.08 = \$1.854 \times 1.08$). Using the standard Gordon growth model, $V_5 = \$74.14 = 2.002/(0.107 - 0.08)$. The present value of the terminal value is $44.60 = 74.14/1.107^5$. The total estimated value of GIS is $50.14 using this model. Notice that almost 90 percent of this value, $44.60, is the present value of V_5, and the balance, $50.14 - \$44.60 = \$5.54$, is the present value of the first five dividends. Recalling our discussion of the sensitivity of the Gordon growth model to changes in the inputs, we might calculate an interval for the intrinsic value of GIS by varying the mature growth rate over the range of plausible values.

The two-stage DDM is very useful because many scenarios exist in which a company can achieve a supernormal growth rate for a few years, after which time the growth rate falls to a more sustainable level. For example, a company may achieve supernormal growth through possession of a patent, first-mover advantage, or another factor that provides a temporary lead in a specific marketplace. Subsequently, earnings must descend to a level that is more consistent with competition and the growth in the overall economy. Accordingly, that is why in the two-stage model, extraordinary growth is often forecast for a few years, and then normal growth is forecast thereafter. The accurate estimation of V_n, the **terminal value of the stock**,[29] is an important part of correct use of DDMs. In practice, analysts estimate the terminal value either by applying a multiple to a projected terminal value of a fundamental, such as earnings per share or book value per share, or they estimate V_n using the Gordon growth model. In the chapter on market multiples, we will discuss using price–earnings multiples in this context.

In our examples, we use a single discount rate, r, for all phases, reflecting both a desire for simplicity and lack of a clear objective basis for adjusting the discount rate for different phases. Some analysts, however, use different discount rates for different phases.

The following example values E.I. duPont de Nemours and Company by combining the dividend discount model and a P/E valuation model.

EXAMPLE 2-18   Combining a DDM and P/E Model to Value a Stock

In the past year, DuPont (NYSE: DD) paid a $1.40 dividend that an analyst expects to grow at 9.3 percent annually for the next four years. At the end of Year 4, the analyst expects the dividend to equal 40 percent of earnings per share and the trailing P/E for DD to be 11. If the required return on DD common stock is 11.5 percent, calculate the per-share value of DD common stock.

Table 2.8 summarizes the relevant calculations. When the dividends are growing at 9.3 percent, the expected dividends and the present value of each (discounted at 11.5 percent) are shown. The terminal stock price, V_4, deserves some explanation. As shown in the table, the Year 4 dividend is $1.40(1.093)^4 = 1.9981$. Because dividends at that time are assumed to be 40 percent of earnings, the EPS projection for Year 4 is $EPS_4 = D_4/0.40 = 1.9981/0.40 = 4.9952$. With a trailing P/E of 11.0, the value of DD at the end of Year 4 should be $11.0(4.9952) = \$54.95$. Discounted at 11.5 percent for four years, the present value of V_4 is $35.55.

The present values of the dividends for Years 1 through 4 sum to $5.33. The present value of the terminal value of $54.95 is $35.55. The estimated total value of DD is the sum of these, or $40.88 per share.

---

[29]The terminal value of a stock has also been called the stock's continuing value.

TABLE 2-8   Value of DuPont Common Stock

Time	Value	Calculation	D_t or V_t	Present Values $D_t/(1.115)^t$ or $V_t/(1.115)^t$
1	D_1	$1.40(1.093)^1$	1.5302	1.3724
2	D_2	$1.40(1.093)^2$	1.6725	1.3453
3	D_3	$1.40(1.093)^3$	1.8281	1.3188
4	D_4	$1.40(1.093)^4$	1.9981	1.2927
4	V_4	$11 \times [1.40(1.093)^4/0.40]$ $= 11 \times [1.9981/0.40]$ $= 11 \times 4.9952$	54.9472	35.5505
Total				40.88

5.2. Valuing a Non-Dividend-Paying Company (First-Stage Dividend = 0)

The fact that a stock is currently paying no dividends does not mean that the principles of the dividend discount model do not apply. Even though D_0 and/or D_1 may be zero, and the company may not begin paying dividends for some time, the present value of future dividends may still capture the value of the company. Of course, if a company pays no dividends and will never be able to distribute cash to shareholders, the stock is worthless.

EXAMPLE 2-19   Valuing a Non-Dividend-Paying Stock

Assume that a company is currently paying no dividend and will not pay one for several years. If the company begins paying a dividend of $1.00 five years from now, and the dividend is expected to grow at 5 percent thereafter, we can discount this future dividend stream back to find the value of the company. This company's required rate of return is 11 percent. Because the expression

$$V_n = \frac{D_{n+1}}{r - g}$$

values a stock at period n using the next period's dividend, the $t = 5$ dividend is used to find the value at $t = 4$:

$$V_4 = \frac{D_5}{r - g} = \frac{1.00}{0.11 - 0.05} = \$16.67$$

To find the value of the stock today, we simply discount V_4 back for four years:

$$V_0 = \frac{V_4}{(1 + r)^4} = \frac{16.67}{(1.11)^4} = \$10.98$$

The value of this stock, even though it will not pay a dividend until Year 5, is $10.98.

If a company is not paying a dividend but is very profitable, an analyst might be willing to forecast its future dividends. Of course, for non-dividend-paying, unprofitable companies, such a forecast would be very difficult. Furthermore, as discussed in Section 2.2 (Streams of Expected Cash Flows), it is usually difficult for the analyst to estimate the timing of the initiation of dividends and the dividend policy that will then be established by the company. Thus the analyst may prefer a free cash flow or residual income model for valuing such companies.

5.3. The H-Model

The basic two-stage model assumes a constant, extraordinary rate for the supernormal growth period that is followed by a constant, normal growth rate thereafter. In Example 2-17, the growth rate for General Mills was 11 percent annually for 5 years, followed by a precipitous drop to 8 percent growth in Year 6 and thereafter. Fuller and Hsia (1984) developed a variant of the two-stage model in which growth begins at a high rate and declines linearly throughout the supernormal growth period until it reaches a normal rate at the end. The value of the dividend stream in the H-model is

$$V_0 = \frac{D_0(1 + g_L)}{r - g_L} + \frac{D_0 H(g_S - g_L)}{r - g_L} \qquad (2\text{-}27)$$

or

$$V_0 = \frac{D_0(1 + g_L) + D_0 H(g_S - g_L)}{r - g_L}$$

where

V_0 = value per share at $t = 0$
D_0 = current dividend
r = required rate of return on equity
H = half-life in years of the high-growth period (i.e., high-growth period = $2H$ years)
g_S = initial short-term dividend growth rate
g_L = normal long-term dividend growth rate after Year $2H$

The first term on the right-hand side of Equation 2-27 is the present value of the company's dividend stream if it were to grow at g_L forever. The second term is an approximation to the extra value (assuming $g_S > g_L$) accruing to the stock because of its supernormal growth for Years 1 through $2H$ (see Fuller and Hsia for technical details).[30] Logically, the longer the supernormal growth period (i.e., the larger the value of H, which is one-half the length of the supernormal growth period) and the larger the extra growth rate in the supernormal growth period (measured by g_S minus g_L), the higher the share value, all else equal.

---

[30] We can provide some intuition on the expression, however. On average, the expected excess growth rate in the supernormal period will be $(g_S - g_L)/2$. Over $2H$ periods, we expect a total excess amount of dividends (compared with the level given g_L) of $2H D_0(g_S - g_L)/2 = D_0 H(g_S - g_L)$. This term is the H-model upward adjustment to the first dividend term, reflecting the extra expected dividends as growth declines from g_S to g_L over the first period. Note, however, that the timing of the individual dividends in the first period is not reflected by individually discounting them; the expression is thus an approximation.

EXAMPLE 2-20   Valuing a Stock with the H-Model

You are valuing Siemens AG (Frankfurt: SIE) with the H-model approach. The relevant inputs to your valuation are as follows:

- Current dividend is €1.00.
- The dividend growth rate is 29.28 percent, declining linearly over a 16-year period to a final and perpetual growth rate of 7.26 percent.
- The risk-free rate is 5.34 percent, the market risk premium is 5.32 percent, and SIE's beta, estimated against the DAX, is 1.37.

The required rate of return for SIE is

$$R_F + \beta_i[E(R_M) - R_F] = 0.0534 + (1.37 \times 0.0532) = 0.1263, \text{ or } 12.63\%$$

Using the H-model, the per-share value estimate of the company is

$$V_0 = \frac{D_0(1 + g_L)}{r - g_L} + \frac{D_0 H(g_S - g_L)}{r - g_L}$$

$$= \frac{1.00(1.0726)}{0.1263 - 0.0726} + \frac{1.00(8)(0.2928 - 0.0726)}{0.1263 - 0.0726}$$

$$= 19.97 + 32.80 = €52.77$$

If SIE experienced normal growth starting now, its value would be €19.97. The extraordinary growth adds €32.80 to its value, which results in a SIE share being worth an estimated total of €52.77.

The H-model is an approximation model, which estimates the valuation that would result from discounting all of the future dividends individually. In many circumstances, this approximation is very close. For a long extraordinary growth period (a high H) or for a large difference in growth rates (the difference between g_S and g_L), however, the analyst might abandon the approximation model for the more exact model. Fortunately, the many tedious calculations of the exact model are made fairly easy using a spreadsheet program.

5.4. Three-Stage Dividend Discount Models

There are two popular versions of the three-stage DDM. In the first version, the company is assumed to have a constant dividend growth rate in each of the three stages. For example, Stage 1 could assume 20 percent growth for three years, Stage 2 could have 10 percent growth for four years, and Stage 3 could have 5 percent growth thereafter. In the second version, in the middle (second) period, the growth rate is assumed to decline linearly. The example below shows how the first type of three-stage model can be used to value a stock, in this case IBM.

EXAMPLE 2-21   The Three-Stage DDM with Three Distinct Stages

IBM currently pays a dividend of $0.55 per year. We estimate the current required rate of return at 12 percent. Assume we believe that dividends will grow at 7.5 percent for the next two years, 13.5 percent for the following four years, and 11.25 percent into perpetuity. What is the current estimated value of IBM using a three-stage approach? We show our calculations in Table 2-9.

TABLE 2-9   Estimated Value of IBM

Time	Value	Calculation	D_t or V_t	Present values $D_t/(1.12)^t$ or $V_t/(1.12)^t$
1	D_1	$0.55(1.075)$	0.5913	0.5279
2	D_2	$0.55(1.075)^2$	0.6356	0.5067
3	D_3	$0.55(1.075)^2(1.135)$	0.7214	0.5135
4	D_4	$0.55(1.075)^2(1.135)^2$	0.8188	0.5204
5	D_5	$0.55(1.075)^2(1.135)^3$	0.9293	0.5273
6	D_6	$0.55(1.075)^2(1.135)^4$	1.0548	0.5344
6	V_6	$0.55(1.075)^2(1.135)^4(1.1125)/$ $(0.12-0.1125)$	156.4595	79.2673
Total				82.3975

Given these assumptions, the three-stage model indicates that a fair price should be $82.40. Nevertheless, an analyst might well question whether an 11.25 percent long-term growth rate is plausible.

A second version of the three-stage DDM has a middle stage similar to the first stage in the H-model. In the first stage, dividends grow at a high, constant (supernormal) rate for the whole period. In the second stage, dividends decline linearly as they do in the H-model. Finally, in Stage 3, dividends grow at a sustainable, constant growth rate. The process of using this model is illustrated in Example 2-22, valuing Hormel Foods.

EXAMPLE 2-22   The Three-Stage DDM with Declining Growth Rates in Stage 2

Elaine Bouvier is evaluating HRL (addressed earlier in Example 2-2). She wishes to value HRL using the three-stage dividend growth model with a linearly declining dividend growth rate in Stage 2. After considerable study, Bouvier has decided to use the following information in her valuation (as of the beginning of 2003):

- The current dividend is $0.39.
- Bouvier estimates the required rate of return on HRL stock at 8.72 percent.
- In Stage 1, the dividend will grow at 11.3 percent annually for the next five years.
- In Stage 2, which will last 10 years, the dividend growth rate will decline linearly, starting at the Stage 1 rate and ending at the Stage 3 rate.
- The equilibrium long-term dividend growth rate (in Stage 3) will be 5.7 percent.

Bouvier values HRL by computing the five dividends in Stage 1 and finding their present values at 8.72 percent. The dividends in Stages 2 and 3 can be valued with the H-model, which estimates their value at the beginning of Stage 2. This value is then discounted back to find the dividends' present value at $t = 0$.

TABLE 2-10   Hormel Foods Corp.

Time	D_t or V_t	Value of D_t or V_t	PV at 8.72%	Explanation of D_t or V_t
1	D_1	0.4341	0.3993	$0.39(1.113)^1$
2	D_2	0.4831	0.4087	$0.39(1.113)^2$
3	D_3	0.5377	0.4184	$0.39(1.113)^3$
4	D_4	0.5985	0.4284	$0.39(1.113)^4$
5	D_5	0.6661	0.4385	$0.39(1.113)^5$
5	V_5	29.4893	19.4141	H-model explained above
Total			21.5074	

The calculation of the five dividends in Stage 1 and their present values are given in Table 2.10. The H-model for calculating the value of the Stage 2 and Stage 3 dividends at the beginning of Stage 2 ($t = 5$) would be

$$V_5 = \frac{D_5(1 + g_L)}{r - g_L} + \frac{D_5 H(g_S - g_L)}{r - g_L}$$

where

$$
\begin{aligned}
D_5 &= D_0(1 + g_S)^5 = 0.39(1.113)^5 = \$0.6661 \\
g_S &= 11.3\% \\
g_L &= 5.7\% \\
r &= 8.72\% \\
H &= 5 \text{ (the second stage lasts } 2H = 10 \text{ years)}
\end{aligned}
$$

Substituting these values into the equation for the H-model gives us V_5:

$$V_5 = \frac{0.6661(1.057)}{0.0872 - 0.057} + \frac{0.6661(5)(0.113 - 0.057)}{0.0872 - 0.057}$$

$$= 23.3135 + 6.1758$$

$$= \$29.4893$$

The present value of V_5 is $\$29.4893/(1.0872)^5 = \$19.4141$.

   According to this three-stage DDM model, the total value of HRL is $21.51. The dividends in Stages 2 and 3 have a total present value of $19.41, and the five dividends in Stage 1 have a total present value of about $2.10 ($21.51− $19.41).

The three-stage DDM with declining growth in Stage 2 has been widely used among companies using a DDM approach to valuation. An example is the DDM adopted by Bloomberg L.P., a financial services company that provides "Bloomberg terminals" to professional investors and analysts. The Bloomberg DDM is a model that provides an estimated value for any stock that the user selects. The DDM is a three-stage model with declining growth in Stage 2. The model uses fundamentals about the company for assumed Stage 1 and Stage 3 growth rates, and then assumes that the Stage 2 rate is a linearly declining rate between the Stage 1 and Stage 3 rates. The model also makes estimates of the lengths of the three stages and the required rate of return. Because the Bloomberg DDM value is just a mouse click away, the analyst can easily compare the Bloomberg value to the analyst's own model value or to the stock's current market price.

5.5. Spreadsheet Modeling

DDMs such as the Gordon growth model and the multistage models presented earlier assume stylized patterns of dividend growth. With the computational power of personal computers, calculators, and personal digital assistants, however, *any* assumed dividend pattern is easily valued.

   Spreadsheets allow the analyst to build complicated models that would be very cumbersome to describe using algebra. Furthermore, built-in spreadsheet functions (such as those to find rates of return) use algorithms to get a numerical answer when a mathematical solution would be impossible or extremely challenging. Because of spreadsheets' widespread use, several analysts can work together or exchange information through the sharing of their spreadsheet models. The example below presents the results of using a spreadsheet to value a stock with dividends changing substantially through time.

EXAMPLE 2-23   Finding the Value of a Stock Using a Spreadsheet Model

Yang Co. is expected to pay a $21.00 dividend next year. The dividend will decline by 10 percent annually for the following three years. In Year 5, Yang will sell off assets worth $100 per share. The Year 5 dividend, which includes a distribution of some of the proceeds of the asset sale, is expected to be $60. In Year 6, we expect the dividend to decrease to $40. We expect that this dividend will be maintained at $40 for one additional year. It is then expected to grow by 5 percent annually thereafter. If the required rate of return is 12 percent, what is the value of one share of Yang?

The value is shown in Table 2-11. Each dividend, its present value discounted at 12 percent, and an explanation are included in the table. The final row treats the dividends from $t = 8$ forward as a Gordon growth model because after Year 7, the dividend grows at a constant 5 percent annually. V_7 is the value of these dividends at $t = 7$.

TABLE 2-11   Value of Yang Co. Stock

Year	D_t or V_t	Value of D_t or V_t	Present Value at 12%	Explanation of D_t or V_t
1	D_1	21.00	18.75	Dividend set at $21
2	D_2	18.90	15.07	Previous dividend × 0.90
3	D_3	17.01	12.11	Previous dividend × 0.90
4	D_4	15.31	9.73	Previous dividend × 0.90
5	D_5	60.00	34.05	Set at $60
6	D_6	40.00	20.27	Set at $40
7	D_7	40.00	18.09	Set at $40
7	V_7	600.00	271.41	$V_7 = D_8/(r - g)$ $V_7 = (40.00 \times 1.05)/(0.12 - 0.05)$
Total			399.48	

As the table shows, the total present value of Yang Co.'s dividends is $399.48. In this example, the terminal value of the company (V_n) at the end of the first stage was found using the Gordon growth model using a mature growth rate of 5 percent. Several alternative approaches to estimating g are available in this context:

- Use the formula $g = (b$ in the mature phase$) \times$ (ROE in the mature phase). We will discuss the expression $g = b \times$ ROE in Section 6. We have several ways to estimate ROE. We can use the DuPont expression for ROE, also presented in Section 6. Some analysts assume that ROE $= r$, the required rate of return on equity, in the mature phase. An alternative assumption is that ROE in the mature phase equals the median industry ROE. The earnings retention ratio, b, may be empirically based. For example, Bloomberg assumes that $b = 0.55$ in the mature phase, equivalent to a dividend payout ratio of 45 percent, a long-run average payout ratio for mature dividend-paying companies in the United States. In addition, sometimes analysts project the dividend payout ratio for the company individually.
- The analyst may estimate the growth rate g with other models relating the mature growth rate to macroeconomic, including industry, growth projections.

5.6. Finding Rates of Return for Any DDM

This chapter has focused on finding the value of a security using assumptions for dividends, required rates of return, and expected growth rates. The models are also useful for other purposes. Given the current price as shown in Section 4.3, we can calculate the implied expected rate of return as an input to security selection. For example, given a current stock price, dividend estimates, and forecasts of growth, we can derive the implied expected rate of return. Finding value and finding expected rates of return are two sides of the same coin. If you know what is on one side, you can deduce what is on the other. In the following discussion, keep in mind that if price does not equal intrinsic value, the expected return will need to be adjusted to reflect the additional component of return that accrues when the mispricing is corrected, as discussed in Section 4.3.

In some cases, it is very easy to find the expected rate of return. With a one-period investment horizon, the expected return was simply $r = (D_1 + P_1)/P_0 - 1$. This calculation requires a forecast of next year's stock price (P_1) in addition to knowledge of the current price (P_0).

In the Gordon growth model, $r = D_1/P_0 + g$. The expected rate of return is the dividend yield plus the expected growth rate. For a security with a current price of $10, an expected dividend of $0.50, and expected growth of 8 percent, the expected rate of return would be 13 percent.

For the H-model, the expected rate of return can be derived as[31]

$$r = \left(\frac{D_0}{P_0}\right)[(1 + g_L) + H(g_S - g_L)] + g_L \tag{2-28}$$

When the short- and long-term growth rates are the same, this model reduces to the Gordon growth model. For a security with a current dividend of $1, a current price of $20, and an expected short-term growth rate of 10 percent declining over 10 years $(H = 5)$ to 6 percent, the expected rate of return would be

$$r = \left(\frac{\$1}{\$20}\right)[(1 + 0.06) + 5(0.10 - 0.06)] + 0.06 = 12.3\%$$

For multistage models and spreadsheet models, it can be more difficult to find a single equation for the rate of return. The process generally used is similar to that of finding the internal rate of return for a series of varying cash flows. Using a computer or trial and error, the analyst must find the rate of return such that the present value of future expected dividends equals the current stock price.

EXAMPLE 2-24   Finding the Expected Rate of Return for Varying Expected Dividends

An analyst expects JNJ's (Johnson & Johnson, from Example 2-4) current dividend of $0.70 to grow by 14.5 percent for six years and then grow by 8 percent into perpetuity. JNJ's current price is $53.28. What is the expected return on an investment in JNJ's stock?

---

[31] Fuller and Hsia (1984).

In performing trial and error with the two-stage model to estimate the expected rate of return, it is important to have a good initial guess. We can use the expected rate of return formula from the Gordon growth model and JNJ's long-term growth rate to find a first approximation: $r = (\$0.70 \times 1.08)/\$53.28 + 0.08 = 9.42\%$. Because we know that the growth rate in the first six years is more than 8 percent, the estimated rate of return must be above 9.42 percent. Using 9.42 percent and 10.0 percent, we calculate the implied price in Table 2-12:

TABLE 2-12   Johnson & Johnson

Time	D_t	Present Value of D_t and V_6 at $r = 9.42\%$	Present Value of D_t and V_6 at $r = 10.0\%$
1	$0.8015	$0.7325	$0.7286
2	$0.9177	$0.7665	$0.7584
3	$1.0508	$0.8021	$0.7895
4	$1.2032	$0.8394	$0.8218
5	$1.3776	$0.8783	$0.8554
6	$1.5774	$0.9191	$0.8904
7	$1.7035		
6		$69.90	$48.0805
Total		$74.84	$52.9246
Market Price		$53.28	$53.28

The present value of the terminal value is $V_6/(1+r)^6 = [D_7/(r-g)]/(1+r)^6$. For $r = 9.42$ percent, the present value is $[1.7035/(0.0942 - 0.08)]/(1.0942)^6 = \$69.90$. The present value for other values of r is found similarly. Apparently, the expected rate of return is slightly less than 10 percent, assuming efficient prices.

5.7. Strengths and Weaknesses of Multistage DDMs

The multistage dividend discount models have several strengths and weaknesses.

Strengths:

- The multistage DDMs can accommodate a variety of patterns of future streams of expected dividends.
- Even though the multistage DDMs may use stylized assumptions about growth, they can provide useful approximations.
- In addition to valuing dividend streams with a DDM, the expected rates of return can be imputed by finding the discount rate that equates the present value of the dividend stream to the current stock price. These expected return values can be adjusted to reflect the expected market correction of mispricing.
- Because of the variety of DDMs available, the analyst is both enabled and compelled to carefully evaluate the assumptions about the stock under examination. The valuation model

should fit the assumptions (because the analyst is not forced to accept a set of assumptions that fit a specific model).

- Spreadsheets are widely available, allowing the analyst to construct and examine an almost limitless number of models.
- Using a model forces the analyst to specify assumptions, rather than simply using subjective assessments. Analysts can thus use common assumptions, understand the reasons for differing valuations when they occur, and react to changing market conditions in a systematic manner.

Weaknesses:

- Garbage in, garbage out. If the inputs are not economically meaningful and appropriate for the company being valued, the outputs from the model will not be useful.
- Analysts sometimes employ models that they do not understand fully. For example, the H-model is an approximation model. An analyst may think it is exact and misuse it.
- As a sensitivity analysis usually shows, valuations are very sensitive to the models' inputs.
- Programming and data errors in spreadsheet models are very common. Spreadsheet models should be checked thoroughly.

6. THE FINANCIAL DETERMINANTS OF GROWTH RATES

In a number of examples earlier in this chapter, we have implicitly used the relationship that the dividend growth rate (g) equals the earning retention ratio (b) times the return on equity (ROE). In this section, we explain this relationship and show how we can combine it with a method of analyzing return on equity, called DuPont analysis, as a simple tool for forecasting dividend growth rates.

6.1. Sustainable Growth Rate

We define the **sustainable growth rate** as the rate of dividend (and earnings) growth that can be sustained for a given level of return on equity, keeping the capital structure constant over time and without issuing additional common stock. The reason to study this concept is that it can help us estimate the stable growth rate in a Gordon growth model valuation, or the mature growth rate in a multistage DDM in which we use the Gordon growth formula for the terminal value of the stock.

The expression to calculate the sustainable growth rate is

$$g = b \times \text{ROE} \tag{2-29}$$

where

$$
\begin{aligned}
g &= \text{dividend growth rate} \\
b &= \text{earnings retention rate } (1 - \text{Dividend payout ratio}) \\
\text{ROE} &= \text{return on equity}
\end{aligned}
$$

Example 2-25 is an illustration of the fact that growth in shareholders' equity is driven by reinvested earnings alone (no new issues of equity, and debt growing at the rate g).[32]

EXAMPLE 2-25   Example Showing $g = b \times$ ROE

In the year just ended, a company began with shareholders' equity of $1,000,000, earned $250,000 net income, and paid dividends of $100,000. Its ROE is 25 percent and its retention rate is 60 percent. The company begins the next year with $1,150,000 of shareholders' equity because it retained $150,000. There are no additions to equity from an increase in shares outstanding.

   If the company again earns 25 percent on equity in the next year, net income will be $287,500, which is a 15 percent increase. The increase in earnings is $287,500 − $250,000 = $37,500. This is 15 percent above the previous year's earnings of $250,000. The company retains 60 percent of earnings (60% × $287,500 = $172,500) and pays out the other 40 percent (40% × $287,500 = $115,000) as dividends.

   The formula for the dividend growth rate is $g = b \times$ ROE, which is $g = 0.60 \times 25\% = 15\%$. Notice that dividends for the company grew from $100,000 to $115,000, which is exactly a 15 percent growth rate.

Equation 2-29 implies that the higher the return on equity, the higher the dividend growth rate, all else constant. The expression also implies that the higher the earnings retention ratio, the higher the growth rate in dividends, holding all else constant.[33]

   A practical logic for defining *sustainable* in terms of growth through internally generated funds (retained earnings) is that external equity (secondary issues of stock) is considerably more costly than internal equity (reinvested earnings), because of investment banker fees. Continuous issuance of new stock is not a practical funding alternative for companies, in general.[34] Growth of capital through issuance of new debt can sometimes be sustained for

---

[32] With debt growing at the rate g, the capital structure is constant. If the capital structure is not constant, ROE would not be constant in general because ROE depends on leverage.

[33] ROE is a variable that reflects underlying profitability as well as the use of leverage or debt. The retention ratio or dividend policy, in contrast, is not a fundamental variable in the same sense as ROE. A higher dividend growth rate through a higher retention ratio (lower dividend payout ratio) is neutral for share value in and of itself. Holding investment policy (capital projects) constant, the positive effect on value from an increase in g will just be offset by the negative effect from a decrease in dividend payouts in the expression for the value of the stock in any DDM. Sharpe, Alexander, and Bailey (1999) discuss this concept in more detail.

[34] As a long-term average, about 2 percent of U.S. publicly traded companies issue new equity in a given year, which corresponds to a secondary equity issue once every 50 years, on average. Businesses may be rationed in their access to secondary issues of equity because of the costs associated with informational asymmetries between management and the public. Because management has more information on the future cash flows of the company than the general public, and equity is an ownership claim to those cash flows, the public may react to additional equity issuance as possibly motivated by an intent to "share (future) misery" rather than "share (future) wealth."

considerable periods, however. Further, if a company manages its capital structure to a target percentage of debt to total capital (debt and common stock), it will need to issue debt to maintain that percentage as equity grows through reinvested earnings. (This approach is one of a variety of observed capital structure policies.) In addition, the earnings retention ratio nearly always shows year-to-year variation in actual companies. For example, earnings may have transitory components that management does not want to reflect in dividends. The analyst may thus observe actual dividend growth rates straying from the growth rates predicted by Equation 2-29 because of these effects, even when his input estimates are unbiased. Nevertheless, the equation can be useful as a simple expression for approximating the average rate at which dividends can grow over a long horizon.

6.2. Dividend Growth Rate, Retention Rate, and ROE Analysis

Thus far we have seen that a company's sustainable growth, as defined above, is a function of its ability to generate return on equity (which depends on investment opportunities) and its retention rate. We now expand this model by examining what drives ROE. Remember that ROE is the return (net income) generated on the equity invested in the company:

$$\text{ROE} = \frac{\text{Net income}}{\text{Stockholders' equity}} \qquad (2\text{-}30)$$

If a company has a ROE of 15 percent, it generates $15 of net income for every $100 invested in stockholders' equity. For purposes of analyzing ROE, we can relate it to several other financial ratios. For example, ROE can be seen as related to return on assets (ROA) and the extent of financial leverage (equity multiplier):

$$\text{ROE} = \frac{\text{Net income}}{\text{Total assets}} \times \frac{\text{Total assets}}{\text{Stockholders' equity}} \qquad (2\text{-}31)$$

Therefore, a company can increase its ROE either by increasing ROA or by the use of leverage (assuming the company can borrow at a rate lower than that it earns on its assets).

We can further expand this model by breaking ROA into two components, profit margin and turnover (efficiency):

$$\text{ROE} = \frac{\text{Net income}}{\text{Sales}} \times \frac{\text{Sales}}{\text{Total assets}} \times \frac{\text{Total assets}}{\text{Stockholders' equity}} \qquad (2\text{-}32)$$

The first term is the company's profit margin. A higher profit margin will result in a higher ROE. The second term measures total asset turnover, which is the company's efficiency. A turnover of 1 indicates that a company generates $1 in sales for every $1 invested in assets. A higher turnover will result in higher ROE. The last term is the equity multiplier, which measures the extent of leverage, as noted earlier. This relationship is widely known as the DuPont model or analysis of ROE. Although ROE can be analyzed further using a five-way analysis, the three-way analysis will provide us with insight into the determinants of ROE that are pertinent to our understanding of the growth rate. Combining Equations 2-29 and

2-32, we find that the dividend growth rate is equal to the retention rate multiplied by ROE:[35]

$$g = \frac{\text{Net income} - \text{Dividends}}{\text{Net income}} \times \frac{\text{Net income}}{\text{Sales}} \times \frac{\text{Sales}}{\text{Assets}} \times \frac{\text{Assets}}{\text{Shareholders' equity}} \quad (2\text{-}33)$$

The model is also useful to the analyst in analyzing the factors that can affect the sustainable growth rate. Higgins (2001) explains this model and calls it the PRAT model (although we have altered the notation and calculations slightly to use averages in the ratios above). Growth is a function of profit margin (P), retention rate (R), asset turnover (A), and financial leverage (T). Two of these factors determine ROA—the profit margin and the asset turnover. The other two factors are based on a company's financial policies—the retention rate and financial leverage. So, the growth rate in dividends can be viewed as determined by the company's ROA and financial policies. The example below illustrates the logic behind this equation.

EXAMPLE 2-26   ROA, Financial Policies, and the Dividend Growth Rate

Baggai Enterprises has an ROA of 10 percent, retains 30 percent of earnings, and has an equity multiplier of 1.25. Mondale Enterprises also has an ROA of 10 percent, but it retains two-thirds of earnings and has an equity multiplier of 2.00. What dividend growth rates should these two companies have?

Baggai's dividend growth rate should be $g = 0.30 \times 10\% \times 1.25 = 3.75\%$

Mondale's dividend growth rate should be $g = (2/3) \times 10\% \times 2.00 = 13.33\%$

Because Mondale has the higher retention rate and higher financial leverage, its dividend growth rate is much higher.

If we are forecasting growth for the next five years, we should use our expectations of the four factors driving growth over this five-year period. If we are forecasting growth into perpetuity, we should use our very long-term forecasts for these variables.

To illustrate the calculation and implications of the sustainable growth rate using the expression for ROE given by the DuPont formula, assume the growth rate is $g = b \times \text{ROE} = 0.60(15\%) = 9\%$. The ROE of 15 percent was based on a profit margin of 5 percent, an asset turnover of 2.0, and an equity multiplier of 1.5. Given fixed ratios of sales-to-assets and assets-to-equity, sales, assets, and debt will also be growing at 9 percent. Because dividends are fixed at 40 percent of income, dividends will grow at the same rate as income, or 9 percent.

---

[35] Strictly speaking, the theoretical expression $g = b \times \text{ROE}$ holds exactly only when ROE is calculated using beginning-of-period shareholders' equity. That assumption is necessary for mathematical simplicity, but assumes that reinvested earnings are not available until the end of the period. Practically, ROE is calculated using average stockholders' equity or sometimes ending stockholders' equity in financial databases, and is preferred for financial analysis.

If the company increases dividends faster than 9 percent, this growth rate would not be sustainable using internally generated funds. Earning retentions would be reduced, and the company would not be able to finance the assets required for sales growth without external financing.

The analyst should be careful in projecting historical financial ratios into the future in using this analysis. Although a company may have grown at 20 percent a year for the last five years, this rate of growth is probably not sustainable indefinitely. Abnormally high ROEs, which may have driven that growth, are unlikely to persist for long periods of time because of competitive forces.

EXAMPLE 2-27   Forecasting Growth with the PRAT Formula

Dell Corporation (NYSE: DELL) is not currently paying a dividend. An analysis of its ROE for the past five years is shown in Table 2-13.

TABLE 2-13   Dell Corporation

Year	ROE (%)	Profit Margin (%)	Asset Turnover	Financial Leverage
2000	39.87 =	6.83	× 2.56	× 2.28
1999	43.74 =	6.60	× 2.75	× 2.41
1998	80.57 =	8.00	× 3.27	× 3.08
1997	90.11 =	7.66	× 3.40	× 3.46
1996	58.50 =	6.68	× 3.02	× 2.90

DELL's ROEs have been very high during this period. Because it is retaining all earnings, the company has grown accordingly. It is unlikely that DELL will sustain these levels indefinitely. Their strong business model and market position, however, are expected by an analyst to maintain above-average performance (relative to the market) during the next five years. Nonetheless, the analyst believes the performance cannot realistically be expected to match prior levels. Further, the analyst assumes that the company will continue to retain all earnings for the next 10 years. The analyst's forecast for profit margin, turnover, and leverage over the next 10 years are

Profit Margin	5%
Asset Turnover	2.50
Leverage	2.00

With a retention rate of 100 percent, the PRAT formula yields Short-term growth = $0.05 \times 1.00 \times 2.50 \times 2.00 = 25\%$.

Although DELL may be able to sustain this level of growth for 10 years, the analyst believes that market conditions may intervene. For example, weak demand for personal computers may result in lower growth. Accordingly, the analyst may elect to lower this growth estimate subjectively.

Assume that the analyst forecasts that after Year 10, DELL will begin to pay out 15 percent of its earnings as dividends (typical for mature technology companies).

Additionally, long-term sustainable estimates for profit margin, asset turnover, and leverage are

Profit Margin	4.5% (reflects declining margins in the industry)
Asset Turnover	1.50 (closer to industry efficiency)
Leverage	2.00 (modest reduction from recent levels)

With a retention rate of 85 percent, the PRAT formula yields Long-term sustainable growth $= 0.045 \times 0.85 \times 1.50 \times 2.00 = 11.48\%$.

Because there are no dividends for the first 10 years, the analyst would use a two-stage DDM with these growth inputs. For the trailing 12 months, DELL has earnings per share excluding non-recurring items of $0.76. Using a risk-free rate of 5.0 percent, an equity risk premium of 5.7 percent, and a beta of 1.45 results in a required rate of return of 13.3 percent. Forecasting earnings in Year 10 at 25 percent annual growth results in E_{10} of $7.08 $= \$0.76 \times 1.25^{10}$. The following year's earnings would be forecasted to grow at 11.48 percent to $7.89. D_{11} would be $7.89 \times 0.15 = \$1.18$. V_{10} would be $1.18/(0.133 − 0.1148)$ or $64.84. Discounting back to V_0 at 13.3 percent yields a current price of $18.60.

This example illustrates the use of a DDM for valuing a non-dividend-paying stock. As noted in Section 2, analysts often select other DCF models in such cases. We will discuss alternative DCF models in later chapters.

6.3. Financial Models and Dividends

Analysts can also forecast dividends by building more-complex models of the company's total operating and financial environment. Because there can be so many aspects to such a model, a spreadsheet is used to build pro forma income statements and balance sheets. The company's ability to pay dividends in the future can be predicted using one of these models. The example below shows the dividends that a highly profitable and rapidly growing company can pay when its growth rates and profit margins decline because of increasing competition over time.

EXAMPLE 2-28   A Spreadsheet Model for Forecasting Dividends

An analyst is preparing a forecast of dividends for Hoshino Distributors for the next five years. He uses a spreadsheet model with the following assumptions:

- Sales are $100 million in Year 1. They grow by 20 percent in Year 2, 15 percent in Year 3, and 10 percent in Years 4 and 5.
- Operating profits (EBIT = earnings before interest and taxes) are 20 percent of sales in Years 1 and 2, 18 percent of sales in Year 3, and 16 percent of sales in Years 4 and 5.
- Interest expenses are 10 percent of total debt for the current year.
- The income tax rate is 40 percent.

- Hoshino pays out 20 percent of earnings in Years 1 and 2, 30 percent in Year 3, 40 percent in Year 4, and 50 percent in Year 5.
- Retained earnings are added to equity in the next year.
- Total assets are 80 percent of the current year's sales in all years.
- In Year 1, debt is $40 million and shareholders' equity is $40 million. Debt equals total assets minus shareholders' equity. Shareholders' equity will equal the previous year's shareholders' equity plus the addition to retained earnings from the previous year.
- Hoshino has 4 million shares outstanding.
- The discount rate is 15 percent, and the value of the company at the end of Year 5 will be 10.0 times earnings.

The analyst wishes to estimate the current value per share of Hoshino. Table 2-14 adheres to the modeling assumptions above. Total dividends and earnings are found at the bottom of the income statement.

TABLE 2-14   Hoshino Distributors Pro Forma Financial Statements (in millions)

	Year 1	Year 2	Year 3	Year 4	Year 5
Income statement					
Sales	$100.00	$120.00	$138.00	$151.80	$166.98
EBIT	$20.00	$24.00	$24.84	$24.29	$26.72
Interest	$4.00	$4.83	$5.35	$5.64	$6.18
EBT	$16.00	$19.17	$19.49	$18.65	$20.54
Taxes	$6.40	$7.67	$7.80	$7.46	$8.22
Net income	$9.60	$11.50	$11.69	$11.19	$12.32
Dividends	$1.92	$2.30	$3.51	$4.48	$6.16
Balance sheet					
Total assets	$80.00	$96.00	$110.40	$121.44	$133.58
Total debt	$40.00	$48.32	$53.52	$56.38	$61.81
Equity	$40.00	$47.68	$56.88	$65.06	$71.77

Dividing the total dividends by the number of outstanding shares gives the dividend per share for each year shown below. The present value of each dividend, discounted at 15 percent, is also shown.

	Year 1	Year 2	Year 3	Year 4	Year 5
DPS	$0.480	$0.575	$0.877	$1.120	$1.540
PV	$0.417	$0.435	$0.577	$0.640	$0.766

The earnings per share in Year 5 are $12.32 million divided by 4 million shares, or $3.08 per share. Given a P/E of 10, the market price in Year 5 is predicted to be $30.80. Discounted at 15 percent (the required rate of return noted above), the present value of this price is $15.31. Adding the present values of the five dividends, which sum to $2.84, gives a total stock value today of $18.15 per share.

6.4. Investment Management and DDMs

Investment management does not involve isolated or occasional valuations of a common stock. An analyst will usually have to do valuations of a number of stocks, and these valuations will be updated regularly or whenever changing circumstances warrant an update. Teams of analysts also have to work together to evaluate the stocks in their investment universe. A competitive environment requires rapid incorporation of the best information, consistent application of valuation principles, and clear communication of investment recommendations (and their justifications).

Investment managers have used DCF models, including dividend discount models, as part of a systematic approach to security selection and portfolio formation. The portfolio formation process has a *planning step*, an *execution step*, and a *feedback step*. Although this chapter has focused on the use of DDM in the execution step, we must put the chapter in the context of the planning step.

In the planning step, risk and return objectives are set. Consider a U.S. domestic core equity portfolio manager with the S&P 500 as a benchmark (the comparison portfolio used to evaluate performance).[36] This investment manager may choose a risk objective in terms of tracking risk relative to the S&P 500. **Tracking risk** is the standard deviation of the differences between the portfolio's and the benchmark's returns. Hypothetically, a tracking risk objective might be set at 5 percent. (For a portfolio with this investment approach, tracking risk would commonly fall in the range of 2 percent to 6 percent.) For this manager, the return objective might be to beat the S&P 500 by 200 basis points. Planning also involves the selection of an investment strategy. DCF models are used in active investment strategies. Active managers hold securities in different-from-benchmark weights in an attempt to produce positive risk-adjusted returns or alphas.

In the execution step, the portfolio manager selects the portfolio, and the trading desk implements the portfolio decisions. Managers use DCF models to identify (select) undervalued securities. If the manager simply chose the most undervalued securities without any risk discipline, his selections might concentrate on a particular (or a few) risk factor. He might often fail to meet his risk objective. A risk-control discipline must be used. Our hypothetical manager might choose sector neutrality with respect to his benchmark as that discipline, defining his investment universe as the S&P 500. A portfolio is **sector neutral** to a benchmark if sectors are represented in the portfolio in the same proportions as in the benchmark, according to market-value weights. (Economic sector membership explains a substantial portion of risk; however, this is an illustration, not a recommendation of a particular risk-control approach.) Then the process continues as follows:

- *Sort stocks into groups according to the risk-control methodology.* In our example, the manager sorts the stocks into groups according to sector membership. As another example, if the manager uses a CAPM risk-control methodology, the sorting is into portfolios of similar beta risk.
- *Rank stocks by expected return within each group using a DCF methodology.* There are several techniques to implement this ranking. The manager may use an expression for r in terms of fundamentals and current market price, using a DCF model. This value of r is an estimate of expected return if price fully reflects value, or if price and value differ but do not converge. As explained earlier, when price (P_0) and intrinsic value (V_0) differ, expected

[36]This illustration is drawn from a composite of several actual investment managers.

return will have an additional component if the two come together. Then the manager's estimate of expected return is the sum of *r* and the return from convergence. In practice, convergence assumptions range from nonconvergence to gradual convergence over five years. At the end of this step, in our example, the manager has ranked stocks from highest to lowest expected return within sector grouping, or whatever grouping approach is used.

- *Select a portfolio from the highest expected return stocks consistent with the risk-control methodology.* This selection is implemented in various ways. As an illustration, the investment manager might preset the number of issues in the portfolio at 80. If the energy sector at the time has a 10 percent weight in the S&P 500, the 8 energy issues (10 percent of 80) in the S&P 500 with the highest expected return enter the portfolio with equal weights. All selected securities are equally weighted, but more-important sectors have a larger number of securities; the result is approximate sector neutrality.

As part of this process, careful investment managers will stress test the expected return inputs with respect to assumptions. Consistency of the assumptions underlying the valuations of different companies is important. For example, if different industry growth forecasts underlie different analysts' earnings projections, then relative valuation differences among stocks may simply reflect different industry forecasts rather than mispricing. As with all active investment strategies, investment results depend on the quality of the inputs. As discussed in Chapter 1, for an active strategy to consistently add value, the manager's expectations (about earnings growth, for example) must differ from consensus expectations and be, on average, correct as well.

Effective and appropriate use of DDMs, as well as the valuation models in the following chapters, is essential for investment management, whether by an individual or by a team of analysts. Analysts can use DDMs to systematically select securities for inclusion in portfolios.

7. SUMMARY

This chapter provided an overview of DCF models of valuation, discussed the estimation of a stock's required rate of return, and presented in detail the dividend discount model.

- In DCF models, the value of any asset is the present value of its (expected) future cash flows

$$V_0 = \sum_{t=1}^{\infty} \frac{CF_t}{(1+r)^t}$$

where V_0 is the value of the asset as of $t = 0$ (today), CF_t is the (expected) cash flow at time t, and r is the discount rate or required rate of return.
- Several alternative streams of expected cash flows can be used to value equities, including dividends, free cash flow, and residual income. A discounted dividend approach is most suitable for dividend-paying stocks, where the company has a discernible dividend policy that has an understandable relationship to the company's profitability, and the investor has a non-control (minority ownership) perspective.
- The free cash flow approach (FCFF or FCFE) might be appropriate when the company does not pay dividends, dividends differ substantially from FCFE, free cash flows align with profitability, or the investor takes a control (majority ownership) perspective.
- The residual income approach can be useful when the company does not pay dividends (as an alternative to a FCF approach), or free cash flow is negative.

- The required rate of return is the minimum rate of return that an investor would anticipate receiving in order to invest in an asset. The two major approaches to determining the cost of equity are an equilibrium method (CAPM or APT) and the bond yield plus risk premium method.
- The equity risk premium for use in the CAPM approach can be based on historical return data or based explicitly on expectational data.
- The DDM with a single holding period gives stock value as

$$V_0 = \frac{D_1}{(1+r)^1} + \frac{P_1}{(1+r)^1} = \frac{D_1 + P_1}{(1+r)^1}$$

where D_t is the expected dividend at time t (here $t = 1$) and V_t is the stock's (expected) value at time t. Assuming that V_0 is equal to today's market price, P_0, the expected holding-period return is

$$r = \frac{D_1 + P_1}{P_0} - 1 = \frac{D_1}{P_0} + \frac{P_1 - P_0}{P_0}$$

- Expected holding-period returns differ from required rates of return when price does not exactly reflect value. When price does not equal value, there will generally be an additional component to the expected holding-period return reflecting the convergence of price to value.
- The expression for the DDM for any given finite holding period n and the general expression for the DDM are, respectively,

$$V_0 = \sum_{t=1}^{n} \frac{D_t}{(1+r)^t} + \frac{P_n}{(1+r)^n} \quad \text{and} \quad V_0 = \sum_{t=1}^{\infty} \frac{D_t}{(1+r)^t}$$

- There are two main approaches to the problem of forecasting dividends: First, we can assign the entire stream of expected future dividends to one of several stylized growth patterns. Second, we can forecast a finite number of dividends individually up to a terminal point, valuing the remaining dividends by assigning them to a stylized growth pattern, or forecasting share price as of the terminal point of our dividend forecasts. The first forecasting approach leads to the Gordon growth model and multistage dividend discount models; the second forecasting approach lends itself to spreadsheet modeling.
- The Gordon growth model assumes that dividends grow at a constant rate g forever, so that $D_t = D_{t-1}(1 + g)$. The dividend stream in the Gordon growth model has a value of

$$V_0 = \frac{D_0(1+g)}{r-g}, \quad \text{or} \quad V_0 = \frac{D_1}{r-g}$$

where $r > g$.
- The value of fixed rate perpetual preferred stock is $V_0 = D/r$, where D is the stock's (constant) annual dividend.
- Assuming that price equals value, the Gordon growth model estimate of a stock's expected rate of return is

$$r = \frac{D_0(1+g)}{P_0} + g = \frac{D_1}{P_0} + g$$

- Given an estimate of the next-period dividend and the stock's required rate of return, we can use the Gordon growth model to estimate the dividend growth rate implied by the current market price (making a constant growth rate assumption).
- The present value of growth opportunities (PVGO) is the part of a stock's total value, V_0, that comes from profitable future growth opportunities in contrast to the value associated with assets already in place. The relationship is $V_0 = E/r + \text{PVGO}$, where E/r is defined as the no-growth value per share.
- We can express the leading price–earnings ratio (P_0/E_1) and the trailing price–earnings ratio (P_0/E_0) in terms of the Gordon growth model as, respectively,

$$\frac{P_0}{E_1} = \frac{D_1/E_1}{r-g} = \frac{1-b}{r-g} \quad \text{and} \quad \frac{P_0}{E_0} = \frac{D_0(1+g)/E_0}{r-g} = \frac{(1-b)(1+g)}{r-g}$$

The above expressions give a stock's justified price–earnings ratio based on forecasts of fundamentals (given that the Gordon growth model is appropriate).

- The Gordon growth model may be useful for valuing broad-based equity indexes and the stock of businesses with earnings that we expect to grow at a stable rate comparable to or lower than the nominal growth rate of the economy.
- Gordon growth model values are very sensitive to the assumed growth rate and required rate of return.
- For many companies, growth falls into phases. In the growth phase, a company enjoys an abnormally high growth rate in earnings per share, called supernormal growth. In the transition phase, earnings growth slows. In the mature phase, the company reaches an equilibrium in which factors such as earnings growth and the return on equity stabilize at levels that can be sustained long term. Analysts often apply multistage DCF models to value the stock of a firm with multistage growth prospects.
- The two-stage dividend discount model assumes different growth rates in Stage 1 and Stage 2

$$V_0 = \sum_{t=1}^{n} \frac{D_0(1+g_S)^t}{(1+r)^t} + \frac{D_0(1+g_S)^n(1+g_L)}{(1+r)^n(r-g_L)}$$

where g_S is the expected dividend growth rate in the first period and g_L is the expected growth rate in the second period.

- The terminal stock value, V_n, is sometimes found with the Gordon growth model or with some other method, such as applying a P/E multiplier to forecasted EPS as of the terminal date.
- The H-model assumes that the dividend growth rate declines linearly from a high supernormal rate to the normal growth rate during Stage 1, and then grows at a constant normal growth rate thereafter:

$$V_0 = \frac{D_0(1+g_L)}{r-g_L} + \frac{D_0 H(g_S - g_L)}{r-g_L} = \frac{D_0(1+g_L) + D_0 H(g_S - g_L)}{r-g_L}$$

- There are two basic three-stage models. In one version, the growth rate is constant in each of the three stages. In the second version, the growth rate is constant in Stage 1, declines linearly in Stage 2, and becomes constant and normal in Stage 3.
- Spreadsheet models are very flexible, providing the analyst with the ability to value any pattern of expected dividends.

- In addition to valuing equities, DDMs are used to find expected rates of return. For simpler models (like the one-period model, the Gordon growth model, and the H-model), well-known formulas may be used to calculate these rates of return. For many dividend streams, however, the rate of return must be found by trial and error, producing a discount rate that equates the present value of the forecasted dividend stream to the current market price. Adjustments to the expected return estimates may be needed to reflect the convergence of price to value.
- Multistage DDM models can accommodate a wide variety of patterns of expected dividends. Even though such models may use stylized assumptions about growth, they can provide useful approximations.
- Values from multistage DDMs are generally sensitive to assumptions. The usefulness of such values reflects the quality of the inputs.
- Dividend growth rates can be obtained from analyst forecasts, from statistical forecasting models, or from company fundamentals. The sustainable growth rate depends on the ROE and the earnings retention rate, b: $g = b \times$ ROE. This expression can be expanded further, using the DuPont formula, as

$$g = \frac{\text{Net income} - \text{Dividends}}{\text{Net income}} \times \frac{\text{Net income}}{\text{Sales}} \times \frac{\text{Sales}}{\text{Assets}} \times \frac{\text{Assets}}{\text{Shareholders' equity}}$$

- Dividend discount models can be used as a discipline for portfolio construction. Potential investments can be screened or selected based on their estimated rates of return, along with other portfolio requirements. Often, the discipline involves three steps: sorting stocks into groups according to a risk-control methodology, ranking stocks by expected return within each group, and selecting a portfolio from the highest expected return stocks consistent with the risk-control methodology.

PROBLEMS

1. The estimated betas for AOL Time Warner (NYSE: AOL), J.P. Morgan Chase & Company (NYSE: JPM), and The Boeing Company (NYSE: BA) are 2.50, 1.50, and 0.80, respectively. The risk-free rate of return is 4.35 percent, and the market risk premium is 8.04 percent. Calculate the required rates of return for these three stocks using the CAPM.

2. The estimated factor sensitivities of Terra Energy to the five macroeconomic factors in the Burmeister, Roll, and Ross (1994) article are given in the table below. The table also gives the market risk premiums to each of these same factors.

	Factor Sensitivity	Risk Premium (%)
Confidence risk	0.25	2.59
Time horizon risk	0.30	−0.66
Inflation risk	−0.45	−4.32
Business-cycle risk	1.60	1.49
Market-timing risk	0.80	3.61

Use the 5-factor BIRR APT model to calculate the required rate of return for Terra Energy using these estimates. The Treasury bill rate is 4.1 percent.

3. Newmont Mining (NYSE: NEM) has an estimated beta of -0.2. The risk-free rate of return is 4.5 percent, and the equity risk premium is estimated to be 7.5 percent. Using the CAPM, calculate the required rate of return for investors in NEM.

4. The expression for the value of a stock given a single-period investment horizon has four variables: $V_0, D_1, P_1,$ and r. Solve for the value of the missing variable for each of the four stocks in the table below.

Stock	Estimated Value (V_0)	Expected Dividend (D_1)	Expected Price (P_1)	Required Rate of Return (r)
1		$0.30	$21.00	10.0%
2	$30.00		32.00	10.0
3	92.00	2.70		12.0
4	16.00	0.30	17.90	

5. General Motors (NYSE: GM) sells for $66.00 per share. The expected dividend for next year is $2.40. Use the single-period DDM to predict GM's stock price one year from today. The risk-free rate of return is 5.3 percent, the market risk premium is 6.0 percent, and GM's beta is 0.90.

6. BP PLC (NYSE: BP) has a current stock price of $50 and current dividend of $1.50. The dividend is expected to grow at 5 percent annually. BP's beta is 0.85. The risk-free interest rate is 4.5 percent, and the market risk premium is 6.0 percent.

   A. What is next year's projected dividend?
   B. What is BP's required rate of return based on the CAPM?
   C. Using the Gordon growth model, what is the value of BP?
   D. Assuming the Gordon growth model is valid, what dividend growth rate would result in a model value of BP equal to its market price?

7. The current market prices of three stocks are given below. The current dividends, dividend growth rates, and required rates of return are also given. The dividend growth rates are perpetual.

Stock	Current Price	Current Dividend ($t = 0$)	Dividend Growth Rate	Required Rate of Return
Que Corp.	$25.00	$0.50	7.0%	10.0%
SHS Company	$40.00	$1.20	6.5	10.5
True Corp.	$20.00	$0.88	5.0	10.0

   A. Find the value of each stock with the Gordon growth model.
   B. Which stock's current market price has the smallest premium or largest discount relative to its DDM valuation?

8. For five utility stocks, the table below provides the expected dividend for next year, the current market price, the expected dividend growth rate, and the beta. The risk-free rate is currently 5.3 percent, and the market risk premium is 6.0 percent.

Stock	Dividend (D_1)	Price (P_0)	Dividend Growth Rate (g)	Beta (β)
American Electric (NYSE: AEP)	2.40	46.17	5.0%	0.60
Consolidated Edison (NYSE: ED)	2.20	39.80	5.0	0.60
Exelon Corp. (NYSE: EXC)	1.69	64.12	7.0	0.80
Southern Co. (NYSE: SO)	1.34	23.25	5.5	0.65
Dominion Resources (NYSE: D)	2.58	60.13	5.5	0.65

A. Calculate the expected rate of return for each stock using the Gordon growth model.

B. Calculate the required rate of return for each stock using the CAPM.

9. Vicente Garcia is a buy-side analyst for a large pension fund. He frequently uses dividend discount models such as the Gordon growth model for the consumer noncyclical stocks that he covers. The current dividend for Procter & Gamble Co. (NYSE: PG) is $1.46, and the dividend eight years ago was $0.585. The current stock price is $80.00.

A. What is the historical dividend growth rate for Procter & Gamble?

B. Garcia assumes that the future dividend growth rate will be exactly half of the historical rate. What is Procter & Gamble's expected rate of return using the Gordon growth model?

C. Garcia uses a beta of 0.53 (computed versus the S&P 500 index) for Procter & Gamble. The risk-free rate of return is 5.56 percent, and the equity risk premium is 3.71 percent. If Garcia continues to assume that the future dividend growth rate will be exactly half of the historical rate, what is the value of the stock with the Gordon growth model?

10. NiSource Preferred B (NYSE: NI-B) is a fixed-rate perpetual preferred stock paying a $3.88 annual dividend. If the required rate of return is 7.88 percent, what is the value of one share? If the price of this preferred stock were $46.00, what would be the yield?

11. R.A. Nixon put out a "strong buy" on DuPoTex (DPT). This company has a current stock price of $88.00 per share. The company has sales of $210 million, net income of $3 million, and 300 million outstanding shares. DPT is not paying a dividend. Dorothy Josephson has argued with Nixon that DPT's valuation is excessive relative to its sales, profits, and any reasonable assumptions about future possible dividends. Josephson also asserts that DPT has a market value equal to that of many large blue-chip companies, which it does not deserve. Nixon feels that Josephson's concerns reflect an archaic attitude about equity valuation and a lack of understanding about DPT's industry.

A. What is the total market value of DPT's outstanding shares? What are the price-to-earnings and price-to-sales ratios?

B. Nixon and Josephson have agreed on a scenario for future earnings and dividends for DPT. Their assumptions are that sales grow at 60 percent annually for four years, and then at 7 percent annually thereafter. In Year 5 and thereafter, earnings will be 10 percent of sales. No dividends will be paid for four years, but in Year 5 and after, dividends will be 40 percent of earnings. Dividends should be discounted at a 12 percent rate. What is the value of a share of DPT using the discounted dividend approach to valuation?

C. Nixon and Josephson explore another scenario for future earnings and dividends for DPT. They assume that sales will grow at 7 percent in Year 5 and thereafter. Earnings will be 10 percent of sales, and dividends will be 40 percent of earnings. Dividends will be initiated in Year 5, and dividends should be discounted at 12 percent. What level of sales is required in Year 4 to achieve a discounted dividend valuation equal to the current stock price?

12. Dole Food (NYSE: DOL) has a current dividend of $0.40, which is expected to grow at 7 percent forever. Felipe Rodriguez has estimated the required rate of return for Dole using three methods. The methods and the estimates are as follows:

Bond yield plus risk premium method	$r = 9.6\%$
CAPM method	$r = 11.2\%$
APT method	$r = 10.4\%$

Using the assumed dividend pattern, what is the value of Dole Food using each of the three estimated required rates of return?

13. The CFO of B-to-C Inc., a retailer of miscellaneous consumer products, recently announced the objective of paying its first (annual) cash dividend of $0.50 in four years. Thereafter, the dividend is expected to increase by 7 percent per year for the foreseeable future. The company's required rate of return is 15 percent.

A. Assuming that you have confidence in the CFO's dividend target, what is the value of the stock of B-to-C today?

B. Suppose that you think that the CFO's outlook is too optimistic. Instead, you believe that the first dividend of $0.50 will not be received until six years from now. What is the value of the stock?

14. FPR is expected to pay a $0.60 dividend next year. The dividend is expected to grow at a 50 percent annual rate for Years 2 and 3, at 20 percent annually for Years 4 and 5, and at 5 percent annually for Year 6 and thereafter. If the required rate of return is 12 percent, what is the value per share?

15. EB Systems is selling for $11.40 and is expected to pay a $0.40 dividend next year. The dividend is expected to grow at 15 percent for the following four years, and then at 7 percent annually after Year 5. If purchased at its current price, what is the expected rate of return on EB Systems? Assume price equals value.

16. Hanson PLC (LSE: HNS) is selling for GBP 472. Hansen has a beta of 0.83 against the FTSE 100 index, and the current dividend is GBP 13.80. The risk-free rate of return is 4.66 percent, and the equity risk premium is 4.92 percent. An analyst covering this stock expects the Hanson dividend to grow initially at 14 percent but to decline linearly to 5 percent over a 10-year period. After that, the analyst expects the dividend to grow at 5 percent.

A. Compute the value of the Hanson dividend stream using the H-model. According to the H-model valuation, is Hanson overpriced or underpriced?

B. Assume that Hanson's dividends follow the H-model pattern the analyst predicts. If an investor pays the current GBP 472 price for the stock, what will be the rate of return?

17. (Adapted from 1995 CFA Level II exam) Your supervisor has asked you to evaluate the relative attractiveness of the stocks of two very similar chemical companies: Litchfield

Chemical Corp. (LCC) and Aminochem Company (AOC). AOC and LCC have June 30 fiscal year ends. You have compiled the data in Table 2-15 for this purpose. Use a one-year time horizon and assume the following:

- Real gross domestic product is expected to rise 5 percent;
- S&P 500 expected total return of 20 percent;
- U.S. Treasury bills yield 5 percent; and
- 30-year U.S. Treasury bonds yield 8 percent.

TABLE 2-15   Selected Data for Litchfield and Aminochem

	Litchfield Chemical (LCC)	Aminochem (AOC)
Current stock price	$50	$30
Shares outstanding (millions)	10	20
Projected earnings per share (FY 1996)	$4.00	$3.20
Projected dividend per share (FY 1996)	$0.90	$1.60
Projected dividend growth rate	8%	7%
Stock beta	1.2	1.4
Investors' required rate of return	10%	11%
Balance sheet data (millions)		
Long-term debt	$100	$130
Stockholders' equity	$300	$320

A. Calculate the value of the common stock of LCC and AOC using the constant-growth DDM. Show your work.
B. Calculate the expected return over the next year of the common stock of LCC and AOC using the CAPM. Show your work.
C. Calculate the internal (implied, normalized, or sustainable) growth rate of LCC and AOC. Show your work.
D. Recommend LCC *or* AOC for investment. Justify your choice using your answers to A, B, and C and the information in Table 2-15.

18. (Adapted from 1999 CFA Level II exam) Scott Kelly is reviewing MasterToy's financial statements in order to estimate its sustainable growth rate. Using the information presented in Table 2-16,

A. i.   Identify the three components of the DuPont formula.
    ii. Calculate the ROE for 1999 using the three components of the DuPont formula.
    iii. Calculate the sustainable growth rate for 1999.

Kelly has calculated actual and sustainable growth for each of the past four years and finds in each year that its calculated sustainable growth rate substantially exceeds its actual growth rate.

B. Cite one course of action (other than ignoring the problem) Kelly should encourage MasterToy to take, assuming the calculated sustainable growth rate continues to exceed the actual growth rate.

TABLE 2-16   MasterToy Inc. Actual 1998 and Estimated 1999 Financial Statements for FY Ending December 31 ($ millions, except per-share data)

	1998	1999e	Change (%)
Income Statement			
Revenue	$4,750	$5,140	8.2
Cost of goods sold	$2,400	$2,540	
Selling, general, and administrative	1,400	1,550	
Depreciation	180	210	
Goodwill amortization	10	10	
Operating income	$760	$830	9.2
Interest expense	20	25	
Income before taxes	$740	$805	
Income taxes	265	295	
Net income	$475	$510	
Earnings per share	$1.79	$1.96	9.5
Average shares outstanding (millions)	265	260	
Balance Sheet			
Cash	$400	$400	
Accounts receivable	680	700	
Inventories	570	600	
Net property, plant, and equipment	800	870	
Intangibles	500	530	
Total assets	$2,950	$3,100	
Current liabilities	$550	$600	
Long-term debt	300	300	
Total liabilities	$850	$900	
Stockholders' equity	2,100	2,200	
Total liabilities and equity	$2,950	$3,100	
Book value per share	$7.92	$8.46	
Annual dividend per share	$0.55	$0.60	

19. (Adapted from 2000 CFA Level II exam) The management of Telluride, an international diversified conglomerate based in the United States, believes that the recent strong performance of its wholly owned medical supply subsidiary, Sundanci, has gone unnoticed. In order to realize Sundanci's full value, Telluride has announced that it will divest Sundanci in a tax-free spin-off.

Sue Carroll, CFA, is Director of Research at Kesson and Associates. In developing an investment recommendation for Sundanci, Carroll has directed four of her analysts to determine a valuation of Sundanci using various valuation disciplines. To assist her analysts, Carroll has gathered the information shown in Tables 2-17 and 2-18 below.

Prior to determining Sundanci's valuation, Carroll analyzes Sundanci's return on equity (ROE) and sustainable growth.

A. i. Calculate the *three* components of ROE in the DuPont formula for the year 2000.

    ii. Calculate ROE for the year 2000.

    iii. Calculate the sustainable rate of growth. Show your work.

Carroll learns that Sundanci's Board of Directors is considering the following policy changes that will affect Sundanci's sustainable growth rate:

- Director A proposes an increase in the quarterly dividend by $0.15 per share.
- Director B proposes a bond issue of $25 million, the proceeds of which will be used to increase production capacity.
- Director C proposes a 2-for-1 stock split.

TABLE 2-17 Sundanci Actual 1999 and 2000 Financial Statements for FY Ending May 31 ($ millions, except per-share data)

Income Statement	1999	2000
Revenue	$474	$598
Depreciation	20	23
Other operating costs	368	460
Income before taxes	86	115
Taxes	26	35
Net income	60	80
Dividends	18	24
Earnings per share	$0.714	$0.952
Dividends per share	$0.214	$0.286
Common shares outstanding (millions)	84.0	84.0
Balance Sheet	**1999**	**2000**
Current assets	$201	$326
Net property, plant, and equipment	474	489
Total assets	675	815
Current liabilities	57	141
Long-term debt	0	0
Total liabilities	57	141
Shareholders' equity	618	674
Total liabilities and equity	675	815
Capital expenditures	34	38

TABLE 2-18 Selected Financial Information

Required rate of return on equity	14%
Growth rate of industry	13%
Industry P/E	26

B. Indicate the effect of each of these proposals on Sundanci's sustainable rate of growth, given that the other factors remain unchanged. Identify which components of the sustainable growth model, if any, are directly affected by each proposal.

Helen Morgan, CFA, has been asked by Carroll to determine the potential valuation for Sundanci using the DDM. Morgan anticipates that Sundanci's earnings and dividends will grow at 32 percent for two years and 13 percent thereafter.

C. Calculate the current value of a share of Sundanci stock using a two-stage dividend discount model and the data from Tables 2-17 and 2-18. Show your work.

20. (Adapted from 2001 CFA Level II exam) Peninsular Research is initiating coverage of a mature manufacturing industry. John Jones, CFA, head of the research department, gathers the information given in Table 2-19 to help in his analysis.

TABLE 2-19   Fundamental Industry and Market Data

Forecasted industry earnings retention rate	40%
Forecasted industry return on equity	25%
Industry beta	1.2
Government bond yield	6%
Equity risk premium	5%

A. Compute the price-to-earnings (P_0/E_1) ratio for the industry based on the fundamental data in Table 2-19. Show your work.

Jones wants to analyze how fundamental P/Es might differ among countries. He gathers the data given in Table 2-20.

TABLE 2-20   Economic and Market Data

Fundamental Factors	Country A	Country B
Forecasted growth in real gross domestic product	5%	2%
Government bond yield	10%	6%
Equity risk premium	5%	4%

B. Determine whether each of the fundamental factors in Table 2-20 would cause P/Es to be generally higher for Country A or higher for Country B. Justify each of your conclusions with one reason. *Note*: Consider each fundamental factor in isolation, with all else remaining equal.

TABLE 2-21   Valuation Information: December 1997

	QuickBrush	SmileWhite
Beta	1.35	1.15
Market price	$45.00	$30.00
Intrinsic value	$63.00	?
Notes:		
Risk-free rate	4.50%	
Expected market return	14.50%	

21. (Adapted from 1998 CFA Level II exam) Janet Ludlow's company requires all its analysts to use a two-stage DDM and the CAPM to value stocks. Using these models, Ludlow has valued QuickBrush Company at $63 per share. She now must value SmileWhite Corporation.

   A. Calculate the required rate of return for SmileWhite using the information in Table 2-21 and the CAPM. Show your work.

   Ludlow estimates the following EPS and dividend growth rates for SmileWhite:

First three years:	12% per year
Years thereafter:	9% per year

   The 1997 dividend per share is $1.72.

   B. Estimate the intrinsic value of SmileWhite using the data above and the two-stage DDM. Show your work.
   C. Recommend QuickBrush or SmileWhite stock for purchase by comparing each company's intrinsic value with its current market price. Show your work.
   D. Describe one strength of the two-stage DDM in comparison with the constant-growth DDM. Describe one weakness inherent in all DDMs.

CHAPTER 3

FREE CASH FLOW VALUATION

LEARNING OUTCOMES

After completing this chapter, you will be able to do the following:

- Discuss the choice of a free cash flow valuation approach.
- Define and interpret free cash flow to the firm (FCFF) and free cash flow to equity (FCFE).
- Describe the FCFF and FCFE approaches to valuation.
- Explain the strengths and limitations of the FCFE model.
- Contrast the ownership perspective implicit in the FCFE approach to the ownership perspective implicit in the dividend discount approach.
- Contrast the appropriate discount rates for the FCFE and FCFF models.
- Discuss the appropriate adjustments to net income, earnings before interest and taxes (EBIT), earnings before interest, taxes, depreciation, and amortization (EBITDA), and cash flow from operations (CFO) to arrive at FCFF and FCFE.
- Calculate FCFF and FCFE given a company's financial statements, prepared according to U.S. Generally Accepted Accounting Principles (GAAP) or International Accounting Standards (IAS).
- Discuss approaches for forecasting FCFF and FCFE.
- Contrast the recognition of value in the FCFE model with the recognition of value in dividend discount models.
- Explain how dividends, share repurchases, share issues, and changes in leverage may affect FCFF and FCFE.
- Contrast FCFF with EBITDA.
- Critique the use of net income and EBITDA as proxies for cash flow in valuation.
- Describe the stable-growth, two-stage, and three-stage FCFF and FCFE models.
- List and discuss the assumptions of the stable-growth, two-stage, and three-stage FCFF and FCFE models.
- Justify the selection of a stable-growth, two-stage, or three-stage FCFF or FCFE model given characteristics of the company being valued.
- Calculate the value of a company using the stable-growth, two-stage, and three-stage FCFF and FCFE models.
- Explain how sensitivity analysis can be used in FCFF and FCFE valuations.
- Discuss approaches for calculating the terminal value in a multistage valuation model.
- Describe the characteristics of companies for which the FCFF model is preferred to the FCFE model.

1. INTRODUCTION TO FREE CASH FLOWS

Discounted cash flow (DCF) valuation views the intrinsic value of a security as the present value of its expected future cash flows. When applied to dividends, the DCF model is the discounted dividend approach or dividend discount model (DDM). This chapter extends DCF analysis to value a company and its equity securities by valuing free cash flow to the firm (FCFF) and free cash flow to equity (FCFE). Although dividends are the cash flows actually paid to stockholders, the free cash flow models are based on the cash flows *available* for distribution.

Unlike dividends, FCFF and FCFE are not published and readily available data. Analysts need to compute these quantities from available financial information, which requires a clear understanding of free cash flows as well as the ability to interpret and use the information correctly. Forecasting future free cash flows is also challenging. The analyst's understanding of a company's financial statements, its operations and financing, and its industry and role in the economy can pay real "dividends" as he or she studies a stock. Finding current cash flows and forecasting future cash flows is a rich and challenging exercise. Because of this richness, it is not surprising that many analysts consider free cash flow models to be more useful than dividend discount models.

Analysts like to use free cash flow as return (either FCFF or FCFE) whenever one or more of the following conditions is present:

- The company is not dividend paying;
- The company is dividend paying but dividends differ significantly from the company's capacity to pay dividends;
- Free cash flows align with profitability within a reasonable forecast period with which the analyst is comfortable; or
- The investor takes a control perspective.

If an investor can take control of the company (or expects another investor to do so), dividends can be changed substantially, possibly coming closer to the company's capacity to pay dividends. Free cash flows can provide an economically sound basis for valuation.

Common equity can be valued directly using FCFE or indirectly by first computing the value of the firm using a FCFF model and then subtracting the value of non-common-stock capital (usually debt)[1] from FCFF to arrive at the value of equity. The purpose of this chapter is to develop the background required to use the FCFF or FCFE approaches to valuing a company's equity. To the extent that free cash flows are more meaningful than dividends and that analysts have a sound economic basis for their free cash flow estimates, free cash flow models have much potential in practical application.

Section 2 defines the concepts of free cash flow to the firm and free cash flow to equity, and then presents the two valuation models based on discounting of FCFF and FCFE. We also explore the constant growth models for valuing FCFF and FCFE, special cases of the general models, in this section. After reviewing the FCFF and FCFE valuation process in Section 2, in Section 3 we turn to the vital task of calculating and forecasting FCFF and FCFE. Section 4 provides more-complicated valuation models and discusses some of the issues associated with their application. Analysts usually value operating assets and nonoperating assets separately and then combine them to find the total value of the firm, an approach described in Section 5.

---

[1] A company's suppliers of capital include stockholders, bondholders, and (sometimes) preferred stockholders.

2. FCFF AND FCFE VALUATION APPROACHES

The purpose of this section is to provide a conceptual understanding of free cash flows and the valuation models based on them. A more detailed accounting treatment of free cash flows and more-complicated valuation models will follow in subsequent sections.

2.1. Defining Free Cash Flow

Free cash flow to the firm is the cash flow available to the company's suppliers of capital after all operating expenses (including taxes) have been paid and necessary investments in working capital (e.g., inventory) and fixed capital (e.g., equipment) have been made. FCFF is the cash flow from operations minus capital expenditures. To calculate FCFF, analysts may use different equations depending on the accounting information available. As mentioned, the company's suppliers of capital include common stockholders, bondholders, and, sometimes, preferred stockholders.

Free cash flow to equity is the cash flow available to the company's common equity holders after all operating expenses, interest, and principal payments have been paid and necessary investments in working and fixed capital have been made. FCFE is the cash flow from operations minus capital expenditures minus payments to (and plus receipts from) debtholders.

How is free cash flow related to a company's net income, cash flow from operations, and measures such as EBITDA (earnings before interest, taxes, depreciation, and amortization)? This question is important: The analyst must understand the relationship between a company's reported accounting data and free cash flow in order to forecast free cash flow and its expected growth. Although a company reports cash flow from operations (CFO) on the statement of cash flows, CFO is *not* free cash flow. Net income and CFO data can be used, however, in determining a company's free cash flow.

The advantage of FCFF and FCFE is that they can be used in a discounted cash flow framework to value the firm or to value equity. Other earnings measures such as net income, EBIT, EBITDA, or CFO do not have this property because they either double-count or omit cash flows in some way. For example, EBIT and EBITDA are before-tax measures, and the cash flows available to investors (in the firm or in equity of the firm) must be after tax. From the stockholders' perspective, these measures do not account for differing capital structures (the after-tax interest expenses or preferred dividends) or for the funds that bondholders supply to finance investments in operating assets. Moreover, these measures do not account for the reinvestment of cash flows that the company makes in capital assets and working capital to maintain or maximize the long-run value of the firm.

Dealing with free cash flow is more challenging than dealing with dividends because the analyst must integrate the cash flows from the company's operations with those from its investing and financing activities. Because FCFF is the after-tax cash flow going to all investors in the firm, the value of the firm is found by discounting FCFF at the weighted-average cost of capital (WACC). The value of equity is then found by subtracting the value of debt from the value of the firm. On the other hand, FCFE is the cash flow going to common stockholders, so the appropriate risk-adjusted discount rate for FCFE is the required rate of return on equity. This section presents the general form of these two valuation models, the FCFF valuation model and the FCFE valuation model.

Depending on the company being analyzed, an analyst may have reasons to prefer using FCFF or FCFE. If the company's capital structure is relatively stable, FCFE is more direct and simpler to use than FCFF. In the case of a levered company with negative FCFE, however, working with FCFF to value stock may be easier. The analyst would discount FCFF to find the present value of operating assets, add cash and marketable securities to get total firm value, and then subtract the market value of debt to find the intrinsic value of equity. If a company has had a history of leverage changes in the past, a growth rate in FCFF may be more meaningful than an ever-changing growth pattern in FCFE.[2]

2.2. Present Value of Free Cash Flow

The two distinct approaches to valuation using free cash flow are the FCFF valuation approach and the FCFE valuation approach. The general expression for these valuation models is similar to the expression for the general dividend discount model. In that model, the value of a share of stock equals the present value of the dividends from Time 1 through infinity, discounted at the required rate of return for equity.

2.2.1. Present Value of FCFF

The FCFF valuation approach estimates the value of the firm as the present value of future FCFF discounted at the weighted-average cost of capital (WACC):

$$\text{Firm value} = \sum_{t=1}^{\infty} \frac{\text{FCFF}_t}{(1 + \text{WACC})^t} \tag{3-1}$$

Because FCFF is the cash flow available to all suppliers of capital, discounting FCFF using WACC gives the total value of all of the company's capital. The value of equity is the value of the firm minus the market value of its debt:

$$\text{Equity value} = \text{Firm value} - \text{Market value of debt} \tag{3-2}$$

Dividing the total value of equity by the number of outstanding shares gives the value per share.

The cost of capital is the required rate of return that investors should demand for a cash flow stream like that generated by the company. WACC depends on the risk of these cash flows. The cost of capital is often considered the opportunity cost of the suppliers of capital: If they can invest elsewhere in investments of similar risk, they will not voluntarily invest in a company unless its rate of return can replicate this opportunity cost.

The most common way to estimate the required rate of return for a company's suppliers of capital is to calculate WACC—a weighted average of required rates of return. If the suppliers of capital are creditors and stockholders, the required rates of return for debt and equity are the after-tax required rates of return for this company under current market conditions. The

---

[2]If a company is projected to change its leverage significantly in the future, the analyst may use the **adjusted present value** (APV) approach to valuing the company. In the APV approach, firm value is the sum of the value of the company assuming no use of debt (unlevered firm value) and the net present value of any effects of debt on firm value (such as any tax benefits of using debt and any costs of financial distress). In this approach, we can estimate unlevered company value by discounting FCFF (assuming no debt) at the unlevered cost of equity (the cost of equity assuming no debt). For more details, see Ross, Westerfield, and Jaffe (2002), who explain APV in a capital budgeting context.

weights used are the proportions of the firm's total market value from each source, debt and equity. The WACC formula is

$$\text{WACC} = \frac{\text{MV(Debt)}}{\text{MV(Debt)} + \text{MV(Equity)}} r_d (1 - \text{Tax rate})$$
$$+ \frac{\text{MV(Equity)}}{\text{MV(Debt)} + \text{MV(Equity)}} r \qquad (3\text{-}3)$$

MV(Debt) and MV(Equity) are the current market values of debt and equity, not their book or accounting values. Dividing MV(Debt) or MV(Equity) by the total market value of the firm, which is MV(Debt) + MV(Equity), gives the proportions of the firm's total capital from debt or equity, respectively. These weights will sum to 1.0.

Because the company's capital structure (the proportions of debt and equity financing) can change over time, WACC may also change over time. In addition, the company's current capital structure may also differ substantially from what it will be in future years. For these reasons, analysts often use *target* weights instead of the current weights when calculating WACC. These target weights incorporate both the analyst's and investors' expectations about the target capital structure that the company will tend to use over time. Target weights provide a good approximation of the WACC for cases in which the current weights misrepresent the company's normal capital structure. Target weights also offer an alternative to using annually changing weights for those companies whose capital structure changes frequently.

The before-tax required return on debt, r_d, is the expected yield to maturity based on the current market value of the company's debt. Multiplying by $(1 - \text{Tax rate})$ gives an after-tax required return on debt. Analysts can choose from several methods to estimate the required return on equity, r, including the capital asset pricing model (CAPM), arbitrage pricing theory, the Gordon growth model, and a build-up method such as the bond yield plus risk premium approach. Because payments to stockholders are usually not tax deductible, no tax adjustment is appropriate for the cost of equity.[3]

2.2.2. Present Value of FCFE

The value of equity can also be found by discounting FCFE at the required rate of return on equity (r):

$$\text{Equity value} = \sum_{t=1}^{\infty} \frac{\text{FCFE}_t}{(1 + r)^t} \qquad (3\text{-}4)$$

Because FCFE is the cash flow remaining for equity holders after all other claims have been satisfied, discounting FCFE by r (the required rate of return on equity) gives the value of the firm's equity. Dividing the total value of equity by the number of outstanding shares gives the value per share.

---

[3]Beginning with Modigliani and Miller (1958), capital structure and the cost of capital have been extensively researched. In addition to the amount of leverage, corporate tax rates, personal tax rates, information asymmetries, agency problems, and signaling issues affect the cost of capital. See a modern corporate finance textbook, such as Brealey and Myers (2000), for a review of capital structure theory.

2.3. Single-Stage FCFF and FCFE Growth Models

In the DDM approach, the Gordon (constant, or stable growth) model makes the assumption that dividends grow at a constant rate. Assuming that free cash flows grow at a constant rate results in the single-stage (stable growth) FCFF and FCFE models.

2.3.1. Constant-Growth FCFF Valuation Model

Assume that FCFF grows at a constant rate g, such that FCFF in any period is equal to FCFF in the previous period multiplied by $(1 + g)$:

$$\text{FCFF}_t = \text{FCFF}_{t-1} \times (1 + g)$$

If FCFF grows at a constant rate,

$$\text{Firm value} = \frac{\text{FCFF}_1}{\text{WACC} - g} = \frac{\text{FCFF}_0(1 + g)}{\text{WACC} - g} \tag{3-5}$$

Subtracting the market value of debt from the firm value gives the value of equity.

EXAMPLE 3-1   Using the Constant-Growth FCFF Valuation Model

Cagiati Enterprises has FCFF of 700 million Swiss francs (CHF) and FCFE of CHF620 million. Cagiati's before-tax cost of debt is 5.7 percent and its required rate of return for equity is 11.8 percent. The company expects a target capital structure consisting of 20 percent debt financing and 80 percent equity financing. The tax rate is 33.33 percent, and FCFF is expected to grow forever at 5.0 percent. Cagiati Enterprises has debt outstanding with a market value of CHF2.2 billion and has 200 million outstanding common shares.

What is Cagiati's weighted average cost of capital? What is the total value of Cagiati's equity using the FCFF valuation approach? What is the value per share using this approach?

Solutions: Using Equation 3-3, WACC is

$$\text{WACC} = 0.20(5.7\%)(1 - 0.3333) + 0.80(11.8\%) = 10.2\%$$

The firm value of Cagiati Enterprises is the present value of FCFF discounted using WACC. For FCFF growing at a constant 5 percent rate, the result is

$$\text{Firm value} = \frac{\text{FCFF}_1}{\text{WACC} - g} = \frac{\text{FCFF}_0(1 + g)}{\text{WACC} - g} = \frac{700(1.05)}{0.102 - 0.05} = \frac{735}{0.052}$$
$$= \text{CHF14,134.6 million}$$

The market value of equity is the value of the firm minus the value of debt:

Equity value $=$ CHF14, 134.6 million $-$ CHF2,200 million $=$ CHF11,934.6 million

Dividing by the number of outstanding shares gives the value per share:

$$V_0 = \text{CHF}11,934.6 \text{ million}/200 \text{ million shares} = \text{CHF}59.67 \text{per share}$$

2.3.2. Constant-Growth FCFE Valuation Model

The constant-growth FCFE valuation model assumes that FCFE grows at a constant rate g. FCFE in any period is equal to FCFE in the preceding period multiplied by $(1 + g)$:

$$\text{FCFE}_t = \text{FCFE}_{t-1} \times (1 + g)$$

The value of equity if FCFE is growing at a constant rate is

$$\text{Equity value} = \frac{\text{FCFE}_1}{r - g} = \frac{\text{FCFE}_0(1 + g)}{r - g} \tag{3-6}$$

The discount rate is r, the required rate of return on equity. Note that the growth rate of FCFF and the growth rate of FCFE are frequently not the same.

3. FORECASTING FREE CASH FLOW

Estimating FCFF or FCFE requires a complete understanding of the company and the financial statements from which those cash flows can be drawn. In order to provide a context for the estimation of FCFF and FCFE, we will first use an extensive example to show the relation between free cash flow and accounting measures of income.

For most of Section 3, we will assume that the company has two sources of capital, debt and common stock. In Section 3.7, we will incorporate preferred stock as a third source of capital. Once the concepts of FCFF and FCFE are understood for a company financed using only debt and common stock, it is easy to incorporate preferred stock for the relatively small number of companies that actually use it.

3.1. Computing FCFF from Net Income

FCFF is the cash flow available to the company's suppliers of capital after all operating expenses (including taxes) have been paid and operating investments have been made. The company's suppliers of capital include bondholders and common stockholders (and occasionally preferred stockholders, which we ignore until later). Understanding that a noncash charge is a charge or expense that does not involve the outlay of cash, the expression for FCFF is as follows:

FCFF = Net income available to common shareholders
Plus: Net noncash charges
Plus: Interest expense × (1 − Tax rate)
Less: Investment in fixed capital[4]
Less: Investment in working capital

---

[4]In this chapter, when we refer to "investment in fixed capital" or "investment in working capital," we are referring to the investments made in the specific period for which the free cash flow is calculated.

This equation can be written more compactly as

$$FCFF = NI + NCC + Int(1 - Tax\ rate) - FCInv - WCInv \qquad (3\text{-}7)$$

Consider each component of FCFF. The starting point in Equation 3-7 is net income available to common shareholders—the bottom line in an income statement. It represents income after depreciation, amortization, interest expense, income taxes, and the payment of dividends to preferred shareholders (but not payment of dividends to common shareholders).

Net noncash charges represent an adjustment for noncash decreases and increases in net income. This adjustment is the first of several that analysts generally perform on a net basis. If noncash decreases in net income exceed the increases, as is usually the case, the adjustment is positive. If noncash increases exceed noncash decreases, the adjustment is negative. The most common noncash charge is depreciation expense. When a company purchases fixed capital such as equipment, the balance sheet reflects a cash outflow at the time of purchase. In subsequent periods, the company records depreciation expense as the asset is used. The depreciation expense reduces net income but is not a cash outflow. Depreciation expense is thus one (the most common) noncash charge that must be added back in computing FCFF. In the case of intangible assets, there is a similar noncash charge, amortization expense, that must also be added back. Other noncash charges vary from company to company and will be discussed in Section 3.3.

After-tax interest expense must be added back to net income to arrive at FCFF. This step is required because interest expense net of the related tax savings was deducted in arriving at net income, and because interest is a cash flow available to one of the company's capital providers. In the United States and many other countries, interest is tax deductible (reduces taxes) for the company and taxable for the recipient. As we shall see later, when we discount FCFF, we do so using an after-tax cost of capital. For consistency, we thus compute FCFF using the after-tax interest paid.[5]

Similar to after-tax interest expense, if a company has preferred stock, dividends on that preferred stock are deducted in arriving at net income available to common shareholders. Because preferred stock dividends are also a cash flow available to one of the company's capital providers, this item is added back to arrive at FCFF. Further discussion of the effects of preferred stock appears in Section 3.7.

Investments in fixed capital represent the outflow of cash necessary to support the company's current and future operations. These investments are capital expenditures for long-term assets such as property, plant, and equipment (PP&E) necessary to support the company. Necessary capital expenditures can also include intangible assets such as trademarks. In the case of cash acquisition of another company in place of a direct acquisition of PP&E, this cash purchase amount can also be treated as a capital expenditure that reduces the company's free cash flow (note that this is the conservative treatment in that it reduces FCFF). In the case of large acquisitions (and all noncash acquisitions), analysts must take care in evaluating the impact on future free cash flow. If a company receives cash in disposing of any of its fixed capital, the analyst must deduct this cash in arriving at investments in fixed capital. For example, suppose we had a sale of equipment for $100,000. This cash inflow reduces the company's cash outflows for investments in fixed capital.

---

[5] Note that we could compute WACC on a pretax basis and compute FCFF by adding back interest paid with no tax adjustment. It is critical, however, that analysts be consistent in their measures of FCFF and WACC.

The company's cash flow statement is an excellent source of information on capital expenditures as well as sales of fixed capital. Analysts should be aware that some companies acquire fixed capital without using cash—for example, through an exchange for stock or debt. Such acquisitions do not appear on a company's cash flow statement but, if material, must be disclosed in the footnotes. Although noncash exchanges do not impact historical FCFF, if the capital expenditures are necessary and may be made in cash in the future, the analyst should use this information in forecasting future FCFF.

Last is an important adjustment for net increases in working capital. As noted in our earlier example, this adjustment represents the net investment in current assets, such as accounts receivable, less current liabilities, such as accounts payable. Analysts can find this information by examining either the company's balance sheet or the cash flow statement.

Although working capital is often defined as current assets minus current liabilities, working capital for cash flow and valuation purposes is defined to exclude cash and short-term debt (which includes notes payable and the current portion of long-term debt). When finding the net increase in working capital for the purpose of calculating free cash flow, we define working capital to exclude cash and cash equivalents, as well as notes payable and the current portion of long-term debt. Cash and cash equivalents are excluded because a change in cash is what we are trying to explain. Notes payable and the current portion of long-term debt are excluded because they are liabilities with explicit interest costs that make them financing, rather than operating, items.

Example 3-2 shows all of the adjustments to net income required to find FCFF.

EXAMPLE 3-2   Calculating FCFF from Net Income

Cane Distribution, Inc., is a distribution company incorporated on December 31, 2000, with initial capital infusions of $224,000 of debt and $336,000 of common stock. This initial capital was immediately invested in fixed capital of $500,000 and working capital of $60,000. Working capital initially consists solely of inventory. The fixed capital consists of nondepreciable property of $50,000 and depreciable property of $450,000. The latter has a 10-year useful life with no salvage value. Tables 3-1, 3-2, and 3-3 provide Cane's financial statements for the three years following incorporation. Starting with net income, calculate Cane's FCFF for each year.

TABLE 3-1   Cane Distribution, Inc., Income Statement (in thousands)

Years Ending December 31	2001	2002	2003
Earnings before interest, taxes, depreciation and amortization (EBITDA)	$200.00	$220.00	$242.00
Depreciation expense	45.00	49.50	54.45
Operating income	155.00	170.50	187.55
Interest expense	15.68	17.25	18.97
Income before taxes	139.32	153.25	168.58
Income taxes (at 30%)	41.80	45.97	50.58
Net income	$97.52	$107.28	$118.00

TABLE 3-2   Cane Distribution, Inc., Balance Sheet (in thousands)

Years Ending December 31	2000	2001	2002	2003
Cash	$0.00	$108.92	$228.74	$360.54
Accounts receivable	0.00	100.00	110.00	121.00
Inventory	60.00	66.00	72.60	79.86
Current assets	60.00	274.92	411.34	561.40
Fixed assets	500.00	500.00	550.00	605.00
Less: Accumulated depreciation	0.00	45.00	94.50	148.95
Total assets	$560.00	$729.92	$866.84	$1,017.45
Accounts payable	$0.00	$50.00	$55.00	$60.50
Current portion of long-term debt	0.00	0.00	0.00	0.00
Current liabilities	0.00	50.00	55.00	60.50
Long-term debt	224.00	246.40	271.04	298.14
Common stock	336.00	336.00	336.00	336.00
Retained earnings	0.00	97.52	204.80	322.80
Total liabilities and equity	$560.00	$729.92	$866.84	$1,017.45

TABLE 3-3   Cane Distribution, Inc., Working Capital (in thousands)

Years Ending December 31	2000	2001	2002	2003
Current assets excluding cash				
Accounts receivable	$0.00	$100.00	$110.00	$121.00
Inventory	60.00	66.00	72.60	79.86
Total current assets excluding cash	60.00	166.00	182.60	200.86
Current liabilities excluding short-term debt				
Accounts payable	0.00	50.00	55.00	60.50
Working capital	$60.00	$116.00	$127.60	$140.36
Increase in working capital		$56.00	$11.60	$12.76

Solution: Following the logic in Equation 3-7, we calculate FCFF from net income as follows:

Years Ending December 31	2001	2002	2003
Net income	$97.52	$107.28	$118.00
Plus: Depreciation and amortization	45.00	49.50	54.45
Plus: Interest expense × (1 − Tax rate)	10.98	12.08	13.28
Less: Investment in fixed capital	0.00	(50.00)	(55.00)
Less: Investment in working capital	(56.00)	(11.60)	(12.76)
Free cash flow to the firm	$97.50	$107.26	$117.97

3.2. Computing FCFF from the Statement of Cash Flows

FCFF is cash flow available to all capital providers (debt and equity). Analysts frequently use cash flow from operations, taken from the statement of cash flows, as a starting point to compute free cash flow because CFO incorporates adjustments for noncash expenses (such as depreciation and amortization) as well as for net investments in working capital.

In a statement of cash flows, cash flows are separated into three components: cash flow from operating activities (or cash flows from operations), cash flows from investing activities, and cash flows from financing activities. Cash flow from operations, which we abbreviate CFO, is the net amount of cash provided from operating activities. The operating section of the cash flow statement shows cash flows related to operating activities, such as cash received from customers and cash paid to suppliers. Investing activities relate to the company's investments in (or sales of) long-term assets, particularly PP&E and long-term investments in other companies. Financing activities relate to the raising or repayment of the company's capital. Interestingly, under U.S. GAAP, interest expense paid to debt capital providers must be classified as part of cash flow from operations (as is interest income), although payment of dividends to equity capital providers is classified as a financing activity. International Accounting Standards (IAS), on the other hand, allow the company to classify interest paid as either an operating or financing activity. Further, IAS allow dividends paid to be classified as either an operating or financing activity. Table 3-4 summarizes U.S. GAAP and IAS treatment of interest and dividends.

TABLE 3-4   U.S. GAAP versus IAS Treatment of Interest and Dividends

	U.S. GAAP	IAS
Interest received	Operating	Operating or Investing
Interest paid	Operating	Operating or Financing
Dividends received	Operating	Operating or Investing
Dividends paid	Financing	Operating or Financing

To estimate FCFF by starting with CFO, we must recognize the treatment of interest paid. If, as with U.S. GAAP, the after-tax interest expense was taken out of net income and out of CFO, after-tax interest expense must be added back in order to get FCFF. In the U.S. case, FCFF can be estimated as follows:

Free cash flow to the firm = Cash flow from operations
Plus: Interest expense $\times$ (1 − Tax rate)
Less: Investment in fixed capital

or

$$FCFF = CFO + Int(1 - \text{Tax rate}) - FCInv \qquad (3\text{-}8)$$

The after-tax interest expense is added back because it was previously taken out of net income. The investment in working capital does not appear in Equation 3-8 because CFO already includes investment in working capital. The following example illustrates the calculation of FCFF using CFO.

EXAMPLE 3-3   Calculating FCFF from CFO

Use the information from the statement of cash flows given in Table 3-5 to calculate FCFF for the three years.

TABLE 3-5   Cane Distribution, Inc., Statement of Cash Flows (in thousands) Indirect Method

Years Ending December 31	2001	2002	2003
Cash flow from operations			
Net income	$97.52	$107.28	$118.00
Plus: Depreciation	45.00	49.50	54.45
Increase in accounts receivable	(100.00)	(10.00)	(11.00)
Increase in inventory	(6.00)	(6.60)	(7.26)
Increase in accounts payable	50.00	5.00	5.50
Cash flow from operations	86.52	145.18	159.69
Cash flow from investing activities			
Purchases of PP&E	0.00	(50.00)	(55.00)
Cash flow from financing activities			
Borrowing (repayment)	22.40	24.64	27.10
Total cash flow	108.92	119.82	131.80
Beginning cash	0.00	108.92	228.74
Ending cash	$108.92	$228.74	$360.54
Notes:			
Cash paid for interest	($15.68)	($17.25)	($18.97)
Cash paid for taxes	($41.80)	($45.98)	($50.57)

Solution: As shown in Equation 3-8, FCFF equals CFO plus after-tax interest minus the investment in fixed capital:

Years Ending December 31	2001	2002	2003
Cash flow from operations	86.52	145.18	159.69
Plus: Interest expense $\times$ (1 − Tax rate)	10.98	12.08	13.28
Less: Investment in fixed capital	0.00	(50.00)	(55.00)
Free cash flow to the firm	97.50	107.26	117.97

3.3. Noncash Charges

The best place to find historical noncash charges is in the company's statement of cash flows. If an analyst wants to use an add-back method, as in FCFF = NI + NCC + Int(1 − Tax rate) − FCInv − WCInv, the analyst should verify the noncash charges to ensure that the FCFF estimate provides a reasonable basis for forecasting. As one example, restructuring charges can involve cash expenditures and noncash charges. For example, severance pay for laid-off employees could be a cash restructuring charge. On the other hand, a write-down in the value of assets as part of a restructuring charge is a noncash item.

EXAMPLE 3-4   An Examination of Noncash Charges

An analyst is attempting to verify Motorola, Inc.'s, historical FCFF as a basis for forecasting. Excerpts from the operating section of Motorola's 1999 statement of cash flow are given in Table 3-6:

TABLE 3-6   Statement of Cash Flows for Motorola (in millions)

Years Ending December 31	1997	1998	1999
Net income (loss)	$1,180	$(962)	$817
Adjustments to reconcile net income (loss) to net cash provided by operating activities:			
Restructuring and other charges	327	1,980	(226)
Iridium charges	178	360	2,119
Depreciation	2,329	2,197	2,182
Deferred income taxes	(98)	(933)	(415)
Amortization of debt discount and issue costs	10	11	11
Gain on disposition of investments and businesses, net of acquisition charges	(116)	(146)	(1,034)
Change in assets and liabilities, net of effects of acquisitions and dispositions:			
Accounts receivable	(812)	(238)	15
Inventories	(880)	254	(661)
Other current assets	(114)	31	(30)
Accounts payable and accrued liabilities	698	(753)	270
Other assets and liabilities	(106)	(780)	(1,120)
Net cash provided by operating activities	$2,596	$1,021	$1,928

Note that in arriving at cash provided by operating activities, Motorola added back "restructuring and other charges" in 1997 and 1998. This item represents the noncash portion of such charges deducted in arriving at net income for those years. In calculating historical FCFF beginning with net income, the analyst would add back the full amount of this item because the item represents noncash charges. For example, for 1998, the full amount of $1,980 million restructuring and other charges should be added back in computing historical FCFF for that year. Asset impairments and losses on asset sales represented the majority of restructuring and other charges for 1998, according to Motorola's financial statements. Motorola's financial statements also disclosed that about $658 million of the $1,980 million restructuring and other charges for 1998 represented an accrual of future employee separation costs.[6]

In contrast to asset impairments and losses on asset sales, which do not represent cash outflows in the current or future years, the $658 million accrual relates to cash outflows in subsequent years. As employees separate from employment with Motorola in subsequent years, Motorola would realize these cash separation expenses, which would result in lower CFO and FCFF in those years. From the perspective of 1998, if the analyst were to use the level of historical FCFF for 1998 to forecast subsequent FCFF, his FCFF forecasts might be biased upward because some of the accrual of separation expenses added back when computing 1998 FCFF would be realized as cash expenses in 1999 and beyond. From the perspective of 1998, the analyst's FCFF forecasts should reflect his expectations concerning the future realization of cash separation expenses.

As noted in Footnote 6, noncash restructuring charges can also cause an increase in net income in some circumstances. Gains and losses are another noncash item that can either increase or decrease net noncash charges. If a company sells a piece of equipment with a book value of $60,000 for $100,000, it reports the $40,000 gain as part of net income. The $40,000 gain is not a cash flow, however, and must be subtracted in arriving at FCFF. Note that the $100,000 is a cash flow and is part of the company's net investment in fixed capital. A loss reduces net income and thus must be added back in arriving at FCFF. Aside from depreciation, gains and losses are the most commonly seen noncash charges that require an adjustment to net income. Analysts should examine the company's cash flow statement to identify items particular to a company and to determine what analyst adjustments might be needed to make the accounting numbers useful for forecasting purposes.

Table 3-7 summarizes the common noncash charges that impact net income and indicates for each item whether to add it to or subtract it from net income in arriving at FCFF.

TABLE 3-7   Noncash Items and FCFF

Noncash Item	Adjustment to NI to Arrive at FCFF
Depreciation	Added back
Amortization of intangibles	Added back
Restructuring charges (expense)	Added back
Restructuring charges (income resulting from reversal)	Subtracted
Losses	Added back
Gains	Subtracted
Amortization of long-term bond discounts	Added back
Amortization of long-term bond premiums	Subtracted
Deferred taxes	Added back but warrants special attention

---

[6]In 1999 Motorola reversed $226 million of the $1,980 million accrual of restructuring and other charges, increasing reported net income by that amount; as a noncash addition to net income, the amount of $226 million must be subtracted to arrive at historical CFO and FCFF for 1999. In 1999, therefore, we see $226 million as a deduction from net income to arrive at CFO, in Motorola's statement of cash flows.

The case of deferred taxes requires special attention. Deferred taxes result from differences in the timing of reporting income and expenses on the company's financial statements and the company's tax return. The income tax expense deducted in arriving at net income for financial reporting purposes is not the same as the amount of cash taxes paid. Over time, these differences between book and taxable income should offset each other and have no impact on aggregate cash flows. If the analyst's purpose is forecasting and he seeks to identify the persistent components of FCFF, then it is not appropriate to add back deferred tax changes that are expected to reverse in the near future. In some circumstances, however, a company may be able to consistently defer taxes until a much later date. If a company is growing and has the ability to indefinitely defer tax liability, an analyst adjustment (add-back) to net income is warranted. An acquirer must be aware, however, that these taxes may be payable at some time in the future.

Conversely, companies often record expenses for financial reporting purposes (e.g., restructuring charges) that are not deductible for tax purposes. In this instance, current tax payments are higher than reported on the income statement, resulting in a deferred tax asset and a subtraction from net income to arrive at cash flow on the cash flow statement. If the deferred tax asset is expected to reverse (e.g., through tax depreciation deductions) in the near future, the analyst would not want to subtract the deferred tax asset in his cash flow forecast to avoid underestimating future cash flows. On the other hand, if the company is expected to have these charges on a continual basis, a subtraction is warranted to lower the forecast of future cash flows.

Employee stock options provide another challenge. Current accounting standards do not require that an expense be recorded in arriving at net income for options provided to employees. Employee options also do not create any operating cash outflow because no cash changes hands when they are granted. When the employee exercises the option, however, the company receives some cash for the strike price. This cash flow is considered a financing cash flow. Also, in some cases, a company may receive a tax benefit from issuing options that increases operating cash flow but not net income.[7] If these cash flows are not expected to persist in the future, analysts should not include them in their forecast of cash flows. An analyst should consider the impact of stock options on the number of shares outstanding. When computing equity value, the analyst may want to use the number of shares expected to be outstanding based on the exercise of employee stock options rather than use currently outstanding shares.

EXAMPLE 3-5   A Further Examination of Noncash Charges

Consider the following cash flow statement of Dell Computer (Nasdaq NMS: DELL) in order to forecast Dell's future cash flows. The special charges relate to restructuring charges and purchased research and development expenses.

---

[7]For a more detailed discussion of the tax versus accounting treatment of employee stock option plans, see Phillips, Munter, and Robinson (2002).

Years Ending	January 29, 1999	January 28, 2000	February 2, 2001
Cash flows from operating activities:			
Net income	$1,460	$1,666	$2,177
Adjustments to reconcile net income to net cash provided by operating activities:			
Depreciation and amortization	103	156	240
Tax benefits of employee stock plans	444	1,040	929
Special charges	—	194	105
Gain on sale of investments	(9)	(80)	(307)
Other	20	56	109
Changes in:			
Operating working capital	367	812	671
Non-current assets and liabilities	51	82	271
Net cash provided by operating activities	$2,436	$3,926	$4,195

How would you use the tax benefits of employee stock option plans, special charges, and the gain on sale of investments as noncash charges when using the add-back method to calculate free cash flows starting from net income?

Solution: You should make a positive adjustment (add back) to net income for depreciation and amortization, and for special charges. The gain on sale of investments should be subtracted because this gain is included in net income but does not generate operating cash flow. The tax benefits of employee stock plans resulted from the company's ability to deduct the value of options, which were considered taxable to employees. During this three-year period, Dell's stock price rose dramatically, which made employee exercise attractive. In the future, after February 2001, it is unlikely that Dell will continue to achieve this unusual operating cash flow. An analyst would probably not make this last adjustment to net income in forecasting free cash flow.

3.4. Computing FCFE from FCFF

FCFE is cash flow available to equity holders only. It is thus necessary to reduce FCFF by interest paid to debt holders and to add any net increase in borrowing[8] (subtract any net decrease in borrowing).

$$\text{Free cash flow to equity} = \text{Free cash flow to the firm}$$
$$\text{Less: Interest expense} \times (1 - \text{Tax rate})$$
$$\text{Plus: Net borrowing}$$

---

[8]Net borrowing is net debt issued less debt repayments over the period for which we are calculating free cash flow.

or

$$FCFE = FCFF - Int(1 - Tax\ rate) + Net\ borrowing \qquad (3\text{-}9)$$

As Equation 3-9 shows, FCFE is found by starting from FCFF and subtracting after-tax interest expenses and adding net new borrowing. Conversely, the analyst can also find FCFF from FCFE by making the opposite adjustments—by adding after-tax interest expenses and subtracting net borrowing: $FCFF = FCFE + Int(1 - Tax\ rate) - Net\ borrowing$.

Table 3-8 shows the calculation of FCFE starting with FCFF. For the Cane Distribution Company in Example 3-3, FCFE is as follows:

TABLE 3-8   Calculating FCFE from FCFF

Years Ending December 31	2001	2002	2003
Free cash flow to the firm	97.50	107.26	117.97
Less: Interest paid × (1 − Tax rate)	(10.98)	(12.08)	(13.28)
Plus: New debt borrowing	22.40	24.64	27.10
Less: Debt repayment	0	0	0
Free cash flow to equity	108.92	119.82	131.79

As stated earlier, FCFE is the cash flow available to common stockholders—the remaining cash flow after all operating expenses (including taxes) have been paid, capital investments have been made, and other transactions with other suppliers of capital have been made. The company's other capital suppliers include creditors, such as bondholders, and preferred stockholders. The cash flows (net of taxes) that have been transacted with creditors and preferred stockholders are deducted from FCFF to arrive at FCFE.

FCFE is the amount that the company can afford to pay out as dividends. In actuality, companies often pay out substantially more or substantially less than FCFE for many reasons, so FCFE often differs from dividends paid. One reason for this difference is that the dividend decision is a discretionary decision of the board of directors. Most corporations "manage" their dividends, preferring to raise them gradually over time, in part because they are very reluctant to cut dividends. Consequently, earnings are much more volatile than dividends. Companies often raise dividends slowly even when their earnings are increasing rapidly, and companies often maintain their current dividends even when their profitability has declined.

In Equations 3-7 and 3-8 above, we showed the calculation of FCFF starting with net income and cash flow from operations, respectively. As Equation 3-9 shows, $FCFE = FCFF - Int(1 - Tax\ rate) + Net\ borrowing$. By subtracting after-tax interest expense and adding net borrowing to Equations 3-7 and 3-8, we then have equations to calculate FCFE starting with net income or CFO, respectively:

$$FCFE = NI + NCC - FCInv - WCInv + Net\ borrowing \qquad (3\text{-}10)$$

$$FCFE = CFO - FCInv + Net\ borrowing \qquad (3\text{-}11)$$

EXAMPLE 3-6   Adjusting Net Income or CFO to Find FCFF and FCFE

The balance sheet, income statement, and statement of cash flows for the Pitts Corporation are shown in Table 3-9. The Pitts Corporation has net income of $240 million in 2003. Show the calculations required to do each of the following:

1. Calculate FCFF starting with the net income figure.
2. Calculate FCFE starting from the FCFF calculated in Part 1.
3. Calculate FCFE starting with the net income figure.
4. Calculate FCFF starting with CFO.
5. Calculate FCFE starting with CFO.

TABLE 3-9   Financial Statements for Pitts Corporation (in millions, except for per-share data)

Balance Sheet Years Ended December 31	2002	2003
Assets		
Current assets		
Cash and equivalents	$190	$200
Accounts receivable	560	600
Inventory	410	440
Total current assets	1,160	1,240
Gross fixed assets	2,200	2,600
Accumulated depreciation	(900)	(1,200)
Net fixed assets	1,300	1,400
Total assets	$2,460	$2,640
Liabilities and shareholders' equity		
Current liabilities		
Accounts payable	$285	$300
Notes payable	200	250
Accrued taxes and expenses	140	150
Total current liabilities	625	700
Long-term debt	865	890
Common stock	100	100
Additional paid-in capital	200	200
Retained earnings	670	750
Total shareholders' equity	970	1,050
Total liabilities and shareholders' equity	$2,460	$2,640

(*continued*)

TABLE 3-9   *(continued)*

Statement of Income

Year Ended December 31	2003
Total revenues	$3,000
Operating costs and expenses	2,200
EBITDA	800
Depreciation	300
Operating income (EBIT)	500
Interest expense	100
Income before tax	400
Taxes (at 40 percent)	160
Net income	240
Dividends	160
Change in retained earnings	80
Earnings per share	$0.48
Dividends per share	$0.32

Statement of Cash Flows

Year Ended December 31	2003
Operating activities	
Net income	$240
Adjustments	
Depreciation	300
Changes in working capital	
Accounts receivable	(40)
Inventories	(30)
Accounts payable	15
Accrued taxes and expenses	10
Cash provided by operating activities	$495
Investing activities	
Purchases of fixed assets	400
Cash used for investing activities	$400
Financing activities	
Notes payable	(50)
Long-term financing issuances	(25)
Common stock dividends	160
Cash used for financing activities	$85
Cash and equivalents increase (decrease)	10
Cash and equivalents at beginning of year	190
Cash and equivalents at end of year	$200
Supplemental cash flow disclosures	
Interest paid	$100
Income taxes paid	$160

Solution to 1: The analyst can use Equation 3-7 to find FCFF from net income.

Net income available to common shareholders	$240
Plus: Net noncash charges	+300
Plus: Interest expense × (1 − Tax rate)	+60
Less: Investment in fixed capital	−400
Less: Investment in working capital	−45
Free cash flow to the firm	$155

This equation can also be written as

$$FCFF = NI + NCC + Int(1 - Tax\ rate) - FCInv - WCInv$$

$$FCFF = \$240 + 300 + 60 - 400 - 45 = \$155\ million$$

Some of these items need explanation. Capital spending is $400 million, which is the increase in gross fixed assets shown on the balance sheet as well as capital expenditures shown as an investing activity on the statement of cash flows. The increase in working capital is $45 million, which is the increase in accounts receivable of $40 million ($600 million − $560 million) plus the increase in inventories of $30 million ($440 million − $410 million) minus the increase in accounts payable of $15 million ($300 million − $285 million) minus the increase in accrued taxes and expenses of $10 million ($140 million − $130 million). When finding the increase in working capital, we ignore cash because the change in cash is what we are calculating. Furthermore, we also ignore short-term debt, such as notes payable, because it is part of the capital provided to the company and is not considered an operating item. The after-tax interest cost is the interest expense times (1 − Tax rate), or $100 million × (1 − 0.40) = $60 million. The values of the remaining items in Equation 3-7 can be taken directly from the financial statements.

Solution to 2: Finding FCFE from FCFF can be done with Equation 3-9.

Free cash flow to the firm	$155
Less: Interest expense × (1 − Tax rate)	−60
Plus: Net borrowing	+75
Free cash flow to equity	$170

Or, using

$$FCFE = FCFF - Int(1 - Tax\ rate) + Net\ borrowing$$

$$FCFE = 155 - 60 + 75 = \$170\ million$$

Solution to 3: The analyst can use Equation 3-10 to find FCFE from NI.

Net income available to common shareholders	$240
Plus: Net noncash charges	+300
Less: Investment in fixed capital	−400
Less: Investment in working capital	−45
Plus: Net borrowing	+75
Free cash flow to equity	$170

Or, using the equation

$$FCFE = NI + NCC - FCInv - WCInv + Net\ borrowing$$

$$FCFE = 240 + 300 - 400 - 45 + 75 = \$170\ million$$

Because notes payable increased by 50 (250 − 200) and long-term debt increased by 25 (890 − 865), net borrowing is 75.

Solution to 4: Equation 3-8 can be used to find FCFF from CFO.

Cash flow from operations	$495
Plus: Interest expense × (1 − Tax rate)	60
Less: Investment in fixed capital	−400
Free cash flow to the firm	$155

or

$$FCFF = CFO + Int(1 - Tax\ rate) - FCInv$$

$$FCFF = 495 + 60 - 400 = \$155\ million$$

Solution to 5: Equation 3-11 can be used to find FCFE from CFO.

Cash flow from operations	$495
Less: Investment in fixed capital	−400
Plus: Net borrowing	75
Free cash flow to equity	$170

or

$$FCFF = CFO - FCInv + Net\ borrowing$$

$$FCFF = 495 - 400 + 75 = \$170\ million$$

FCFE is usually less than FCFF; in this example, however, FCFE ($170 million) exceeds FCFF ($155 million) because external borrowing was large during this year.

3.5. Finding FCFF and FCFE from EBIT or EBITDA

FCFF and FCFE are most frequently calculated from a starting basis of net income or CFO (as shown above in Sections 3.1 and 3.2). Two other starting points are EBIT or EBITDA from the income statement.

To show the relationship between EBIT and FCFF, we start with Equation 3-7 and assume that the only noncash charge (NCC) is depreciation (Dep):

$$FCFF = NI + Dep + Int(1 - Tax\ rate) - FCInv - WCInv$$

Net income (NI) can be expressed as

$$NI = (EBIT - Int)(1 - Tax\ rate) = EBIT(1 - Tax\ rate) - Int(1 - Tax\ rate)$$

Substituting this equation for NI in Equation 3-7, we have

$$FCFF = EBIT(1 - Tax\ rate) + Dep - FCInv - WCInv \qquad (3\text{-}12)$$

To get FCFF from EBIT, we multiply EBIT by $(1 - Tax\ rate)$, add back depreciation, and then subtract the investments in fixed capital and working capital.

It is also easy to show the relation between FCFF from EBITDA. Net income can be expressed as

$$NI = (EBITDA - Dep - Int)(1 - Tax\ rate) = EBITDA(1 - Tax\ rate)$$
$$- Dep(1 - Tax\ rate) - Int(1 - Tax\ rate)$$

Substituting this equation for NI in Equation 3-7 results in

$$FCFF = EBITDA(1 - Tax\ rate) + Dep(Tax\ rate) - FCInv - WCInv \qquad (3\text{-}13)$$

FCFF equals EBITDA times $(1 - Tax\ rate)$ plus depreciation times the tax rate minus the investments in fixed capital and working capital. In comparing Equations 3-12 and 3-13, note the difference in the handling of depreciation.

Many noncash charge adjustments required to calculate FCFF based on net income are not required when starting from EBIT or EBITDA. In the calculation of net income, many noncash charges are made after computing EBIT or EBITDA, so they do not need to be added back when calculating FCFF based on EBIT or EBITDA. Another important consideration is that some noncash charges, such as depreciation, are tax deductible. A noncash charge that affects taxes must be accounted for. In summary, whether an adjustment for a noncash charge is needed depends on where in the income statement it has been deducted and whether the noncash charge is a tax-deductible expense.

It is also possible to calculate FCFE (instead of FCFF) from EBIT or EBITDA. An easy way to obtain FCFE from EBIT or EBITDA is to derive FCFF using Equation 3-12 or 3-13, and then subtract $Int(1 - Tax\ rate)$ and add net borrowing to end up with FCFE:[9]

$$FCFE = FCFF - Int(1 - Tax\ rate) + Net\ borrowing$$

---

[9]It is also possible to derive equations for FCFE as a function of EBIT or EBITDA. To do so, start with the equation for FCFE as a function of NI (Equation 3-10), again making the assumption that the only noncash charge is depreciation: $FCFE = NI + Dep - FCInv - WCInv + Net\ borrowing$. Substituting $NI = EBIT(1 - Tax\ rate) - Int(1 - Tax\ rate)$ and $NI = EBITDA(1 - Tax\ rate) - Dep(1 - Tax\ rate) - Int(1 - Tax\ rate)$ into Equation 3-10 yields two equations for FCFE as a function of EBIT or EBITDA, respectively:

$FCFE = EBIT(1 - Tax\ rate) - Int(1 - Tax\ rate) + Dep - FCInv - WCInv + Net\ borrowing$

$FCFE = EBITDA(1 - Tax\ rate) + Dep(Tax\ rate) - Int(1 - Tax\ rate)$
$\qquad - FCInv - WCInv + Net\ borrowing$

Example 3-7 uses the Pitts Corporation financial statements to find FCFF and FCFE from EBIT and EBITDA.

EXAMPLE 3-7   Adjusting EBIT and EBITDA to Find FCFF and FCFE

The Pitts Corporation (financial statements provided in Example 3-6) has EBIT of $500 million and EBITDA of $800 million. Show the adjustments that would be required to find FCFF and FCFE:

1. starting from EBIT, and
2. starting from EBITDA.

Solution to 1: To get FCFF from EBIT using Equation 3-12:

EBIT(1 − Tax rate) = 500(1 − 0.40)	$300
Plus: Net noncash charges	300
Less: Net investment in fixed capital	−400
Less: Net increase in working capital	−45
Free cash flow to the firm	$155

or

$$FCFF = EBIT(1 - Tax\ rate) + Dep - FCInv - WCInv$$

$$FCFF = 500(1 - 0.40) + 300 - 400 - 45 = \$155\ million$$

To obtain FCFE, make the appropriate adjustments to FCFF:

$$FCFE = FCFF - Int(1 - Tax\ rate) + Net\ borrowing$$

$$FCFE = 155 - 100(1 - 0.40) + 75 = \$170\ million$$

Solution to 2: To obtain FCFF from EBITDA using Equation 3-13:

EBITDA(1 − Tax rate) = 800(1 − 0.40)	$480
Plus: Depreciation(Tax rate) = 300(0.40)	120
Less: Net investment in fixed capital	−400
Less: Net increase in working capital:	−45
Free cash flow to the firm	$155

or

$$FCFF = EBITDA(1 - Tax\ rate) + Dep(Tax\ rate) - FCInv - WCInv$$

$$FCFF = 800(1 - 0.40) + 300(0.40) - 400 - 45 = \$155\ million$$

Again, to obtain FCFE, make the appropriate adjustments to FCFF:

$$FCFE = FCFF - Int(1 - Tax\ rate) + Net\ borrowing$$

$$FCFE = 155 - 100(1 - 0.40) + 75 = \$170\ million$$

3.6. Forecasting FCFF and FCFE

Computing FCFF and FCFE based on historical accounting data is relatively straightforward. Often, these data are then used directly in a single-stage DCF valuation model. On other occasions, an analyst may desire to forecast future FCFF or FCFE directly. In this case, the analyst must forecast the individual components of free cash flow. This section extends our previous presentation on computing FCFF and FCFE to the more complex task of forecasting FCFF and FCFE. We present FCFF and FCFE valuation models in the next section.

Given the variety of ways to derive free cash flow on a historical basis, it should come as no surprise that several methods exist for forecasting free cash flow. One approach is to calculate historical free cash flow and apply some constant growth rate. This approach would be appropriate if a company's free cash flow tended to grow at a constant rate and if historical relationships between free cash flow and fundamental factors were expected to be maintained.

EXAMPLE 3-8   Constant Growth in FCFF

Use Pitts Corporation data to compute its FCFF for the next three years. Assume growth in FCFF remains at historical levels of 15 percent a year.

	2003A	2004E	2004E	2005E
FCFF	155.00	178.25	204.99	235.74

A more complex approach is to forecast the components of free cash flow. This approach can better capture the complex relationships among the components. For example, one popular method[10] is to forecast the individual components of free cash flow—EBIT(1 − Tax rate), net noncash charges, investment in fixed capital, and investment in working capital. EBIT can be forecasted directly or by forecasting sales and the company's EBIT margin based on an analysis of historical data and the current and expected economic environment. Similarly, analysts can examine the historical relationship between increases in sales and investments in fixed and working capital.

In the case of investments in fixed capital, a popular shortcut method is to combine net noncash charges and investments in fixed capital. This approach works well when the only noncash charge to be added back is depreciation expense. In this approach, FCFF is calculated by forecasting EBIT(1 − Tax rate) and subtracting incremental fixed capital expenditures and incremental working capital expenditures.[11] In order to estimate FCInv and WCInv, we

---

[10] See Rappaport (1997) for a variation of this model.
[11] See Rappaport (1997).

multiply their past proportion to sales' increases by the forecasted sales' increases. Incremental fixed capital expenditures as a proportion of sales increases are computed as follows:

$$\frac{\text{Capital expenditures} - \text{Depreciation expense}}{\text{Increase in sales}}$$

Similarly, incremental working capital expenditures as a proportion of sales increases are

$$\frac{\text{Increase in working capital}}{\text{Increase in sales}}$$

When depreciation is the only significant net noncash charge, this method yields the same results as the previous equations for estimating FCFF or FCFE. Rather than adding back all depreciation and subtracting all capital expenditures when starting with EBIT(1 − Tax rate), this approach simply subtracts the net capital expenditures in excess of depreciation.

Although it may not be obvious, this approach recognizes that capital expenditures have two components: those expenditures necessary to maintain existing capacity (fixed capital replacement) and those incremental expenditures necessary for growth. In forecasting, the former are likely to be related to the current level of sales and the latter are likely related to the forecast of sales growth.

When forecasting FCFE, analysts often make an assumption that there is a target ratio of debt financing. They often assume that a specified percentage of the net new investment in fixed capital (new fixed capital minus depreciation) and of the increase in working capital is financed with a target ratio of debt. This leads to a simplification of FCFE calculations. Recalling Equation 3-10 and assuming that depreciation is the only noncash charge, Equation 3-10, FCFE = NI + NCC − FCInv − WCInv + Net borrowing, becomes

$$\text{FCFE} = \text{NI} - (\text{FCInv} - \text{Dep}) - \text{WCInv} + \text{Net borrowing}$$

Note that FCInv − Dep represents the incremental fixed capital expenditure net of depreciation. By assuming a target debt ratio (DR), we eliminate the need to forecast net borrowing and can use the expression

$$\text{Net borrowing} = \text{DR}(\text{FCInv} - \text{Dep}) + \text{DR} \times \text{WCInv}$$

Using this expression, we do not need to forecast debt issuance and repayment on an annual basis to estimate net borrowing. Equation 3-10 then becomes

$$\text{FCFE} = \text{NI} - (\text{FCInv} - \text{Dep}) - \text{WCInv} + (\text{DR})(\text{FCInv} - \text{Dep}) + (\text{DR})(\text{WCInv})$$

or

$$\text{FCFE} = \text{NI} - (1 - \text{DR})(\text{FCInv} - \text{Dep}) - (1 - \text{DR})(\text{WCInv}) \qquad (3\text{-}14)$$

We again assume that the only noncash charge is depreciation.

EXAMPLE 3-9   Free Cash Flow Tied to Sales

At the end of 2003, Carla Espinosa is an analyst following Pitts Corporation. Assume from Example 3-6 that the company's sales for 2003 are $3,000 million. Espinosa expects Pitts Corporation's sales to increase by 10 percent a year thereafter. Furthermore, Pitts is a stable company in many respects, and Espinosa expects it to maintain its historical EBIT margin and proportions of incremental investments in fixed and working capital. Sales in the previous year grew by $300 million. Pitts Corporation's EBIT for 2003 is $500 million; its EBIT margin is 16.67 percent (500/3000), and its tax rate is 40 percent. Incremental fixed capital investment in the previous year was

(Capital expenditures − Depreciation expense)/(Increase in sales) or

(400 − 300)/(300) = 33.33%

Incremental working capital investment in the past year was

(Increase in working capital)/(Increase in sales) or

45/300 = 15%

So for every $100 increase in sales, Pitts Corporation invests $33.33 in new equipment in addition to replacement of depreciated equipment and $15 in working capital. Espinosa forecasts FCFF for 2004 as shown below:

Sales	$3,300	Up 10%
EBIT	550	16.67% of sales
EBIT(1 − Tax rate)	330	Adjusted for 40% tax rate
Incremental FC	(100)	33.33% of sales increase
Incremental WC	(45)	15% of sales increase
FCFF	$185	

This model can be used to forecast multiple periods and is flexible enough to allow varying sales growth rates, EBIT margins, tax rates, and incremental capital increase rates.

EXAMPLE 3-10   Free Cash Flow Growth Tied to Sales Growth

Continuing her work, Espinosa wants to forecast FCFF for the next five years. Espinosa is concerned that Pitts will not be able to maintain its historical EBIT margin and that the EBIT margin will decline from the current 16.67 percent to 14.5 percent in the next five years. Table 3-10 summarizes her forecasts.

TABLE 3-10   Free Cash Flow Growth for Pitts Corporation

	Year 1	Year 2	Year 3	Year 4	Year 5
Sales growth	10.00%	10.00%	10.00%	10.00%	10.00%
EBIT margin	16.67%	16.00%	15.50%	15.00%	14.50%
Tax rate	40.00%	40.00%	40.00%	40.00%	40.00%
Incremental FC investment	33.33%	33.33%	33.33%	33.33%	33.33%
Incremental WC investment	15.00%	15.00%	15.00%	15.00%	15.00%
Prior year sales	3,000.00				
Sales forecast	3,300.00	3,630.00	3,993.00	4,392.30	4,831.53
EBIT forecast	550.00	580.80	618.92	658.85	700.57
EBIT(1 − Tax rate)	330.00	348.48	371.35	395.31	420.34
Incremental FC	(100.00)	(110.00)	(121.00)	(133.10)	(146.41)
Incremental WC	(45.00)	(49.50)	(54.45)	(59.90)	(65.88)
FCFF	185.00	188.98	195.90	202.31	208.05

The model need not begin with sales; it could start with net income, cash flow from operations, or EBITDA.

A similar model can be designed for FCFE. In the case of FCFE, the analyst can begin with net income and must also forecast any net new borrowing or net preferred stock issue.

EXAMPLE 3-11   Finding FCFE

Espinosa decides to forecast FCFE for the year 2004. She uses the same expectations derived in the example above. Additionally, she expects

- the profit margin to remain at 8 percent (= 240/3000), and
- the company to finance incremental fixed and working capital investments with 50 percent debt—the target debt ratio.

Sales	$3,300	Up 10%
NI	264	8.0% of sales
Incremental FC	(100)	33.33% of sales increase
Incremental WC	(45)	15% of sales increase
Net borrowing	72.50	(100 FCInv + 45 WCInv) × 50%
FCFE	$191.50	

When the company has significant noncash charges other than depreciation expense, the approach just illustrated will result in a less accurate estimate of FCFE than one obtained by forecasting all the individual components of FCFE.

In some cases, the analyst will have specific forecasts of planned components, such as capital expenditures. In other cases, the analyst studies historical relationships, such as previous capital expenditures and sales levels, to develop a forecast.

3.7. Other Issues with Free Cash Flow Analysis

3.7.1. Analyst Adjustments to CFO

Although corporate financial statements are often straightforward, frequently they are not transparent. Sometimes, difficulties in analysis arise because the companies and their trans-actions are simply more complicated than the example provided by the Pitts Corporation (above).

For instance, in many corporate financial statements, the changes in balance sheet items (the increase in an asset or the decrease in a liability) differ from those reported on the statement of cash flows. Likewise, depreciation in the statement of cash flows may differ from depreciation expense in the income statement. How do such problems arise?

Two factors can cause discrepancies between changes in balance sheet accounts and the changes reported in the statement of cash flows: acquisitions and divestitures, and foreign subsidiaries. For example, an increase in an inventory account can result from purchases from suppliers (which is an operating activity) or from an acquisition or merger with another company that has inventory on its balance sheet (which is an investing activity). Discrepancies can also occur from currency translations of foreign subsidiaries.

As discussed in Section 3.2, the CFO figure from the statement of cash flows may be contaminated by cash flows arising from financing and/or investing activities. As a consequence, when analysts use CFO in a valuation context, ideally they should remove such contaminations and produce an analyst-adjusted CFO before using it as a starting point for free cash flow calculations.

3.7.2. Free Cash Flow versus Dividends and Other Earnings Components

Many analysts have a strong preference for free cash flow valuation models over dividend discount models (DDMs). Although perhaps no theoretical advantage exists for one type of model over another, legitimate reasons to prefer one model can arise in the process of applying free cash flow models versus DDMs. First, many corporations pay no, or very low, cash dividends. Using dividend discount models to value these companies puts the analyst in an awkward situation, forcing her to speculate about when dividends will be initiated and established at a material level. Second, dividend payments are at the discretion of the corporation's board of directors. As such, they may imperfectly signal the company's long-run profitability. Some corporations clearly pay dividends that are substantially less than their free cash flow, and others pay dividends that are substantially more. Finally, as mentioned in Section 1, dividends are the cash flow going to shareholders, and free cash flow to equity is the cash flow available to shareholders if they controlled the company. If a company is being analyzed as a takeover target, free cash flow is the appropriate cash flow measure; once the company is taken over, the new owners will have discretion over free cash flow.

We have defined FCFF and FCFE and presented alternative (equivalent) ways to calculate both of them. So you should have a good feel for what is included in FCFF or FCFE. You may wonder why some cash flows are not included. Specifically, what role do dividends, share repurchases, share issuance, or leverage changes have on FCFF and FCFE? The simple answer is: not much. Recall two formulas for FCFF and FCFE:

$$FCFF = NI + NCC + Int(1 - Tax\ rate) - FCInv - WCInv$$

$$FCFE = NI + NCC - FCInv - WCInv + Net\ borrowing$$

 Notice that dividends and these other transactions are absent from the formulas. The reason is that FCFF and FCFE are the cash flows *available* to investors or to stockholders; dividends and share repurchases are *uses* of these cash flows. So the simple answer is that transactions between the company and its shareholders (through cash dividends, share repurchases, and share issuances) do not affect free cash flow. Leverage changes, such as using more debt financing, would have some impact because they would increase the interest tax shield (reduce corporate taxes because of the tax deductibility of interest) and reduce the cash flow available to equity. In the long run, however, investing and financing decisions made today will affect future cash flows.

If all inputs were known and mutually consistent, a dividend discount model and a FCFE model would result in identical valuations for a stock. One possibility is that FCFE, from Equation 3-10 above, equals cash dividends each year. Both cash flow streams are discounted at the required return for equity and would thus have the same present value. Generally, FCFE and dividends will differ. FCFE recognizes value as the cash flow available to stockholders (NI + NCC − FCInv − WCInv + Net borrowing) even if it is not paid out in dividends. The company's board of directors, because of its discretion over dividends, can choose to pay dividends that are lower or higher than FCFE. Generally, however, the same economic forces that lead to low (high) dividends lead to low (high) FCFE. For example, a rapidly growing company with superior investment opportunities will retain a high proportion of earnings and pay low dividends. This same company would have high investments in fixed capital and working capital (in Equation 3-10, for example) and have a low FCFE. Conversely, a mature company that is investing relatively little might have high dividends and high FCFE. In spite of this tendency, however, FCFE and dividends will usually differ.

FCFF and FCFE, as defined in this book, are measures of cash flow designed for valuation of the firm or its equity. Other definitions of "free cash flow" frequently appear in textbooks, articles, and vendor-supplied databases of financial information on public companies. In many cases, these other definitions of free cash flow are not designed for valuation purposes and thus should not be used for valuation. Using numbers supplied by others without knowing exactly how they are defined increases the likelihood of making errors in valuation. As consumers and producers of research, analysts are well advised to clarify the definition of free cash flow being used because so many versions exist.

Because free cash flow analysis requires considerable care and understanding in its use, some practitioners erroneously use earnings components such as NI, EBIT, EBITDA, or CFO in a discounted cash flow valuation. Such mistakes may lead the analyst to systematically overstate or understate the value of a stock. Shortcuts can be costly.

One common shortcut is to use EBITDA as a proxy for the cash flow to the firm. Equation 3-13 clearly showed the differences between EBITDA and FCFF:

$$FCFF = EBITDA(1 - \text{Tax rate}) + Dep(\text{Tax rate}) - FCInv - WCInv$$

Depreciation charges as a percentage of EBITDA vary substantially for different companies and industries, as does the depreciation tax shield (the depreciation charge times the tax rate). Although FCFF captures this difference, EBITDA does not. EBITDA also does not account for the investments a company makes in fixed capital or working capital. Hence, EBITDA is a very poor measure of the cash flow available to the company's investors. Using EBITDA in a discounted cash flow model (instead of an actual cash flow) has another important aspect as well: EBITDA is a before-tax measure, so the discount rate applied to EBITDA would need to be a before-tax rate. The WACC used to discount FCFF is an after-tax rate.

EBITDA is a poor proxy for FCFF because it does not account for the depreciation tax shield and the investment in fixed capital and working capital, but it is an even poorer proxy for free cash flow to equity. From a stockholder's perspective, additional defects of EBITDA include its failure to account for the after-tax interest costs or cash flows from new borrowing or debt repayments. Example 3-12 shows the mistakes sometimes made in discussions of cash flows.

EXAMPLE 3-12   The Mistake of Using Net Income for FCFE and EBITDA for FCFF

A recent job applicant made some interesting comments about FCFE and FCFF: "I don't like the definitions for FCFE and FCFF because they are unnecessarily complicated and confusing. The best measure of FCFE, the funds available to pay dividends, is simply net income. You take the net income number straight off the income statement and don't need to make any further adjustments. Likewise, the best measure of FCFF, the funds available to the company's suppliers of capital, is EBITDA. You can take EBITDA straight off the income statement and don't need to consider using anything else."

How would you respond to the job applicant's definition of (1) FCFE and (2) FCFF?

Solution to 1: The FCFE is the cash generated by the business's operations less the amounts it must reinvest in additional assets plus the amounts it is borrowing. Equation 3-10, which starts with net income to find FCFE, shows these items:

Free cash flow to equity = Net income available to common shareholders
                   Plus: Net noncash charges
                   Less: Investment in fixed capital
                   Less: Investment in working capital
                   Plus: Net borrowing

Net income does not include several cash flows. Investments in fixed or working capital reduce the cash available to stockholders, as do loan repayments. New borrowing increases the cash available. FCFE includes the cash generated from operating the business and also accounts for the investing and financing activities of the company. So, net income tells only part of the overall story. Of course, a special case exists in which net income and FCFE are the same. This case occurs when new investments exactly equal depreciation and the company is not investing in working capital or engaging in any net borrowing.

Solution to 2: Assuming that EBITDA equals FCFF introduces several possible mistakes. Equation 3-13 highlights these mistakes:

$$\text{Free cash flow to the firm} = \text{EBITDA}(1 - \text{Tax rate})$$
$$\text{Plus: Depreciation}(\text{Tax rate})$$
$$\text{Less: Investment in fixed capital}$$
$$\text{Less: Investment in working capital}$$

The job applicant is ignoring taxes, which obviously reduce the cash available to the company's suppliers of capital.

3.7.3. Free Cash Flow and More-Complicated Capital Structures

For the most part, the discussion of FCFF and FCFE above assumes a simple capital structure in which the company has two sources of capital, debt and equity. Including preferred stock as a third source of capital would cause the analyst to add terms to the equations for FCFF and FCFE for the dividends paid on preferred stock and for the issuance or repurchase of preferred shares. Instead of including those terms in all of the equations, we chose to leave preferred stock out because only a minority of corporations use preferred stock. For companies that do have preferred stock, however, its effects can be incorporated where appropriate. For example, in Equation 3-7, which calculates FCFF starting with net income available to common shareholders, preferred dividends paid would have to be added to the cash flows to obtain FCFF. In Equation 3-10, which calculates FCFE starting with net income available to common shareholders, if preferred dividends were already subtracted when arriving at net income available to common, no further adjustment for preferred dividends would be required. Issuing (redeeming) preferred stock increases (decreases) the cash flow available to common stockholders, however, so this term must be added in. In many respects, the existence of preferred stock in the capital structure has many of the same effects as the existence of debt, except that unlike interest payments on debt, preferred stock dividends paid are not tax deductible.

EXAMPLE 3-13   FCFF Valuation with Preferred Stock in the Capital Structure

Welch Corporation uses bond, preferred stock, and common stock financing. The market value of each of these sources of financing and the before-tax required rates of return for each are given below:

	Market Value	Required Return
Bonds	$400,000,000	8.0%
Preferred stock	$100,000,000	8.0%
Common stock	$500,000,000	12.0%
Total	$1,000,000,000	

Other financial information:

- Net income available to common shareholders = $110,000,000
- Interest expenses = $32,000,000
- Preferred dividends = $8,000,000
- Depreciation = $40,000,000
- Investment in fixed capital = $70,000,000
- Investment in working capital = $20,000,000
- Net borrowing = $25,000,000
- Tax rate = 30 percent
- Stable growth rate of FCFF = 4.0 percent
- Stable growth rate of FCFE = 5.0 percent

1. Calculate Welch Corporation's WACC.
2. Calculate the current value of FCFF.
3. Based on forecasted FCFF, what is the total value of the firm and the value of equity?
4. Calculate the current value of FCFE.
5. Based on forecasted FCFE, what is the value of equity?

Solution to 1: Based on the weights and after-tax costs of each source of capital, the WACC is

$$\text{WACC} = \frac{400}{1,000}8\%(1 - 0.30) + \frac{100}{1,000}8\% + \frac{500}{1,000}12\% = 9.04\%$$

Solution to 2: If the company did not issue preferred stock, FCFF would be

$$\text{FCFF} = \text{NI} + \text{NCC} + \text{Int}(1 - \text{Tax rate}) - \text{FCInv} - \text{WCInv}$$

If preferred stock dividends have been paid (and net income is income available to common), the preferred dividends must be added back just as after-tax interest expenses are above. The modified equation (including preferred dividends) for FCFF would be

$$\text{FCFF} = \text{NI} + \text{NCC} + \text{Int}(1 - \text{Tax rate}) + \text{Preferred dividends} - \text{FCInv} - \text{WCInv}$$

For Welch Corporation, FCFF is

$$\text{FCFF} = 110 + 40 + 32(1 - 0.30) + 8 - 70 - 20 = \$90.4 \text{ million}$$

Solution to 3: The total value of the firm is

$$\text{Firm} = \frac{\text{FCFF}_1}{\text{WACC} - g} = \frac{90.4(1.04)}{0.0904 - 0.04} = \frac{94.016}{0.0504} = \$1{,}865.40 \text{ million}$$

The value of equity is the total value of the company minus the value of debt and preferred stock:

$$\text{Equity} = 1{,}865.40 - 400 - 100 = \$1{,}365.40 \text{ million}$$

Solution to 4: With no preferred stock, FCFE is

$$\text{FCFE} = \text{NI} + \text{NCC} - \text{FCInv} - \text{WCInv} + \text{Net borrowing}$$

If the company has preferred stock, the FCFE equation is essentially the same. Net borrowing would be the total of new debt borrowing and net issuances of new preferred stock. For Welch Corporation, FCFE is

$$\text{FCFE} = 110 + 40 - 70 - 20 + 25 = \$85 \text{ million}$$

Solution to 5: Valuing FCFE, which is growing at 5.0 percent, we have a value of equity of

$$\text{Equity} = \frac{\text{FCFE}_1}{r - g} = \frac{85(1.05)}{0.12 - 0.05} = \frac{89.25}{0.07} = \$1{,}275.00 \text{ million}$$

Paying cash dividends on common stock does not affect FCFF or FCFE, the amounts of cash *available* to all investors or to common stockholders. It is simply a use of the available cash. Share repurchases of common stock also do not affect FCFF or FCFE. Share repurchases, in many respects, are substitutes for cash dividends. Similarly, issuing shares of common stock does not affect FCFF or FCFE. On the other hand, changing leverage (changing the amount of debt financing in the company's capital structure) does have some effects. An increase in leverage will not affect FCFF (although it might affect the calculations you use to arrive at FCFF). An increase in leverage affects FCFE in two ways. In the year the debt is issued, it increases the FCFE by the amount of debt issued. After the debt is issued, FCFE is then reduced by the after-tax interest expense.

   Section 3 has discussed the concepts of FCFF and FCFE and their estimation. The next section presents additional valuation models using forecasts of FCFF or FCFE to value the firm or its equity. These DCF models are similar to the dividend discount models discussed in the previous chapter, although the analyst must face the reality that estimating free cash flows is a more time-consuming exercise than estimating dividends.

4. FREE CASH FLOW MODEL VARIATIONS

Section 4 presents several extensions of the FCF models presented earlier. In many cases, especially when inflation rates are volatile, analysts will value real cash flows instead of nominal values. As with dividend discount models, free cash flow models are very sensitive to the data inputs, and analysts routinely perform sensitivity analyses on their valuations. Previously, in Section 2, we presented single-stage free cash flow models, which have a constant growth rate. This section presents two-stage and three-stage free cash flow valuation models.

4.1. An International Application of the Single-Stage Model

Valuation using real values instead of nominal values has much appeal when inflation rates are high and volatile. Many analysts use this adaptation for both domestic and foreign stocks, but the use of real values is especially helpful for valuing international stocks. Special challenges to valuing equities from multiple countries include incorporating economic factors such as interest rate, inflation rate, and growth rate differences across countries as well as dealing with variable accounting standards. Furthermore, performing analyses in multiple countries challenges the analyst, and most particularly a team of analysts, to use consistent assumptions for all countries.

Several securities firms have adapted the single-stage FCFE model to address some of these challenges of international valuation. They choose to analyze companies using real cash flows and real discount rates instead of using nominal values. To estimate real discount rates, they use a modification of the build-up method mentioned in Chapter 2. Starting with a "country return," which is a real required rate of return for stocks from a particular country, they then make adjustments to the country return for the stock's industry, size, and leverage:

Country return (real)	x.xx%
+/− Industry adjustment	x.xx%
+/− Size adjustment	x.xx%
+/− Leverage adjustment	x.xx%
Required rate of return (real)	x.xx%

The adjustments in the model should have sound economic justification. They should reflect factors expected to impact the relative risk and return associated with an investment.

The growth rate of FCFE also is predicted in real terms. These securities firms supply all analysts with estimates of the real growth rates for each country. The analyst then chooses a real growth rate for the stock benchmarked against the real country growth rate. This approach is particularly useful for countries with high or variable inflation rates. The value of the stock is found with an equation essentially like Equation 3-6 except that all terms in the equation are in real terms. If $FCFE_0$ is for the current year, say 2002, then the value of the stock will be in 2002 currency.

$$V_0 = \frac{FCFE_0(1 + g_{real})}{r_{real} - g_{real}}$$

Whenever real discount rates and real growth rates can be estimated more reliably than nominal discount rates and nominal growth rates, this method is worth using. Example 3-14 below shows how this procedure can be applied.

EXAMPLE 3-14   Using Real Cash Flows and Discount Rates for International Stocks

---

YPF Sociedad Anonima (NYSE: YPF) is an integrated oil and gas company headquartered in Buenos Aires, Argentina. Although cash flows have been volatile, an analyst has estimated a normalized FCFE of 1.05 Argentine pesos (ARS) per share for the year just ended. The real country return for Argentina is 7.30 percent; adjustments to the country return for YPF S.A. are an industry adjustment of +0.80 percent, a size adjustment of −0.33 percent, and a leverage adjustment of −0.12 percent. The long-term real growth rate for Argentina is estimated to be 3.0 percent, and the real growth rate of YPF S.A. is expected to be about 0.5 percent below the country rate. The real required rate of return for YPF S.A. is

Country return (real)	7.30%
Industry adjustment	+0.80%
Size adjustment	−0.33%
Leverage adjustment	−0.12%
Required rate of return	7.65%

The real growth rate of FCFE is expected to be 2.5 percent (3.0% − 0.5%), so the value of one share is

$$V_0 = \frac{\text{FCFE}_0(1 + g_{\text{real}})}{r_{\text{real}} - g_{\text{real}}} = \frac{1.05(1.025)}{0.0765 - 0.025} = \frac{1.07625}{0.0515} = \text{ARS}20.90$$

4.2. Sensitivity Analysis of FCFF and FCFE Valuations

In large measure, growth in FCFF and in FCFE depend on a company's future profitability. Sales growth and changes in net profit margins dictate future net profits. Sales growth and profit margins depend on the growth phase of the company and the profitability of the industry. A highly profitable company in a growing industry can enjoy years of profit growth. Eventually, its profit margins are likely to be eroded by increased competition, and sales growth is likely to abate as well because of fewer opportunities for expansion of market size and market share. Growth rates and the duration of growth are difficult to forecast.

The base-year values for the FCFF or FCFE growth models are also critical. Given the same required rates of return and growth rates, the value of the firm or the value of equity will increase or decrease proportionately with the initial value of FCFF or FCFE employed.

Valuing a company involves forecasts of the company's future cash flows as well as estimates of the opportunity cost of funds that should be used to find the present value of the future cash flows. Analysts can perform a sensitivity analysis, which shows how sensitive the final valuation is to changes in each of a valuation model's input variables. Some input variables have a much larger impact on stock valuation than others. Example 3-15 shows the sensitivity of the valuation of Anheuser-Busch Companies to five input variables.

EXAMPLE 3-15   Sensitivity Analysis of a FCFE Valuation

Steve Bono has valued Anheuser-Busch Companies (NYSE: BUD) using the FCFE constant-growth approach. His best estimates of the input values for the analysis are that $FCFE_0$ is \$1.64 per share, the FCFE growth rate is 5.20 percent forever, the risk-free return is 5.5 percent, the equity risk premium is also 5.5 percent, and the company's beta is 0.60. The required rate of return for BUD is

$$r = E(R_i) = R_F + \beta_i[E(R_M) - R_F] = 5.5\% + 0.60(5.5\%) = 8.80\%$$

The value per share is

$$\text{Value} = \frac{FCFE_0(1 + g)}{r - g} = \frac{1.64(1.052)}{0.088 - 0.052} = \frac{1.7253}{0.036} = \$47.92$$

Bono has also collected other reasonable estimates for the variables. Bono's original estimates are given in the table as the "base case" estimates, and the highest and lowest of the alternative estimates are shown in Table 3-11 as the high and low estimates. The column "Valuation with Low Estimate" gives the estimated value of BUD using the low estimate for the variable on the same row of the first column and the base case estimates for the remaining four variables. "Valuation with High Estimate" performs a similar exercise using the high estimate for the variable at issue.

TABLE 3-11   Sensitivity Analysis for Anheuser-Busch Valuation

Variable	Base Case Estimate	Low Estimate	High Estimate	Valuation with Low Estimate	Valuation with High Estimate
Free cash flow to equity	\$1.64	\$1.55	\$1.75	\$45.29	\$51.14
Beta	0.60	0.40	0.70	\$69.01	\$41.57
Risk-free rate of return	5.5%	5.3%	5.7%	\$50.74	\$45.40
Equity risk premium	5.5%	4.5%	6.0%	\$57.51	\$44.23
FCFE growth rate	5.2%	3.8%	6.0%	\$34.05	\$62.09

As the table shows, the value of Anheuser-Busch is very sensitive to the inputs. Of the five variables in the valuation model, the stock valuation was least sensitive to the range of estimates of FCFE and of the risk-free rate. The range of estimates for the risk-free rate of return and for FCFE gave the smallest ranges of stock values (from \$50.74 to \$45.40 for the risk-free rate and from \$45.29 to \$51.14 for FCFE). The stock value was most sensitive to the extreme values for beta and for the FCFE growth rate. These ranges were roughly \$28 (from \$69.01 to \$41.57 for beta and from \$34.05 to \$62.09 for the FCFE growth rate).

Of course, the variables to which the stock price is most sensitive vary from case to case. A sensitivity analysis gives the analyst a guide as to which variables are most critical to the final valuation.

4.3. Two-Stage Free Cash Flow Models

Several two-stage and multistage models exist for valuing FCF streams, just as several such models are available for valuing dividend streams. The free cash flow models are much more complex than the discounted dividend models because the analyst usually incorporates sales, profitability, investments, financing costs, and new financing to find FCFF or FCFE.

In two-stage FCF models, the growth rate in the second stage is a long-run sustainable growth rate. For a declining industry, the second-stage growth rate could be slightly below the GDP growth rate. For an industry that will grow in the future relative to the overall economy, the second-stage growth rate could be slightly greater than the GDP growth rate.

The two most popular versions of the two-stage FCFF and FCFE models are distinguished by the pattern of the growth rates in Stage 1. In one version, the growth rate is constant in Stage 1 before dropping to the long-run sustainable rate in Stage 2. In the other version, the growth rates decline in Stage 1, reaching the sustainable rate at the beginning of Stage 2. The latter model is like the H-model for dividend valuation in Chapter 2, in which dividend growth rates decline in Stage 1 and are constant in Stage 2.

The growth rates can be applied to different variables. The growth rate could be the growth rate for FCFF or FCFE, or the growth rate for income (such as net income), or the growth rate for sales. If the growth rate were for net income, the changes in FCFF or FCFE would also depend on investments in operating assets and financing of these investments. When the growth rate in income declines, such as between Stage 1 and Stage 2, investments in operating assets will probably decline at the same time. If the growth rate is for sales, changes in net profit margins as well as investments in operating assets and financing policies will determine FCFF and FCFE.

A general expression for the two-stage FCFF valuation model is

$$\text{Firm value} = \sum_{t=1}^{n} \frac{\text{FCFF}_t}{(1 + \text{WACC})^t} + \frac{\text{FCFF}_{n+1}}{(\text{WACC} - g)} \frac{1}{(1 + \text{WACC})^n} \qquad (3\text{-}15)$$

The summation gives the present value of the first n years of FCFF. The terminal value of the FCFF from Year $n + 1$ onward is $\text{FCFF}_{n+1}/(\text{WACC} - g)$, which is discounted at the WACC for n periods to obtain its present value. Subtracting the value of outstanding debt gives the value of equity. The value per share is then found by dividing the total value of equity by the number of outstanding shares.

The general expression for the two-stage FCFE valuation model is

$$\text{Equity} = \sum_{t=1}^{n} \frac{\text{FCFE}_t}{(1 + r)^t} + \frac{\text{FCFE}_{n+1}}{r - g} \frac{1}{(1 + r)^n} \qquad (3\text{-}16)$$

The summation is the present value of the first n years of FCFE, and the terminal value of $\text{FCFE}_{n+1}/(r - g)$ is discounted at the required rate of return on equity for n years. The value per share is found by dividing the total value of equity by the number of outstanding shares.

In Equation 3-16, the terminal value of the stock at $t = n$ is found using the constant-growth model. In this case, $\text{TV}_n = \text{FCFE}_{n+1}/(r - g)$. Of course, the analyst might choose to estimate the terminal value, TV_n, another way, such as using a P/E multiplied by the company's forecasted EPS. The terminal value estimation is critical for a simple reason: The present value of the terminal value often represents a substantial portion of the total value of the stock. For example, in Equation 3-16 above, when calculating the total present value of the first n cash flows (FCFE) and the present value of the terminal value, the latter is often substantial. In the examples that follow, the terminal value is usually very important. The same is true in practice.

4.3.1. Fixed Growth Rates in Stage 1 and Stage 2

The simplest two-stage FCFF or FCFE growth model has a constant growth rate in each stage. Example 3-16 finds the value of a firm that has a 20 percent sales growth rate in Stage 1 and a 6 percent sales growth rate in Stage 2.

EXAMPLE 3-16   A Two-Stage FCFE Valuation Model with a Constant Growth Rate in Each Stage

Uwe Henschel is doing a valuation of TechnoSchaft using the following information:

- Year 0 sales per share = €25
- Sales growth rate = 20 percent annually for three years and 6 percent annually thereafter
- Net profit margin = 10 percent forever
- Net investment in fixed capital (net of depreciation) = 50 percent of the sales increase
- Annual increase in working capital = 20 percent of the sales increase
- Debt financing = 40 percent of the net investments in capital equipment and working capital
- TechnoSchaft beta = 1.20, risk-free rate of return = 7 percent, equity risk premium = 4.5 percent

The required rate of return for equity is

$$r = E(R_i) = R_F + \beta_i[E(R_M) - R_F] = 7\% + 1.2(4.5\%) = 12.4\%$$

Table 3-12 shows the calculations for FCFE.

TABLE 3-12   FCFE Estimates for TechnoSchaft

Year	1	2	3	4	5	6
Sales growth rate	20%	20%	20%	6%	6%	6%
Sales per share	30.000	36.000	43.200	45.792	48.540	51.452
Net profit margin	10%	10%	10%	10%	10%	10%
Earnings per share	3.000	3.600	4.320	4.579	4.854	5.145
Net FCInv per share	2.500	3.000	3.600	1.296	1.374	1.456
WCInv per share	1.000	1.200	1.440	0.518	0.550	0.582
Debt financing per share	1.400	1.680	2.016	0.726	0.769	0.815
FCFE per share	0.900	1.080	1.296	3.491	3.700	3.922
Growth rate of FCFE		20%	20%	169%	6%	6%

In the table, sales grow at 20 percent annually for the first three years and then at 6 percent thereafter. Profits, which are 10 percent of sales, grow at the same rates. The net investments in fixed capital and working capital are 50 percent of the increase in sales and 20 percent of the increase in sales, respectively. New debt financing equals 40 percent of the total increase in net fixed capital and working capital. FCFE is EPS minus the net investment in fixed capital per share minus the investment in working capital per share plus the debt financing per share.

Notice that FCFE grows by 20 percent annually for the first three years. Then, between Year 3 and Year 4, when the sales growth rate drops from 20 percent to 6 percent, FCFE increases substantially. In fact, FCFE increases by 169 percent from Year 3 to Year 4. This large increase in FCFE occurs because profits grow at 6 percent but the investments in capital equipment and working capital (and the increase in debt financing) drop substantially from the previous year. In Years 5 and 6 in the table, sales, profit, investments, financing, and FCFE all grow at 6 percent.

The stock value is the present value of the first three years' FCFE plus the present value of the terminal value of the FCFE from Year 4 and later. The terminal value is

$$\text{TV}_3 = \text{FCFE}_4/(r - g) = 3.491/(0.124 - 0.06) = 54.55$$

The present values are

$$V_0 = \frac{0.900}{1.124} + \frac{1.080}{(1.124)^2} + \frac{1.296}{(1.124)^3} + \frac{54.55}{(1.124)^3}$$
$$= 0.801 + 0.855 + 0.913 + 38.415 = \text{€}40.98$$

The estimated value of this stock is €40.98 per share.

As mentioned previously, the terminal value may account for a large fraction of the value of a stock. For this case, the present value of the terminal value is €38.415 out of a total value of €40.98. The present value of the terminal value is almost 94 percent of the total value of TechnoSchaft stock.

4.3.2. Declining Growth Rates in Stage 1 and Constant Growth in Stage 2

Growth rates usually do not drop precipitously from one rate to another as they do between the stages in the two-stage model above, but growth rates can decline over time for many reasons. Sometimes, a small company has a high growth rate that is not sustainable as its market share increases. A highly profitable company also can attract competition that makes it harder for the company to sustain its high profit margins.

In this section, we present two examples of the two-stage model with declining growth rates in Stage 1. In the first example, the growth rate of EPS declines during Stage 1. As a company's profitability declines and the company is no longer generating very high returns, the company will usually reduce its net new investment in operating assets. The debt financing accompanying the new investments will also decline. It is not unusual for highly profitable, growing companies to have negative or low cash flows. Later, when growth in profits slows, investments will tend to slow and the company will experience positive cash flows. Of course, the negative cash flows incurred in the high-growth stage help determine the cash flows that occur in future years.

Example 3-17 below models FCFE per share as a function of EPS, which declines constantly during Stage 1. Because of declining earnings growth rates, the company in the example reduces its new investments over time as well. The value of the company depends on these free cash flows, which are substantial after the high-growth (and high-profitability) period has largely elapsed.

EXAMPLE 3-17   A Two-Stage FCFE Valuation Model with Declining Net Income Growth in Stage 1

Vishal Noronha needs to prepare a valuation of Sindhuh Enterprises. Noronha has assembled the following information for his analysis. It is now the first day of 2003.

- EPS for 2002 is $2.40.
- For the next five years, the growth rate in EPS is given below. After 2007, the growth rate will be 7 percent.

Year	2003	2004	2005	2006	2007
Growth rate for EPS	30%	18%	12%	9%	7%

- Net investment in fixed capital (net of depreciation) for the next five years are given below. After 2007, capital expenditures are expected to grow at 7 percent annually.

Year	2003	2004	2005	2006	2007
Net capital expenditure per share	3.000	2.500	2.000	1.500	1.000

- The investment in working capital each year will equal 50 percent of the net investment in capital items.
- Thirty percent of the net investment in fixed capital and investment in working capital will be financed with new debt financing.
- Current market conditions dictate a risk-free rate of 6.0 percent, an equity risk premium of 4.0 percent, and a beta of 1.10 for Sindhuh Enterprises.

  1. What is the per-share value of Sindhuh Enterprises on the first day of 2003?
  2. What should be the trailing P/E on the first day of 2003 and the first day of 2007?

Solution to 1: The required return for Sindhuh should be

$$r = E(R_i) = R_F + \beta_i[E(R_M) - R_F] = 6\% + 1.1(4\%) = 10.4\%$$

The FCFEs for the company for years 2003 through 2007 are given in Table 3-13 below. Earnings are $2.40 in 2002. Earnings increase each year by the growth rate given in the table. Net capital expenditures (capital expenditures minus depreciation) are the amounts that Noronha assumed. The increase in working capital each year is 50 percent

TABLE 3-13   FCFE Estimates for Sindhuh Enterprises

Year	2003	2004	2005	2006	2007
Growth rate for EPS	30%	18%	12%	9%	7%
Earnings per share	$3.120	$3.682	$4.123	$4.494	$4.809
Net FCInv per share	3.000	2.500	2.000	1.500	1.000
WCInv per share	1.500	1.250	1.000	0.750	0.500
Debt financing per share*	1.350	1.125	0.900	0.675	0.450
FCFE per share**	−0.030	1.057	2.023	2.919	3.759
PV of FCFE discounted at 10.4%	−0.027	0.867	1.504	1.965	

*30 percent of (Net FCInv + WCInv)

**EPS − Net FCInv per share − WCInv per share + Debt financing per share

of the increase in net capital expenditures. Debt financing is 30 percent of the total outlays for net capital expenditures and working capital each year. The FCFE each year is net income minus net capital expenditures minus increase in working capital plus new debt financing. Finally, for years 2003 through 2006, the present value of FCFE is found by discounting FCFE by the 10.4 percent required rate of return for equity.

After 2006, FCFE will grow by a constant 7 percent annually, so the constant growth FCFE valuation model can be used to value this cash flow stream. At the end of 2006, the value of the future FCFE is

$$V_{2006} = \frac{FCFE_{2007}}{r - g} = \frac{3.759}{0.104 - 0.07} = \$110.56$$

To find the present value of V_{2006} as of the end of 2002, V_{2002}, we discount V_{2006} at 10.4 percent for four years:

$$PV = 110.56/(1.104)^4 = \$74.425$$

The total present value of the company is the present value of the first four years' FCFE plus the present value of the terminal value, or

$$V_{2002} = -0.027 + 0.867 + 1.504 + 1.965 + 74.42 = \$78.73$$

Solution to 2: Using the estimated $78.73 stock value, the trailing P/E at the beginning of 2003 would be

$$P/E = 78.73/2.40 = 32.8$$

At the beginning of 2007, the expected stock value is $110.56 and the previous year's earnings per share is $4.494, so the trailing P/E at this time would be

$$P/E = 110.56/4.494 = 24.6$$

After its high-growth phase has ended, the P/E for the company declines substantially.

FCFE in this example was based on forecasts of future earnings per share. Analysts often model a company by forecasting future sales and then estimating the profits, investments, and financing associated with those sales levels. For large companies, analysts may estimate the sales, profitability, investments, and financing for each division or large subsidiary. The free cash flows for all of the divisions or subsidiaries are aggregated to get the free cash flow for the company as a whole.

Example 3-18 below is a two-stage FCFE model with declining sales growth rates in Stage 1, with profits, investments, and financing keyed to sales. In Stage 1, the growth rate of sales and the profit margin on sales both decline as the company matures and faces more competition and lower growth.

EXAMPLE 3-18   A Two-Stage FCFE Valuation Model with Declining Sales Growth Rates

Medina Werks has a competitive advantage that will probably deteriorate over time. Flavio Torino expects this deterioration to be reflected in declining sales growth rates as well as declining profit margins. To value the company, Torino has accumulated the following information:

- Current sales are $600 million. Over the next six years, the annual sales growth rate and the net profit margin are projected to be as follows:

Year	1	2	3	4	5	6
Sales growth rate	20%	16%	12%	10%	8%	7%
Net profit margin	14%	13%	12%	11%	10.50%	10%

Beginning in Year 6, the 7 percent sales growth rate and 10 percent net profit margin should persist indefinitely.
- Capital expenditures (net of depreciation) in the amount of 60 percent of the sales increase will be required each year.
- Investments in working capital equal to 25 percent of the sales increase will also be required each year.
- Debt financing will be used to fund 40 percent of the investments in net capital items and working capital.
- The beta for Medina Werks is 1.10. The risk-free rate of return is 6.0 percent and the equity risk premium is 4.5 percent.
- There are 70 million outstanding shares.

What is the estimated total market value of equity and the value per share?

Solution: The required return for Medina is

$$r = E(R_i) = R_F + \beta_i[E(R_M) - R_F] = 6\% + 1.10(4.5\%) = 10.95\%$$

The annual sales and net profit can be found readily as shown in Table 3-14 below.

TABLE 3-14   FCFE Estimates for Medina Werks

Year	1	2	3	4	5	6
Sales growth rate	20%	16%	12%	10%	8%	7%
Net profit margin	14%	13%	12%	11%	10.50%	10%
Sales	720.000	835.200	935.424	1028.966	1111.284	1189.074
Net profit	100.800	108.576	112.251	113.186	116.685	118.907
Net FCInv	72.000	69.120	60.134	56.125	49.390	46.674
WCInv	30.000	28.800	25.056	23.386	20.579	19.447
Debt financing	40.800	39.168	34.076	31.804	27.988	26.449
FCFE	39.600	49.824	61.137	65.480	74.703	79.235
PV of FCFE at 10.95%	35.692	40.475	44.763	43.211	44.433	

Sales increase each year by the sales growth rate in Table 3-14. Net profit each year is the year's net profit margin times the year's sales. Capital investment (net of depreciation) equals 60 percent of the sales increase from the previous year. The investment in working capital is 25 percent of the sales increase from the previous year. The debt financing each year is equal to 40 percent of the total net investment in capital items and working capital for that year. FCFE is net income minus the net capital investment minus the working capital investment plus the debt financing. The present value of each year's FCFE is found by discounting FCFE at the required rate of return for equity, 10.95 percent.

In Year 6 and beyond, sales will increase at 7 percent annually. Net income will be 10 percent of sales, so net profit will also grow at a 7 percent annual rate. Because they are pegged to the 7 percent sales increase, the investments in capital items and working capital and debt financing will also grow at the same 7 percent rate. The amounts in Year 6 for net income, investment in capital items, investment in working capital, debt financing, and FCFE will grow at 7 percent.

The terminal value of FCFE in Year 6 and beyond is

$$TV_5 = \frac{FCFE_6}{r - g} = \frac{79.235}{0.1095 - 0.07} = 2,005.95 \text{ million}$$

The present value of this amount is

$$PV = 2,005.95/(1.1095)^5 = 1,193.12 \text{ million}$$

The estimated total market value of the firm is the present value of FCFE for Years 1 through 5 plus the present value of the terminal value: Market value = 35.692 + 40.475 + 44.763 + 43.211 + 44.433 + 1,193.12 = $1,401.69 million. Dividing by the 70 million outstanding shares gives the estimated value per share of $20.02.

4.4. Three-Stage Growth Models

Three-stage models are a straightforward extension of the two-stage models. One common version of a three-stage model is to assume a constant growth rate in each of the three stages.

The growth rates could be for sales; and profits, investments in fixed and working capital, and external financing could be a function of the level of sales or changes in sales. A more simplistic model would apply the growth rate to FCFF or FCFE.

A second common model is a three-stage model with constant growth rates in Stages 1 and 3 and a declining growth rate in Stage 2. Again, the growth rates could be applied to sales or to FCFF or FCFE. Although it is unlikely that future FCFF and FCFE will follow the assumptions of either of these three-stage growth models, analysts often consider such models to provide useful approximations.

Example 3-19 is a three-stage FCFF valuation model with declining growth rates in Stage 2. The model is directly forecasting FCFF instead of deriving FCFF from a more complicated model that estimates cash flow from operations and investments in fixed capital and working capital. Because Marathon Oil spun off substantial assets in 2001, the analyst is unsure how much value remains in the company. Hence, he is updating his valuation of the firm with a new model and estimated parameters.

EXAMPLE 3-19   A Three-Stage FCFF Valuation Model with Declining Growth in Stage 2

Charles Jones is evaluating Marathon Oil Company (NYSE: MRO) using a three-stage growth model. He has accumulated the following information:

- Current FCFF = $745 million
- Outstanding shares = 309.39 million
- Equity beta = 0.90, risk-free rate = 5.04 percent, and equity risk premium = 5.5 percent
- Cost of debt = 7.1 percent
- Marginal tax rate = 34 percent
- Capital structure = 20 percent debt, 80 percent equity
- Long-term debt = $1.518 billion
- Growth rate of FCFF =

  - 8.8 percent annually in Stage 1, Years 1-4
  - 7.4 percent in Year 5, 6.0 percent in Year 6, 4.6 percent in Year 7
  - 3.2 percent in Year 8 and thereafter

Using the information that Jones has accumulated, estimate the following:

1. WACC
2. Total value of the firm
3. Total value of equity
4. Value per share

Solution to 1: The required return for equity is

$$r = E(R_i) = R_F + \beta_i[E(R_M) - R_F] = 5.04\% + 0.9(5.5\%) = 9.99\%$$

WACC is

$$\text{WACC} = 0.20(7.1\%)(1 - 0.34) + 0.80(9.99\%) = 8.93\%$$

Solution to 2: Table 3-15 displays the projected FCFF over the next eight years and the present values of each, discounted at 8.93 percent:

TABLE 3-15   Forecasted FCFF for Marathon Oil

Year	1	2	3	4	5	6	7	8
Growth rate	8.80%	8.80%	8.80%	8.80%	7.40%	6.00%	4.60%	3.20%
FCFF	811	882	959	1,044	1,121	1,188	1,243	1,283
PV at 8.93%	744	743	742	741	731	711	683	

The terminal value at the end of Year 7 is

$$\text{TV}_7 = \text{FCFF}_8/(\text{WACC} - g) = 1,283/(0.0893 - 0.032) = \$22,391 \text{ million}$$

The present value of this amount, discounted at 8.93 percent for seven years, is

$$\text{PV of TV}_7 = 22,391/(1.0893)^7 = \$12,304 \text{ million}$$

The total present value of the first seven years' FCFF is $5,097 million. The total value of the firm is $12,304 million + $5,097 million = $17,401 million.

Solution to 3: The value of equity is the value of the firm minus the market value of debt: $17,401 million − $1,518 million = $15,883 million.

Solution to 4: Dividing the equity value by the number of shares yields the value per share: $15,883 million/309.39 million = $51.33.

5. NONOPERATING ASSETS AND FIRM VALUE

If a company has significant nonoperating assets such as excess cash, excess marketable securities, or land held for investment, then analysts often calculate the value of the firm as the value of its operating assets plus the value of its nonoperating assets:

$$\text{Value of firm} = \text{Value of operating assets} + \text{Value of nonoperating assets} \qquad (3\text{-}17)$$

Recall that when calculating FCFF or FCFE, investments in working capital do not include any investments in cash and marketable securities. The value of cash and marketable securities should be added to the value of the company's operating assets to find the total firm value. Some companies have substantial noncurrent investments in stocks and bonds that are not operating subsidiaries but financial investments. These investments should be reflected at their current market value. Those securities reported at book values based on accounting conventions should be revalued to market values.

6. SUMMARY

Discounted cash flow models are used widely by analysts to value companies.

- Free cash flow to the firm (FCFF) and free cash flow to equity (FCFE) are the cash flows available to all of the investors in the company and to common stockholders, respectively.
- Analysts like to use free cash flow as return (either FCFF or FCFF)
  - if the company is not dividend paying,
  - if the company is dividend paying but dividends differ significantly from the company's capacity to pay dividends,
  - if free cash flows align with profitability within a reasonable forecast period with which the analyst is comfortable, or
  - if the investor takes a control perspective.
- The FCFF valuation approach estimates the value of the firm as the present value of future FCFF discounted at the weighted average cost of capital (WACC):

$$\text{Firm value} = \sum_{t=1}^{\infty} \frac{\text{FCFF}_t}{(1 + \text{WACC})^t}$$

The value of equity is the value of the firm minus the value of the firm's debt:

$$\text{Equity value} = \text{Firm value} - \text{Market value of debt}$$

Dividing the total value of equity by the number of outstanding shares gives the value per share.

The WACC formula is

$$\text{WACC} = \frac{\text{MV(Debt)}}{\text{MV(Debt)} + \text{MV(Equity)}} r_d (1 - \text{Tax rate}) + \frac{\text{MV(Equity)}}{\text{MV(Debt)} + \text{MV(Equity)}} r$$

- The value of the firm if FCFF is growing at a constant rate is

$$\text{Firm value} = \frac{\text{FCFF}_1}{\text{WACC} - g} = \frac{\text{FCFF}_0 (1 + g)}{\text{WACC} - g}$$

- With the FCFE valuation approach, the value of equity can be found by discounting FCFE at the required rate of return on equity (r):

$$\text{Equity value} = \sum_{t=1}^{\infty} \frac{\text{FCFE}_t}{(1 + r)^t}$$

Dividing the total value of equity by the number of outstanding shares gives the value per share.

- The value of equity if FCFE is growing at a constant rate is

$$\text{Equity value} = \frac{\text{FCFE}_1}{r - g} = \frac{\text{FCFE}_0(1 + g)}{r - g}$$

- FCFF and FCFE are frequently calculated starting with net income:

$$\text{FCFF} = \text{NI} + \text{NCC} + \text{Int}(1 - \text{Tax rate}) - \text{FCInv} - \text{WCInv}$$

$$\text{FCFE} = \text{NI} + \text{NCC} - \text{FCInv} - \text{WCInv} + \text{Net borrowing}$$

- FCFF and FCFE are related to each other as follows:

$$\text{FCFE} = \text{FCFF} - \text{Int}(1 - \text{Tax rate}) + \text{Net borrowing}$$

- FCFF and FCFE can be calculated starting from cash flow from operations:

$$\text{FCFF} = \text{CFO} + \text{Int}(1 - \text{Tax rate}) - \text{FCInv}$$

$$\text{FCFE} = \text{CFO} - \text{FCInv} + \text{Net borrowing}$$

- FCFF can also be calculated from EBIT or EBITDA:

$$\text{FCFF} = \text{EBIT}(1 - \text{Tax rate}) + \text{Dep} - \text{FCInv} - \text{WCInv}$$

$$\text{FCFF} = \text{EBITDA}(1 - \text{Tax rate}) + \text{Dep}(\text{Tax rate}) - \text{FCInv} - \text{WCInv}$$

FCFE can then be found by using $\text{FCFE} = \text{FCFF} - \text{Int}(1 - \text{Tax rate}) + \text{Net borrowing}$.
- Finding CFO, FCFF, and FCFE can require careful interpretation of corporate financial statements. In some cases, the needed information may not be transparent.
- Earnings components such as net income, EBIT, EBITDA, and CFO should not be used as cash flow measures to value a firm. These earnings components either double-count or ignore parts of the cash flow stream.
- More-complicated capital structures, such as those with preferred stock, are easily adapted to find FCFF or FCFE.
- A general expression for the two-stage FCFF valuation model is

$$\text{Firm value} = \sum_{t=1}^{n} \frac{\text{FCFF}_t}{(1 + \text{WACC})^t} + \frac{\text{FCFF}_{n+1}}{(\text{WACC} - g)} \frac{1}{(1 + \text{WACC})^n}$$

- A general expression for the two-stage FCFE valuation model is

$$\text{Equity value} = \sum_{t=1}^{n} \frac{\text{FCFE}_t}{(1 + r)^t} + \frac{\text{FCFE}_{n+1}}{r - g} \frac{1}{(1 + r)^n}$$

- One common two-stage model assumes a constant growth rate in each stage, and a second common model assumes declining growth in Stage 1 followed by a long-run sustainable growth rate in Stage 2.

- To forecast FCFF and FCFE, analysts build a variety of models of varying complexity. A common approach is to forecast sales, with profitability, investments, and financing derived from changes in sales.
- Three-stage models are often considered to be good approximations for cash flow streams that, in reality, fluctuate from year to year.
- Nonoperating assets such as excess cash and marketable securities, noncurrent investment securities, and nonperforming assets are usually segregated from the company's operating assets. They are valued separately and then added to the value of the company's operating assets to find total firm value.

PROBLEMS

1. Indicate the effect on this period's FCFF and FCFE of a change in each of the items listed below. Assume a $100 increase in each case and a 40 percent tax rate.
   A. Net income
   B. Cash operating expenses
   C. Depreciation
   D. Interest expense
   E. EBIT
   F. Accounts receivable
   G. Accounts payable
   H. Property, plant, and equipment
   I. Notes payable
   J. Cash dividends paid
   K. Proceeds from issuing new common shares
   L. Common stock share repurchases

2. LaForge Systems, Inc., has net income of $285 million for the year 2003. Using information from the company's financial statements below, show the adjustments to net income that would be required to find:
   A. FCFF, and
   B. FCFE.
   C. In addition, show the adjustments to FCFF that would result in FCFE.

LaForge Systems, Inc.
Balance Sheet

In millions	December 31, 2002	2003
Assets		
Current assets		
Cash and equivalents	$210	$248
Accounts receivable	474	513
Inventory	520	564
Total current assets	1,204	1,325
Gross fixed assets	2,501	2,850
Accumulated depreciation	(604)	(784)
Net fixed assets	1,897	2,066
Total assets	$3,101	$3,391

Liabilities and shareholders' equity
Current liabilities

Accounts payable	$295	$317
Notes payable	300	310
Accrued taxes and expenses	76	99
Total current liabilities	671	726
Long-term debt	1,010	1,050
Common stock	50	50
Additional paid-in capital	300	300
Retained earnings	1,070	1,265
Total shareholders' equity	1,420	1,615
Total liabilities and shareholders' equity	$3,101	$3,391

Statement of Income

In millions, except per share data	December 31, 2003
Total revenues	$2,215
Operating costs and expenses	1,430
EBITDA	785
Depreciation	180
EBIT	605
Interest expense	130
Income before tax	475
Taxes (at 40 percent)	190
Net income	285
Dividends	90
Addition to retained earnings	195

Statement of Cash Flows

In millions	December 31, 2003
Operating activities	
Net income	$285
Adjustments	
Depreciation	180
Changes in working capital	
Accounts receivable	(39)
Inventories	(44)
Accounts payable	22
Accrued taxes and expenses	23
Cash provided by operating activities	$427
Investing activities	
Purchases of fixed assets	349
Cash used for investing activities	$349
Financing activities	
Notes payable	(10)
Long-term financing issuances	(40)
Common stock dividends	90
Cash used for financing activities	$40

Cash and equivalents increase (decrease)	38
Cash and equivalents at beginning of year	210
Cash and equivalents at end of year	$248
Supplemental cash flow disclosures	
Interest paid	$130
Income taxes paid	$190

3. For LaForge Systems, whose financial statements are given in Problem 2 above, show the adjustments from the current levels of CFO (which is 427), EBIT (605), and EBITDA (785) to find

   A. FCFF, and
   B. FCFE.

4. The term "free cash flow" is frequently applied to cash flows that differ from the definition for FCFF that should be used to value a firm. Two such definitions of "free cash flow" are given below. Compare the definitions given for FCF to FCFF.

   A. FCF = Net income + Depreciation and amortization − Cash dividends − Capital expenditures
   B. FCF = Cash flow from operations (from the statement of cash flows) − Capital expenditures

5. Proust Company has FCFF of $1.7 billion and FCFE of $1.3 billion. Proust's WACC is 11 percent and its required rate of return for equity is 13 percent. FCFF is expected to grow forever at 7 percent and FCFE is expected to grow forever at 7.5 percent. Proust has debt outstanding of $15 billion.

   A. What is the total value of Proust's equity using the FCFF valuation approach?
   B. What is the total value of Proust's equity using the FCFE valuation approach?

6. Quinton Johnston is evaluating Taiwan Semiconductor Manufacturing Co., Ltd., (NYSE: TSM) headquartered in Hsinchu, Taiwan. In 2001, when Johnston is performing his analysis, the company—and indeed, the whole industry—is unprofitable. Furthermore, TSM pays no dividends on its common shares. Johnston decides to value TSM using his forecasts of FCFE and makes the following assumptions:

   - The company has 17.0 billion outstanding shares.
   - Sales will be $5.5 billion in 2002, increasing at 28 percent annually for the next four years (through 2006).
   - Net income will be 32 percent of sales.
   - Investment in fixed assets will be 35 percent of sales, investment in working capital will be 6 percent of sales, and depreciation will be 9 percent of sales.
   - 20 percent of the investment in assets will be financed with debt.
   - Interest expenses will be only 2 percent of sales.
   - The tax rate will be 10 percent.
   - TSM's beta is 2.1, the risk-free government bond rate is 6.4 percent, and the equity risk premium is 5.0 percent.
   - At the end of 2006, Johnston projects TSM will sell for 18 times earnings.

   What is the value of one ordinary share of Taiwan Semiconductor Manufacturing Co., Ltd.?

7. Do Pham is evaluating Phaneuf Accelerateur using the FCFF and FCFE valuation approaches. Pham has collected the following information (currency in euro):

   - Phaneuf has net income of 250 million, depreciation of 90 million, capital expenditures of 170 million, and an increase in working capital of 40 million.
   - Phaneuf will finance 40 percent of the increase in net fixed assets (capital expenditures less depreciation) and 40 percent of the increase in working capital with debt financing.
   - Interest expenses are 150 million. The current market value of Phaneuf's outstanding debt is 1,800 million.
   - FCFF is expected to grow at 6.0 percent indefinitely, and FCFE is expected to grow at 7.0 percent.
   - The tax rate is 30 percent.
   - Phaneuf is financed with 40 percent debt and 60 percent equity. The before-tax cost of debt is 9 percent and the before-tax cost of equity is 13 percent.
   - Phaneuf has 10 million outstanding shares.

     A. Using the FCFF valuation approach, estimate the total value of the firm, the total market value of equity, and the value per share.
     B. Using the FCFE valuation approach, estimate the total market value of equity and the value per share.

8. PHB Company currently sells for $32.50 per share. In an attempt to determine if PHB is fairly priced, an analyst has assembled the following information:

   - The before-tax required rates of return on PHB debt, preferred stock, and common stock are 7.0 percent, 6.8 percent, and 11.0 percent, respectively.
   - The company's target capital structure is 30 percent debt, 15 percent preferred stock, and 55 percent common stock.
   - The market value of the company's debt is $145 million, and its preferred stock is valued at $65 million.
   - PHB's FCFF for the year just ended is $28 million. FCFF is expected to grow at a constant rate of 4 percent for the foreseeable future.
   - The tax rate is 35 percent.
   - PHB has 8 million outstanding common shares.

   What is PHB's estimated value per share? Is PHB's stock underpriced?

9. Watson Dunn is planning to value BHP Billiton Ltd. (NYSE: BHP) using a single-stage FCFF approach. BHP Billiton, headquartered in Melbourne, Australia, provides a variety of industrial metals and minerals. The financial information Dunn has assembled for his valuation is as follows:

   - The company has 1,852 million shares outstanding.
   - Market value of debt is $3.192 billion.
   - FCFF is currently $1.1559 billion.
   - Equity beta is 0.90, the equity risk premium is 5.5 percent, and the risk-free rate is 5.5 percent.
   - The before-tax cost of debt is 7.0 percent.
   - The tax rate is 40 percent.
   - To calculate WACC, assume the company is financed 25 percent with debt.
   - FCFF growth rate is 4 percent.

Using Dunn's information, calculate the following:

A. WACC

B. Value of the firm

C. Total market value of equity

D. Value per share

10. Kenneth McCoin is valuing McDonald's Corporation and performing a sensitivity analysis on his valuation. He uses a single-stage FCFE growth model. The "base case" values for each of the parameters in the model are given in the table below, along with possible "low" and "high" estimates for each variable.

Variable	Base Case Value	Low Estimate	High Estimate
Normalized $FCFE_0$	$0.88	$0.70	$1.14
Risk-free rate	5.08%	5.00%	5.20%
Equity risk premium	5.50%	4.50%	6.50%
Beta	0.70	0.60	0.80
FCFE growth rate	6.40%	4.00%	7.00%

A. Use the base case values to estimate the current value of McDonald's Corporation.

B. Calculate the range of stock prices that would occur if the base case value for $FCFE_0$ were replaced by the low and high estimates for $FCFE_0$. Similarly, using the base case values for all other variables, calculate the range of stock prices caused by the using the low and high values for beta, the risk-free rate, the equity risk premium, and the growth rate. Rank the sensitivity of the stock price to each of the five variables based on these ranges.

11. An aggressive financial planner who claims to have a superior method for picking undervalued stocks is courting one of your clients. The planner claims that the best way to find the value of a stock is to divide EBITDA by the risk-free bond rate. The planner is urging your client to invest in Alcan, Inc. (NYSE: AL). Alcan is the parent of a group of companies engaged in all aspects of the aluminum business. The planner says that Alcan's EBITDA of $1,580 million divided by the long-term government bond rate of 7 percent gives a total value of $22,571 million. With 318 million outstanding shares, Alcan's value per share using this method is $70.98. Shares of Alcan currently trade for $36.50, and the planner wants your client to make a large investment in Alcan through him.

A. Provide your client with an alternative valuation of Alcan based on a two-stage FCFE valuation approach. Use the following assumptions:

- Net income is currently $600 million. Net income will grow by 20 percent annually for the next three years.
- The net investment in operating assets (capital expenditures less depreciation plus investment in working capital) will be $1,150 million next year and grow at 15 percent for the following two years.
- Forty percent of the net investment in operating assets will be financed with net new debt financing.
- Alcan's beta is 1.3, the risk-free bond rate is 7 percent, and the equity risk premium is 4 percent.

- After three years, the growth rate of net income will be 8 percent and the net investment in operating assets (capital expenditures minus depreciation plus increase in working capital) each year will drop to 30 percent of net income.
- Debt is, and will continue to be, 40 percent of total assets.
- Alcan has 318 million outstanding shares.

  Find the value per share of Alcan.
  B. Criticize the valuation approach that the aggressive financial planner used.

12. Bron has earnings per share of $3.00 in 2002 and expects earnings per share to increase by 21 percent in 2003. Earnings per share are expected to grow at a decreasing rate for the following five years, as shown in the table below. In 2008, the growth rate will be 6 percent and is expected to stay at that rate thereafter. Net capital expenditures (capital expenditures minus depreciation) will be $5.00 per share in 2002 and then follow the pattern predicted in the table. In 2008, net capital expenditures are expected to be $1.50 and will then grow at 6 percent annually. The investment in working capital parallels the increase in net capital expenditures and is predicted to equal 25 percent of net capital expenditures each year. In 2008, investment in working capital will be $0.375 and is predicted to grow at 6 percent thereafter. Bron will use debt financing to fund 40 percent of net capital expenditures and 40 percent of the investment in working capital.

Year	2003	2004	2005	2006	2007	2008
Growth rate for earnings per share	21%	18%	15%	12%	9%	6%
Net capital expenditure per share	$5.00	$5.00	$4.50	$4.00	$3.50	$1.50

The required rate of return for Bron is 12 percent. Find the value per share using a two-stage FCFE valuation approach.

13. (Adapted from CFA Level II exam, 2000) The management of Telluride, an international diversified conglomerate based in the United States, believes that the recent strong performance of its wholly owned medical supply subsidiary, Sundanci, has gone unnoticed. To realize Sundanci's full value, Telluride announced that it will divest Sundanci in a tax-free spinoff.

    Sue Carroll, CFA, is Director of Research at Kesson and Associates. In developing an investment recommendation for Sundanci, Carroll has gathered the information shown in Tables 3-16 and 3-17 below.

    Abbey Naylor, CFA, has been directed by Carroll to determine the value of Sundanci's stock using the FCFE model. Naylor believes that Sundanci's FCFE will grow at 27 percent for two years, and 13 percent thereafter. Capital expenditures, depreciation, and working capital are all expected to increase proportionately with FCFE.

    A. Calculate the amount of FCFE per share for 2000 using the data from Table 3-16. Show your work.
    B. Calculate the current value of a share of Sundanci stock based on the two-stage FCFE model. Show your work.
    C. Describe limitations that the two-stage DDM and FCFE models have in common.

TABLE 3-16   Sundanci Actual 1999 and 2000 Financial Statements for
Fiscal Years Ending 31 May (in millions, except per-share data)

Income Statement	1999	2000
Revenue	$474	$598
Depreciation	20	23
Other operating costs	368	460
Income before taxes	86	115
Taxes	26	35
Net income	60	80
Dividends	18	24
Earnings per share	$0.714	$0.952
Dividends per share	$0.214	$0.286
Common shares outstanding	84.0	84.0

Balance Sheet	1999	2000
Current assets (includes $5 cash in 1999 and 2000)	$201	$326
Net property, plant, and equipment	474	489
Total assets	675	815
Current liabilities (all non-interest bearing)	57	141
Long-term debt	0	0
Total liabilities		
Shareholders' equity	618	674
Total liabilities and equity	675	815
Capital expenditures	34	38

TABLE 3-17   Selected Financial Information

Required rate of return on equity	14%
Industry growth rate	13%
Industry P/E	26

14. (Adapted from CFA Level II exam, 2001) John Jones, CFA, is head of the research department of Peninsular Research. One of the companies he is researching, Mackinac Inc., is a U.S.–based manufacturing company. Mackinac has released its June 2001 financial statements, shown in Tables 3-18, 3-19, 3-20.

Mackinac has announced that it has finalized an agreement to handle North American production of a successful product currently marketed by a foreign company. Jones decides to value Mackinac using the dividend discount model (DDM) and the free cash flow to equity (FCFE) model. After reviewing Mackinac's financial statements and forecasts related to the new production agreement, Jones concludes the following:

- Mackinac's earnings and FCFE are expected to grow 17 percent a year over the next three years before stabilizing at an annual growth rate of 9 percent.
- Mackinac will maintain the current payout ratio.
- Mackinac's beta is 1.25.
- The government bond yield is 6 percent, and the market equity risk premium is 5 percent.

TABLE 3-18   Mackinac Inc. Annual Income Statement
June 30, 2001 (in thousands, except per-share data)

Sales	$250,000
Cost of goods sold	125,000
Gross operating profit	125,000
Selling, general, and administrative expenses	50,000
EBITDA	75,000
Depreciation and amortization	10,500
EBIT	64,500
Interest expense	11,000
Pretax income	53,500
Income taxes	16,050
Net income	$37,450
Shares outstanding	13,000
EPS	$2.88

TABLE 3-19   Mackinac Inc. Balance Sheet June 30, 2001 (in thousands)

Current Assets		
Cash and equivalents	$20,000	
Receivables	40,000	
Inventories	29,000	
Other current assets	23,000	
Total current assets		$112,000
Noncurrent Assets		
Property, plant, and equipment	$145,000	
Less: Accumulated depreciation	(43,000)	
Net property, plant, and equipment	102,000	
Investments	70,000	
Other noncurrent assets	36,000	
Total noncurrent assets		208,000
Total assets		$320,000
Current Liabilities		
Accounts payable	$41,000	
Short-term debt	12,000	
Other current liabilities	17,000	
Total current liabilities		$70,000
Noncurrent Liabilities		
Long-term debt	100,000	
Total noncurrent liabilities		100,000
Total liabilities		170,000
Shareholders' Equity		
Common equity	40,000	
Retained earnings	110,000	
Total equity		150,000
Total liabilities and equity		$320,000

TABLE 3-20   Mackinac Inc. Cash Flow Statement June 30, 2001
(in thousands)

Cash Flow from Operating Activities		
Net income		$37,450
Depreciation and amortization		10,500
Change in Working Capital		
(Increase) Decrease) in receivables	($5,000)	
(Increase) Decrease in inventories	(8,000)	
Increase (Decrease) in payables	6,000	
Increase (Decrease) in other current liabilities	1,500	
Net change in working capital		(5,500)
Net cash from operating activities		$42,450
Cash Flow from Investing Activities		
Purchase of property, plant, and equipment	($15,000)	
Net cash from investing activities		($15,000)
Cash Flow from Financing Activities		
Change in debt outstanding	$4,000	
Payment of cash dividends	(22,470)	
Net cash from financing activities		(18,470)
Net change in cash and cash equivalents		$8,980
Cash at beginning of period		11,020
Cash at end of period		$20,000

A. Calculate the value of a share of Mackinac's common stock using the two-stage DDM. Show your calculations.
B. Calculate the value of a share of Mackinac's common stock using the two-stage FCFE model. Show your calculations.
C. Jones is discussing with a corporate client the possibility of that client acquiring a 70 percent interest in Mackinac. Discuss whether the DDM or FCFE model is more appropriate for this client's valuation purposes.

15. SK Telecom Co. is a cellular telephone paging and computer communication services company in Seoul, South Korea. The company is traded on the Korea, New York, and London stock exchanges (NYSE: SKM). Sol Kim has estimated the normalized FCFE for SK Telecom to be 1,300 Korean won (per share) for the year just ended. The real country return for South Korea is 6.50 percent. To estimate the required return for SK Telecom, the adjustments to the real country return are an industry adjustment of +0.60 percent, a size adjustment of −0.10 percent, and a leverage adjustment of +0.25 percent. The long-term real growth rate for South Korea is estimated at 3.5 percent, and Kim expects the real growth rate of SK Telecom to track the country rate.
A. What is the real required rate of return for SK Telecom?
B. Using the single-stage FCFE valuation model and real values for the discount rate and FCFE growth rate, estimate the value of one share of SK Telecom.

16. Lawrence McKibben is preparing a valuation of Tele Norte Leste Participacoes SA (NYSE: TNE), a telecom services company headquartered in Rio de Janeiro, Brazil. McKibben has decided to use a three-stage FCFE valuation model and the following estimates. The FCFE per share for the current year is $0.75. FCFE is expected to grow at 10 percent

for next year, then at 26 percent annually for the following three years, and then grow at 6 percent in Year 5 and thereafter. TNE's estimated beta is 2.00, and McKibben feels that current market conditions dictate a 4.5 percent risk-free rate of return and a 5.0 percent equity risk premium. Given McKibben's assumptions and approach, what is the value of Tele Norte Leste Participacoes?

17. Clay Cooperman has valued the operating assets of Johnson Extrusion at $720 million. The company also has short-term cash and securities with a market value of $60 million. The noncurrent investments have a book value of $30 million and a market value of $45 million. The company also has an overfunded pension plan, with plan assets of $210 million and plan liabilities of $170 million. Johnson Extrusion has $215 million of notes and bonds outstanding and 100 million outstanding shares. What is the value per share?

CHAPTER 4

MARKET-BASED VALUATION: PRICE MULTIPLES

LEARNING OUTCOMES

After completing this chapter, you will be able to do the following:

- Distinguish among types of valuation indicators.
- Distinguish between the method of comparables and the method based on forecasted fundamentals as approaches to using price multiples in valuation.
- Define a justified price multiple.
- Discuss the economic rationales for the method of comparables and the method based on forecasted fundamentals.
- List and discuss rationales for each price multiple and dividend yield in valuation.
- Discuss possible drawbacks to the use of each price multiple and dividend yield.
- Define and calculate each price multiple and dividend yield.
- Define underlying earnings, and calculate underlying earnings given earnings per share (EPS) and nonrecurring items in the income statement.
- Define normalized EPS, discuss the methods of normalizing EPS, and calculate normalized EPS by each method.
- Explain and justify the use of earnings yield (E/P).
- Identify and discuss the fundamental factors that influence each price multiple and dividend yield.
- Calculate the justified price-to-earnings ratio (P/E), price-to-book ratio (P/B), and price-to-sales ratio (P/S) for a stock, based on forecasted fundamentals.
- Calculate a predicted P/E given a cross-sectional regression on fundamentals and explain limitations to the cross-sectional regression methodology.
- Define the benchmark value of a multiple.
- Evaluate a stock using the method of comparables.
- Discuss the importance of fundamentals in using the method of comparables.
- Define and calculate the P/E-to-growth (PEG) ratio and explain its use in relative valuation.
- Calculate and explain the use of price multiples in determining terminal value in a multistage discounted cash flow (DCF) model.
- Discuss alternative definitions of cash flow used in price multiples and explain the limitations of each.

- Discuss the sources of differences in cross-border valuation comparisons.
- Describe the main types of momentum indicators and their use in valuation.
- Explain the use of stock screens in investment management.

1. INTRODUCTION

Among the most familiar and widely used valuation tools are price multiples. **Price multiples** are ratios of a stock's market price to some measure of value per share. The intuition behind price multiples is that we cannot evaluate a stock's price—judge whether it is fairly valued, overvalued, or undervalued—without knowing what a share buys in terms of assets, earnings, or some other measure of value. As valuation indicators (measures or indicators of value), price multiples have the appealing qualities of simplicity in use and ease in communication. A price multiple summarizes in a single number the valuation relationship between a stock's price and a familiar quantity such as earnings, sales, or book value per share. Among the questions we will study in this chapter that will help us use price multiples professionally are the following:

- What accounting issues affect particular price multiples, and how can analysts address them?
- How do price multiples relate to fundamentals, such as earnings growth rates, and how can analysts use this information when making valuation comparisons among stocks?
- For which types of valuation problems is a particular price multiple appropriate or inappropriate?
- What challenges arise in applying price multiples internationally?

According to surveys of professional practice, **momentum indicators** are popular. These relate either price or a fundamental (such as earnings) to the time series of its own past values, or in some cases to its expected value. The logic behind the use of momentum indicators is the proposition that such indicators may provide information on future patterns of returns over some time horizon. Because the purpose of valuation is to help select rewarding investments, momentum indicators are also a class of valuation indicators, with a focus different from and complementary to that of price multiples.

The chapter is organized as follows: In Section 2, we put the use of price multiples in its economic context and present certain themes common to the use of any price multiple. We then begin a treatment of individual ratios: Section 3 presents price-to-earnings multiples (P/Es), Section 4 presents price-to-book multiples (P/Bs), Section 5 presents price-to-sales multiples (P/Ss), and Section 6 presents price-to-cash flow multiples.

Enterprise value is the total market value of all sources of financing including common stock (a more technical definition will follow); EBITDA (earnings before interest, tax, depreciation, and amortization) is an accounting concept related to cash flow from operations. We present valuation using the ratio of enterprise value to EBITDA in Section 7. Dividends in relation to price have been used as a valuation indicator. Because the ratio of price to dividends is not defined for stocks that do not pay dividends, we discuss valuation in terms of dividend yield (D/P) in Section 8. Section 9 presents issues in using price multiples internationally. In Section 10, we turn to a discussion of momentum valuation indicators. We present some practical aspects of using valuation indicators in investment management in Section 11, and we summarize the chapter in Section 12.

2. PRICE MULTIPLES IN VALUATION

In practice, analysts use price multiples in two ways: the method of comparables and the method based on forecasted fundamentals. Each of these methods relates to a definite economic rationale. In this section, we introduce the two methods and their associated economic rationales.

The idea behind price multiples is that we need to evaluate a stock's price in relation to what it buys in terms of earnings, assets, or some other measure of value. Obtained by dividing price by a measure of value per share, a price multiple gives the price to purchase one unit of value, however value is measured. For example, a price-to-sales ratio of 2 means that it takes two units of currency (for example, €2) to buy one unit of sales (for example, €1 of sales).

This scaling of price per share by value per share also makes comparisons possible among different stocks. For example, an investor pays more for a unit of sales for a stock with a P/S of 2.5 than for another stock with a P/S of 2. If the securities are otherwise closely similar (if they have similar risk, profit margins, and growth prospects, for example), the investor might conclude that the second security is undervalued relative to the first.

So, price multiples are price scaled by a measure of value, which provides the basis for the method of comparables. The **method of comparables** involves using a price multiple to evaluate whether an asset is relatively fairly valued, relatively undervalued, or relatively overvalued when compared to a benchmark value of the multiple. The word *relatively* is necessary. An asset may be undervalued relative to a comparison asset or group of assets, and an analyst may expect the asset to outperform the comparison asset or assets on a relative basis. If the comparison asset or assets themselves are not efficiently priced, however, the stock may not be undervalued—it could be fairly valued or even overvalued (on an absolute basis).

Many choices for the benchmark value of a multiple have appeared in stock valuation, including the multiple of a closely matched individual stock as well as the average or median value of the multiple for the stock's company or industry peer group. The economic rationale underlying the method of comparables is the law of one price—the economic principle that two identical assets should sell at the same price.[1] The method of comparables is perhaps the most widely used approach for analysts reporting valuation judgments on the basis of price multiples.

Because cash flows are related to fundamentals, we can also relate multiples to company fundamentals through a discounted cash flow (DCF) model. Expressions for price multiples in terms of fundamentals permit analysts to examine how valuation differences across stocks relate to different expectations concerning fundamentals such as earnings growth rates.

Recall that DCF models view the intrinsic value of stock as the present value of all its expected future returns or cash flows. Fundamentals—characteristics of a business related to profitability or financial strength—drive cash flows. Price multiples are calculated with respect to a single value of a fundamental, such as earnings per share (EPS). For example, we calculate what we will later discuss as a leading price–earnings multiple (P/E) on the basis of a forecast of EPS for the next year. Despite being stated with respect to only a single value of a fundamental, we can relate any price multiple to the entire future stream of expected cash flows

---

[1]In practice, analysts can at best only approximately match characteristics across companies. To keep our classification simple, we treat comparisons with a market index and with historical values of a stock's multiple under the rubric of the method of comparables. Nevertheless, the law of one price is the idea driving the method of comparables.

through its DCF value. We do this by first taking the present value of the stream of expected future cash flows; we then divide that present value by the fundamental (e.g., forecasted EPS).

For example, if the DCF value of a U.K. stock is GBP10.20 and forecasted EPS is GBP1.2, the P/E consistent with the DCF value is GBP10.20/GBP1.2 = 8.5. We can do this exercise using any DCF model (defining cash flows as dividends, free cash flow, or residual income) and any definition of price multiple. We illustrated this concept in Chapter 2, where we explained P/E in terms of perhaps the simplest DCF model, the Gordon growth dividend discount model, in an expression that includes the expected dividend growth rate (among other variables). We call the approach relating a price multiple to fundamentals through a DCF model the **method based on forecasted fundamentals**.[2] DCF valuation, because it incorporates forecasts of all future returns or cash flows, is the most basic valuation approach in theory. That characteristic of DCF models and the possibility of relating price multiples to DCF models provide the economic rationale for the method based on forecasted fundamentals.

We can also usefully incorporate the insights from the method based on forecasted fundamentals in explaining valuation differences based on comparables, because we seldom find other than approximate comparables. In the sections covering each multiple, we will present the method based on forecasted fundamentals first so we can refer to it when using the method of comparables.

In summary, we can approach valuation using multiples from two perspectives. First, we can use the method of comparables, which involves comparing a stock's multiple to a standard of comparison. Similar assets should sell at similar prices. Second, we can use the method based on forecasted fundamentals, which involves forecasting the stock's fundamentals rather than making comparisons with other stocks. The price multiple of an asset should be related to the prospective cash flows from holding it.

Using either method, how can an analyst express his view of the value of a stock? Of course the analyst can offer just the qualitative judgment that the stock appears to be fairly valued, overvalued, or undervalued (and offer definite reasons for the view). The analyst may also be more precise, communicating a **justified price multiple** for the stock: the estimated fair value of that multiple.[3] An analyst can justify a multiple based on the method of comparables or the method based on forecasted fundamentals.

For example, suppose that we are using the price-to-book multiple (P/B) in a valuation and that the mean P/B for the company's peer group, the standard of comparison, is 2.3. The stock's justified P/B, based on the method of comparables, is 2.3 (without making possible adjustments for differences in fundamentals). We can compare the justified with the actual P/B based on market price to form an opinion on value. If the justified P/B is larger (smaller) than the actual P/B, the stock may be undervalued (overvalued). We can also translate the justified P/B based on comparables into an estimate of absolute fair value of the stock, on the assumption that the comparison assets are fairly priced. If the current book value per share is $23, then the fair value of the stock is 2.3 × $23 = $52.90, which can be compared with its market price.

On the other hand, suppose that on the basis of a residual income model valuation (which we will present in Chapter 5), the DCF value of the stock is $46. Then the justified P/B based on forecasted fundamentals is $46/$23 = 2.0, which we can again compare with the actual value of the stock's ratio. We can also state our estimate of the stock's absolute fair value as

---

[2]For brevity, we sometimes use the phrase "based on fundamentals" in describing multiples calculated according to this approach.

[3]The justified price multiple is also called the **warranted price multiple** or the **intrinsic price multiple**.

2 × $23 = $46. (Note that the analyst could report valuation judgments related to a DCF model in terms of the DCF value directly; however, price multiples are a familiar form in which to state valuations.)

In the next section, we begin our discussion of specific implementations of the price multiple approach to valuation.

3. PRICE TO EARNINGS

In the first edition of *Security Analysis*, Benjamin Graham and David L. Dodd (1934, p. 351) described common stock valuation based on P/Es as the standard method of that era, and the price-to-earnings ratio is doubtless still the most familiar valuation measure today.

We begin our discussion of the P/E with rationales offered by analysts for its use, as well as possible drawbacks. We then define the two chief variations of the P/E: the trailing P/E and the leading P/E. The multiple's numerator, market price, is (as in other multiples) definitely determinable; it presents no special problems of interpretation. But the denominator, EPS, is based on the complex rules of accrual accounting and presents important interpretation issues. We discuss those issues and the adjustments analysts can make to obtain more-meaningful P/Es. Finally, we conclude the section by examining how analysts use P/Es to value a stock using the method of forecasted fundamentals and the method of comparables. As mentioned earlier, we discuss fundamentals first so that we can draw from that discussion's insights when using comparables.

Analysts have offered several rationales for using P/Es:

- Earnings power is a chief driver of investment value, and EPS, the denominator of the P/E ratio, is perhaps the chief focus of security analysts' attention. In Block's 1999 survey, earnings ranked first among four variables—earnings, cash flow, book value, and dividends—as an input in valuation.
- The P/E ratio is widely recognized and used by investors.
- Differences in P/Es may be related to differences in long-run average returns, according to empirical research.[4]

Drawbacks to using P/Es derive from the characteristics of EPS:

- EPS can be negative, and the P/E ratio does not make economic sense with a negative denominator.
- The ongoing or recurring components of earnings are the most important in determining intrinsic value. Earnings often have volatile, transient components, however, making the analyst's task difficult.
- Management can exercise its discretion within allowable accounting practices to distort EPS as an accurate reflection of economic performance. Distortions can affect the comparability of P/Es across companies.

Analysts have developed methods to attempt to address these potential drawbacks, and we will discuss these methods later. In the next section, we discuss the definition and calculation of EPS for use in P/Es.

---

[4]Block (1999) documented a belief among CFA Institute members that low–P/E stocks tend to outperform the market. See Bodie, Kane, and Marcus (2001) for a brief summary of the related academic research, which has wide ramifications and is the subject of continuing active debate.

3.1. Determining Earnings

In calculating a P/E, the current price for publicly traded companies is generally easily obtained and unambiguous. Determining the earnings figure to be used in the denominator, however, is not as straightforward. The following two issues must be considered:

- the time horizon over which earnings are measured, which results in two chief alternative definitions of the P/E, and
- adjustments to accounting earnings that the analyst may make, so that P/Es can be compared across companies.

The two chief alternative definitions of P/E are trailing P/E and leading P/E. A stock's **trailing P/E** (sometimes referred to as a **current P/E**) is its current market price divided by the most recent four quarters' EPS. In such calculations, EPS is sometimes referred to as trailing 12 months (TTM) EPS. Trailing P/E is the P/E published in financial newspapers' stock listings. The **leading P/E** (also called the **forward P/E** or **prospective P/E**) is a stock's current price divided by next year's expected earnings. Other names and time horizon definitions also exist: First Call/Thomson Financial reports as the "current P/E" a stock's market price divided by the last reported annual EPS; Value Line reports as the "P/E" a stock's market price divided by the sum of the preceding two quarters' trailing earnings and the next two quarters' expected earnings.

In using the P/E, the same definition should be applied to all companies and time periods under examination. Otherwise the P/Es are not comparable, either for a given company over time or for different companies at a specific point in time. The differences in P/E calculated using different methods could be systematic (as opposed to random). For example, for companies with rising earnings, the leading P/E will be smaller than the trailing P/E because the denominator in the leading P/E calculation will be larger.

Logic sometimes indicates that a particular definition of the P/E is not relevant. For example, a major acquisition or divestiture may change the nature of a business so that the trailing P/E based on past EPS is not informative about the future and thus not relevant to a valuation. In such a case, the leading P/E is the appropriate measure. Valuation is a forward-looking process; and the analyst, when she has earnings forecasts, usually features the leading P/E in analyses. If a company's future earnings are not readily predictable, however, then a trailing P/E (or alternative valuation metric) may be more appropriate. In the following sections, we address issues that arise in calculating trailing and leading P/Es.

3.1.1. Calculating the Trailing P/E

When calculating a P/E using trailing earnings, care must be taken in determining the EPS used in the denominator. An analyst must consider the following:

- transitory, nonrecurring components of earnings that are company specific,
- transitory components of earnings due to cyclicality (business or industry cyclicality),
- differences in accounting methods, and
- potential dilution of EPS.

Example 4-1 illustrates the first bullet point. Items in earnings that are not expected to recur in the future (nonrecurring earnings) are generally removed by analysts. Such items are not expected to reappear in future earnings, and valuation looks to the future as concerns cash flows. The analyst's focus is on estimating **underlying earnings**: earnings excluding nonrecurring components.[5] An increase in underlying earnings reflects an increase in earnings that the analyst expects to persist into the future.

EXAMPLE 4-1   Adjusting EPS for Nonrecurring Items

You are calculating a trailing P/E for American Electric Power (NYSE: AEP) as of November 9, 2001, when the share price closed at $44.50. In its fiscal year ended December 13, 2000, AEP recorded EPS of $0.83 that included an extraordinary loss of $0.11. Additionally, AEP took an expense of $203 million for merger costs during that calendar year, which are not expected to recur, and had unusual deficits in two out of four quarters. As of November 2001, the trailing 12 months' EPS was $2.16, including three quarters in 2001 and one quarter in 2000. The fourth quarter of calendar year 2000 had $0.69 per share in nonrecurring expenses. Without making an adjustment for nonrecurring items, the trailing P/E was $44.50/$2.16 = 20.6. Adjusting for these items, you arrive at a figure for trailing EPS of $2.85 using an underlying earnings concept, and a trailing P/E of $44.50/$2.85 = 15.6. This number is the P/E an analyst would use in valuation, being consistent in the treatment of earnings for all stocks under review. In the course of this chapter, we will illustrate adjustments to earnings in many examples.

The identification of nonrecurring items often requires detailed work, in particular the examination of the income statement, the footnotes to the income statement, and management's discussion and analysis. The analyst cannot rely only on income statement classifications in identifying the nonrecurring components of earnings. Nonrecurring items (for example, gains and losses from the sale of assets, asset write-downs, provisions for future losses, and changes in accounting estimates) often appear in the income from continuing operations portion of a business's income statement.[6] An analyst taking the income statement classification at face value could draw incorrect conclusions in a valuation.

Besides company-specific effects such as restructuring costs, transitory effects on earnings can come from business-cycle or industry-cycle influences, as stated in the second bullet point above. These effects are somewhat different in nature. Because business cycles repeat, such effects (although transitory) can be expected to recur over subsequent cycles.

Because of cyclic effects, the most recent four quarters of earnings may not accurately reflect the average or long-term earnings power of the business, particularly for **cyclical businesses**—businesses with high sensitivity to business- or industry-cycle influences. Trailing EPS for such stocks are often depressed or negative at the bottom of the cycle and unusually

---

[5]Other names for underlying earnings include **persistent earnings, continuing earnings**, and **core earnings**.

[6]An asset **write-down** is a reduction in the value of an asset as stated in the balance sheet. The timing and amount of write-downs often are at least in part discretionary. **Accounting estimates** include the useful lives of assets (depreciable lives), warranty costs, and the amount of uncollectible receivables.

high at the top of the cycle. Empirically, P/Es for cyclical companies are often highly volatile over a cycle without any change in business prospects: high P/Es on depressed EPS at the bottom of the cycle and low P/Es on unusually high EPS at the top of the cycle, a countercyclical property of P/Es known as the **Molodovsky effect**.[7] Analysts address this problem by normalizing EPS—that is, calculating the level of EPS that the business could achieve currently under mid-cyclical conditions (**normalized earnings per share** or **normal earnings per share**).[8] Two of several available methods to calculate normal EPS are as follows:

- *The method of historical average EPS.* Normal EPS is calculated as average EPS over the most recent full cycle.
- *The method of average return on equity.* Normal EPS is calculated as the average return on equity (ROE) from the most recent full cycle, multiplied by current book value per share.

The first method is one of several possible statistical approaches to the problem of cyclical earnings; however, this method does not account for changes in the business's size. The second alternative, by using recent book value per share, reflects more accurately the effect on EPS of growth or shrinkage in the company's size. For that reason, the method of average ROE is sometimes preferred.[9] When reported current book value does not adequately reflect company size in relation to past values (because of items such as large write-downs), the analyst can make the appropriate accounting adjustment. The analyst can also estimate normalized earnings by multiplying total assets by an estimate of the long-run return on total assets.[10]

EXAMPLE 4-2   Normalizing EPS for Business-Cycle Effects

You are researching the valuation of Koninklijke Philips Electronics N.V. (NYSE: PHG), Europe's largest electronics company, as of the beginning of November 2001. On November 8, 2001, PHG stock closed at $25.72. PHG experienced a severe cyclical contraction in its Consumer Electronics division in 2001, resulting in a loss of $1.94 per share; you thus decide to normalize earnings. You believe the 1995–2000 period (which excludes 2001) reasonably captures average profitability over a business cycle.

---

[7]Named after Nicholas Molodovsky, who wrote on this subject in the 1950s. We can state the Molodovsky effect another way: P/Es may be negatively related to the recent earnings growth rate but positively related to the anticipated future growth rate, because of expected rebounds in earnings.

[8]The wording is based on a definition in Kisor and Whitbeck (1963, p. 57). Some writers describe the removal of any one-time or nonrecurring items from earnings as normalizing earnings as well.

[9]This approach has appeared in valuation research, as in Michaud (1999), who calculated a normalized earnings yield rather than a normalized P/E. (Earnings yield is earnings per share divided by price.)

[10]An example of the application of this method is Lee, Myers, and Swaminathan (1999), who used 6 percent of total assets as an estimate of normal earnings levels when current earnings for a company were negative, in their study of the intrinsic value of the Dow Jones Industrial Average, a U.S. equity index. According to the authors, the long-run return on total assets in the United States is approximately 6 percent.

Table 4-1 supplies data on EPS, book value per share (BVPS), and return on equity (ROE).[11]

TABLE 4-1   Koninklijke Philips (EPS and BVPS in U.S. Dollars)

	2001	2000	1999	1998	1997	1996	1995
EPS	(1.94)	2.11	1.15	0.87	1.16	0.55	1.14
BVPS	13.87	16.62	9.97	11.68	6.57	6.43	6.32
ROE	NM	0.129	0.104	0.072	0.168	0.083	0.179

NM = not meaningful.
Sources: www.philips.com for 2001 data; *The Value Line Investment Survey* for other data.

Using the data in Table 4-1,

1. Calculate a normal EPS for PHG based on the method of historical average EPS, and then calculate the P/E based on that estimate of normal EPS.
2. Calculate a normal EPS for PHG based on the method of average ROE and the P/E based on that estimate of normal EPS.
3. Explain the source of the differences in the normal EPS calculated by the two methods, and contrast the impact on the estimate of a normal P/E.

Solution to 1: Averaging EPS over the 1995–2000 period, we find that ($1.14 + $0.55 + $1.16 + $0.87 + $1.15 + $2.11)/6 = $1.16. According to the method of historical average EPS, PHG's normal EPS is $1.16. The P/E based on this estimate is $25.72/1.16 = 22.2.

Solution to 2: Averaging ROE over the 1995–2000 period, we find that (0.179 + 0.083 + 0.168 + 0.072 + 0.104 + 0.129)/6 = 0.1225, or 12.25%. For current BVPS, we use the 2001 value of $13.87. According to the method of average ROE, we have 0.1225 × $13.87 = $1.70 as normal EPS. The P/E based on this estimate is $25.72/$1.70 = 15.1.

Solution to 3: From 1995 to 2001, BVPS increased from $6.32 to $13.87, an increase of about 219 percent. The estimate of $1.70 from the average ROE method compared with $1.16 from the historical average EPS method reflects the use of information on the current size of the company. Because of that difference, PHG appears more conservatively valued (as indicated by a lower P/E) using the method based on average ROE.

We also need to adjust EPS for differences in accounting methods between the company and its standard of comparison or benchmark, so that the P/Es are comparable.

---

[11] EPS and BVPS are based on EUR/USD translation rates for 2001 and 2000 and on Dutch guilder/USD translation rates for earlier years, as given by Value Line.

EXAMPLE 4-3   Adjusting for Differences in Accounting Methods

In late October 1999, Coachmen Industries (NYSE: COA) was trading at a price of $16 per share and had trailing 12 months EPS of $1.99. COA's P/E was thus 8.04. At the same time, Winnebago Industries (NYSE: WGO) was trading at a price of $17 per share and had trailing 12 months EPS of $1.99 for a P/E of 8.54. COA uses the first-in, first-out (FIFO) method of accounting for its inventory. WGO uses the last-in, first-out (LIFO) method of accounting for its inventory. Adjusting WGO's results for differences between the LIFO and FIFO methods produces an adjusted EPS of $2.02 and an adjusted P/E of 8.42. Adjusting EPS for WGO for consistency with COA's inventory accounting method narrows the difference between the two companies' P/Es.

In addition to adjustments for nonrecurring items and accounting methods, the analyst should consider the impact of potential dilution on EPS.[12] Companies are required to present both basic EPS and diluted EPS. **Basic earnings per share** reflects total earnings divided by the weighted-average number of shares actually outstanding during the period. **Diluted earnings per share** reflects division by the number of shares that would be outstanding if holders of securities such as executive stock options, equity warrants, and convertible bonds exercised their options to obtain common stock.

EXAMPLE 4-4   Basic versus Diluted Earnings Per Share

For the fiscal year ended June 31, 2001, Microsoft (Nasdaq NMS: MSFT) had basic EPS of $1.38 and diluted EPS of $1.32. Based on a stock price of $60 shortly after the release of the annual report, Microsoft's trailing P/E is 43.5 using basic EPS and 45.5 using diluted EPS.

Two issues concerning P/Es that relate to their use in investment management and research are (1) negative earnings and (2) look-ahead bias in calculating trailing P/Es. (**Look-ahead bias** is the use of information that is not contemporaneously available in computing a quantity.)

Stock selection disciplines that use P/Es or other price multiples often involve ranking stocks from highest value of the multiple to lowest value of the multiple. The security with the lowest positive P/E has the lowest purchase cost per currency unit of earnings among the securities ranked. Negative earnings, however, result in a negative P/E. A negative-P/E

---

[12]Dilution refers to the reduction in the proportional ownership interests as a result of the issuance of new shares.

TABLE 4-2   P/E and E/P for Four Personal Computer Manufacturers
(as of November 13, 2001; in U.S. Dollars)

	Current Price	Trailing EPS	Trailing P/E	E/P
Dell Computer Corporation (Nasdaq NMS: DELL)	26.00	0.49	53.06	1.9%
Apple Computer (Nasdaq NMS: AAPL)	19.20	−0.11	NM	−0.6%
Compaq Computer Corporation (NYSE: CPQ)	8.59	−0.40	NM	−4.7%
Gateway (NYSE: GTW)	8.07	−3.15	NM	−39.0%

Source: Morningstar, Inc.

security will rank below the lowest positive-P/E security but, because earnings are negative, the negative-P/E security is actually the most costly in terms of earnings purchased.[13]

Negative P/Es are not meaningful. In some cases, an analyst might handle negative EPS by using normal EPS in its place. Also, when trailing EPS is negative, year-ahead EPS and thus the leading P/E may be positive. If the analyst is interested in a ranking, an available solution (applicable to any ratio involving a quantity that can be negative or zero) is to restate the ratio with price in the denominator, because price is never negative.[14] In the case of the P/E, the associated ratio is E/P, the **earnings yield** ratio. Ranked by earnings yields from highest to lowest, the securities are correctly ranked from cheapest to most costly in terms of the amount of earnings one unit of currency buys.

Table 4-2 illustrates the above points for a group of personal computer manufacturers, three of which have negative EPS. When reporting a P/E based on negative earnings, analysts should report such P/Es as NM (not meaningful).

Investment analysts often research investment strategies involving P/Es and other price multiples using historical data. When doing so, analysts must be aware that time lags in the reporting of financial results create the potential for look-ahead bias in the research. For example, as of early January 2003, most companies have not reported EPS for the last quarter of 2002, so a trailing P/E would be based on EPS for first, second, and third quarters of 2002 and the last quarter of 2001. An investment strategy based on a trailing P/E calculated using actual EPS for the last quarter of 2002 could be examined with hindsight, but because the portfolio manager could not implement the strategy in practice, it would involve look-ahead bias. The correction is to calculate the trailing P/E based on four quarters of EPS, lagged by a sufficient amount of time relative to the time at which stock price is observed, so that the EPS information would be contemporaneously available. The same principle applies to other multiples calculated on a trailing basis.

---

[13]Some research indicates that stocks with negative P/Es have special risk−return characteristics (see Fama and French 1992), so care should be exercised in interpreting such rankings.
[14]Earnings yield can be based on normal EPS and expected next-year EPS as well as on trailing EPS. In these cases, too, earnings yield provides a consistent ranking.

3.1.2. Calculating a Leading P/E

In the definition of leading P/E, analysts have interpreted "next year's expected earnings" as

- expected EPS for the next four quarters, or
- expected EPS for the next fiscal year.

We can take the first definition, which is closer to how cash flows are dated in our discussion of DCF valuation, as what we understand by leading P/E, unless stated otherwise.[15] To illustrate the calculation, suppose the current market price of a stock is $15 as of March 1, 2003, and the most recently reported quarterly EPS (for the quarter ended December 31, 2002) is $0.22. Your forecasts of EPS are as follows:

- $0.15 for the quarter ending March 31, 2003
- $0.18 for the quarter ending June 30, 2003
- $0.18 for the quarter ending September 30, 2003
- $0.24 for the quarter ending December 31, 2003

The sum of the forecasts for the next four quarters to report is $0.15 + $0.18 + $0.18 + $0.24 = $0.75, and the leading P/E for this stock is $15/$0.75 = 20.0.

For examples of the fiscal year concept, First Call/Thomson Financial reports a stock's "forward P/E" (leading P/E) in two ways: first, based on the mean of analysts' current fiscal year (FY1 = Fiscal Year 1) forecasts, in which analysts may have actual EPS in hand for some quarters; and second, based on analysts' following fiscal year (FY2 = Fiscal Year 2) forecasts, which must be based entirely on forecasts. For First Call, "forward P/E" contrasts with "current P/E," which is based on the last reported annual EPS, as mentioned earlier. Clearly, analysts must be consistent in the definition of leading P/E when comparing stocks.

EXAMPLE 4-5   Calculating a Leading P/E Ratio (1)

A market price for the common stock of American Electric Power (NYSE: AEP) in mid-November 2001 was $44.55. AEP's fiscal year coincides with the calendar year. According to Zacks Investment Research, the consensus EPS forecast for 2001 (FY1 as of November 2001) was $3.87. The consensus EPS forecast for 2002 (FY2 as of November 2001) was $3.69.

1. Calculate AEP's leading P/E based on a fiscal year definition and FY1 consensus forecasted EPS.
2. Calculate AEP's leading P/E based on a fiscal year definition and FY2 consensus forecasted EPS.

---

[15] Analysts have developed DCF expressions incorporating fractional time periods. In practice, uncertainty in forecasts is the more limiting factor to accuracy in estimating justified P/Es.

Solution to 1: AEP's leading P/E is $44.55/$3.87 = 11.5 based on FY1 forecasted EPS. Note that this EPS number involves the forecast of only one quarter as of November 2001.

Solution to 2: AEP's leading P/E is $44.55/$3.69 = 12.1 based on FY2 forecasted EPS.

In Example 4-5, the business's EPS was expected to be relatively stable, and the leading P/Es based on the two different EPS specifications presented did not vary substantially from each other. Example 4-6 presents the calculation of leading P/Es for the company examined in Example 4-2, Koninklijke Philips. Valuations according to leading P/E can vary dramatically depending on the definition of earnings for businesses with volatile earnings. The analyst was probably justified in normalizing EPS in Example 4-2.

EXAMPLE 4-6   Calculating a Leading P/E Ratio (2)

In Example 4-2, we calculated a normalized EPS for Koninklijke Philips (NYSE: PHG) and a P/E based on normalized EPS. In this example, we compute leading P/Es for PHG using alternative definitions. Table 4-3 presents PHG's actual and forecasted EPS, which reflect a severe downturn in its Consumer Electronics division.

TABLE 4-3   Quarterly EPS for PHG (in US Dollars, excluding nonrecurring items)

	March 31	June 30	September 30	December 31
2001	0.08	(0.34)	(0.27)	E0.00
2002	E(0.05)	E0.10	E0.15	E0.30

Source: *The Value Line Investment Survey.*

On November 8, 2001, PHG stock closed at $25.72. PHG's fiscal year ends on December 31. As of November 8, 2001, solve the following problems using the information in Table 4-3:

1. Calculate PHG's leading P/E based on the next four quarters of forecasted EPS.
2. Calculate PHG's leading P/E based on a fiscal year definition and current fiscal year (2001) forecasted EPS.
3. Calculate PHG's leading P/E based on a fiscal year definition and next fiscal year (2002) forecasted EPS.

Solution to 1: We sum forecasted EPS as follows:

4Q:2001 EPS (estimate)	$0.00
1Q:2002 EPS (estimate)	($0.05)
2Q:2002 EPS (estimate)	$0.10
3Q:2002 EPS (estimate)	$0.15
Sum	$0.20

The leading P/E by this definition is $25.72/$0.20 = 128.6.

Solution to 2: We sum EPS as follows:

1Q:2001 EPS (actual)	$0.08
2Q:2001 EPS (actual)	($0.34)
3Q:2001 EPS (actual)	($0.27)
4Q:2001 EPS (estimate)	$0.00
Sum	($0.53)

The leading P/E is $25.72/($0.53) = −48.5 or not meaningful (NM).

Solution to 3: We sum EPS as follows:

1Q:2002 EPS (estimate)	($0.05)
2Q:2002 EPS (estimate)	$0.10
3Q:2002 EPS (estimate)	$0.15
4Q:2002 EPS (estimate)	$0.30
Sum	$0.50

The leading P/E by this definition is $25.72/$0.50 = 51.4.

Having explored the issues involved in calculating P/Es, we turn to using them in valuation.

3.2. Valuation Based on Forecasted Fundamentals

The analyst who understands DCF valuation models can use them not only to develop an estimate of the justified P/E for a stock but also to gain insight into possible sources of valuation differences using the method of comparables. The simplest of all DCF models is the Gordon growth form of the dividend discount model. In Chapter 2, we related the P/E to the Gordon growth model value of the stock through the expressions

$$\frac{P_0}{E_1} = \frac{D_1/E_1}{r - g} = \frac{1 - b}{r - g}$$

which was Equation 2-21 for the leading P/E, and

$$\frac{P_0}{E_0} = \frac{D_0(1 + g)/E_0}{r - g} = \frac{(1 - b)(1 + g)}{r - g}$$

which was Equation 2-22 for the trailing P/E. Note that both expressions state P/E as a function of two fundamentals: the stock's required rate of return, r, reflecting its risk, and the expected (stable) dividend growth rate, g. The dividend payout ratio, $1 - b$, also enters into the expression. A particular value of the P/E is associated with a set of forecasts of the fundamentals (and dividend payout ratio). This value is the stock's justified P/E based on forecasted fundamentals (that is, the P/E justified by fundamentals). The higher the expected dividend growth rate or the lower the stock's required rate of return, the higher the stock's intrinsic value and the higher its justified P/E, all else equal. This intuition carries over to more-complex DCF models. Using any DCF model, all else equal, justified P/E is

- inversely related to the stock's required rate of return, and
- positively related to the growth rate(s) of future expected cash flows, however defined.

We illustrate the calculation of a justified leading P/E in Example 4-7.

EXAMPLE 4-7   Leading P/E Based on Fundamental Forecasts (1)

FPL Group (NYSE: FPL) is a southeastern U.S. utility. Jan Unger, a utility analyst, forecasts a long-term earnings retention rate (b) of 50 percent and a long-term growth rate of 5 percent. Unger also calculates a required rate of return of 9 percent. Based on Unger's forecasts of fundamentals and the equation above, FPL's justified leading P/E is

$$\frac{P_0}{E_1} = \frac{1 - b}{r - g} = \frac{1 - 0.50}{0.09 - 0.05} = 12.5$$

When assuming a complex DCF model for valuing the stock, we may not be able to express the P/E as a function of fundamental variables. Nevertheless, we can still calculate a justified P/E by dividing the DCF value by the fundamental used in the multiple, as illustrated in Example 4-8.

EXAMPLE 4-8   Leading P/E Based on Fundamental Forecasts (2)

Hyundai Motor Company Ltd. (KSE: 05380.KS) manufactures and sells cars, trucks, and commercial vehicles. As of the beginning of February 2002, you are valuing Hyundai stock (which closed at Korean won 29,300 on that day). Using a spreadsheet free-cash-flow-to-equity model in which you have forecasted FCFE individually for

2002 and 2003, and valuing the final piece using a P/E, you obtain a FCFE value for the stock of KRW31,500. For ease of communication, you want to express your valuation in terms of a leading P/E based on forecasted year 2002 EPS of KRW4,446.

1. What is Hyundai's justified P/E based on forecasted fundamentals?
2. State whether the stock appears to be fairly valued, overvalued, or undervalued, based on your answer to Problem 1.

Solution to 1: KRW31,500/KRW4,446 = 7.1 is the justified leading P/E.

Solution to 2: The justified P/E of 7.1 is slightly larger than the leading P/E based on market price, KRW29,300/KRW4,446 = 6.6. Consequently, the stock appears to be slightly undervalued.

Although related to a justified P/E, a predicted P/E can be estimated from cross-sectional regressions of P/E on the fundamentals believed to drive security valuation. Kisor and Whitbeck (1963) and Malkiel and Cragg (1970) pioneered this approach. The P/Es, and the stock and company characteristics thought to determine P/E, are measured as of a given year for a group of stocks. The P/Es are regressed against the stock and company characteristics. The estimated equation shows the relationships in the data set between P/E and the characteristics for that group of stocks and for that time period. The Kisor and Whitbeck study included the historical growth rate in earnings, the dividend payout ratio, and the standard deviation of EPS changes as explanatory (independent) variables. Malkiel and Cragg (1970) introduced explanatory variables based on expectations (alongside regressions on historical values). The analyst can in fact conduct such cross-sectional regressions using any set of variables he believes determines investment value. Other DCF models besides the dividend discount model (DDM) can provide ideas for such variables.

EXAMPLE 4-9 Predicted P/E Based on a Cross-Sectional Regression

You are valuing a food company with a beta of 0.9, a dividend payout ratio of 0.45, and an earnings growth rate of 0.08. The estimated regression for a group of other stocks in the same industry is

$$\text{Predicted P/E} = 12.12 + (2.25 \times \text{DPR}) - (0.20 \times \text{beta}) + (14.43 \times \text{EGR})$$

where

DPR = the dividend payout ratio

beta = the stock's beta

EGR = the five-year earnings growth rate

> 1. What is the predicted P/E for the food company based on the above cross-sectional regression?
> 2. If the stock's actual trailing P/E is 18, is the stock fairly valued, overvalued, or undervalued?
>
> *Solution to 1*:   Predicted P/E $= 12.12 + (2.25 \times 0.45) - (0.20 \times 0.9) + (14.43 \times 0.08) = 14.1$. The predicted P/E is 14.1.
>
> *Solution to 2*:   Because the predicted P/E of 14.1 is less than the actual P/E of 18, the stock appears to be overvalued (selling at a higher multiple than is justified by its fundamentals).

The cross-sectional regression method summarizes a large amount of data in a single equation and can provide a useful additional perspective on a valuation. It is infrequently used as a main tool, however, because it is subject to at least three limitations:

- The method captures valuation relationships for a specific time period and sample of stocks. The predictive power of the regression for a different stock and different time period is not known.
- The regression coefficients and explanatory power of the regressions tend to change substantially over a number of years. The relationships between P/E and fundamentals may thus change over time.
- Because regressions using this method are prone to the problem of multicollinearity (correlation within linear combinations of the independent variables), interpreting individual regression coefficients is difficult.

3.3. Valuation Using Comparables

The most common application of the P/E approach to valuation is to compare a stock's price multiple with a benchmark value of the multiple. This section explores these comparisons for P/Es. To apply the method of comparables using any multiple, an analyst must follow these steps:

- Select and calculate the price multiple that will be used in the comparison.
- Select the comparison asset or assets.
- Calculate the value of the multiple for the comparison asset. For a group of comparison assets, calculate a mean or median value of the multiple for the assets. The result in either case is the **benchmark value of the multiple**.
- Compare the subject stock's actual multiple with the benchmark value.
- When feasible, assess whether differences between the actual and benchmark values of the multiple are explained by differences in the fundamental determinants of the price multiple, and modify conclusions about relative valuation accordingly.

The above bullet points provide the structure for this chapter's presentation of the method of comparables. Some practitioners will take the benchmark value of the multiple, possibly subjectively adjusted for differences in fundamentals, as the basis for a point estimate of value.

This variation is illustrated in Example 4-11, Problem 2. We can apply this discussion to P/Es. Choices for the P/E benchmark value that have appeared in practice include

- the P/E of the most closely matched individual stock,
- the average or median value of the P/E for the company's peer group of companies within an industry,
- the average or median value of the P/E for the company's industry or sector,
- the P/E for a representative equity index, and
- an average past value of the P/E for the stock.

Because of averaging, valuation errors are probably less likely to occur when we use an equity index or a group of stocks than when we use a single stock. Hence, the focus of the following discussion will be the last four methods (we will illustrate a comparison with a closely matched individual stock in the section on price to cash flow).

Economists and investment analysts have long attempted to group companies by similarities and differences in their business operations. A country's economy overall is grouped most broadly into **economic sectors** or large industry groupings. These groupings can change over time. As one example, Standard & Poor's once divided the U.S. economy into 11 sectors, shown in Table 4-4 (beginning with Basic Materials).[16]

Companies in an economic sector share some characteristics that distinguish them from companies in other sectors; however, a given sector usually contains businesses with very distinct business operations. Analysts thus further sort companies into industries within a sector. Many different government and investment industry classification schemes exist. According to Standard & Poor's, however, Consumer Cyclicals contains 23 industries, including Textiles with a P/E of 17.9 and Leisure Time Products with a P/E of 46.6.[17] Within Textiles, there is a subgroup—Textiles (Apparel). Within Textiles (Apparel), Standard & Poor's distinguishes peer groups of companies, or companies that are most similar within an industry. For example, one Standard & Poor's peer group in Textiles (Apparel) is Hosiery/Intimate/Bridal Apparel, composed of nine companies that manufacture and sell apparel in these categories.

An analyst could form even more narrowly defined peer groups within the S&P peer group. One tool for identifying similarities and differences among businesses being used as comparables is financial ratio analysis. Financial ratios can point to contrasts in

- a company's ability to meet short-term financial obligations (liquidity ratios),
- the efficiency with which assets are being used to generate sales (asset turnover ratios),
- the use of debt in financing the business (leverage ratios),
- the degree to which fixed charges such as interest on debt are met by earnings or cash flow (coverage ratios), and
- profitability (profitability ratios).

---

[16] Standard & Poor's has since revised its sector classifications to the following 10 sectors: Consumer Discretionary, Consumer Staples, Energy, Financials, Health Care, Industrials, Information Technology, Materials, Telecommunication, and Utilities. Consumer Discretionary, Industrials, and Information Technology largely correspond to the old sectors Consumer Cyclicals, Capital Goods, and Technology, respectively; the former Transportation sector has been folded into the new Industrial sector. Within the sectors, Standard & Poor's has also made revisions to its industry classifications. For more information, visit www.spglobal.com/gics.html.

[17] According to the June 2001 issue of the *Industry Surveys: Monthly Investment Review*.

TABLE 4-4   Valuation of U.S. Sectors: P/E (as of May 31, 2001)

	2000	2001E	Long-Term Average
S&P 1500	22.4	23.5	26.5
S&P 500	25.1	23.8	17.8
Mid-Cap 400	22.6	20.4	23.8
Small-Cap 600	21.9	18.8	23.8
Basic Materials	24.7	26.4	26.3
Capital Goods	28.6	24.1	33.1
Communications Services	22.7	31.0	26.9
Consumer Cyclicals	24.2	22.5	21.3
Consumer Staples	31.7	28.9	28.7
Energy	14.7	14.3	21.6
Financial	19.4	16.7	13.0
Health Care	37.7	28.5	24.9
Technology	30.6	43.1	28.8
Transportation	18.3	16.3	20.7
Utilities	28.6	16.5	13.4

Source: Standard & Poor's *Industry Surveys: Monthly Investment Review* (June 2001).

With this understanding of terms in hand, we turn to presenting the method of comparables, beginning with industry peer groups and moving to comparison assets that are progressively less closely matched to the stock. We then turn to using historical P/Es in comparisons. Finally, we sketch how both fundamentals- and comparables-driven models for P/Es can be used to calculate a value for the mature phase in a multistage DCF valuation.

3.3.1. Peer Company Multiples

A business's peer group of companies is frequently used for comparison assets. The advantage to using a peer group is that the constituent companies are typically similar in their business mix. This approach is consistent with the idea underlying the method of comparables—that similar assets should sell at similar prices. The subject stock's P/E is then compared to the mean or median P/E for the peer group to arrive at a relative valuation. Multiplying the justified P/E by EPS, we can also arrive at an absolute value that can be compared with the stock's market price. The absolute value represents an estimate of intrinsic value if the comparison assets were efficiently (fairly) priced.

EXAMPLE 4-10   A Simple Peer Group Comparison

As a housing industry analyst at a brokerage firm, you are valuing Lennar Corporation (NYSE: LEN), a U.S. builder of moderately priced homes with nationwide operations. The valuation metric that you have selected is the trailing P/E. You are evaluating the P/E using the median trailing P/E of peer group companies as the benchmark value.

LEN is in the homebuilding industry, and its peer group is Homebuilders–National. Table 4-5 presents the relevant data.

TABLE 4-5   Trailing P/Es of U.S. National Homebuilders (as of November 9, 2001)

Company	Trailing P/E
Beazer Homes USA (NYSE: BZH)	6.83
Centex Corporation (NYSE: CTX)	7.36
D.R. Horton (NYSE: DHI)	7.99
Lennar Corporation (NYSE: LEN)	7.20
MDC Holdings (NYSE: MDC)	4.91
Pulte Homes (NYSE: PHM)	5.94
Ryland Group (NYSE: RYL)	6.70
Toll Brothers (NYSE: TOL)	6.29
Mean	6.65
Median (midway between 6.70 and 6.83)	6.77

Source: Morningstar, Inc.

Based on the data in Table 4-5, answer the following questions:

1. Given the definition of the benchmark stated above, state the benchmark value of the P/E for LEN.
2. State whether LEN is relatively fairly valued, relatively overvalued, or relatively undervalued, assuming no differences in fundamentals among the peer group companies. Justify your answer.
3. Which stocks in the Homebuilders–National group appear to be relatively undervalued using the mean trailing P/E as a benchmark? What further analysis may be appropriate to confirm your answer?

Solution to 1:   The median trailing P/E for the group is 6.77, so 6.77 represents the benchmark value of the multiple (the analyst chose to use the median rather than the mean).

Solution to 2:   LEN appears to be overvalued because its P/E is greater than the median P/E of 6.77.

Solution to 3:   MDC, PHM, and TOL appear to be undervalued relative to their peers because their trailing P/Es are lower than the mean P/E of 6.65. The apparent differences in valuation may be explained by differences in risk and expected growth rates compared with their peers. In addition, financial ratio analysis may help analysts determine the precise dimensions along which businesses may differ by risk and expected return.

In actual practice, analysts often find that the stock being valued has some significant differences from the median or mean fundamental characteristics of the comparison assets. In applying the method of comparables, analysts usually attempt to judge whether differences from the benchmark value of the multiple can be explained by differences in the fundamental factors believed to influence the multiple. The following relationships for P/E hold, all else equal:

- If the subject stock has higher-than-average (or median) expected earnings growth, a higher P/E than the benchmark P/E is justified.
- If the subject stock has higher-than-average (or median) risk (operating or financial), a lower P/E than the benchmark P/E is justified.

Another perspective on the above two points is that for a group of stocks with comparable relative valuations, the stock with the greatest expected growth rate (or the lowest risk) is the most attractively valued, all else equal. Example 4-11, Problem 1, illustrates this principle.

One metric that appears to address the impact of earnings growth on P/E is the P/E-to-growth (**PEG**) ratio. PEG is calculated as the stock's P/E divided by the expected earnings growth rate. The ratio in effect calculates a stock's P/E per unit of expected growth. Stocks with lower PEGs are more attractive than stocks with higher PEGs, all else equal. PEG is useful but must be used with care for several reasons:

- PEG assumes a linear relationship between P/Es and growth. The model for P/E in terms of DDM shows that in theory the relationship is not linear.
- PEG does not factor in differences in risk, a very important component of P/Es.
- PEG does not account for differences in the duration of growth. For example, dividing P/Es by short-term (five-year) growth forecasts may not capture differences in growth in long-term growth prospects.

The way in which fundamentals can add insight to comparables is illustrated in Example 4-11.

EXAMPLE 4-11   A Peer Group Comparison Modified by Fundamentals

Continuing with the valuation of homebuilders, you gather information on fundamentals related to risk (beta[18]), profitability (five-year earnings growth forecast), and valuation (trailing and leading P/E). These data are reported in Table 4-6, which lists companies in order of descending earnings growth forecasts. The use of leading P/Es recognizes that differences in trailing P/Es could be the result of transitory effects on earnings.

---

[18]In comparables work, analysts may also use other measures of risk, for example, financial leverage.

TABLE 4-6   Valuation Data for U.S. National Homebuilders (as of November 9, 2001)

	Trailing P/E	Leading P/E	Five-Year EPS Growth Forecast	Leading PEG	Beta
TOL	6.29	6.43	14.60%	0.44	1.05
DHI	7.99	7.37	14.20%	0.52	1.40
LEN	7.20	7.12	14.00%	0.51	1.45
BZH	6.83	7.29	14.00%	0.52	1.00
CTX	7.36	7.63	13.30%	0.57	1.20
MDC	4.91	5.93	13.30%	0.45	1.05
RYL	6.70	7.76	11.80%	0.66	1.20
PHM	5.94	6.08	11.70%	0.52	1.05
Mean	6.65	6.95	13.36%	0.52	1.18
Median	6.77	7.21	13.65%	0.52	1.13

Source: Morningstar, Inc.

Based on the data in Table 4-6, answer the following questions:

1. In Example 4-10, Problem 3, MDC, PHM, and TOL were identified as possibly relatively undervalued compared with the peer group as whole. Using information relating to profitability and risk, which of the three stocks appears to be the relatively *most* undervalued? Justify your answer with three reasons.
2. TOL has a consensus year-ahead EPS forecast of $5.48. Suppose that the median P/E of 7.21 for the peer group is subjectively adjusted upward to 7.5 for the justified P/E for TOL, reflecting TOL's lower risk and superior fundamentals. Estimate TOL's intrinsic value.
3. TOL's current market price is $35.25. State whether TOL appears to be fairly valued, overvalued, or undervalued on an absolute basis, given your answer to Problem 2 above.

Solution to 1: Among MDC, PHM, and TOL, TOL appears to represent the greatest undervaluation, according to the data in Table 4-6. Of the three stocks, TOL has

- the highest five-year consensus earnings growth forecast,
- the lowest PEG based on leading P/E, and
- the same level of risk as measured by beta.

Solution to 2: $5.48 \times 7.50 = 41.10 is an estimate of intrinsic value. Because the adjustment is subjective, we might prefer to say that TOL should trade at a premium to $5.48 \times 7.21 = 39.51.

Solution to 3: Because $41.10 is greater than $35.25, TOL appears to be undervalued on an absolute basis.

Analysts frequently compare a stock's multiple with the median or mean value of the multiple for larger sets of assets than a company's peer group. As one example, Value Line reports a relative P/E that is calculated as the stock's current P/E divided by the median P/E under Value Line review. The less closely matched the stock is to the comparison assets, the more dissimilarities are likely to be present to complicate the interpretation. Arguably, however, the larger the number of assets, the more likely it is that mispricings of individual assets cancel out. For example, during the 1998–2000 Internet boom, valuation relative to the overall market was more likely to point to the possibility of a crash in 2000–2001 than valuation relative to other Internet stocks alone. The next sections examine these larger groups.

3.3.2. Industry and Sector Multiples

Mean or median industry P/Es, as well as economic sector P/Es, are frequently used in relative valuation. The median is insensitive to outliers. Many databases, however, report only mean values of multiples for industries. The mechanics of using industry multiples are identical to the case of peer group comparisons. We make a comparison of a stock's multiple to the mean or median multiple for the company's industry, taking account of relevant fundamental information.

The analyst may want to explore whether the comparison assets themselves are efficiently priced. This will give insight into whether the relative valuation (justified P/E based on comparables) accurately reflects absolute intrinsic value.

EXAMPLE 4-12   Relative Industry Valuation

In general, the U.S. pharmaceutical industry traded at a substantial premium to the market (S&P 500) in the years 1951 to 1993.[19] In the early 1990s, the industry's relative valuation was at its lowest level and priced at a discount to the market. Had the U.S. pharmaceutical industry prospects changed?

To some extent, the industry outlook had changed due to the prospect of U.S. health care reform and secular changes in the industry in the early 1990s. Nevertheless, stocks in this sector continued to rise dramatically through the year 2000. Recent S&P industry data indicate that as of May 31, 2001, the U.S. pharmaceutical industry was trading at an average P/E of 33.7 compared to an S&P 500 P/E of 25.1—once again, at a premium to the market.

3.3.3. Overall Market Multiple

Although the logic of the comparables approach points to industry and peer companies as comparison assets, equity market indexes also have been used as comparison assets. The mechanics of using the method of comparables are not changed, although the user should be cognizant of any size differences between the subject stock and the stocks in the selected index. The question of whether the overall market is fairly priced has captured analyst interest over the entire history of investments. We mentioned one approach to market valuation (using a DDM) in Chapter 2. We end the discussion of using an equity market index as a comparison asset with two topical developments in market valuation.

---

[19]The example draws on information in Haley (1993).

EXAMPLE 4-13   Valuation Relative to the Market

You are analyzing three large-cap European stock issues with approximately equal earnings growth prospects and risk. As one step in your analysis, you have decided to check valuations relative to the Financial Times Stock Exchange (FTSE) Eurotop 300, an index of Europe's 300 largest companies. Table 4-7 provides the data.

TABLE 4-7   Comparison with an Index Multiple (prices and EPS in €)

As of February 28, 2002	Stock A	Stock B	Stock C	FTSE Eurotop 300
Current price	23	50	260	1229
P/E 2003E	20	25.5	20	23.2
Five-year average P/E (as a percent of Eurotop 300 P/E)	80	110	105	

Source: Bank Leu *Stock Guide* (March 2002) for FTSE Eurotop 300 data.

Based only on the data in Table 4-7, answer the following questions:

1. Which stock appears relatively undervalued against the FTSE Eurotop 300?
2. State the assumption underlying the five-year average P/E comparisons.

Solution to 1: Stock C appears to be undervalued against the FTSE Eurotop 300. Stock A and Stock C both are trading at a P/E of 20 relative to 2003 estimated earnings, versus a P/E of 23.2 for the market. But Stock A has historically traded at a P/E reflecting a 20 percent discount to the market (which would equal a P/E of $0.8 \times 23.2 = 18.6$). In contrast, Stock C has usually traded at a premium to the market P/E but now trades at a discount to it. Stock B trades at a high P/E, in line with its historical relationship to the market P/E ($1.1 \times 23.2 = 25.5$).

Solution to 2: Using historical relative valuation information in investment decisions relies on an assumption of stable underlying economic relationships (that the past is relevant for the future).

Because many equity indexes are market capitalization weighted, most vendors report the average market P/E with the individual P/Es weighted by the company's market capitalization. As a consequence, the largest constituent stocks heavily influence the calculated P/E. To the extent there are systematic differences in the P/Es by market capitalization, differences from the index's multiple may be explained by such effects. For stocks in middle capitalization ranges in particular, the analyst should favor using the median P/E for the index as the benchmark value of the multiple.[20]

---

[20]The differences can be substantial. For example, as of October 31, 2001, including only stocks with positive earnings, the market-cap-weighted mean P/E for the S&P 500 was 25.8 but the median P/E was 22.

As with other comparison assets, the analyst may be interested in whether the equity index itself is efficiently priced. A common comparison is the index's P/E in relation to historical values. For example, the current P/E of 27.83 for the Dow Jones Industrial Average as of October 31, 2001 was well above the 10-year average P/E of 17.4 reported by Value Line through 2000. Using a broader index of stocks over the 1871–1996 period, Siegel (1998) computed a long-term median P/E for U.S. stocks of 13.70. Two potential justifications for a higher P/E are lower interest rates and higher expected growth rates. An alternative hypothesis is that the market as a whole is currently overvalued or, alternatively, that earnings are abnormally low. The use of past data relies on the key assumption that the past (sometimes the distant past) is relevant for the future.

Other methods of examining market valuation have been used as well. Chapter 2 mentioned the use of DCF models. Examples 4-14 and 4-15 illustrate other approaches.

EXAMPLE 4-14   The Fed Model

One of the main drivers of P/E for the market as a whole is the level of interest rates. The inverse relationship between value and interest rates can be seen from the expression of P/E in terms of fundamentals, because the risk-free rate is one component of the required rate of return that is inversely related to value. The U.S. Federal Reserve Board of Governors uses one such valuation model that relates the inverse of the S&P 500 P/E, the earnings yield, to the yield to maturity on 10-year Treasury bonds. As already defined in Section 3.1.1, Earnings yield = E/P, where the Fed uses expected earnings for the next 12 months in calculating this ratio.

The model asserts that the market is overvalued when the stock market's current earnings yield is less than the 10-year Treasury bond yield. The intuition is that when Treasury bonds yield more than the earnings yield on the stock market, which is riskier than bonds, stocks are an unattractive investment. Figure 4-1 shows the historical indications of market overvaluation by performance of this model.

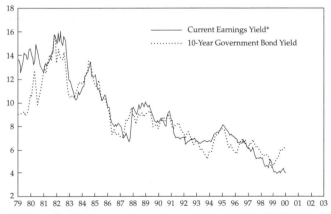

* I/B/E/S consensus estimates of earnings over the coming 12 months divided by S&P 500 Index.
Reprinted with permission of Dr. Edward Yardeni.

FIGURE 4-1   The Fed Stock Valuation Model

Figure 4-1 shows that, in general, the earnings yield has tracked the 10-year Treasury bond yield quite closely. Interestingly, the model indicated that the S&P 500 was overvalued at the beginning of 2000, a year in which the S&P 500 returned −9.1 percent. According to the model, the justified or fair-value P/E for the S&P 500 is the reciprocal of the 10-year T-bond yield. As of March 1, 2002, with a 10-year T-bond yielding 4.975 percent, the justified P/E on the S&P 500 was $1/0.04975 = 20.1$, according to the model. The leading P/E for the S&P 500 as of same date based on the consensus 2002 EPS from First Call/Thomson Financial was 29.6.

Earlier, we presented an expression for the justified P/E in terms of the Gordon growth model. That expression indicates that the expected growth rate in dividends or earnings is a variable entering into the intrinsic value of a stock (or an index of stocks). That variable is lacking in the Fed model.[21] Example 4-15 presents a model that takes a step toward addressing these concerns.

EXAMPLE 4-15   The Yardeni Model

Yardeni (2000) developed a model that incorporates the expected growth rate in earnings—a variable that is missing in the Fed model.[22] Yardeni's model is

$$CEY = CBY - b \times LTEG + Residual$$

CEY is the current earnings yield on the market index, CBY is the current Moody's A-rated corporate bond yield, and LTEG is the consensus five-year earnings growth rate forecast for the market index. The coefficient b measures the weight the market gives to five-year earnings projections (recall that the expression for P/E in terms of the Gordon growth model is based on the long-term sustainable growth rate and that five-year forecasts of growth may not be sustainable). Note that although CBY incorporates a default risk premium relative to T-bonds, it does not incorporate an equity risk premium per se (for example, in the bond yield plus risk premium model for the cost of equity, presented in Chapter 2, we added 300 to 400 basis points to a corporate bond yield).

Yardeni has found that the historical coefficient b has averaged 0.10. Noting that CEY is E/P and taking the inverse of both sides of this equation, Yardeni obtains the following expression for the justified P/E on the market:

---

[21] The earnings yield is in fact the expected rate of return on a no-growth stock (under the assumption that price equals value). See Equation 2-20 in Chapter 2, setting price equal to value: $P_0 = E/r + PVGO$. Setting the present value of growth opportunities equal to zero and rearranging, $r = E/P_0$.

[22] This model is presented as one example of more-complex models than the Fed model. Economic analysts at most investment companies have their own models that incorporate growth and historical relationships of market indexes and government bonds.

$$\frac{P}{E} = \frac{1}{(CBY - b \times LTEG)}$$

Consistent with valuation theory, in Yardeni's model, higher current corporate bond yields imply a lower justified P/E, and higher expected long-term growth results in a higher justified P/E. Yardeni's model uses a five-year growth forecast as a proxy for longer-term growth. Figure 4-2 illustrates the fair value predictions of the Yardeni model for the S&P 500.

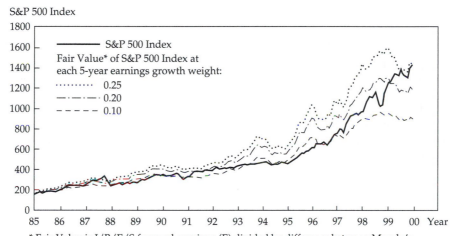

S&P 500 Index

* Fair Value is I/B/E/S forward earnings (E) divided by difference between Moody's A-rated corporate bond yield (CBY) and fraction (*b*) (as shown above) of consensus 5-year earnings growth (LTEG)
P = E/(CBY - *b* x LTEG)
Reprinted with permission of Dr. Edward Yardeni.

FIGURE 4-2   The Yardeni Stock Valuation Model

Figure 4-2 shows that in the years 1997 through 1999, the S&P 500 appeared to be overvalued using the historical weighting of 0.10 on growth; at the end of 1999, the model required a 0.25 weighting on growth to justify the market valuation, possibly indicating too much optimism was built into prices. As of March 1, 2002, with 10-year A rated corporates yielding 5.65 percent and LTEG equal to 7 percent based on First Call/Thomson Financial data, using the historical weighting of 0.10, the justified P/E on the S&P 500 was $1/(0.0565 - 0.10 \times 0.07) = 20.2$, essentially the same as the Fed model prediction.

3.3.4. Own Historical P/E Comparisons

As an alternative to comparing a stock's valuation with that of other stocks, another tradition uses past values of a stock's own P/E as a basis for comparison. Underlying this use is the idea that a stock's P/E may regress to historical average levels. A benchmark value can be obtained in a variety of ways with this approach. Value Line reports as a "P/E median" a rounded average of four middle values of a stock's average annual P/E for the previous 10 years. The five-year average trailing P/E is another reasonable alternative. In general, trailing P/Es are more commonly used than leading P/Es in such computations. Besides "higher" and "lower" comparisons with this benchmark, justified price based on this approach may be calculated as follows:

Justified price = (Benchmark value of own historical P/Es) × (Most recent EPS)   (4-1)

Normalized EPS replaces most recent EPS in Equation 4-1 when EPS is negative and as otherwise appropriate (see Section 3.1.1).

EXAMPLE 4-16   Valuation Relative to Own Historical P/Es

As of the beginning of 2001, you are valuing the Bank of Nova Scotia (TSE: BNS.TO), Canada's fourth-largest bank in terms of assets. You are investigating the method of comparables using BNS.TO's five-year average P/E as the benchmark value of the multiple. Table 4-8 presents the data.

TABLE 4-8   Historical P/Es for BNS.TO

	2000	1999	1998	1997	1996	Overall Mean
Average annual P/E	9.7	11.1	12.8	11.0	8.0	10.5

Source: The Value Line Investment Survey.

1. State a benchmark value for BNS.TO's P/E.
2. Given 2000 EPS of CAD3.55, calculate a justified price for BNS.

Solution to 1: From Table 4-8, this benchmark value is 10.5.

Solution to 2: The calculation is 10.5 × CAD3.55 = CAD37.28.

Changes in the interest rate environment and economic fundamentals over different time periods are a limitation to using an average past value of P/E for a stock as a benchmark. One specific caution is that inflation can distort the economic meaning of reported earnings. Consequently, comparisons of own P/E with average P/E, calculated with respect to a period with a different inflationary environment, can be misleading.[23] Further, analysts should be

---

[23] In the presence of inflation, reported earnings can overstate the real economic value of earnings that investors in principle are concerned about. Investors may value a given amount of reported earnings less during inflationary periods, tending to lower observed P/Es during such periods. For more details, see Bodie, Kane, and Marcus (2001).

alert to the impact of changes in a company's business mix over time on valuation levels. If the company's business has changed substantially over the time period examined, the method based on own past P/Es is prone to error.

3.3.5. Using P/Es to Obtain Terminal Value in Multistage Dividend Discount Models

In valuing a stock using a DDM, whether using a multistage model or modeling within a spreadsheet (forecasting cash flows individually up to some horizon), the accurate estimation of the terminal value of the stock is important. The key condition that must be satisfied is that terminal value reflects earnings growth that the company can sustain in the long run. Analysts frequently use price multiples to estimate terminal value, in particular P/Es and P/Bs. We can call such multiples **terminal price multiples**. Some choices available to the analyst in the multiples approach (where n is the point in time at which the final stage begins) include the following:

Terminal price multiple based on fundamentals
Analysts may restate the Gordon growth model value as a multiple by dividing it by B_n or E_n (for a trailing terminal price multiple) or by B_{n+1} or E_{n+1} (for a leading terminal price multiple). Of course, multiplying by the same value of the fundamental gives estimated terminal value. Because of their familiarity, multiples may be a useful way to communicate an estimate of terminal value.

Terminal price multiple based on comparables
The expression for terminal value (using P/E as an example) is

$$V_n = \text{Benchmark value of trailing P/E} \times E_n$$

or

$$V_n = \text{Benchmark value of leading P/E} \times E_{n+1}$$

Analysts have used various choices for the benchmark value, including

- median industry P/E,
- average industry P/E, and
- average of own past P/Es.

The use of a comparables approach has the strength that it is entirely grounded in market data. In contrast, the Gordon growth model calls for specific estimates (the required rate of return, the dividend payout ratio, and the expected mature growth rate) and is very sensitive to perturbations in those estimates. A possible disadvantage to the comparables approach, however, is that when the benchmark value reflects mispricing (over- or undervaluation), so will the estimate of terminal value.

EXAMPLE 4-17   Valuing the Mature Growth Phase Using P/Es

As an energy analyst, you are valuing the stock of an oil exploration company. You have projected earnings and dividends three years out (to $t = 3$), and you have gathered the following data and estimates:

- Required rate of return = 0.10
- Average dividend payout rate for mature companies in the market = 0.45
- Industry average ROE = 0.13
- $E_3 = 3.00
- Industry average P/E = 14.3

On the basis of the above information, answer the following questions:

1. Calculate terminal value based on comparables.
2. Contrast your answer in Problem 1 to an estimate of terminal value using the Gordon growth model.

Solution to 1: $V_n = $ Benchmark value of P/E $\times E_n = 14.3 \times \$3.00 = \$42.90$

Solution to 2:   In the sustainable growth rate expression, $g = b \times$ ROE, we can use $(1 - 0.45) = 0.55 = b$, and ROE $= 0.13$ (the industry average), obtaining $g = b \times$ ROE $= 0.55 \times 0.13 = 0.0715$. Given the required rate of return of 0.10, we obtain the estimate $\$3.00(0.45)(1.0715)/(0.10 - 0.0715) = \$50.76$. In this case, the Gordon growth model estimate of terminal value is $(\$50.76 - \$42.90)/\$42.90 = 0.1832$, or 18.3 percent higher than the estimate based on multiples.

4. PRICE TO BOOK VALUE

The ratio of market price per share to book value per share (P/B), like P/E, has a long history of use in valuation practice (as discussed in Graham and Dodd 1934). In Block's 1999 survey of CFA Institute members, book value ranked distinctly behind earnings and cash flow, but ahead of dividends, of the four factors surveyed.[24] According to the *Merrill Lynch Institutional Factor Survey*, in the years 1989 to 2001, P/B has been only slightly less popular than P/E as a factor consistently used among institutional investors.[25]

In the P/E ratio, the measure of value (EPS) in the denominator is a flow variable relating to the income statement. In contrast, the measure of value in the P/B's denominator (book value per share) is a stock or level variable coming from the balance sheet. Intuitively, book value per share attempts to represent the investment that common shareholders have made in the company, on a per-share basis. (*Book* refers to the fact that the measurement of value comes from accounting records or books, in contrast to market value.) To define book value per share more precisely, we first find **shareholders' equity** (total assets minus total liabilities). Because our purpose is to value common stock, we subtract from shareholders' equity any

---

[24]Earnings received a ranking of 1.55, cash flow a ranking of 1.65, book value a ranking of 3.29, and dividends a ranking of 3.51, where 1, 2, 3, and 4 were assigned to inputs ranked first, second, third, and last in importance in averaging responses.
[25]From 1989 to 2001, an average of 37.3 percent of respondents reported consistently using P/B in valuation, compared with 40.4 percent for earnings yield (the reciprocal of P/E rather than P/E was the actual variable surveyed by Merrill Lynch).

value attributable to preferred stock; we thus obtain common shareholders' equity or the **book value of equity** (often called simply **book value**).[26] Dividing book value by the number of common stock shares outstanding, we obtain **book value per share**, the denominator in the P/B.

In the balance of this section, we present the reasons analysts have offered for using P/B as well as possible drawbacks to its use. We then illustrate the calculation of P/B and discuss the fundamental factors that drive P/B. We end the section by showing the use of P/B based on the method of comparables.

Analysts have offered several rationales for the use of the P/B:

- Because book value is a cumulative balance sheet amount, book value is generally positive even when EPS is negative. We can generally use P/B when EPS is negative, whereas P/E based on a negative EPS is not meaningful.
- Because book value per share is more stable than EPS, P/B may be more meaningful than P/E when EPS is abnormally high or low, or is highly variable.
- As a measure of net asset value per share, book value per share has been viewed as appropriate for valuing companies composed chiefly of liquid assets, such as finance, investment, insurance, and banking institutions (Wild, Bernstein, and Subramanyam 2001, p. 233). For such companies, book values of assets may approximate market values.
- Book value has also been used in the valuation of companies that are not expected to continue as a going concern (Martin 1998, p. 22).
- Differences in P/Bs may be related to differences in long-run average returns, according to empirical research.[27]

Possible drawbacks of P/Bs in practice include the following:

- Other assets besides those recognized in accounting may be critical operating factors. For example, in many service companies, **human capital**—the value of skills and knowledge possessed by the workforce—is more important than physical capital as an operating factor.
- P/B can be misleading as a valuation indicator when significant differences exist among the level of assets used by the companies under examination. Such differences may reflect differences in business models, for example.
- Accounting effects on book value may compromise book value as a measure of shareholders' investment in the company. As one example, book value can understate shareholders' investment as a result of the expensing of investment in research and development (R&D). Such expenditures often positively affect income over many periods and in principle create assets. Accounting effects such as these can impair the comparability of P/B across companies and countries.[28]
- In the accounting of most countries, including the United States, book value largely reflects the historical purchase costs of assets, as well as accumulated accounting depreciation expenses. Inflation as well as technological change eventually drive a wedge between the book value and the market value of assets. As a result, book value per share often poorly

---

[26] If we were to value a company as a whole, rather than just the common stock, we would not exclude the value of preferred stock from the computation.

[27] See Bodie, Kane, and Marcus (2001) for a brief summary of the empirical research.

[28] For example, in some countries the values of brand name assets created by advertising are recognized on the balance sheet; in the United States, they are not.

reflects the value of shareholders' investments. Such effects can impair the comparability of P/Bs across companies, for example, when significant differences exist in the average age of assets among companies being compared.

Example 4-18 illustrates one possible disadvantage to using P/B in valuation.

EXAMPLE 4-18   Differences in Business Models Reflected in Differences in P/Bs

Dell Computer Corporation (Nasdaq NMS: DELL), Apple Computer (Nasdaq NMS: AAPL), Gateway (NYSE: GTW), and Compaq Computer Corporation (NYSE: CPQ) compete with each other in the personal computer industry. Table 4-9 gives valuation data for these companies according to P/B, as of the end of 2001.

TABLE 4-9   P/Bs for Four
Peer Companies

Company	P/B
Dell	14.42
Apple	1.76
Gateway	1.83
Compaq	1.23

Source: Morningstar, Inc.

Dell is an assembler rather than a manufacturer, uses a just-in-time inventory system for parts needed in assembly, and sells built-to-order computers directly to the end consumer. Just-in-time inventory systems attempt to minimize the amount of time that parts needed for building computers are held in inventory. How can these practices explain the much higher P/B of Dell compared with the P/Bs of peer group stocks?

Because Dell assembles parts manufactured elsewhere, it requires smaller investments in fixed assets than it would if it were a manufacturer; this translates into a smaller book value per share. The just-in-time inventory system reduces Dell's required investment in working capital. Because Dell does not need to respond to the inventory needs of large resellers, its need to invest in working capital is reduced. The overall effect of this business model is that Dell generates its sales on a comparatively small base of assets. As a result, Dell's P/B is not comparable with those of its peer group, and the question of relative valuation is not resolved by the comparison in Table 4-9. Using P/B as a valuation indicator effectively penalizes Dell's efficient business model.[29]

---

[29] There is a second reason for Dell's relatively high P/B; Dell's substantial share repurchases have reduced its book value per share in the years preceding this data.

4.1. Determining Book Value

In this section, we illustrate the calculation of book value and how analysts may adjust book value to improve the comparability of P/B ratios across companies. To compute book value per share, we need to refer to the business's balance sheet, which has a shareholders' (or stockholders') equity section. The computation of book value is as follows:

- (Shareholders' equity) − (Total value of equity claims that are senior to common stock) = Common shareholders' equity
- (Common shareholders' equity)/(Number of common stock shares outstanding) = Book value per share

Possible senior claims to common stock include the value of preferred stock and dividends in arrears on preferred stock.[30] Example 4-19 illustrates the calculation.

EXAMPLE 4-19   Computing Book Value per Share

Ennis Business Forms (NYSE: EBF), a wholesale manufacturer of custom business forms and other printed business products, reported the balance sheet given in Table 4-10 for its fiscal year ending February 28, 2001.

TABLE 4-10   Ennis Business Forms Balance Sheet
(in thousands, except per-share amounts)

	February 28, 2001
Assets	
Current Assets:	
Cash and cash equivalents	$ 8,964
Short-term investments	980
Net receivables	29,957
Inventory	13,088
Unbilled contract revenue	364
Other current assets	4,910
Total Current Assets	58,263
Noncurrent Assets:	
Investment securities	2,170
Net property, plant, and equipment	57,781
Goodwill	23,615
Other assets	1,025
Total Assets	**$ 142,854**

---

[30] Some preferred stock issues have the right to premiums (liquidation premiums) if they are liquidated. If present, these premiums should be deducted as well.

TABLE 4-10   *(continued)*

Liabilities and Shareholders' Equity	
Current Liabilities:	
Current installments of long-term debt	$ 4,176
Accounts payable	6,067
Accrued expenses	7,665
Total Current Liabilities	17,908
Noncurrent Liabilities:	
Long-term debt	23,555
Deferred credits	9,851
Total Liabilities	51,314
Shareholders' Equity:	
Common stock ($2.50 par value. Authorized 40,000,000; issued 21,249,860)	53,125
Additional paid-in capital	1,040
Retained earnings	127,817
Treasury stock (cost of 4,979,095 shares repurchased in 2001)	(90,442)
Total Shareholders' Equity	91,540
Total Liabilities and Shareholders' Equity	**$ 142,854**

The entries in the balance sheet should be familiar. Treasury stock results from share repurchases (or buybacks) and is a deduction (recorded at cost above) to reach shareholders' equity. For the number of shares to be used in the divisor, we take 21,249,860 shares issued (under Common stock) and subtract 4,979,095 shares repurchased in 2001 to get 16,270,765 shares outstanding.

1. Using the data in Table 4-10, calculate book value per share as of February 28, 2001.
2. Given a closing price per share for EBF of $8.42 as of June 4, 2001, and your answer to Problem 1, calculate EBF's P/B as of June 4, 2001.

Solution to 1: (Common shareholders' equity)/(Number of common stock shares outstanding) = $91,540,000/16,270,765 = $5.63

Solution to 2: P/B = $8.42/$5.63 = 1.5

Example 4-19 illustrated the calculation of book value per share without any adjustments. Adjusting P/B has two purposes: (1) to make P/B more accurately reflect the value of shareholders' investment and (2) to make P/B more useful for comparisons among different stocks.

- Some services and analysts report a **tangible book value per share**. Computing tangible book value per share involves subtracting reported intangible assets from the balance sheet from common shareholders' equity. The analyst should be familiar with the calculation. However, from the viewpoint of financial theory, the general exclusion of all intangibles may not be warranted. In the case of individual intangible assets such as patents, which can be separated from the entity and sold, exclusion may not be justified. Exclusion may be appropriate, however, for goodwill from acquisitions. **Goodwill** represents the excess of the purchase price of an acquisition over the net asset value of tangible assets and specifically identifiable intangibles. Many analysts feel that goodwill does not represent an asset, because it is not separable and may reflect overpayment for an acquisition.

- For book value per share to most accurately reflect current values, the balance sheet should be adjusted for significant off-balance-sheet assets and liabilities and for differences in the fair value of these assets/liabilities from recorded accounting amounts.[31] Internationally, accounting methods currently report some assets/liabilities at historical cost (with some adjustments) and others at fair value.[32] For example, assets such as land or equipment are reported at their historical acquisitions cost, and in the case of equipment are being depreciated over their useful lives. These assets may have appreciated over time, or they may have declined in value more than is reflected in the depreciation computation. Other assets such as investments in marketable securities are reported at fair market value. Reporting assets at fair value would make P/B more relevant for valuation (including comparisons among companies).
- Certain adjustments may be appropriate for comparability. For example, one company may use FIFO and a peer company may use LIFO, which in an inflationary environment will generally understate inventory values. To more accurately assess the relative valuation of the two companies, the analyst should restate the book value of the company using LIFO to what it would be on a FIFO basis. Example 4-20 illustrates this and other adjustments to book value.[33]

Regarding the second bullet point, over the last few years, there has been a trend among accounting standard setters toward a fair value model—more assets/liabilities are stated at fair value. If this trend continues, the need for adjustments will be reduced (but not eliminated).

EXAMPLE 4-20   Adjusting Book Value

Edward Stavros is a junior analyst at a major U.S. pension fund. Stavros is researching Harley Davidson (NYSE: HDI) for the fund's Consumer Cyclical portfolio. Stavros is particularly interested in determining Harley Davidson's relative P/B. He obtains the condensed balance sheet for Harley Davidson from Edgar Online (a computerized database of U.S. SEC filings); his data are shown in Table 4-11.

---

[31] An example of an off-balance-sheet liability is a guarantee to pay a debt of another company in the event of that company's default. See Chapter 11 of White, Sondhi, and Fried (1998).

[32] **Fair value** has been defined as the price at which an asset or liability would change hands between a willing buyer and a willing seller when the former is not under any compulsion to buy and the latter is not under any compulsion to sell.

[33] For a complete discussion of balance sheet adjustments, see "Analysis of Financial Statements: A Synthesis," in White, Sondhi, and Fried (1998).

TABLE 4-11   Harley Davidson Condensed Consolidated
Balance Sheet (in thousands)

	December 31, 2000
Assets	
Current Assets:	
Cash and cash equivalents	$ 419,736
Accounts receivable, net	98,311
Finance receivables, net	530,859
Inventories	191,931
Other current assets	56,427
Total Current Assets	1,297,264
Noncurrent Assets:	
Finance receivables, net	234,091
Property, plant, and equipment, net	754,115
Goodwill	54,331
Other assets	96,603
Total Assets	$ 2,436,404
Liabilities and Shareholders' Equity	
Current Liabilities:	
Accounts payable	$ 169,844
Accrued and other liabilities	238,390
Current portion of finance debt	89,509
Total Current Liabilities	497,743
Noncurrent Liabilities:	
Finance debt	355,000
Other long-term liabilities	97,340
Postretirement health care benefits	80,666
Contingencies	
Shareholders' Equity:	1,405,655
Total Liabilities and Shareholders' Equity	$ 2,436,404

Stavros computes book value per share initially by dividing total shareholders' equity ($1,405,655,000) by the number of shares outstanding at December 31, 2000 (302,070,745). The resulting book value per share is $4.65. Stavros then realizes that he must examine the full set of financial statements to assess the impact of accounting methods on balance sheet data. Harley Davidson's footnotes indicate that the company uses the LIFO inventory method. Inventories on a FIFO basis are presented in the company's footnotes at $210,756,000. Additionally, an examination of Harley's pension footnotes indicates that the pension plan is currently overfunded but that accounting rules require the recognition of a net liability of $21,705,000. This overstatement of a liability is somewhat offset by an underfunded post-retirement health care plan that understates liabilities by $15,400,000.

Stavros makes the following adjustments on an after-tax basis (HDI's average tax rate is 37 percent) to his book value computation (in dollars):

Total Shareholders Equity	$1,405,655,000
Plus Inventory Adjustment	$18,825,000 \times 0.63 = 11,859,750$

Plus Pension Adjustment $21,705,000 \times 0.63 = 13,674,150$

Less Post-Retirement
    Adjustment $15,400,000 \times 0.63 = (9,702,000)$

Adjusted Book Value $1,421,486,900

Adjusted Book Value
    per Share $4.71

In the above calculations, the after-tax amount is found by multiplying the pretax amount by $(1 - 0.37) = 0.63$. Stavros is putting all the company's inventory valuation on a FIFO basis for comparability. Using after-tax amounts is necessary because if Harley Davidson were to change its inventory method to FIFO, the change would result in higher taxes as HDI liquidates old inventory. Although inventory on the balance sheet would increase by $18,825,000, taxes payable would also increase (or cash would decrease). As a result, the net effect on book value equals the change in inventory less the associated tax increase.

In conclusion, adjusted book value per share is $4.71.[34] Based on a price of $42.00 shortly after year-end, HDI has a P/B (adjusted basis) of $42/$4.71 = 8.9. Outstanding stock options could dilute both book value per share figures by $0.07, which would have a small impact on these ratios.

4.2. Valuation Based on Forecasted Fundamentals

We can use fundamental forecasts to estimate a stock's justified P/B. For example, assuming the Gordon growth model and using the expression $g = b \times \text{ROE}$ for the sustainable growth rate, the expression for the justified P/B based on the most recent book value (B_0) is[35]

$$\frac{P_0}{B_0} = \frac{\text{ROE} - g}{r - g} \qquad (4\text{-}2)$$

For example, if a business's ROE is 12 percent, its required rate of return is 10 percent, and its expected growth rate is 7 percent, then its justified P/B based on fundamentals is $(0.12 - 0.07)/(0.10 - 0.07) = 1.7$.

Equation 4-2 states that the justified P/B is an increasing function of ROE, all else equal. Because the numerator and denominator are differences of ROE and r, respectively, from the

---

[34]The calculation of tangible book value per share (adjusted basis for inventory accounting method) is as follows:

Adjusted Book Value	$1,421,486,900
Less Goodwill	(54,331,000)
Tangible Adjusted Book Value	$1,367,155,900
Tangible Adjusted Book Value per Share	$4.53

and price to tangible book value is 9.3.

[35]According to the Gordon growth model, $V_0 = E_1 \times (1 - b)/(r - g)$. Defining $\text{ROE} = E_1/B_0$, so $E_1 = B_0 \times \text{ROE}$, and substituting for E_1 in the prior expression, we have $V_0 = B_0 \times \text{ROE} \times (1 - b)/(r - g)$, giving $V_0/B_0 = \text{ROE} \times (1 - b)/(r - g)$. The sustainable growth rate expression is $g = b \times \text{ROE}$. Substituting $b = g/\text{ROE}$ into the expression just given for V_0/B_0, we have $V_0/B_0 = (\text{ROE} - g)/(r - g)$. Because justified price is intrinsic value, V_0, we obtain Equation 4-2.

same quantity, g, what determines the justified P/B in Equation 4-2 is ROE in relation to the required rate of return, r. The larger ROE is in relation to r, the higher the justified P/B based on fundamentals.[36]

A practical insight from Equation 4-2 is that we cannot evaluate whether a particular value of the P/B reflects undervaluation without taking into account the business's profitability. Equation 4-2 suggests as well that given two stocks with the same P/B, the one with the higher ROE is relatively undervalued, all else equal. These relationships have been confirmed using cross-sectional regression analysis.[37]

Further insight into the P/B comes from the residual income model, which was mentioned in Chapter 2 and which we will discuss in detail in Chapter 5. The expression for the justified P/B based on the residual income valuation is[38]

$$\frac{P_0}{B_0} = 1 + \frac{\text{Present value of expected future residual earnings}}{B_0} \tag{4-3}$$

Equation 4-3, which makes no special assumptions about growth, states the following:

- If the present value of expected future residual earnings is zero—for example, if the business just earns its required return on investment in every period—the justified P/B is 1.
- If the present value of expected future residual earnings is positive (negative), the justified P/B is greater than (less than) 1.

4.3. Valuation Using Comparables

To use the method of comparables for valuing stocks using a P/B, we follow the same steps given in Section 3.3, illustrated there with P/Es. In contrast to EPS, however, analysts' forecasts of book value are not aggregated and widely disseminated by vendors such as First Call/Thomson Financial and Zacks; in practice, most analysts use trailing book value

---

[36]This relationship can be seen clearly if we set $g = 0$ (the no-growth case): $P_0/B_0 = \text{ROE}/r$.

[37]Harris and Marston (1994) perform a regression of B/MV (book to market, the inverse of the P/B) against variables for growth (mean analyst forecasts) and risk (beta) for a large sample of companies over the period July 1982 to December 1989. The estimated regression was

$$\text{B/MV} = 1.172 - 4.15 \times \text{Growth} + 0.093 \times \text{Risk} \ (R^2 = 22.9\%)$$

The coefficient of -4.15 indicates that expected growth was negatively related to B/MV, and, as a consequence, positively related to P/B. Risk was positively related to B/MV and thus negatively related to P/B. Both variables were statistically significant with growth having the greatest impact. Fairfield (1994) also found that P/Bs are related to future expectations of ROE in the predicted fashion.

[38]Noting that $(\text{ROE} - r) \times B_0$ would define a level residual income stream, we can show that Equation 4-2 is consistent with Equation 4-3 (a general expression) as follows. In $P_0/B_0 = (\text{ROE} - g)/(r - g)$, we can successively rewrite the numerator $(\text{ROE} - g) + r - r = (r - g) + (\text{ROE} - r)$, so $P_0/B_0 = [(r - g) + (\text{ROE} - r)]/(r - g) = 1 + (\text{ROE} - r)/(r - g)$, which can be written $P_0/B_0 = 1 + [\text{ROE} - r)/(r - g)] \times B_0/B_0 = 1 + [(\text{ROE} - r) \times B_0/(r - g)]/B_0$; the second term in the final expression is the present value of residual income divided by B_0 as in Equation 4-3.

in calculating P/Bs.[39] Evaluation of relative P/Bs should consider differences in return on invested capital (as measured by ROE in this context), risk, and expected earnings growth.

EXAMPLE 4-21   P/B Comparables Approach

John Todd, CFA, is a portfolio manager with Midland Value, a mid-cap value mutual fund. Recently, a property and casualty company owned by the fund was acquired by a large-cap insurance company. Todd is seeking a mid-cap replacement for this position. Given the fund's value orientation, Todd is particularly interested in mid-cap property and casualty companies selling at a reasonable multiple to book value. Todd's initial research has resulted in a short list of four candidates: Allmerica Financial Corporation (NYSE: AFC), American Financial Group (NYSE: AFG), Safeco Corporation (Nasdaq NMS: SAFC), and Old Republic International Corporation (NYSE: ORI). Table 4-12 presents information on these companies.[40]

TABLE 4-12   P/B Comparables

Year	Price to Book Value							Forecasted ROE	Beta
	1996	1997	1998	1999	2000	Five-Year Average	Current		
AFC	1.0	1.1	1.4	1.4	1.6	1.3	0.8	9.5%	1.10
AFG	1.5	1.5	1.6	1.2	1.0	1.4	1.0	13.5%	0.95
SAFC	1.2	1.2	1.1	0.8	0.9	1.0	1.1	10%	1.05
ORI	1.4	1.6	1.4	0.6	1.6	1.3	1.2	11%	0.90
Property/ casualty industry (mean value)							2.2	11%	

Sources: Morningstar; *The Value Line Investment Survey* for ROE forecasts.

Based only on the information in Table 4-12, answer the following questions:

1. Discuss the valuation of ORI relative to the industry.
2. Discuss the valuation of AFG relative to the industry and peer companies.

Solution to 1: ORI is selling at a P/B that is only 55 percent of the industry mean, although its forecasted ROE equals the mean forecasted ROE for the industry, 11 percent. ORI appears to be relatively undervalued based on an industry benchmark.

---

[39] Because equity in successive balance sheets is linked by net income from the income statement, however, the analyst could, given dividend forecasts, translate EPS forecasts into corresponding book value forecasts, taking account of any anticipated ownership transactions.

[40] Forecasted ROE refers to forecasts for 2004 to 2006.

Solution to 2: AFG is selling at a P/B that is only 45 percent of the industry mean P/B. At the same time, its expected ROE is distinctly higher than the industry's. On the basis of the data given, AFG appears to be undervalued relative to the industry benchmark. AFG also appears to be undervalued with respect to SAFC and probably AFC and ORI as well, based on the data given:

- AFG has a lower P/B, a higher expected ROE, and a lower beta than SAFC.
- Although the P/B of AFG is 25 percent higher than that of AFC, its expected ROE is 42 percent higher than AFC, with lower risk as judged by beta.
- With a P/B that is about 17 percent smaller than ORI's, a higher expected ROE, and only a 0.05 difference in beta, AFG also may be relatively undervalued with respect to ORI.

5. PRICE TO SALES

Certain types of privately held companies, including investment management companies and companies in partnership form, have long been valued as a multiple of annual revenues. In recent decades, the ratio of price to sales has become well known as a valuation indicator for publicly traded companies as well. According to the *Merrill Lynch Institutional Factor Survey*, from 1989 to 2001, on average, slightly more than one-quarter of respondents consistently used the P/S in their investment process.

Analysts have offered the following rationales for using P/S:

- Sales are generally less subject to distortion or manipulation than are other fundamentals, such as EPS or book value. Through discretionary accounting decisions concerning expenses, for example, management can distort EPS as a reflection of economic performance. In contrast, total sales, as the top line in the income statement, is prior to any expenses.
- Sales are positive even when EPS is negative. Therefore, analysts can use P/S when EPS is negative, whereas the P/E based on a negative EPS is not meaningful.
- Because sales are generally more stable than EPS, which reflects operating and financial leverage, P/S is generally more stable than P/E. P/S may be more meaningful than P/E when EPS is abnormally high or low.
- P/S has been viewed as appropriate for valuing the stock of mature, cyclical, and zero-income companies (Martin 1998).
- Differences in P/Ss may be related to differences in long-run average returns, according to empirical research.[41]

Possible drawbacks of using P/S in practice include the following:

- A business may show high growth in sales even when it is not operating profitably as judged by earnings and cash flow from operations. To have value as a going concern, a business must ultimately generate earnings and cash.

---

[41] See Nathan, Sivakumar, and Vijayakumar (2001), O'Shaughnessy (1997), and Senchack and Martin (1987).

- P/S does not reflect differences in cost structures among different companies.
- Although relatively robust with respect to manipulation, revenue recognition practices offer the potential to distort P/S.

5.1. Determining Sales

P/S is calculated as price per share divided by annual net sales per share (net sales is total sales less returns and customer discounts). Analysts usually use annual sales from the company's most recent fiscal year in the calculation, as illustrated in Example 4-22. Because valuation is forward-looking in principle, the analyst may also develop and use P/Ss based on forecasts of next year's sales.

EXAMPLE 4-22   Calculating P/S

In 2001, Abitibi-Consolidated (Toronto Stock Exchange: A.TO), a manufacturer of newsprint and groundwood papers, reported 2001 net sales of CAD6,032,000,000 with 440 million shares outstanding. Calculate the P/S for Abitibi based on a closing price of CAD13.38 on February 14, 2002.

$$\text{Sales per share} = \text{CAD6,032,000,000/440,000,000} = \text{CAD13.71}$$

So, P/S = CAD13.38/CAD13.71 = 0.9759 or 1.0.

Although the determination of sales is more straightforward than the determination of earnings, the analyst should evaluate a company's revenue recognition practices, in particular those tending to speed up the recognition of revenues. An analyst using a P/S approach who does not also assess the quality of accounting for sales may be led to place too high a value on such companies' shares. Example 4-23 illustrates the problem.

EXAMPLE 4-23   Revenue Recognition Practices (1)

Analysts label stock markets as *bubbles* when market prices appear to lose contact with intrinsic value. The run-up of the prices of Internet stocks in U.S. markets in the 1998–2000 period, in the view of many, represented a bubble. During this period, many analysts adopted P/S as a metric for valuing Internet stocks with negative earnings and cash flow. Perhaps at least partly as a result of this practice, some Internet companies engaged in questionable revenue recognition practices to justify their high valuations. In order to increase sales, some companies engaged in activities such as bartering Web site advertising with other Internet companies. For example, InternetRevenue.com might barter $1,000,000 worth of banner advertising with RevenueIsUs.com. Each would show $1,000,000 of revenue and $1,000,000 of expense. Although neither had any net income or cash flow, each company's revenue growth and market valuation was enhanced (at least temporarily). The value placed on the advertising was also questionable. As a result of these and other questionable activities, the U.S. SEC issued a stern warning to companies. International accounting standard setters have begun a study to define revenue recognition principles. The analyst should review footnote disclosures to assess whether the company may be recognizing revenue prematurely or otherwise aggressively.

Example 4-24 illustrates another instance in which an analyst would need to look behind the accounting numbers.

EXAMPLE 4-24   Revenue Recognition Practices (2)

Sales on a **bill-and-hold basis** involve selling products but not delivering those products until a later date.[42] Sales on this basis have the effect of accelerating sales into an earlier reporting period. The following is a case in point. In its Form 10K filed March 6, 1998, for fiscal year ended December 28, 1997, Sunbeam Corporation listed the following footnote:

> *1. Operations and Significant Accounting Policies Revenue Recognition*   The Company recognizes revenues from product sales principally at the time of shipment to customers. In limited circumstances, at the customer's request the Company may sell seasonal product on a bill and hold basis provided that the goods are completed, packaged and ready for shipment, such goods are segregated and the risks of ownership and legal title have passed to the customer. The amount of such bill and hold sales at December 29, 1997, was approximately 3 percent of consolidated revenues. Net sales are comprised of gross sales less provisions for expected customer returns, discounts, promotional allowances and cooperative advertising.

After internal and SEC investigations, the company restated its financial results, including a restated revenue recognition policy:

> *Revenue Recognition*   The Company recognizes sales and related cost of goods sold from product sales when title passes to the customers which is generally at the time of shipment. Net sales is comprised of gross sales less provisions for estimated customer returns, discounts, promotional allowances, cooperative advertising allowances and costs incurred by the Company to ship product to customers. Reserves for estimated returns are established by

---

[42]For companies whose reports must conform to U.S. SEC accounting regulations, revenue from bill-and-hold sales cannot be reported unless the risk of loss on the products transfers to the buyer and additional criteria are met (see SEC Staff Accounting Bulletin 101 for criteria).

the Company concurrently with the recognition of revenue. Reserves are established based on a variety of factors, including historical return rates, estimates of customer inventory levels, the market for the product and projected economic conditions. The Company monitors these reserves and makes adjustment to them when management believes that actual returns or costs to be incurred differ from amounts recorded. In some situations, the Company has shipped product with the right of return where the Company is unable to reasonably estimate the level of returns and/or the sale is contingent upon the resale of the product. In these situations, the Company does not recognize revenue upon product shipment, but rather when it is reasonably expected the product will not be returned.

The company had originally reported revenue of $1,168,182,000 for the fiscal year ended December 31, 1997. After restatement, the company reported revenue of $1,073,000,000 for the same period—a more than 8 percent reduction in revenue. The analyst reading the footnote in the original report would have noted the bill-and-hold practices and reduced revenue by 3 percent. This company engaged in other accounting practices tending to inflate revenue, which did not come to light until the investigation.

Sometimes, as in Example 4-24, it is not possible to determine precisely by how much sales may be overstated. If a company is engaged in questionable revenue recognition practices of an unknown amount, the analyst may well suggest avoiding that security. At the very least, the analyst should be skeptical and assess a higher risk premium, which would result in a lower justified P/S.

5.2. Valuation Based on Forecasted Fundamentals

Like other multiples, P/S can be linked to DCF models. In terms of the Gordon growth model, we can state P/S as[43]

$$\frac{P_0}{S_0} = \frac{(E_0/S_0)(1-b)(1+g)}{r-g} \tag{4-4}$$

where E_0/S_0 is the business's profit margin PM_0. Although the profit margin is stated in terms of trailing sales and earnings, the analyst may use a long-term forecasted profit margin in Equation 4-4. Equation 4-4 states that the justified P/S is an increasing function of its profit margin and earnings growth rate, and the intuition generalizes to more complex DCF models. Profit margin is a determinant of the justified P/S not only directly, but also through its effect on g. We can illustrate this concept by restating Equation 2-33 from Chapter 2 for the sustainable growth rate, g:

$$g = b \times PM_0 \times \frac{Sales}{Assets} \times \frac{Assets}{Shareholders' \ equity}$$

---

[43] The Gordon growth model is $P_0 = D_0(1+g)/(r-g)$. Substituting $D_0 = E_0(1-b)$ into the previous equation produces $P_0 = E_0(1-b)(1+g)/(r-g)$. Dividing both sides by S_0 gives $P_0/S_0 = (E_0/S_0)(1-b)(1+g)/(r-g)$.

where the last three terms come from the DuPont analysis of ROE. An increase (decrease) in the profit margin produces a higher (lower) sustainable growth rate, so long as sales do not decrease (increase) proportionately.[44]

EXAMPLE 4-25   Justified P/S Based on Forecasted Fundamentals

As an automobile analyst, you are valuing the stocks of three automobile manufacturers including General Motors (NYSE: GM) as of the end of 2001. You estimate that GM's required rate of return is 11 percent based on an average of a capital asset pricing model (CAPM) estimate and a bond yield plus risk premium estimate. Your other forecasts are as follows:

- long-term profit margin = 3.5 percent,
- dividend payout ratio = 30 percent, and
- earnings growth rate = 5 percent.

Although you forecast that GM's profit margin for 2001 will be 1 percent, you recognize that 2001 was a year of economic contraction. A profit margin of 3.5 percent is close to GM's long-term average, and an earnings growth rate of 5 percent is close to the median analyst forecast, according to First Call/Thomson Financial. As a first estimate of GM's justified P/S based on forecasted fundamentals, you decide to use Equation 4-4.

1. Based on the above data, calculate GM's justified P/S.
2. Given an estimate of GM's sales per share for 2001 of $295, what is the intrinsic value of GM stock?
3. Given a market price for GM of $53 as of December 6, 2001, and your answer to Problem 2, state whether GM stock appears to be fairly valued, overvalued, or undervalued.

Solution to 1: Using Equation 4-4, we calculate GM's justified P/S as follows:

$$\frac{P_0}{S_0} = \frac{0.035 \times 0.30 \times 1.05}{0.11 - 0.05} = 0.1838$$

Solution to 2: An estimate of intrinsic value is $0.1838 \times \$295 = \$54.22$. Rounding P/S to two decimal places, we can calculate intrinsic value as $0.18 \times \$295 = \$53.10$.

Solution to 3:   GM stock appears to be approximately fairly valued, or slightly undervalued.

---

[44]That is, it is possible that an increase (decrease) in the profit margin could be offset by a decrease (increase) in total asset turnover (Sales/Assets).

5.3. Valuation Using Comparables

Using the method of comparables for valuing stocks using P/S follows the steps given in Section 3.3, which we earlier illustrated using P/E and P/B. As mentioned earlier, P/Ss are usually reported based on trailing sales. The analyst may also base a relative valuation on P/Ss calculated on forecasted sales, given that the analyst has developed models for forecasting sales.[45] In valuing stocks using the method of comparables, analysts should also gather information on profit margin, expected earnings growth, and risk. As always, the quality of accounting merits investigation as well.

EXAMPLE 4-26   P/S Comparables Approach

Continuing with the valuation project, you have compiled the information on GM and peer companies Ford Motor Corporation (NYSE: F) and DaimlerChrysler (NYSE: DCX) given in Table 4-13.

TABLE 4-13   P/S Comparables (as of December 6, 2001)

	Price to Sales			2000 Profit Margin	Forecast Profit Margin	Median Analyst Long-Term EPS Growth Forecast	Beta
	Current Close	YTD High	YTD Low				
General Motors (GM)	0.16	0.21	0.12	3.0%	2.5%	5.0%	1.11
Ford (F)	0.19	0.29	0.16	2.8%	3.0%	5.0%	0.99
DaimlerChrysler (DCX)	0.32	0.37	0.18	2.2%	2.6%	7.0%	1.23

Sources: Bloomberg LLC; *The Value Line Investment Survey* for profit margin and ROE forecasts; First Call/Thomson Financial for EPS growth forecasts.

Answer the following questions using the data in Table 4-13:

1. Based on the P/S (using the current close) and referencing no other information, does GM appear to be relatively undervalued?
2. State whether GM or DCX is most closely comparable to Ford. Justify your answer.
3. As of the end of 2001, the S&P 500 had a weighted average P/S of 2.5 and a median P/S of 1.27. GM, F, and DCX have traded at P/Ss that represent

---

[45] Unlike EPS forecasts, analysts' sales forecasts are not generally gathered and disseminated.

discounts of as much as 90 percent from the weighted average P/S for the S&P 500. Can you conclude from this fact alone that, as a group, the three automobile makers were undervalued in absolute terms? Explain your answer.

Solution to 1: Because the P/S for GM, 0.16, is the lowest of the three P/Ss, GM appears to be relatively undervalued, referencing no other information.

Solution to 2: Ford appears to be more closely matched to GM than to DaimlerChrysler on the basis of the information given. The profit margin, the growth rate *g*, and risk are key fundamentals in the P/S approach. Ford closely matches GM along the dimension of expected growth. The risk of Ford stock as measured by beta is closer to GM than to DaimlerChrysler. The comparison of profit margins, reflecting cost structure, is less conclusive but does not contradict the general conclusion. The current profit margin of Ford is close to that of General Motors (2.8%/3% = 0.933 or 93% of GM's) but well above that of DaimlerChrysler (2.8%/2.2% = 1.27 or 127% of DCX's). The forecast is for Ford to take the lead in profit margin over GM and DCX by about an equal amount.

    An interesting point arises here. DCX's actual net profit margin per the unadjusted numbers in its Form 20-F Annual Report filing with the U.S. SEC was 4.86%, and some vendors report that number. Using 4.86%, the analyst might conclude that DCX had the lowest cost structure among the three companies, rather than the highest, in 2000. This percentage, however, includes gains from the sales of business units in 2000, which are nonrecurring. The comparisons in Table 4-13 better reflect underlying earnings.

Solution to 3: No, such a conclusion would not be warranted. Before concluding that the automakers as a group were undervalued in absolute terms, the analyst would need to establish that

- the automakers were relatively undervalued given differences in profit margin, earnings growth prospects, and risk, in relation to the S&P 500; and
- the S&P 500 itself was fairly valued at a weighted average P/S of 2.5.

6. PRICE TO CASH FLOW

Price to cash flow is a widely reported valuation indicator. In Block's 1999 survey, cash flow ranked behind only earnings in importance. According to the *Merrill Lynch Institutional Factor Survey*, price to cash flow on average saw wider use in investment practice than P/E, P/B, P/S, or dividend yield in the 1989–2001 period, among the institutional investors surveyed.[46]

    In this section, we present price to cash flows based on alternative major cash flow concepts. With the wide variety of cash flow concepts in use, the analyst should be especially

---

[46]On average, 46.1 percent of respondents reported consistently using price to cash flow over this period. In one year (2001), price to cash flow ranked first among the 23 factors surveyed.

careful that she understands (and communicates, as a writer) the exact definition of *cash flow* that is the basis for the analysis.

Analysts have offered the following rationales for the use of price to cash flow:

- Cash flow is less subject to manipulation by management than earnings.[47]
- Because cash flow is generally more stable than earnings, price to cash flow is generally more stable than P/E.
- Using price to cash flow rather than P/E addresses the issue of differences in accounting conservatism between companies (differences in the quality of earnings).
- Differences in price to cash flow may be related to differences in long-run average returns, according to empirical research.[48]

Possible drawbacks to the use of price to cash flow include the following:

- When the EPS plus noncash charges approximation to cash flow from operations is used, items affecting actual cash flow from operations, such as noncash revenue and net changes in working capital, are ignored.[49]
- Theory views free cash flow to equity (FCFE) rather than cash flow as the appropriate variable for valuation. We can use P/FCFE ratios but FCFE does have the possible drawback of being more volatile compared to cash flow, for many businesses. FCFE is also more frequently negative than cash flow.

EXAMPLE 4-27   Accounting Methods and Cash Flow

One approximation of cash flow in practical use is EPS plus depreciation, amortization, and depletion. Even this simple approximation can point to issues of interest to the analyst in valuation, as this stylized illustration shows. Hypothetical companies A and B have constant cash revenues and cash expenses (as well as a constant number of shares outstanding) in 2000, 2001, and 2002. Company A incurs total depreciation of $15.00 per share during the three-year period, which it spreads out evenly (straight-line depreciation, SLD). Because revenues, expenses, and depreciation are constant over the period, EPS for Company A is also constant, say at $10, as given in Column 1 in Table 4-14. Company B is identical to Company A except that it uses accelerated depreciation: Depreciation is 150 percent of SLD in 2000, declining to 50 percent of SLD in 2002, as given in Column 5. (We assume both A and B use the same depreciation method for tax purposes.)

---

[47] Cash flow from operations, precisely defined, can be manipulated only through "real" activities, such as the sale of receivables.

[48] See, for example, O'Shaughnessy (1997), who examined price to cash flow, and Hackel, Livnat, and Rai (1994) and Hackel and Livnat (1991), who examined price to average free cash flow.

[49] For example, aggressive recognition (front-end loading) of revenue would not be captured in the earnings-plus-noncash-charges definition.

TABLE 4-14   Earning Growth Rates and Cash Flow (all amounts per share)

Year	Company A			Company B		
	Earnings (1)	Depreciation (2)	Cash Flow (3)	Earnings (4)	Depreciation (5)	Cash Flow (6)
2000	$10.00	$5.00	$15.00	$7.50	$7.50	$15.00
2001	$10.00	$5.00	$15.00	$10.00	$5.00	$15.00
2002	$10.00	$5.00	$15.00	$12.50	$2.50	$15.00
	Sum	$15.00		Sum	$15.00	

Because of different choices in how Companies A and B depreciate for financial reporting purposes, Company A's EPS is flat at $10.00 (Column 1) whereas Company B's shows 29 percent compound growth, $(\$12.50/\$7.50)^{1/2} - 1.00 = 0.29$ (Column 4). Company B shows apparent positive earnings momentum. As analysts comparing Companies A and B, we might be misled using EPS numbers as reported (without putting EPS on a comparable basis). For both companies, however, cash flow per share is level at $15. Depreciation may be the simplest noncash charge to understand; write-offs and other noncash charges may offer more latitude for the management of earnings. Hawkins (1998) summarizes many corporate accounting issues for analysts, including how accounting choices can create the effect of earnings momentum.

6.1. Determining Cash Flow

In practice, analysts and data vendors often use simple approximations to cash flow from operations in calculating cash flow in price to cash flow. For many companies, depreciation and amortization are the major noncash charges regularly added to net income in the process of calculating cash flow from operations by the add-back method. A representative approximation specifies cash flow per share as EPS plus per-share depreciation, amortization, and depletion.[50] We call this estimation the earnings-plus-noncash-charges definition and use the symbol CF for it, understanding that this definition is one common usage in calculating price to cash flow rather than a technically accurate definition from an accounting perspective. We will also introduce more technically accurate cash flow concepts: cash flow from operations (CFO), free cash flow to equity (FCFE), and EBITDA, an estimate of pre-interest, pre-tax operating cash flow.[51]

Most frequently, trailing price to cash flows are reported. A trailing price to cash flow is calculated as the current market price divided by the sum of the most recent four quarters' cash flow per share. A fiscal year definition is also possible, just as in the case of EPS.

---

[50] This representation is, for example, the definition in Value Line (2001). Value Line states its definition of cash flow in terms of "net income minus preferred dividends (if any)," which is net income to common shareholders, to which it adds the above three noncash charges. The resulting sum is then divided by the number of shares outstanding. Note that depletion is an expense only for natural resource companies.
[51] See Grant and Parker (2001). Grant and Parker point out that EBITDA as a cash flow approximation assumes that changes in working capital accounts are immaterial. The EPS-plus-noncash-charges definition makes the same assumption (it is essentially earnings before depreciation and amortization).

EXAMPLE 4-28   Calculating Earnings-Plus-Noncash Charges (CF)

In 2000, Koninklijke Philips Electronics N.V. reported net income of €9,602 million, equal to basic EPS of €7.31, as well as depreciation and amortization of €2,320 million or €1.75 per share. Koninklijke Philips trades both on the New York Stock Exchange (NYSE: PHG) and Euronext Amsterdam (AEX: PHIA). An AEX price for Koninklijke Philips as of early March 2001 was €30. Calculate the P/CF ratio for PHIA.

EPS plus per-share depreciation, amortization, and depletion is €7.31 + €1.75 = €9.06 per share. Thus P/CF = €30/€9.06 = 3.31, or 3.3.

Rather than use an approximate EPS-plus-noncash-charges concept of cash flow, analysts can use cash flow from operations (CFO) in a price multiple. CFO is found in the statement of cash flows. Careful analysts often adjust CFO as reported to remove the effects of any items related to financing or investing activities. For example, when CFO includes cash outflows for interest expense and cash inflows for interest income, as in U.S. GAAP accounting, one common adjustment is to add back to CFO the quantity (Net cash interest outflow) × (1 − Tax rate).[52] Analysts also adjust CFO for components not expected to persist into future time periods.

In addition, the analyst can relate price to FCFE, the cash flow concept with the strongest link to valuation theory. Because the amount of capital expenditures as a fraction of CFO will generally differ among companies being compared, the analyst may find that rankings by P/CFO (as well as P/CF) will differ from rankings by P/FCFE. Because period-by-period FCFE can be more volatile than CFO (or CF), however, a trailing P/FCFE is not necessarily more informative in a valuation. As an example, consider two similar businesses with the same CFO and capital expenditures over a two-year period. If the first company times the expenditures toward the beginning of the period and the second times the expenditures toward the end, the P/FCFE ratios for the two stocks may differ sharply without pointing to a meaningful economic difference between them.[53] This concern can be addressed at least in part by using price to average free cash flow, as in Hackel, Livnat, and Rai (1994).

Another ratio sometimes reported is P/EBITDA.[54] EBITDA is earnings before interest, taxes, depreciation, and amortization. To calculate EBITDA, as discussed in Chapter 3, analysts usually start with earnings from continuing operations excluding nonrecurring items. To that earnings number, interest, taxes, depreciation, and amortization are added. When per-share price is in the numerator, per-share EBITDA is used in the denominator. EBITDA, as already mentioned, is a pre-tax and pre-interest number. Because EBITDA is pre-interest, it is a flow to both debt and equity. As a result, with EBITDA in the denominator of a ratio, total company value (debt plus equity) is more appropriate than common stock value in the

---

[52]Under International Accounting Standards (IAS), interest income and interest expense may or may not be in CFO. Therefore, an adjustment may be necessary to match U.S. GAAP and IAS. Consistency in treatment is important.

[53]The analyst could appropriately use the FCFE discounted cash flow model value, which incorporates all expected future free cash flows to equity, however.

[54]Another concept that has become popular is cash earnings, which has been defined in various ways, such as earnings plus amortization of intangibles or EBITDA less net financial expenses.

numerator. In Section 7, we present a multiple, enterprise value to EBITDA, that is consistent with this observation.

EXAMPLE 4-29   Alternative Price to Cash Flow Concepts

In Example 4-18, we concluded that the P/B was inappropriate for valuing Dell Computer (Nasdaq NMS: DELL) relative to peer companies. In particular, Dell's relatively efficient use of assets penalizes it in P/B comparisons. Because Dell's business model results in relatively strong cash flow, we might compare Dell with its peers on the basis of one or more cash flow measures or related concepts:

- EPS-plus-noncash charges (CF),
- CFO,
- FCFE, and/or
- EBITDA.

In this example, we illustrate the calculation of price multiples based on these concepts from actual financials. The two financial statements needed to calculate any of these concepts are the income statement and the statement of cash flows, given in Tables 4-15(A) and 4-15(B).

TABLE 4-15 (A)   Dell Computer Corporation Consolidated Statement of Income (in millions, except per-share amounts)

	February 2, 2001
Net revenue	$31,888
Cost of revenue	25,445
Gross margin	6,443
Operating Expenses	
Selling, general, and administrative	3,193
Research, development, and engineering	482
Special charges	105
Total Operating Expenses	3,780
Operating income	2,663
Investment and other income, net	531
Income before income taxes and cumulative effect of change in accounting principle	3,194
Provision for income taxes	(958)
Cumulative effect of change in accounting principle, net	(59)
Net Income	$2,177
Earnings per common share:	
Before cumulative effect of change in accounting principle:	
Basic	$0.87
Diluted	$0.81

TABLE 4-15 (A)   *(continued)*

After cumulative effect of change in accounting principle:	
Basic	$0.84
Diluted	$0.79
Weighted average shares outstanding:	
Basic	2,582
Diluted	2,746

TABLE 4-15 (B)   Dell Computer Corporation Consolidated Statement
of Cash Flows (in millions)

	February 2, 2001
Cash Flows from Operating Activities:	
Net income	$ 2,177
Adjustments to reconcile net income to net cash provided by operating activities:	
Depreciation and amortization	240
Tax benefits of employee stock plans	929
Special charges	105
Gain on sale of investments	(307)
Other	109
Changes in:	
Operating working capital	671
Non-current assets and liabilities	271
Net Cash Provided by Operating Activities	4,195
Cash Flows from Investing Activities:	
Investments	
Purchases	(2,606)
Maturities and sales	2,331
Capital expenditures	(482)
Net Cash Used in Investing Activities	(757)
Cash Flows from Financing Activities:	
Purchase of common stock	(2,700)
Issuance of common stock under employee plans	404
Proceeds from issuance of long-term debt, net of issuance costs	—
Other	(9)
Net Cash Used in Financing Activities	(2,305)
Effect of exchange rate changes on cash	(32)
Net increase in cash	1,101
Cash and cash equivalents at beginning of period	3,809
Cash and cash equivalents at end of period	$4,910

Other information for Dell is as follows:

- In the last three years, Dell has had a cash flow "tax benefits of employee stock plans," which it has classified as an operating cash flow. This item, amounting to $929 million in 2001, relates to tax benefits from the exercise of employee stock options during a period of rising stock prices. The amount of such benefits in the future is related to continuing rising stock prices for Dell.
- Net investment income of $531 million included $47 million in interest expense. Actual cash interest paid for the year was $49 million. Cash flow from operations as reported incorporates such financing effects. The effective tax rate per the income statement was 30 percent.
- Dell stock closed at $27.11 on April 16, 2001.

Based on the above data, answer the following questions:

1. Calculate P/CF.
2. Calculate P/CFO, adjusting CFO for the "tax benefits of employee stock plans" and for financing effects.
3. Calculate P/FCFE consistent with your work in Problem 2.
4. Calculate P/EBITDA.

Solution to 1: Net income = $2,177 million; depreciation and amortization = $240 million; so CF = 2,177 + 240 = $2,417 million. There are 2,582 million shares outstanding. Thus CF = 2,417/2,582 = 0.94 and P/CF = 27.11/0.94 = 28.8.

Solution to 2: Cash flow from operations is $4,195 million. Excluding $929 million associated with tax benefits of employee stock plans gives 4,195 − 929 = 3,266. To further adjust CFO for the effect of actual cash interest paid, we have $3,266 + 49(1 − 0.30) = $3,266 + $34.3 = $3,300.3. So $3,300.3/2,582 = $1.28. So P/CFO based on adjusted per-share CFO of $1.28 equals $27.11/$1.28 = 21.2.[55] The logic of excluding the $929 million is that because such tax benefits depend on stock price performance, they may not persist into the future.

Solution to 3: Recall that FCFE is cash flow from operations less net investment in fixed capital plus net borrowing. Net cash used in fixed capital (reported above as capital expenditures) was $482 million and net borrowing was zero. Because FCFE is a flow to equity, we must subtract the add-back of $34.3 million that we made in Problem 2. So FCFE is $3,300.3 − $482 − $34.3 = $2,784. Per share we have $2,784/2,582 = $1.08. P/FCFE = $27.11/$1.08 = 25.1.

Solution to 4: Net income = $2,177 million, Interest expense = $47 million, Depreciation and amortization = $240 million, Taxes = $958 million. EBITDA = $2,177 +

---

[55]Although 30 percent was the effective tax rate per the income statement, interestingly Dell actually paid no taxes for the year because of the effect of the employee stock options. The adjustment we just illustrated would be appropriate for use in forecasting; adding back the full $49 million (reflecting no taxes) would better reflect actual cash flow for the year purged of financing items.

$47 + $240 + $958 = $3,422$. Per share EBITDA $= $3,422/2,582 = 1.32. P/EBITDA $= $27.11/$1.32 = 20.5$.

In summary, this exercise produced multiples ranging from 20.5 for P/EBITDA to 28.8 for P/CF. Consistency in definition is important. Furthermore, if the analyst were featuring diluted EPS in her analysis, she would report cash flow multiples based on 2,746 million diluted shares.

6.2. Valuation Based on Forecasted Fundamentals

The relationship between the justified price to cash flow and fundamentals follows from the familiar mathematics of the present value model. The justified price to cash flow is inversely related to the stock's required rate of return and positively related to the growth rate(s) of expected future cash flows (however defined), all else equal. We can find a justified price to cash flow based on fundamentals by finding the value of a stock using the most suitable DCF model and dividing that number by cash flow, using our chosen definition of cash flow. Example 4-30 illustrates the process.

EXAMPLE 4-30   Justified Price to Cash Flow Based on Forecasted Fundamentals

As a technology analyst, you are working on the valuation of Dell Computer (Nasdaq NMS: DELL). You have calculated per-share FCFE for DELL of 1.39. As a first estimate of value, you are applying a FCFE model under the assumption of a stable long-term growth rate in FCFE:

$$V_0 = \frac{(1+g)\text{FCFE}_0}{r-g}$$

where g is the expected growth rate of FCFE. You estimate trailing FCFE at $1.39 per share and trailing CF (based on the earnings-plus-noncash-charges definition) at $0.75. Your other estimates are a 14.5 percent required rate of return and an 8.5 percent expected growth rate of FCFE.

1. What is the intrinsic value of DELL, according to a constant-growth FCFE model?
2. What is the justified P/CF, based on forecasted fundamentals?
3. What is the justified P/FCFE, based on forecasted fundamentals?

Solution to 1: Calculate intrinsic value as $(1.085 \times $1.39)/(0.145 - 0.085) = 25.14.

Solution to 2: Calculate a justified P/CF based on forecasted fundamentals as $25.14/$0.75 = 33.5$.

Solution to 3: The justified P/FCFE ratio is $25.14/$1.39 = 18.1$.

6.3. Valuation Using Comparables

Using the method of comparables for valuing stocks based on price to cash flow follows the steps given in Section 3.3, which we earlier illustrated using P/E, P/B, and P/S.

EXAMPLE 4-31   Price to Cash Flow and Comparables

As a technology analyst, you have been asked to compare the valuation of Compaq Computer Corporation (NYSE: CPQ) with Gateway, Inc. (NYSE: GTW).[56] One valuation metric you are considering is P/CF. Table 4-16 gives information on P/CF, P/FCFE, and selected fundamentals as of April 16, 2001.

TABLE 4-16   A Comparison Between Two Companies (all amounts per share)

	Current Price	Trailing CF per Share	P/CF	Trailing FCFE per Share	P/FCFE	Consensus Five-Year Growth Forecast	Beta
CPQ	$17.98	$1.84	9.8	$0.29	62	13.4%	1.50
GTW	$15.65	$1.37	11.4	−$1.99	NM	10.6%	1.45

Source: The Value Line Investment Survey.

Using the information in Table 4-16, compare the valuations of CPQ and GTW using the P/CF multiple, assuming that the two stocks have approximately equal risk.

Solution: CPQ is selling at a P/CF (9.8) approximately 14 percent smaller than the P/CF of GTW (11.4). We would expect on that basis that, all else equal, investors anticipate a higher growth rate for GTW. In fact, the consensus five-year earnings growth forecast for CPQ is 280 basis points higher than for GTW. As of the date of the comparison, CPQ appears to be relatively undervalued compared with GTW, as judged by P/CF. The information in Table 4-16 on FCFE supports the proposition that CPQ may be relatively undervalued. Positive FCFE for CPQ suggests that growth was funded internally; negative FCFE for GTW suggests the need for external funding of growth.

---

7. ENTERPRISE VALUE TO EBITDA

In Section 6, when presenting the P/EBITDA multiple, we stated that because EBITDA is a flow to both debt and equity, a multiple using total company value in the numerator was logically more appropriate. Enterprise value to EBITDA responds to this need. **Enterprise**

---

[56]In 2002, Compaq Computer Corporation merged with Hewlett-Packard Corporation.

value (EV) is total company value (the market value of debt, common equity, and preferred equity) minus the value of cash and investments. Because the numerator is enterprise value, EV/EBITDA is a valuation indicator for the overall company rather than common stock. If the analyst can assume that the business's debt and preferred stock (if any) are efficiently priced, the analyst can also draw an inference about the valuation of common equity. Such an assumption is often reasonable.

Analysts have offered the following rationales for using EV/EBITDA:

- EV/EBITDA may be more appropriate than P/E for comparing companies with different financial leverage (debt), because EBITDA is a pre-interest earnings figure, in contrast to EPS, which is post-interest.
- By adding back depreciation and amortization, EBITDA controls for differences in depreciation and amortization across businesses. For this reason, EV/EBITDA is frequently used in the valuation of capital-intensive businesses (for example, cable companies and steel companies). Such businesses typically have substantial depreciation and amortization expenses.
- EBITDA is frequently positive when EPS is negative.

Possible drawbacks to EV/EBITDA include the following:

- EBITDA will overestimate cash flow from operations if working capital is growing. EBITDA also ignores the effects of differences in revenue recognition policy on cash flow from operations.[57]
- Free cash flow to the firm (FCFF), which directly reflects the amount of required capital expenditures, has a stronger link to valuation theory than does EBITDA. Only if depreciation expenses match capital expenditures do we expect EBITDA to reflect differences in businesses' capital programs. This qualification to EBITDA comparisons can be meaningful for the capital-intensive businesses to which EV/EBITDA is often applied.

7.1. Determining EBITDA

We illustrated the calculation of EBITDA in Chapter 3 as well as in Section 6 of this chapter. As discussed above, analysts commonly define enterprise value as follows:

> Market value of common equity (Number of shares outstanding × Price per share)
> Plus: Market value of preferred stock (if any)
> Plus: Market value of debt
> Less: Cash and investments
> Equals: Enterprise value

Cash and investments (sometimes termed nonearning assets) are subtracted because EV is designed to measure the price an acquirer would pay for a company as a whole. The acquirer must buy out current equity and debt providers but then gets access to the cash and investments, which lower the net cost of the acquisition. The same logic explains the use of market values: In repurchasing debt, an acquirer would have to pay market prices. Some debt, however, may be private and not trade, or be publicly traded but trade infrequently. When the analyst does not have market values, he uses book values (values as given in the balance sheet). Example 4-32 illustrates the calculation of EV/EBITDA.

---

[57] See Moody's Investors Service (2000) and Grant and Parker (2001) for additional issues and concerns.

EXAMPLE 4-32   Calculating EV/EBITDA

Comcast Corporation is principally engaged in the development, management, and operation of hybrid fiber-coaxial broadband cable networks, cellular and personal communications systems, and the provision of content. Table 4-17 gives excerpts from the consolidated balance sheet (as of December 31, 2000).

TABLE 4-17   Comcast Corporation Liabilities and Shareholders' Equity (in millions, except per share)

	December 31, 2000
Liabilities and Shareholders' Equity	
Current Liabilities:	
Accounts payable and accrued expenses	$ 2,852.9
Accrued interest	105.5
Deferred income taxes	789.9
Current portion of long-term debt	293.9
Total Current Liabilities	4,042.2
Noncurrent Liabilities:	
Long-term debt, less current portion	10,517.4
Deferred income taxes	5,786.7
Minority interest and other commitments and contingencies	1,257.2
Common equity put options	54.6
Total Noncurrent Liabilities	17,615.9
Shareholders' Equity:	
Preferred Stock: Authorized, 20,000,000 shares 5.25%	
Series B mandatorily redeemable convertible, $1,000 par value; issued, 59,450 at redemption value	59.5
Class A special common stock, $1 par value: Authorized, 2,500,000,000 shares; issued, 931,340,103; outstanding, 908,015,192	908.0
Class A common stock, $1 par value: Authorized, 200,000,000 shares; issued and outstanding, 21,832,250	21.8
Class B common stock, $1 par value: Authorized, 50,000,000 shares; issued and outstanding, 9,444,375	9.4
Additional capital	11,598.8
Retained earnings (accumulated deficit)	1,056.5
Accumulated other comprehensive income	432.4
Total Shareholders' Equity	14,086.4
Total Liabilities and Shareholders' Equity	$35,744.5

An unusual item in the balance sheet is "common equity put options," which were issued as part of a share repurchase program. Because the value of these puts should be reflected in the price of the common stock, the $54.6 million should not be included in calculating EV. The balance sheet shows that Comcast has three classes of common stock:

- Class A Special Common Stock (Nasdaq NMS: CMCSK) is generally nonvoting; this issue is a component of the S&P 500;
- Class A (Nasdaq NMS: CMCSA) is entitled to one vote; and
- Class B is entitled to 15 votes and is convertible, share for share, into Class A or Class A Special Common Stock. This issue is not publicly traded.

Closing share prices as of March 7, 2001, were $45.875 for CMCSK and $45.25 for CMCSA. "Minority interest and other" is to be viewed as an equity item.[58]

The asset side of the balance sheet (as of December 31, 2000) gave the following items (in millions):

Cash and cash equivalents	$651.5
Investments	$3,059.7

The income statement for the year ending December 31, 2000, gave the following items (in millions):

Net income	$2,021.5
Net income for common stockholders	$1,998.0
Interest expense	$691.4
Taxes	$1,441.3
Depreciation	$837.3
Amortization	$1,794.0

Based on the above information, calculate EV/EBITDA.

Solution:

- We first calculate EBITDA. We always select net income (which is net income available to both preferred and common equity) in the EBITDA calculation:

	2000
Net income	$2,021.5
Interest	$691.4
Taxes	$1,441.3
Depreciation	$837.3
Amortization	+ $1,794.0
EBITDA	$6,785.5

- We calculate the value of all equity, adding to it "minority interest and other."

	Millions
CMCSK issue ($45.875 × 908.015192 million shares)	41,655.20
CMCSA issue ($45.25 × 21.83225 million shares)	987.91
Class B stock (per books)	9.4
Common equity value	42,652.51
Preferred equity (per books)	59.5
Total equity	42,712.01
Minority interest and other	1,257.2
Common equity plus minority interest	43,969.21

- The value of long-term debt (per the books) is $10,517.4 million.
- The sum of cash and cash equivalents plus investments is $651.5 million + $3,059.7 million = $3,711.2 million.

So, EV = $43,969.21 million + $10,517.4 million − $3,711.2 million = $50,775.41 million. We conclude that EV/EBITDA = ($50,775.41 million)/($6,785.5 million) = 7.5.

---

[58]Minority interest represents the proportionate stake of minority shareholders in a company's consolidated, majority-owned subsidiary.

TABLE 4-18   EV/EBITDA Multiples Are Well Below Recent Averages Calendar 2002E Cash Flow Multiples (in millions, except per share)

	CMCSK^c	CHTR^d	COX	ADLAC^e	CVC	MCCC^f	ICCI^g	Average
Rating	Strong Buy	Strong Buy	Buy	Strong Buy	Buy	Buy	Buy	
Size ranking	3	4	5	6	7	8	9	
Price	$33.98	$17.62	$39.65	$28.97	$40.00	$16.10	$20.25	
Times . . . Diluted shares outstanding^a	964	657	620	173	178	119.9	61.3	
Equals . . . Equity market capitalization	$32,754	$11,583	$24,576	$5,016	$7,104	$1,930	$1,242	
Plus . . . Debt at 12/02	$10,852	$17,618	$8,988	$13,936	$6,147	$3,059	$1,055	
Plus . . . Preferred	$0	$0	$281	$148	$2,630	$0	$0	
Less . . . Nonearning assets at 12/02	$15,726	$144	$5,792	($139)	$3,885	$7	$19	
Less . . . Options exercise	$507	$0	$80	$0	$481	$0	$21	
Equals . . . **Enterprise value**	**$27,373**	**$29,057**	**$27,973**	**$19,239**	**$11,514**	**$4,982**	**$2,257**	
Adjusted Cable EBITDA^b	**$2,455**	**$2,134**	**$1,822**	**$1,616**	**$1,012**	**$387**	**$185**	
Equals . . .								
Cable Cash Flow Multiple	**11.1 ×**	**13.6 ×**	**15.4 ×**	**11.9 ×**	**11.4 ×**	**12.9 ×**	**12.2 ×**	**12.6 ×**

Pro forma subscribers at 12/02	8,475	7,130	6,402	5,858	3,059	1,593	592	
Pro forma homes passed at 12/02	13,610	12,161	10,016	9,503	4,417	2,595	1,035	
Enterprise value per subscriber	**$3,230**	**$4,075**	**$4,369**	**$3,284**	**$3,764**	**$3,127**	**$3,809**	**$3,665**
Enterprise value per homes passed	**$2,011**	**$2,389**	**$2,793**	**$2,024**	**$2,607**	**$1,920**	**$2,181**	
Percent of Plant > 550 MHz at 12/02	98%	95%	96%	96%	95%	86%	95%	

Notes:

[a] Includes primary shares plus in-the-money employee/management options and convertible instruments.

[b] Adjusted Cable EBITDA includes allocated corporate overhead.

[c] Pro forma the AT&T and Adelphia system swaps and AT&T system acquisitions as if all were completed prior to January 1, 2001.

[d] Pro forma the Kalamazoo and AT&T systems acquisitions as if they occurred January 1, 2000.

[e] Pro forma the Century, Frontier, Harron, Coaxial, Benchmark, Cablevision (Cleveland), Prestige, and GS Communications acquisitions as if they took place on January 1, 2000.

[f] Pro forma the AT&T acquisition as if it occurred before January 1, 2000.

[g] All numbers proportional of Insight's 50% stake in the Insight Midwest JV. Pro forma the JV rollup as if it occurred before January 1, 2000.

Source: Shapiro, Savner, and Toohig (2001).

7.2. Valuation Based on Forecasted Fundamentals

As with other multiples, intuition concerning the fundamental drivers of enterprise value to EBITDA can help when applying the method of comparables. All else equal, the justified EV/EBITDA based on fundamentals should be positively related to expected growth rate in FCFF and negatively related to the business's weighted-average cost of capital. The analyst should review the statement of cash flows to get a better picture of the relationship of EBITDA to the company's underlying cash flow from operations.

7.3. Valuation Using Comparables

A recent equity research report on the cable industry, excerpted in Table 4-18, illustrates a format for the presentation of relative valuations using EV/EBITDA, which is informally called a "cash flow multiple" in the report. All else equal, a lower EV/EBITDA value relative to peers indicates relative undervaluation. The analyst's recommendations are clearly not completely determined by relative EV/EBITDA, however; from the analyst's perspective, EV/EBITDA is simply one piece of information to consider.

8. DIVIDEND YIELD

Total return has a capital appreciation component and a dividend yield component. Dividend yield is frequently reported to supply the investor with an estimate of the dividend yield component of total return. Dividend yield is also used as a valuation indicator. According to the *Merrill Lynch Institutional Factor Survey*, from 1989 to 2001, on average slightly less than one-quarter of respondents reported using dividend yield as a factor in the investment process.

Analysts have offered the following rationales for using dividend yields in valuation:

- Dividend yield is a component of total return.
- Dividends are a less risky component of total return than capital appreciation.

Possible drawbacks of dividend yield include the following:

- Dividend yield is only one component of total return; not using all information related to expected return is suboptimal.
- Dividends paid now displace earnings in all future periods (a concept known as the **dividend displacement of earnings**). Investors trade off future earnings growth to receive higher current dividends.
- The argument about the relative safety of dividends presupposes that the market prices reflect in a biased way differences in the relative risk of the components of return.

8.1. Calculation of Dividend Yield

This chapter thus far has presented multiples with market price in the numerator. Price to dividend (P/D) ratios have occasionally appeared in valuation, particularly with respect to indexes. Many stocks, however, do not pay dividends, and the P/D ratio is undefined with zero in the denominator; for such stocks, dividend yield is defined. For practical purposes, dividend yield is the preferred way to present this variable. **Trailing dividend yield** is generally calculated as four times the most recent quarterly per-share dividend divided by the current market price per share. (The most recent quarterly dividend times four is known as the **dividend rate**.) The **leading dividend yield** is calculated as forecasted dividends per share over the next year divided by the current market price per share.

EXAMPLE 4-33   Calculating Dividend Yield

Table 4-19 gives dividend data for Ford Motor Company (NYSE: F).

TABLE 4-19   Dividend Data for
Ford Motor Company

	Dividends per Share
1Q:2002	$0.10
4Q:2001	$0.15
3Q:2001	$0.30
2Q:2001	$0.30
Total	$0.85

Source: Standard & Poor's Stock Reports.

Given a price per share of $14.62, calculate the trailing dividend yield of Ford.

Solution: The dividend rate is $0.10 × 4 = $0.40. The dividend yield is $0.40/$14.62 = 0.0274 or 2.7%. This percentage is the yield reported by Standard & Poor's in a stock report on Ford Motor Company dated February 16, 2002.

8.2. Valuation Based on Forecasted Fundamentals

The relationship of dividend yield to fundamentals can be illustrated in the context of the Gordon growth model. From that model we obtain the expression

$$\frac{D_0}{P_0} = \frac{r - g}{1 + g} \tag{4-5}$$

Equation 4-5 shows that dividend yield is negatively related to the expected rate of growth in dividends and positively related to the stock's required rate of return. The first point implies that the selection of stocks with relatively high dividend yields is consistent with an orientation to a value rather than growth investment style.

8.3. Valuation Using Comparables

Using dividend yield with comparables is similar to the process that has been illustrated for other multiples. An analyst compares a company with its peers to determine whether it is attractively priced considering its dividend yield and risk. The analyst should examine whether differences in expected growth explain difference in dividend yield. Another consideration used by some investors is the security of the dividend (the probability that it will be cut).

EXAMPLE 4-34   Dividend Yield Comparables

William Leiderman is a portfolio manager for a U.S. pension fund's domestic equity portfolio. The portfolio is exempt from taxes, so any differences in the taxation of dividends and capital gains are not relevant. Leiderman's client has a high current income requirement. Leiderman is considering the purchase of utility stocks for the fund as of early April 2002. He has narrowed down his selection to three large-cap utilities serving the southeastern United States, given in Table 4-20.

TABLE 4-20   Using Dividend Yield to Compare Stocks

Company	Consensus Forecast Growth	Beta	Dividend Yield
Florida Power and Light (NYSE: FPL)	6.95%	0.13	3.7%
Progress Energy (NYSE: PGN)	6.79%	0.09	4.4%
Southern Company (NYSE: SO)	5.44%	−0.06	4.7%

Source: First Call/Thomson Financial.

All of the securities exhibit similar and low market risk. Although Southern Company has the highest dividend yield, it also has the lowest expected growth rate. Leiderman determines that Progress Energy provides the greatest combination of dividend yield and growth, amounting to 11.19 percent.

---

9. INTERNATIONAL VALUATION CONSIDERATIONS

Clearly, to perform a relative value analysis, an analyst must use comparable companies and underlying financial data prepared using comparable methods. Using relative valuation methods in an international setting is thus difficult. Comparing companies across borders frequently involves accounting method differences, cultural differences, economic differences, and resulting differences in risk and growth opportunities. P/Es for individual companies in the same industry across borders have been found to vary widely.[59] Furthermore, national market P/Es often vary substantially at any single point in time. As of November 30, 1998,

---

[59]Copeland, Koller, and Murrin (1994, p. 375) provide an interesting example.

P/Es in 10 markets around the world ranged from a low of 18.1 in Hong Kong to a high of 191.0 in Japan.[60]

Although international accounting standards are beginning to converge, significant differences across borders still exist, making comparisons difficult. Even if harmonization of accounting principles is achieved, the need to adjust accounting data for comparability will always remain. As we have seen in earlier sections, even within a single country's accounting standards, differences between companies result from management's accounting choices (e.g., FIFO versus LIFO). The U.S. SEC requires that foreign companies whose securities trade in U.S. markets provide a reconciliation of their earnings from home country accounting principles to U.S. GAAP. This requirement not only assists the analyst in making necessary adjustments but also provides some insight into appropriate adjustments for other companies not required to provide this data. Table 4-21 (on page 228) presents a reconciliation from International Accounting Standards to U.S. GAAP for Nokia Corporation (NYSE: NOK).

In a study of companies filing such reconciliations to U.S. GAAP, Harris and Muller (1999) classify common differences into seven categories:

	Mean Adjustment Direction	
Category	Earnings	Equity
Differences in the treatment of goodwill	Minus	Plus
Deferred income taxes	Plus	Plus
Foreign exchange adjustments	Plus	Minus
Research and development costs	Minus	Minus
Pension expense	Minus	Plus
Tangible asset revaluations	Plus	Minus
Other	Minus	Minus

Although the mean adjustments are presented above, adjustments for individual companies can vary considerably. This list, however, provides the analyst with common adjustments that should be made.

International accounting differences affect the comparability of all price multiples. Of the price multiples examined in this chapter, P/CFO and P/FCFE will generally be least affected by accounting differences. P/Bs and P/Es will generally be more severely affected, as will multiples based on concepts such as EBITDA, which start from accounting earnings.

10. MOMENTUM VALUATION INDICATORS

The valuation indicators we call momentum indicators relate either price or a fundamental such as earnings to the time series of their own past values, or in some cases to the fundamental's expected value. One style of growth investing uses positive momentum in various senses as a selection criterion, and practitioners sometimes refer to such strategies as growth/momentum investment strategies. Momentum indicators based on price, such as the relative strength indicator discussed below, have also been referred to as **technical indicators**. According to

---

[60] See Schieneman (2000).

TABLE 4-21   Principal Differences between IAS and U.S. GAAP for
Nokia Corporation (years ended December 31; in millions)

	1999	1998
Reconciliation of net income		
Net income reported under IAS	€2,577	€1,750
U.S. GAAP adjustments:		
Deferred income taxes	0	−70
Pension expense	9	16
Development costs	−47	−18
Marketable securities	−15	29
Sale-leaseback transaction	4	1
Deferred tax effect of U.S. GAAP adjustments	14	−19
Net income under U.S. GAAP	€2,542	€1,689
Reconciliation of shareholders' equity		
Total shareholders' equity reported under IAS	€7,378	€5,109
U.S. GAAP adjustments:		
Pension expense	54	45
Development costs	−186	−138
Marketable securities	142	89
Sale-leaseback transaction	0	−4
Deferred tax effect of U.S. GAAP adjustments	−4	1
Total shareholders' equity under U.S. GAAP	€7,384	€5,102

Source: Nokia Corporation Annual Report, 1999.

the *Merrill Lynch Institutional Factor Survey*, momentum indicators were among the most popular valuation indicators over 1989 to 2001.[61] In this section, we review three representative momentum group indicators: earnings surprise, standardized unexpected earnings, and relative strength.

To define standardized unexpected earnings, we define **unexpected earnings** (also called **earnings surprise**) as the difference between reported earnings and expected earnings:

$$UE_t = EPS_t - E(EPS_t)$$

where UE_t is the unexpected earnings for quarter t, EPS_t is the reported EPS for quarter t, and $E(EPS_t)$ is the expected EPS for the quarter. For example, a stock with reported quarterly earnings of $1.05 and expected earnings of $1.00 would have a positive earnings surprise of $0.05. Often the percent earnings surprise, earnings surprise divided by expected EPS, is reported; in this example, percent earning surprise would be $0.05/$1.00 = 0.05 or 5%. When used directly as a valuation indicator, earnings surprise is generally scaled by a measure reflecting the variability or range in analysts' EPS estimates. The principle is that a given size EPS forecast error in relation to the mean is more meaningful the less the disagreement

---

[61] During the time period, the percentage of respondents who indicated that they used EPS surprise (surprise relative to consensus forecasts), EPS momentum (defined as 12-month trailing EPS divided by year-ago 12-month trailing EPS), and relative strength (defined as the difference between 3-month and 12-month price performance) was 51.5 percent, 46.3 percent, and 39.1 percent, respectively. EPS surprise was the most popular factor of the 23 surveyed over the entire time period.

among analysts' forecasts. A way to accomplish such scaling is to divide unexpected earnings by the standard deviation of analysts' earnings forecasts, which we can call **scaled earnings surprise**.

EXAMPLE 4-35   Calculating Scaled Earnings Surprise Using Analyst Forecasts

As of the end of November, the mean December 2001 quarterly consensus earnings forecast for International Business Machines (NYSE: IBM) was $1.32. For the 18 analysts covering the stock, the low forecast is $1.22 and the high is $1.37, and the standard deviation of the forecasts is $0.03. If reported earnings come in $0.04 above the mean forecast, what is the earnings surprise for IBM, scaled to reflect the dispersion in analysts' forecasts?

In this case, scaled earnings surprise is $0.04/$0.03 = 1.33.

The rationale behind using earnings surprises is the thesis that positive surprises may be associated with persistent positive abnormal returns, or alpha. The same rationale lies behind a momentum indicator that is closely related to earnings surprise but more highly researched: **standardized unexpected earnings** (SUE). SUE is defined as

$$SUE_t = \frac{EPS_t - E(EPS_t)}{\sigma[EPS_t - E(EPS_t)]}$$

where the numerator is the unexpected earnings for t and the denominator, $\sigma[EPS_t - E(EPS_t)]$, is the standard deviation of past unexpected earnings over some period prior to time t—for example, the 20 quarters prior to t as in Latané and Jones (1979), the article that introduced the SUE concept. In SUE, the magnitude of unexpected earnings is scaled by a measure of the size of historical forecast errors or surprises. The principle is that a given size EPS forecast error is more (less) meaningful the smaller (the larger) the historical size of forecast errors.

Suppose that for a stock that had a $0.05 earnings surprise, the standard deviation of past surprises is $0.20. The $0.05 surprise is relatively small compared to past forecast errors, reflected in a SUE of $0.05/$0.20 = 0.25. If the standard error of past surprises were smaller, say $0.07, the SUE would be $0.05/$0.07 = 0.71. SUE has been the subject of a number of studies.[62]

Another set of indicators, **relative strength** (RSTR) indicators, compare a stock's performance during a particular period either to its own past performance[63] or to the performance of some group of stocks. The simplest relative strength indicator of the first type is the stock's

---

[62] See Reilly and Brown (2000) and Sharpe, Alexander, and Bailey (1999) for a summary.
[63] Other definitions relate a stock's return over a recent period to its return over a longer period that includes the more recent period.

compound rate of return over some specified time horizon, such as six months or one year.[64] Despite its simplicity, this measure has appeared in numerous recent studies including Chan, Jegadeesh, and Lakonishok (1999) and Lee and Swaminathan (2000). The rationale behind its use is the thesis that patterns of persistence or reversal exist in stock returns, which may depend empirically on the investor's time horizon (Lee and Swaminathan 2000).

A simple relative strength indicator of the second type is the stock's performance divided by the performance of an equity index. If the value of this ratio increases, the stock price increases relative to the index and displays positive relative strength. Often the relative strength indicator may be scaled to 1.0 at the beginning of the study period. If the stock goes up at a higher (lower) rate than the index, for example, then relative strength will be above (below) 1.0. Relative strength in this sense is often calculated for industries as well as for individual stocks.

EXAMPLE 4-36   Relative Strength in Relation to an Equity Index

Table 4-22 shows the values of the utility and the finance components of the NYSE Common Stock Indexes for the end of each of 12 months from November 2000 through October 2001. Values for the NYSE Composite Index are also given.

TABLE 4-22   NYSE Indexes

	Utility	Finance	Composite
November	434.95	592.35	629.78
December	440.54	646.95	656.87
January	442.51	641.37	663.64
February	406.01	603.76	626.94
March	394.69	585.48	595.66
April	421.41	604.65	634.83
May	406.49	625.11	641.67
June	376.61	626.65	621.76
July	370.92	616.58	616.94
August	346.92	585.54	597.84
September	340.74	549.41	543.84
October	323.46	543.16	546.34

To produce the information for Table 4-23, we divide each industry index value by the NYSE Composite value for the same month and then scale those results so that relative strength for November 2001 equals 1.0.

On the basis of Tables 4-22 and 4-23, answer the following questions:

1. State the relative strength of utilities and finance over the entire time period November 2000 through October 2001. Interpret the relative strength for each sector over that period.

---

[64]This concept has also been referred to as **price momentum** in the academic literature.

TABLE 4-23   Relative Strength Indicators

	RSTR Utility	RSTR Finance
November	1.000	1.000
December	0.971	1.047
January	0.965	1.028
February	0.938	1.024
March	0.959	1.045
April	0.961	1.013
May	0.917	1.036
June	0.877	1.072
July	0.871	1.063
August	0.840	1.041
September	0.907	1.074
October	0.857	1.057

2. Discuss the relative performance of utilities and finance in the month of April 2001.

Solution to 1:   The relative strength of utilities was 0.857. This number represents $1 - 0.857 = 0.143$ or 14.3% underperformance relative to the NYSE Composite over the time period. The relative strength of finance was 1.057. This number represents $1.057 - 1.000 = 0.057$ or 5.7% outperformance relative to the NYSE Composite over the time period.

Solution to 2:   April 2001 utilities' RSTR at 0.961 was higher than in the prior month, but finance's RSTR at 1.013 was lower than in the prior month. In contrast to performance for the entire period, utilities outperformed finance in April.

Momentum group indicators have substantial followings among professional investors. The rigorous study of the use of such indicators is a subject of current active research both in industry and business schools.

11. VALUATION INDICATORS AND INVESTMENT MANAGEMENT

All the valuation indicators discussed in this chapter are quantitative aids, but not necessarily solutions, to the problem of security selection. Because each carefully selected and calculated price multiple, momentum indicator, or fundamental may supply some piece of the puzzle of stock valuation, many investors use more than one valuation indicator (in addition to other criteria) in stock selection.[65] The application of a set of criteria to reduce an investment

---

[65]According to the *Merrill Lynch Institutional Factor Survey* for 2001, from 1989 to 2001 responding institutional investors on average used about 8 factors (of the 23 surveyed) in selecting stocks. The survey factors include not only price multiples, momentum indicators, and DDM, but the fundamentals ROE, debt to equity, projected five-year EPS growth, EPS variability, EPS estimate dispersion, size, beta, foreign exposure, low price, and neglect.

universe to a smaller set of investments is called **screening**. Stock screens often include not only criteria based on the valuation measures discussed in this chapter but fundamental criteria that may explain differences in such measures. Computerized stock screening is an efficient way to narrow a search for investments and is a part of many stock-selection disciplines. The limitations to such screens usually relate to the lack of control over the calculation of important inputs (such as EPS) when using many commercial databases and screening tools; the absence of qualitative factors in most databases is another important limitation.

EXAMPLE 4-37   Using Screens to Find Stocks for a Portfolio

Janet Larsen manages an institutional portfolio and is currently looking for new stocks to add to the portfolio. Larsen has a commercial database with information on 7,532 U.S. stocks. She has designed several screens to select stocks with low P/E, P/CF, and Enterprise Value/EBITDA multiples. She also wants stocks that are currently paying a cash dividend and have positive earnings, and stocks with a total market capitalization between $1 billion and $5 billion. Table 4-24 shows the number of stocks that meet each of six screens reflecting these desires, as well as the number of stocks meeting all screens simultaneously, as of January 2002.

TABLE 4-24   A Stock Screen

Screen	Stocks Meeting Screen	
	Number	Percent
P/E < 20.0	2,549	33.8%
P/CF < 12.0	4,209	55.9%
Enterprise value/EBITDA < 10.0	4,393	58.3%
Dividends > 0	2,411	32.0%
EPS > 0	4,116	54.6%
Market capitalization from 1 billion to 5 billion	1,009	13.4%
All six screens simultaneously	117	1.6%

- The product of the fractions of stocks passing each screen individually is $0.338 \times 0.559 \times 0.583 \times 0.32 \times 0.546 \times 0.134 = 0.0026$, or 0.26%.
- The P/E of the S&P 500 was 24.4, the P/E of S&P 500/BARRA Growth Index was 32.4, and the P/E of the S&P 500/BARRA Value Index was 19.2 as of January 2002, excluding companies with negative earnings from the calculation of P/E.

Answer the following questions using the information supplied above:

1. What type of valuation indicators does Larsen not include in her stock screen?
2. Characterize the overall orientation of Larsen as to investment style.
3. Why is the fraction of stocks passing all six screens simultaneously, 1.6 percent, larger than the product of the fraction of stocks passing each screen individually, 0.26 percent?
4. State two limitations of Larsen's stock screen.

Solution to 1: Larsen has not included momentum indicators in the screen.

Solution to 2: Larsen can be characterized as a mid-cap value investor. Her screen does not include explicit growth rate criteria or include momentum indicators, such as positive earnings surprise, usually associated with a growth orientation. Larsen also specifies a cutoff for P/E that is consistent with the S&P 500/BARRA Value Index. Note that her multiples criteria are all "less than" criteria.[66]

Solution to 3: The fraction of stocks passing all screens simultaneously is greater than 0.26 percent because the criteria are not all independent. For example, we expect that some stocks that pass the P/CF criterion also will pass the P/E criteria because cash flow is positively correlated with earnings, on average.

Solution to 4: Larsen does not include any fundamental criteria. This is a limitation because a stock's expected low growth rate or high risk may explain its low P/E. A second limitation of her screen is that the computations of the value indicators in a commercial database may not reflect the appropriate adjustments to inputs. The absence of qualitative criteria is also a possible limitation.

Investors also apply all the metrics that we have illustrated in terms of individual stocks to industries and economic sectors. For example, average price multiples and momentum indicators can be used in sector rotation strategies to determine relatively under- or overvalued sectors.[67] (A sector rotation strategy is an investment strategy that overweights economic sectors that are anticipated to outperform or lead the overall market.)

12. SUMMARY

In this chapter, we have defined and explained the most important valuation indicators in professional use and illustrated their application to a variety of valuation problems.

- Price multiples are ratios of a stock's price to some measure of value per share.
- Momentum indicators relate either price or a fundamental to the time series of their own past values (or in some cases to their expected value).
- Price multiples are most frequently applied to valuation using the method of comparables. This method involves using a price multiple to evaluate whether an asset is relatively undervalued, fairly valued, or overvalued in relation to a benchmark value of the multiple.

---

[66] In using multiples such as P/E or P/B in this widely used fashion to characterize a portfolio, an analyst should be aware of the limitations. A high-P/E stock is usually labeled as a growth stock but may actually be an overpriced low-growth stock in the sense of future earnings growth.

[67] See Salsman (1997) for an example.

- The benchmark value of the multiple may be the multiple of a similar company or the median or average value of the multiple for a peer group of companies, an industry, an economic sector, an equity index, or the median or average own past values of the multiple.
- The economic rationale for the method of comparables is the law of one price.
- Price multiples may also be applied to valuation using the method based on forecasted fundamentals. Discounted cash flow models provide the basis and rationale for this method. Fundamentals also interest analysts who use the method of comparables, because differences between a price multiple and its benchmark value may be explained by differences in fundamentals.
- The key idea behind the use of P/Es is that earning power is a chief driver of investment value and EPS is probably the primary focus of security analysts' attention. EPS, however, is frequently subject to distortion, often volatile, and sometimes negative.
- The two alternative definitions of P/E are trailing P/E, based on the most recent four quarters of EPS, and leading P/E, based on next year's expected earnings.
- Analysts address the problem of cyclicality by normalizing EPS—that is, calculating the level of EPS that the business could achieve currently under mid-cyclical conditions (normal EPS).
- Two methods to normalize EPS are the method of historical average EPS (over the most recent full cycle) and the method of average ROE (average ROE multiplied by current book value per share).
- Earnings yield (E/P) is the reciprocal of the P/E. When stocks have negative EPS, a ranking by earnings yield is meaningful whereas a ranking by P/E is not.
- Historical trailing P/Es should be calculated with EPS lagged a sufficient amount of time to avoid look-ahead bias. The same principle applies to other multiples calculated on a trailing basis.
- The fundamental drivers of P/E are expected earnings growth rate(s) and the required rate of return. The justified P/E based on fundamentals bears a positive relationship to the first factor and an inverse relationship to the second factor.
- PEG (P/E to growth) is a tool to incorporate the impact of earnings growth on P/E. PEG is calculated as the ratio of the P/E to the consensus growth forecast. Stocks with lower PEGs are more attractive than stocks with higher PEGs, all else equal.
- We can estimate terminal value in multistage DCF models using price multiples based on comparables. The expression for terminal value is (using P/E as an example)

$$V_n = \text{Benchmark value of trailing P/E} \times E_n$$

or

$$V_n = \text{Benchmark value of leading P/E} \times E_{n+1}$$

- Book value per share attempts to represent the investment that common shareholders have made in the company, on a per-share basis. Inflation, technological change, and accounting distortions, however, can impair book value for this purpose.
- Book value is calculated as common shareholders' equity divided by the number of shares outstanding. Analysts adjust book value to more accurately reflect the value of shareholders' investment and to make P/B more useful for comparing different stocks.
- The fundamental drivers of P/B are ROE and the required rate of return. The justified P/B based on fundamentals bears a positive relationship to the first factor and an inverse relationship to the second factor.

- An important rationale for the price-to-sales ratio (P/S) is that sales, as the top line in an income statement, are generally less subject to distortion or manipulation than other fundamentals such as EPS or book value. Sales are also more stable than earnings and never negative.
- P/S fails to take into account differences in cost structure between businesses, may not properly reflect the situation of companies losing money, and can be subject to manipulation through revenue recognition practices.
- The fundamental drivers of P/S are profit margin, growth rate, and the required rate of return. The justified P/S based on fundamentals bears a positive relationship to the first two factors and an inverse relationship to the third factor.
- A key idea behind the use of price-to-cash-flow ratios is that cash flow is less subject to manipulation than are earnings. Price to cash flow are often more stable than P/E. Some common approximations to cash flow from operations have limitations, however, because they ignore items that may be subject to manipulation.
- The major cash flow and related concepts used in multiples are earnings plus noncash charges (CF), cash flow from operations (CFO), free cash flow to equity (FCFE), and earnings before interest, taxes, depreciation, and amortization (EBITDA).
- In calculating price to cash flow, the earnings-plus-noncash-charges concept is traditionally used, although the FCFE has the strongest link to financial theory.
- CF and EBITDA are not strictly cash flow numbers because they do not account for noncash revenue and net changes in working capital.
- The fundamental drivers of price to cash flow, however defined, are the expected growth rates of future cash flows and the required rate of return. The justified price to cash flow based on fundamentals bears a positive relationship to the first factor and an inverse relationship to the second.
- Enterprise value (EV) is total company value (the market value of debt, common equity, and preferred equity) minus the value of cash and investments.
- EV/EBITDA is preferred to P/EBITDA because EBITDA as a pre-interest number is a flow to all providers of capital.
- EV/EBITDA may be more appropriate than P/E for comparing companies with different amounts of financial leverage (debt).
- EV/EBITDA is frequently used in the valuation of capital-intensive businesses.
- The fundamental drivers of EV/EBITDA are the expected growth rate in free cash flow to the firm and the weighted-average cost of capital. The justified EV/EBITDA based on fundamentals bears a positive relationship to the first factor and an inverse relationship to the second.
- Dividend yield has been used as a valuation indicator because it is a component of total return, and is less risky than capital appreciation. However, investors trade off future earnings growth to receive higher current dividends.
- Trailing dividend yield is calculated as four times the most recent quarterly per-share dividend divided by the current market price.
- The fundamental drivers of dividend yield are the expected growth rate in dividends and the required rate of return.
- Comparing companies across borders frequently involves accounting method differences, cultural differences, economic differences, and resulting differences in risk and growth opportunities.
- Momentum valuation indicators include earnings surprise, standardized unexpected earnings, and relative strength.

- Unexpected earnings (or earnings surprise) equals the difference between reported earnings and expected earnings.
- Standardized unexpected earnings (SUE) are unexpected earnings divided by the standard deviation in past unexpected earnings.
- Relative-strength indicators compare a stock's performance during a period either with its own past performance (first type) or with the performance of some group of stocks (second type). The rationale behind using relative strength is the thesis of patterns of persistence or reversal in returns.
- Screening is the application of a set of criteria to reduce an investment universe to a smaller set of investments and is a part of many stock selection disciplines. In general, limitations of such screens include the lack of control over the calculation of important inputs and the absence of qualitative factors.

PROBLEMS

1. As of February 2002, you are researching Smith International (NYSE: SII), an oil field services company subject to cyclical demand for its services. You believe the 1997–2000 period reasonably captures average profitability. SII closed at $57.98 on February 2, 2002.

	2001	2000	1999	1998	1997
EPS	E$3.03	$1.45	$0.23	$2.13	$2.55
BVPS	E19.20	16.21	14.52	13.17	11.84
ROE	E16%	8.9%	1.6%	16.3%	21.8%

Source: The Value Line Investment Survey.

A. Define normal EPS.
B. Calculate a normal EPS for SII based on the method of historical average EPS, and then calculate the P/E based on that estimate of normal EPS.
C. Calculate a normal EPS for SII based on the method of average ROE and the P/E based on that estimate of normal EPS.

2. An analyst plans to use P/E and the method of comparables as a basis for recommending one of two peer group companies in the personal digital assistant business. Data on the companies' prices, trailing EPS, and expected growth rates in sales (five-year compounded rate) are given in the table below. Neither business has been profitable to date, and neither is anticipated to have positive EPS over the next year.

	Price	Trailing EPS	P/E	Expected Growth (Sales)
Hand	$22	−$2.20	NM	45%
Somersault	$10	−$1.25	NM	40%

Unfortunately, because the earnings for both companies were negative, the P/Es were not meaningful. On the basis of the above information, answer the following questions.

A. State how the analyst might make a relative valuation in this case.
B. Which stock should the analyst recommend?

3. May Stewart, CFA, a retail analyst, is performing a P/E-based comparison of two jewelry stores as of early 2001. She has the following data for Hallwhite Stores (HS) and Ruffany (RUF).

   • HS is priced at $44. RUF is priced at $22.50.
   • HS has a simple capital structure, earned $2.00 per share in 2000, and is expected to earn $2.20 in 2001.
   • RUF has a complex capital structure as a result of its outstanding stock options. Moreover, it had several unusual items that reduced its basic EPS in 2000 to $0.50 (versus the $0.75 that it earned in 1999).
   • For 2001, Stewart expects RUF to achieve net income of $30 million. RUF has 30 million shares outstanding and options outstanding for an additional 3,333,333 shares.

   A. Which P/E (trailing or leading) should Stewart use to compare the two companies' valuation?
   B. Which of the two stocks is relatively more attractively valued on the basis of P/Es (assuming that all other factors are approximately the same for both stock)?

4. You are researching the valuation of the stock of a company in the food processing industry. Suppose you intend to use the mean value of the leading P/Es for the food processing industry stocks as the benchmark value of the multiple. That mean P/E is 18.0. The leading or expected EPS for the next year for the stock you are studying is $2.00. You calculate $18.0 \times \$2.00 = \$36$, which you take to be the intrinsic value of the stock based only on the information given above. Comparing $36 with the stock's current market price of $30, you conclude the stock is undervalued.

   A. Give two reasons why your conclusion that the stock is undervalued may be in error.
   B. What additional information about the stock and the peer group would support your original conclusion?

5. A. Identify two significant differences between Yardeni's model of stock market valuation and the Fed model.
   B. Suppose an analyst uses an equity index as a comparison asset in valuing a stock. Which price multiple(s) would cause concern about the impact of potential overvaluation of the equity index on a decision to recommend purchase of an individual stock?

6. (Adapted from 2000 CFA Level II exam) Christie Johnson, CFA, has been assigned to analyze Sundanci. Johnson assumes that Sundanci's earnings and dividends will grow at a constant rate of 13 percent. Tables 4-25 and Tables 4-26 provide financial statements and other information for Sundanci.

   A. Calculate a justified P/E based on information in Tables 4-25 and 4-26 (on page 238) and on Johnson's assumptions for Sundanci. Show your work.
   B. Identify, within the context of the constant dividend growth model, how *each* of the fundamental factors shown below would affect the P/E.

TABLE 4-25 Sundanci Actual 1999 and 2000 Financial
Statements For Fiscal Years Ending May 31
(in millions, except per-share data)

Income Statement	1999	2000
Revenue	$474	$598
Depreciation	20	23
Other operating costs	368	460
Income before taxes	86	115
Taxes	26	35
Net income	60	80
Dividends	18	24
Earnings per share	$0.714	$0.952
Dividends per share	$0.214	$0.286
Common shares outstanding	84.0	84.0

Balance Sheet	1999	2000
Current assets	$201	$326
Net property, plant, and equipment	474	489
Total assets	675	815
Current liabilities	57	141
Long-term debt	0	0
Total liabilities		
Shareholders' equity	618	674
Total liabilities and equity	675	815
Capital expenditures	34	38

TABLE 4-26 Selected Financial Information

Required rate of return on equity	14%
Growth rate of industry	13%
Industry P/E	26

   i. The risk (beta) of Sundanci increases substantially.
  ii. The estimated growth rate of Sundanci's earnings and dividends increases.
 iii. The market risk premium increases.

Note: A change in a fundamental factor is assumed to happen in isolation; interactive effects between factors are ignored. Every other item of the company is unchanged.

7. At a meeting of your company's investment policy committee, Bill Yu presents a recommendation based on a P/E analysis. He presents the case for Connie's Sporting Goods (CSG), a small chain of retail stores that receives almost no coverage by analysts. Yu begins by noting that CSG appeared to be fairly valued compared with its peers on a P/E basis. CSG's 10-Q filing revealed, however, that an initiative at CSG to offer sports

instruction (e.g., golf lessons) along with equipment should immediately raise the earnings growth rate at the company from 5 percent to 6 percent. Yu thus expects the company's trailing P/E to rise from 10.5 to 13.25, a 26 percent increase, as soon as the investment community recognizes this development. The computations supporting his analysis follow.

Currently the justified P/E based on fundamentals is

$$\frac{P_0}{E_0} = \frac{(1-b)(1+g)}{r-g} = \frac{(1-0.5)(1.05)}{0.10-0.05} = 10.5$$

He points out that when g rises to 0.06, the trailing P/E should increase to 13.25, providing investors with appreciation in excess of 20 percent. When asked if he expects CSG's ROE to improve with the initiative, Yu indicated that it would likely be flat for the first several years. A colleague argues that because of the flat ROE, CSG's justified P/E will not increase to 13.25 because b must increase to be consistent with the sustainable growth rate expression for g. Only companies with at least 20 percent near-term appreciation potential are candidates for inclusion on your company's focus list of stocks.

A. How would you expect the new initiative to affect the trailing P/E accorded to CSG's stock, assuming Yu's assumptions are correct? (Growth will increase as indicated above and ROE will be steady.)

B. Is CSG a good candidate for your company's focus list?

8. Tom Smithfield is valuing the stock of a food processing business. He has projected earnings and dividends to four years (to $t = 4$). Other information and estimates are

- Required rate of return = 0.09
- Average dividend payout rate for mature companies in the market = 0.45
- Industry average ROE = 0.10
- $E_3 = \$3.00$
- Industry average P/E = 12

On the basis of the above, answer the following questions:

A. Compute terminal value based on comparables.

B. Contrast your answer in Part A to an estimate of terminal value using the Gordon growth model.

9. Discuss three types of stocks or investment problems for which an analyst could appropriately use P/B in valuation.

10. Avtech is a multinational distributor of semiconductor chips and related products to businesses. Its leading competitor around the world is Target Electronics. Avtech has a current market price of $10, 20 million shares outstanding, annual sales of $1 billion, and a 5 percent profit margin. Target has a market price of $20, 30 million shares outstanding, annual sales of $1.6 billion, and a profit margin of 4.9 percent. Based on the information given, answer the following questions:

A. Which of the two companies has a more attractive valuation based on P/S?

B. Identify and explain one advantage of P/S over P/E as a valuation tool.

11. Wilhelm Müller, CFA, has organized the selected data on four food companies that appear below (TTM stands for trailing 12 months):

	Hormel Foods	Tyson Foods	IBP Corp	Smithfield Foods
Stock price	$25.70	$11.77	$23.65	$24.61
Shares out (1,000s)	138,923	220,662	108,170	103,803
Market cap ($ mil)	3,570	2,597	2,558	2,523
Sales ($ mil)	4,124	10,751	17,388	6,354
Net income ($ mil)	182	88	122	252
TTM EPS	$1.30	$0.40	$1.14	$2.31
Return on equity	19.20%	4.10%	6.40%	23.00%
Net profit margin	4.41%	0.82%	0.70%	3.99%

On the basis of the data given, answer the following questions:

A. Calculate the trailing P/E and P/S for each company.

B. Explain on the basis of fundamentals why these stocks have different P/Ss.

12. (Adapted from 2001 CFA Level II exam) John Jones, CFA, is head of the research department at Peninsular Research. Peninsular has a client who has inquired about the valuation method best suited for comparison of companies in an industry with the following characteristics:

   - Principal competitors within the industry are located in the United States, France, Japan, and Brazil.
   - The industry is currently operating at a cyclical low, with many companies reporting losses.

   Jones recommends that the client consider the following valuation ratios:

   1. P/E
   2. P/B
   3. P/S

   Determine which *one* of the three valuation ratios is most appropriate for comparing companies in this industry. Support your answer with *one* reason that makes that ratio superior to either of the other two ratios in this case.

13. General Electric (NYSE: GE) is currently selling for $38.50, with trailing 12-month earnings and dividends of $1.36 and $0.64, respectively. P/E is 28.3, P/B is 7.1, and P/S is 2.9. The return on equity is 27.0 percent, and the profit margin on sales is 10.9 percent. The Treasury bond rate is 4.9 percent, the equity risk premium is 5.5 percent, and GE's beta is 1.2.

   A. What is GE's required rate of return, based on the capital asset pricing model?

   B. Assume that the dividend and earnings growth rates are 9 percent. What P/Es, P/Bs, and P/Ss would be justified given the required rate of return in Part A and current values of the dividend payout ratio, ROE, and profit margin?

   C. Given that the assumptions and constant growth model are appropriate, state whether GE appears to be fairly valued, overvalued, or undervalued based on fundamentals.

14. Jorge Zaldys, CFA, is researching the relative valuation of two companies in the aerospace/defense industry, NCI Heavy Industries (NCI) and Relay Group International (RGI). He has gathered relevant information on the companies in the following table.

EBITDA Comparisons
(in € millions except for per-share)

Company	RGI	NCI
Price per share	150	100
Shares outstanding	5 million	2 million
Market value of debt	50	100
Book value of debt	52	112
Cash and investments	5	2
Net income	49.5	12
Net income from continuing operations	49.5	8
Interest expense	3	5
Depreciation and amortization	8	4
Taxes	2	3

Using the information in the above table, answer the following questions:

A. Calculate P/EBITDA for NCI and RGI.

B. Calculate EV/EBITDA for NCI and RGI.

C. Select NCI or RGI for recommendation as relatively undervalued. Justify your selection.

15. Define the major alternative cash flow concepts, and state one limitation of each.

16. Data for two hypothetical companies in the pharmaceutical industry, DriveMed and MAT Technology, are given in the table below. For both companies, expenditures in fixed capital and working capital during the previous year reflected anticipated average expenditures over the foreseeable horizon.

	DriveMed	MAT Tech.
Current price	$46.00	$78.00
Trailing CF per share	$3.60	$6.00
P/CF	12.8	13.0
Trailing FCFE per share	$1.00	$5.00
P/FCFE	46.0	15.6
Consensus five-year growth forecast	15%	20%
Beta	1.25	1.25

On the basis of the information supplied, discuss the valuation of MAT Technology relative to DriveMed. Justify your conclusion.

17. Your value-oriented investment management company recently hired a new analyst, Bob Westard, because of his expertise in the life sciences and biotechnology areas. At the company's weekly meeting, during which each analyst proposes a stock idea for inclusion on the company's approved list, Westard recommends Human Cloning International (HCI). He bases his recommendation to the Investment Committee on two considerations. First, HCI has pending patent applications but a P/E that he judges to be low given

the potential earnings from the patented products. Second, HCI has had high relative strength versus the S&P 500 over the past month.

A. Explain the difference between price multiples and relative strength approaches.
B. State which, if any, of the bases for Westard's recommendation is consistent with the investment orientation of your company.

18. Kirstin Kruse, a portfolio manager, has an important client who wants to alter the composition of her equity portfolio, which is currently a diversified portfolio of 60 global common stocks. The client wants a portfolio that meets the following criteria:

- Stocks must be in the Dow Jones Industrial Average, Transportation Average, or Utilities Average.
- Stocks must have a dividend yield of at least 5.0 percent.
- Stocks must have a P/E no greater than 20.
- Stocks must have a total market capitalization of at least $2.0 billion.

The table below shows how many stocks satisfied each screen, which was run in November 2001.

Screen	Number Satisfying
In Dow Jones Industrial Average, Transportation Average, or Utilities Average	65
Dividend yield of at least 5.0%	10
P/E less than 20	27
Total market cap of at least $2.0 billion	52
Satisfies all four screens	6

Other facts are:

- In total, there are 65 stocks in these three indexes (30 in the Industrial Average, 20 in the Transportation Average, and 15 in the Utilities Average).
- The stocks meeting all four screens were Southern Co. (utility), TXU Corporation (utility), Eastman Kodak Co. (consumer goods), Public Service Enterprise Group (utility), Reliant Energy (utility), and Consolidated Edison (utility).

A. Which valuation indicator or fundamental in Kruse's screen is most restrictive?
B. Critique the construction of the screen.
C. Do these screens identify an appropriate replacement portfolio for the client?

CHAPTER 5

RESIDUAL INCOME VALUATION

LEARNING OUTCOMES

After completing this chapter, you will be able to do the following:

- Define and calculate residual income.
- Describe alternative measures of residual earnings, such as economic value added.
- Discuss the uses of residual income models.
- Calculate future values of residual income given current book value, earnings growth estimates, and an assumed dividend payout ratio.
- Calculate the intrinsic value of a share of common stock using the residual income model.
- Contrast the recognition of value in the residual income model to value recognition in other present value models.
- Discuss the strengths and weaknesses of the residual income model.
- Justify the selection of the residual income model for equity valuation, given characteristics of the company being valued.
- Identify and discuss the fundamental determinants or drivers of residual income.
- Explain the relationship between the justified price-to-book ratio and residual income.
- Explain the relationship of the residual income model to the dividend discount and free cash flow to equity models.
- Discuss the major accounting issues in applying residual income models.
- Calculate an implied growth rate in residual income given the market price-to-book ratio and an estimate of the required rate of return on equity.
- Define continuing residual income and list the common assumptions regarding continuing residual income.
- Justify an estimate of continuing residual income at the earnings forecast horizon given company and industry prospects.
- Calculate the intrinsic value of a share of common stock using a multistage residual income model, given the required rate of return, forecasted earnings per share over a finite horizon, and forecasted continuing residual earnings.

1. INTRODUCTION

Residual income models of equity value have become widely recognized tools in both investment practice and research. Conceptually, residual income is net income less a charge (deduction) for common shareholders' opportunity cost in generating net income. As an economic concept, residual income has a long history. As far back as the 1920s, General Motors employed the concept in evaluating business segments.[1] More recently, residual income has received renewed attention and interest, sometimes under names such as economic profit, abnormal earnings, or economic value added.

The appeal of residual income models stems from a shortcoming of traditional accounting. Specifically, although a company's income statement includes a charge for the cost of debt capital in the form of interest expense, it does not include a charge for the cost of equity capital. A company can have positive net income but may still not be adding value for shareholders if it does not earn more than the cost of equity capital. Residual income concepts have been used in a variety of contexts, including the measurement of internal corporate performance. This chapter, however, will focus on the residual income model for estimating the intrinsic value of common stock. Among the questions we will study to help us use residual income models professionally are the following:

- How is residual income measured, and how can an analyst use residual income in valuation?
- How does residual income relate to fundamentals, such as return on equity and earnings growth rates?
- How is residual income linked to other valuation methods, such as a price-multiple approach?
- What challenges arise in applying residual income valuation internationally?

The chapter is organized as follows: In Section 2, we develop the concept of residual income and present alternative measures used in practice. In Section 3, we derive the residual income valuation model and illustrate its use in valuing common stock. Section 4 addresses accounting and international issues in the use of residual income valuation. In subsequent sections, we present practical applications of residual income models: Section 5 presents the single-stage (constant-growth) residual income model, and Section 6 presents multistage residual income models. We summarize the chapter in Section 7.

2. RESIDUAL INCOME

Traditional financial statements, particularly the income statement, are prepared to reflect earnings available to owners. As a result, net income includes an expense to represent the cost of debt capital in the form of interest expense. Dividends or other charges for equity capital, however, are not deducted. Traditional accounting lets the owners decide whether earnings cover their opportunity costs. The economic concept of residual income, on the other hand, explicitly deducts the estimated cost of equity capital, the finance concept that measures shareholders' opportunity costs. Residual income models have been used to value both individual stocks[2] and the Dow Jones Industrial Average[3] and have been proposed as a solution to measuring goodwill impairment by accounting standard setters.[4] Residual

---

[1] See, for example, Young (1999) and Lo and Lys (2000).
[2] See Fleck, Craig, Bodenstab, Harris, and Huh (2001).
[3] See Lee and Swaminathan (1999) and Lee, Myers, and Swaminathan (1999).
[4] See American Accounting Association Financial Accounting Standards Committee (2001). **Impairment** in an accounting context means downward adjustment. **Goodwill**, in this context, is an intangible asset that may appear on a company's balance sheet as a result of its purchase of another company.

income models have been found more useful than some other major present value models of equity value in explaining stock prices (American Accounting Association 2001). Example 5-1 illustrates, in a stylized setting, the calculation and interpretation of residual income.[5]

EXAMPLE 5-1   The Calculation of Residual Income

Axis Manufacturing Company, Inc. (AXCI), a very small company in terms of market capitalization, has total assets of €2,000,000 financed 50 percent with debt and 50 percent with equity capital. The cost of debt capital is 7 percent before taxes (4.9 percent after taxes) and the cost of equity capital is 12 percent.[6] The company has earnings before interest and taxes (EBIT) of €200,000 and a tax rate of 30 percent. Net income for AXCI can be determined as follows:

EBIT	€200,000
Less: Interest Expense	70,000
Pretax Income	€130,000
Less: Income Tax Expense	39,000
Net Income	€ 91,000

With earnings of €91,000, AXCI is clearly profitable in an accounting sense. But was the company profitable enough to satisfy its owners? Unfortunately, it was not. To incorporate the cost of equity capital, we compute residual income. One approach to calculating residual income is to deduct an **equity charge** (the estimated cost of equity capital in money terms) from net income. We compute the equity charge as follows:

$$\text{Equity charge} = \text{Equity capital} \times \text{Cost of equity capital in percent}$$

$$= €1,000,000 \times 12\% = €120,000$$

As stated, residual income is equal to net income minus the equity charge:

Net Income	€91,000
Equity Charge	120,000
Residual Income	€(29,000)

AXCI did not earn enough to cover the cost of equity capital. As a result, it has negative residual income. Although AXCI is profitable in an accounting sense, it is not profitable in an economic sense.

In Example 5-1, we calculated residual income based on net income and a charge for the cost of equity capital. Analysts will also encounter another approach to calculating residual income

---

[5]To simplify the following introduction, we assume here that net income accurately reflects *clean surplus accounting*, which we will explain later in this chapter. Our discussions in this chapter assume that companies' financing consists of common equity and debt only. In the case of a company that also has preferred stock financing, the calculation of residual income would reflect the deduction of preferred stock dividends from net income.

[6]See Chapter 2 for a discussion of estimating required rates of return for equity.

that yields the same results. In this second approach, which takes the perspective of all providers of capital (both debt and equity), we subtract a **capital charge** (the company's total cost of capital in money terms) from the company's after-tax operating profit. In the case of AXCI in Example 5-1, net operating profit after taxes (NOPAT) is €140,000 (€200,000 less 30 percent taxes). AXCI's after-tax weighted-average cost of capital (WACC) is 8.45 percent, computed as 50 percent (capital structure weight of equity) times the cost of equity of 12 percent plus 50 percent (capital structure weight of debt) times the after-tax cost of debt, 4.9 percent.[7] The capital charge is €169,000 (= 8.45% × €2,000,000), which is higher than its after-tax operating profit of €140,000 by €29,000, the same figure obtained in Example 5-1. That the company is not profitable in an economic sense can also be seen by comparing the company's WACC, 8.45 percent, with after-tax operating profits as a percent of total assets (the after-tax net operating return on total assets or capital). The after-tax net operating return on total assets is €140,000/€2,000,000 = 7 percent, which is less than WACC by 1.45 percentage points.[8]

We can illustrate the impact of residual income on equity valuation using the case of AXCI presented in Example 5-1. Assume the following:

- Initially, AXCI equity is selling for book value or €1,000,000, with 100,000 shares outstanding. Thus, AXCI's book value per share and initial share price are both €10.
- Earnings per share (EPS) are €91,000/100,000 = €0.91.
- Earnings will continue at the current level indefinitely.
- All net income is distributed as dividends.

Because AXCI is not earning its cost of equity, as shown in Example 5-1, the company's share price should fall. In Chapter 2, we explained that for a no-growth company, as here, the earnings yield (E/P) is an estimate of the expected rate of return. Therefore, when price reaches the point at which E/P equals the required rate of return on equity, an investment in the stock is expected to just cover the stock's required rate of return. With EPS of €0.91, the earnings yield is exactly 12 percent (AXCI's cost of equity) when share price is €7.58333. At a share price of €7.58333, the total market value of AXCI equity is €758,333. At this level, the equity charge is €91,000 (€758,333 × 12%) and residual income is zero. When a company has negative residual income, we expect shares to sell at a discount to book value. In this example, AXCI's price-to-book ratio (P/B) would be 0.7583. Conversely, if we changed the data in Example 5-1 so that AXCI earned positive residual income, we would conclude that its shares would sell at a premium to book value. In summary, we expect higher residual income to be associated with higher market prices (and higher P/Bs), all else equal.

Residual income and residual income valuation models have been referred to by a variety of names. Residual income has sometimes been called **economic profit** because it represents the economic profit of the company after deducting the cost of all capital, debt, and equity. In forecasting future residual income, the term **abnormal earnings** is also used. Assuming that in the long term the company is expected to earn its cost of capital (from all sources), any earnings

---

[7]This example of the weighted-average cost of capital assumes that interest is tax deductible. In countries where corporate interest is not tax deductible, the after-tax cost of debt would equal the pretax cost of debt. In the rest of the chapter, we will refer to *after-tax cost of capital* or *after-tax WACC* as *cost of capital* and *WACC*, respectively, for brevity.

[8]After-tax net operating profits as a percent of total assets or capital has been called **return on invested capital** (ROIC). Residual income can also be calculated as (ROIC − WACC) × (Beginning capital).

in excess of the cost of capital can be termed abnormal earnings. The residual income valuation model has also been called the **discounted abnormal earnings model** (DAE model) and the **Edwards-Bell-Ohlson model** (EBO model) after the names of researchers in the field.[9] This chapter focuses on a presentation of a general residual income valuation model that can be used by analysts using publicly available data and nonproprietary accounting adjustments. A number of commercial implementations of the approach are also very well known, however. Before returning to the general residual income valuation model in Section 3, we briefly discuss one such commercial implementation.

2.1. Commercial Implementations

One example of several competing commercial implementations of the residual income concept is **economic value added** (EVA®), trademarked by Stern Stewart & Company.[10] In the previous section, we illustrated the calculation of residual income starting from net operating profit after taxes, and EVA takes the same broad approach. Specifically, EVA is computed as

$$EVA = NOPAT - (C\% \times TC) \tag{5-1}$$

where NOPAT is the company's net operating profit after taxes, C% is the cost of capital, and TC is total capital. In this model, both NOPAT and TC determined under generally accepted accounting principles are adjusted for a number of items.[11] Some of the more common adjustments follow:

- Research and development expenses are capitalized and amortized rather than expensed (R&D expense is added back to earnings to compute NOPAT).
- In the case of strategic investments that are not expected to generate a return immediately, a charge for capital is suspended until a later date.
- Goodwill is capitalized and not amortized (amortization expense is added back in arriving at NOPAT, and accumulated amortization is added back to capital).
- Deferred taxes are eliminated such that only cash taxes are treated as an expense.
- Any inventory LIFO reserve is added back to capital, and any increase in the LIFO reserve is added in arriving at NOPAT.
- Operating leases are treated as capital leases, and nonrecurring items are adjusted.

Because of the adjustments made under EVA, a different numerical result will be obtained, in general, than that resulting from the use of the simple computation presented in Example 5-1. In practice, general (nonbranded) residual income (RI) valuation also considers the impact of accounting methods on reported results. However, analysts' adjustments to reported accounting results in estimating residual income will generally reflect some differences from the set specified for EVA. Section 4 of this chapter will explore accounting considerations in more detail.

Over time, a company must generate EVA in order for its market value to increase. A related concept is market value added (MVA):

$$MVA = \text{Market value of the company} - \text{Total capital} \tag{5-2}$$

---

[9] More information on the background of the model is given later.
[10] For a complete discussion, see Stern (1991) and Peterson and Peterson (1996).
[11] See, for example, Ehrbar (1998).

A company that generates positive EVA should have a market value in excess of the accounting book value of its capital.

Research on the ability of value-added concepts to explain equity value and stock returns has reached mixed conclusions. Peterson and Peterson (1996) found that value-added measures are slightly more highly correlated with stock returns than traditional measures such as return on assets and return on equity. Bernstein and Pigler (1997) and Bernstein, Bayer, and Pigler (1998) found that value-added measures are no better at predicting stock performance than are measures such as earnings growth.

A variety of commercial models related to the residual income concept have been marketed by other major accounting and consulting firms. Interestingly, the application focus of these models is not, in general, equity valuation. Rather, these implementations of the residual income concept are marketed primarily for measuring internal corporate performance and determining executive compensation.

3. THE RESIDUAL INCOME VALUATION MODEL

In Section 2, we discussed the concept of residual income and briefly introduced the relationship of residual income to equity value. In the long term, companies that earn more than the cost of capital should sell for more than book value, and companies that earn less than the cost of capital should sell for less than book value. The **residual income model** (RIM) of valuation analyzes the intrinsic value of equity into two components:

- the current book value of equity, plus
- the present value of expected future residual income.

Note that when we turn from valuing total shareholders' equity to directly valuing an individual common share, we work with earnings per share rather than net income. According to the residual income model, the intrinsic value of common stock can be expressed as follows:

$$V_0 = B_0 + \sum_{t=1}^{\infty} \frac{RI_t}{(1+r)^t} = B_0 + \sum_{t=1}^{\infty} \frac{E_t - rB_{t-1}}{(1+r)^t} \qquad (5\text{-}3)$$

where

V_0 = value of a share of stock today ($t = 0$)

B_0 = current per-share book value of equity

B_t = expected per-share book value of equity at any time t

r = required rate of return on equity (cost of equity)

E_t = expected EPS for period t

RI_t = expected per-share residual income, equal to $E_t - rB_{t-1}$

The per-share residual income in period t, RI_t, is the EPS for the period, E_t, minus the per-share equity charge for the period, which is the required rate of return on equity times the book value per share at the beginning of the period, or rB_{t-1}. Whenever earnings per share exceed the per-share cost of equity, per-share residual income is positive; and whenever earnings are less, per-share residual income is negative. Example 5-2 illustrates the calculation of per-share residual income.

EXAMPLE 5-2   Per-Share Residual Income Forecasts

David Smith is evaluating the expected residual income for ScottishPower (London Stock Exchange: SPW). Smith determines that SPW has a required rate of return of 8 percent. He obtains the following data from Thomson Financial as of March 4, 2002:

Current market price:	GBP4.00
Book value per share:	GBP3.41
Consensus annual earnings estimates	
March 2002:	GBP0.33
March 2003:	GBP0.39
Annualized dividend per share:	GBP0.26

What is the forecast residual income for fiscal years ended March 2002 and March 2003?

Solution:

TABLE 5-1

Year	2002	2003
Beginning book value (BV_0)	3.41	3.48
Earnings per share forecast (E)	0.33	0.39
Dividend forecast (D)	0.26	0.26
Forecast book value per share ($BV_0 + E - D$)	3.48	3.61
Per-share equity charge ($BV_0 \times r$)	0.27	0.28
Per-share residual income (EPS forecast − Equity charge)	0.06	0.11

We illustrate the use of Equation 5-3, the expression for the estimated intrinsic value of common stock, in Example 5-3.

EXAMPLE 5-3   Using the Residual Income Model (1)

Bugg Properties' expected EPS is $2.00, $2.50, and $4.00 for the next three years, respectively. Analysts expect that Bugg will pay dividends of $1.00, $1.25, and $12.25 for the three years. The last dividend is anticipated to be a liquidating dividend; analysts expect Bugg will cease operations after Year 3. Bugg's current book value is $6.00 per share, and its required rate of return on equity is 10 percent.

   1. Calculate per-share book value and residual income for the next three years.

2. Estimate the stock's value using the residual income model given in Equation 5-3:

$$V_0 = B_0 + \sum_{t=1}^{\infty} \frac{E_t - rB_{t-1}}{(1+r)^t}$$

Solution to 1: The book values and residual incomes for the next three years are as follows:

TABLE 5-2

Year	1	2	3
Beginning book value per share	6.00	7.00	8.25
Retained earnings ($E - D$)	1.00	1.25	−8.25
Ending book value	7.00	8.25	0
Net income	2.00	2.50	4.00
Less equity charge ($r \times$ Beginning BV)	0.60	0.70	0.825
Residual income	1.40	1.80	3.175

Solution to 2: The value using the residual income model is

$$V_0 = 6.00 + \frac{1.40}{(1.10)} + \frac{1.80}{(1.10)^2} + \frac{3.175}{(1.10)^3}$$

$$= 6.00 + 1.2727 + 1.4876 + 2.3854$$

$$= \$11.15$$

Example 5-4 illustrates an important point that the recognition of value in residual income models typically occurs earlier than in dividend discount models.

EXAMPLE 5-4   Valuing a Perpetuity with the Residual Income Model

Assume the following data:

- A company will earn $1.00 per share forever.
- The company pays out all earnings as dividends.
- Book value per share is $6.00.
- The required rate of return on equity (or the percent cost of equity) is 10 percent.

1. Calculate the value of this stock using the dividend discount model (DDM).
2. Calculate the level amount of per-share residual income that will be earned each year.

3. Calculate the value of the stock using a residual income valuation model.
4. Create a table summarizing the recognition of value in the dividend discount model and the residual income model.

Solution to 1: Because the dividend is a perpetuity, $V_0 = D/r = 1.00/0.10 = \$10.00$ per share.

Solution to 2: Because each year all net income is paid out as dividends, book value per share will be constant at $6.00. Therefore, with a required rate of return on equity of 10 percent, for all future years, per-share residual income will be as follows:

$$RI_t = E_t - rB_{t-1} = 1.00 - 0.10(6.00) = 1.00 - 0.60 = \$0.40$$

Solution to 3: Using a residual income model, the estimated value equals the current book value per share plus the present value of future expected residual income (which here can be valued as a perpetuity):

$$V_0 = \text{Book value} + \text{PV of expected future per-share residual income}$$

$$= 6.00 + 0.40/0.10$$

$$= 6.00 + 4.00 = \$10.00$$

Solution to 4: Table 5-3 below summarizes when values are recognized in the DDM and the RI valuation models.

TABLE 5-3   Value Recognition in DDM and RIM Valuation

	Dividend Discount Model		Residual Income Model	
Year	D_t	PV of D_t	B_0 or RI_t	PV of B_0 or RI_t
0			6.00	6.000
1	1.00	0.909	0.40	0.364
2	1.00	0.826	0.40	0.331
3	1.00	0.751	0.40	0.301
4	1.00	0.683	0.40	0.273
5	1.00	0.621	0.40	0.248
6	1.00	0.564	0.40	0.226
7	1.00	0.513	0.40	0.205
8	1.00	0.467	0.40	0.187
⋮	⋮	⋮	⋮	⋮
Total		$10.00		$10.00

Table 5-3 shows that in the residual income valuation, current book value of $6.00 represents 60 percent of the stock's total present value of $10. Most of the total value is recognized now (today) for this stock. The DDM valuation also estimates the value of the stock as $10. As an exercise, suppose we add up the present values of the first five years' dividends. This sum of $3.79 ($0.909 + $0.826 + $0.751 + $0.683 +

$0.621) represents approximately 38 percent of the total present value of $10. In the DDM, value is recognized with the receipt of dividends; typically the recognition of value occurs earlier in a residual income model than in a dividend discount model.

As illustrated in Example 5-4, the dividend discount and residual income models are in theory mutually consistent. Because of the real-world uncertainty in forecasting distant cash flows, however, we may find that the earlier recognition of value in a residual income approach relative to other present value approaches is a practical advantage. In the dividend discount and free cash flow models (discussed in Chapters 2 and 3, respectively), we often model a stock's value as the sum of the present values of individually forecasted dividends or free cash flows up to some terminal point plus the present value of the expected terminal value of the stock. In practice, analysts often find that a large fraction of a stock's total present value, using either the dividend discount or free cash flow to equity model, is represented by the present value of the expected terminal value. However, substantial uncertainty often surrounds the terminal value. In contrast, residual income valuations typically are relatively less sensitive to terminal value estimates. (In some residual income valuation contexts the terminal value may actually be set equal to zero, as we will discuss in a later section.) The early recognition of value is one reason residual income valuation can be a useful analytical tool.

Before we discuss the implementation of the residual income model in detail, it is helpful to have an overview of the strengths and weaknesses of the residual income approach. The strengths of the residual income models include the following:

- Terminal values do not make up a large portion of the total present value, relative to other models.
- The RI models use readily available accounting data.
- The models can be readily applied to companies that do not pay dividends or to companies that do not have positive expected near-term free cash flows.
- The models can be used when cash flows are unpredictable.
- The models have an appealing focus on economic profitability.

The potential weaknesses of residual income models include the following:

- The models are based on accounting data that can be subject to manipulation by management.
- Accounting data used as inputs may require significant adjustments.
- The models require that the clean surplus relation holds, or that the analyst makes appropriate adjustments when the clean surplus relation does not hold. In the next section we will present the clean surplus relation (or clean surplus accounting), previously mentioned in Chapter 2.

The above list of potential weaknesses helps explain the chapter's focus in Section 4 on accounting considerations. In light of its strengths and weaknesses, we state the following broad guidelines for using a residual income model in common stock valuation. A residual income model is most appropriate when

- a company does not pay dividends, or its dividends are not predictable;
- a company's expected free cash flows are negative within the analyst's comfortable forecast horizon; or

- there is great uncertainty in forecasting terminal values using an alternative present value approach.

Residual income models are least appropriate when

- there are significant departures from clean surplus accounting; or
- significant determinants of residual income, such as book value and ROE, are not predictable.

The balance of Section 3 develops the most familiar general expression for the residual income model and illustrates the model's application.

3.1. The General Residual Income Model

The residual income model is conceptually sound and hence will have a clear relationship to other sound models, such as the dividend discount model. In fact, the residual income model given in Equation 5-3 can be derived from the dividend discount model. The general expression for the dividend discount model is

$$V_0 = \frac{D_1}{(1+r)^1} + \frac{D_2}{(1+r)^2} + \frac{D_3}{(1+r)^3} + \cdots$$

The **clean surplus relation** states the relationship among earnings, dividends, and book value as follows:

$$B_t = B_{t-1} + E_t - D_t$$

In other terms, the ending book value of equity equals the beginning book value plus earnings less dividends, apart from ownership transactions. The condition that income (earnings) reflect all changes in the book value of equity other than ownership transactions is known as clean surplus accounting. Rearranging the clean surplus relation, the dividend for each period can be viewed as the net income minus the earnings retained for the period, or net income minus the increase in book value:

$$D_t = E_t - (B_t - B_{t-1}) = E_t + B_{t-1} - B_t$$

Substituting $E_t + B_{t-1} - B_t$ for D_t in the expression for V_0 results in

$$V_0 = \frac{E_1 + B_0 - B_1}{(1+r)^1} + \frac{E_2 + B_1 - B_2}{(1+r)^2} + \frac{E_3 + B_2 - B_3}{(1+r)^3} + \cdots$$

This equation can be rewritten as follows:

$$V_0 = B_0 + \frac{E_1 - rB_0}{(1+r)^1} + \frac{E_2 - rB_1}{(1+r)^2} + \frac{E_3 - rB_2}{(1+r)^3} + \cdots$$

Expressed with summation notation, the following equation restates the residual income model that we gave in Equation 5-3 above:

$$V_0 = B_0 + \sum_{t=1}^{\infty} \frac{\text{RI}_t}{(1+r)^t} = B_0 + \sum_{t=1}^{\infty} \frac{E_t - rB_{t-1}}{(1+r)^t}$$

According to the above expression, the value of a stock equals its book value per share plus the present value of expected future per-share residual income. Note that when the present value of expected future per-share residual income is positive (negative), intrinsic value V_0 is greater (smaller) than book value per share, B_0.

The residual income model used in practice today has largely developed from the recent academic work of Ohlson (1995) and Feltham and Ohlson (1995) and the earlier work of Edwards and Bell (1961), although in the United States this method has been used to value small businesses in tax cases since the 1920s.[12] The general expression for the residual income model based on this work[13] can also be stated as

$$V_0 = B_0 + \sum_{t=1}^{\infty} \frac{(\text{ROE}_t - r) \times B_{t-1}}{(1 + r)^t} \tag{5-4}$$

Equation 5-4 is equivalent to the expressions for V_0 given earlier because in any year t, $\text{RI}_t = (\text{ROE}_t - r) \times B_{t-1}$. Other than the required rate of return on common stock, the inputs to the residual income model come from accounting data. Example 5-5 illustrates the estimation of value using Equation 5-4.

EXAMPLE 5-5   Using the Residual Income Model (2)

To recap the data from Example 5-3, Bugg Properties has expected earnings per share of $2.00, $2.50, and $4.00, and expected dividends per share of $1.00, $1.25, and $12.25 over the next three years. Analysts expect that the last dividend will be a liquidating dividend and that Bugg will cease operating after Year 3. Bugg's current book value per share is $6.00, and its estimated required rate of return on equity is 10 percent.

Using the above data, estimate the value of Bugg Properties stock using a residual income model of the form $V_0 = B_0 + \sum_{t=1}^{\infty} \frac{(\text{ROE}_t - r) \times B_{t-1}}{(1 + r)^t}$.

Solution: To value the stock, we need to forecast residual income. Table 5-4 illustrates the calculation of residual income. (Note that Table 5-4 arrives at the same estimates of residual income as did Table 5-2 in Example 5-3.)

TABLE 5-4

Year	1	2	3
Earnings per share	2.00	2.50	4.00
Beginning book value per share	6.00	7.00	8.25
ROE	0.3333	0.3571	0.4848
Abnormal rate of return (ROE − r)	0.2333	0.2571	0.3848
Residual income (ROE − r) × Beginning BV	1.40	1.80	3.175

---

[12] In tax valuation, the method is known as the excess earnings method. For example, see Hawkins and Paschall (2001) and U.S. IRS Revenue Ruling 68–609.

[13] See, for example, Hirst and Hopkins (2000).

We estimate the stock value as follows:

$$V_0 = 6.00 + \frac{1.40}{(1.10)} + \frac{1.80}{(1.10)^2} + \frac{3.175}{(1.10)^3}$$

$$= 6.00 + 1.2727 + 1.4876 + 2.3854$$

$$= \$11.15$$

Note that the value is identical to the estimate obtained using Equation 5-3, as illustrated in Example 5-3, because the assumptions are the same and Equations 5-3 and 5-4 are equivalent expressions.

Example 5-5 showed that residual income value can be estimated using current book value, forecasts of earnings, forecasts of book value, and an estimate of the required rate of return on equity. The forecasts of earnings and book value translate into ROE forecasts.

EXAMPLE 5-6   Valuing a Company Using the General Residual Income Model

Robert Sumargo, an equity analyst, is considering the valuation of Dell Computer (NYSE: DELL), which closed on April 19, 2002, at $27.34. Sumargo notes that DELL has had very high ROE in the past 10 years and that consensus analyst forecasts for EPS for fiscal years ending in January 2003 and 2004 reflect expected ROEs of 50 percent and 48 percent, respectively. Sumargo expects that high ROEs may not be sustainable in the future. Sumargo often takes a present value approach to valuation. As of the date of the valuation, DELL does not pay dividends; although a discounted dividend valuation is possible, Sumargo does not feel confident about predicting the date of dividend initiation. He decides to apply the residual income model to value DELL, using the following data and assumptions:

- According to the capital asset pricing model (CAPM), DELL has a required rate of return of 14 percent.
- DELL's book value per share at February 1, 2002, was $1.78.
- ROE is expected to be 50 percent for fiscal year-end January 2003. Because of competitive pressures, Sumargo expects ROE to decline by 2 percent each year thereafter until it reaches the CAPM required rate of return.
- DELL does not currently pay a dividend. Sumargo does not expect one to be paid in the foreseeable future, so that all earnings will be reinvested.

1. Compute the value of DELL using the residual income model (Equation 5-4).
2. After reviewing Sumargo's valuation, a colleague points out that DELL has been issuing stock options to employees, which are not recorded as an expense, and repurchasing shares on the market to offset the dilutive impact of the stock

options. These activities have resulted in a large decline in book value per share in recent years. At the same time, the colleague expects that the diminution of book value per share from the use of employee stock options will continue into the future. Discuss the potential impact on Sumargo's estimate of value if the colleague is correct.

Solution to 1: Book value per share is initially $1.78. Based on a ROE forecast of 50 percent in the first year, the forecast EPS would be $0.89. Because no dividends are paid and the clean surplus relation is assumed to hold, book value at the end of the period is forecast at $2.67. For 2003, residual income is measured as the beginning book value per share times the difference between ROE and r or $0.64. The present value of $0.64 at 14 percent for one year is $0.56. This process is continued year by year as presented in Table 5-5. The value of DELL under this residual income model would be the present value of each year's residual income plus the current book value per share. Because residual income is zero starting in 2021, no forecast is required beyond that period. The estimated value under this model is $27.01, as shown in Table 5-5.

TABLE 5-5   Valuation of DELL Using the Residual Income Model

FYE January	Book Value per Share (beginning)	Forecast EPS	Forecast DPS	Forecast ROE (on beg. BV, %)	Required Return (%)	ROE − r (%)	(ROE − r) × BV	PV of (ROE − r) × BV
2003	1.78	0.89	0	50	14	36	0.64	0.56
2004	2.67	1.28	0	48	14	34	0.91	0.70
2005	3.95	1.82	0	46	14	32	1.26	0.85
2006	5.77	2.54	0	44	14	30	1.73	1.02
2007	8.31	3.49	0	42	14	28	2.33	1.21
2008	11.80	4.72	0	40	14	26	3.07	1.40
2009	16.52	6.28	0	38	14	24	3.96	1.58
2010	22.79	8.21	0	36	14	22	5.01	1.76
2011	31.00	10.54	0	34	14	20	6.20	1.91
2012	41.54	13.29	0	32	14	18	7.48	2.02
2013	54.83	16.45	0	30	14	16	8.77	2.08
2014	71.28	19.96	0	28	14	14	9.98	2.07
2015	91.23	23.72	0	26	14	12	10.95	1.99
2016	114.95	27.59	0	24	14	10	11.50	1.84
2017	142.54	31.36	0	22	14	8	11.40	1.60
2018	173.90	34.78	0	20	14	6	10.43	1.28
2019	208.68	37.56	0	18	14	4	8.35	0.90
2020	246.25	39.40	0	16	14	2	4.92	0.47
2021	285.65	39.99	0	14	14	0	0.00	0.00

Total PV 25.23
Initial book value 1.78
Total value 27.01

Solution to 2:   Unless the inputs are corrected to reflect clean surplus accounting, the residual income valuation will probably overstate intrinsic value because forecasted book value growth will not be realized. The clean surplus relation assumes that all changes to book value other than ownership transactions flow through earnings. If that relation is violated, estimated share value can be overstated (or understated). In the case of DELL, in recent years (relative to the date of Sumargo's analysis) many transactions have affected book value per share without flowing through the income statement. DELL has made wide use of employee stock options, which have not been recorded as an expense on the income statement. DELL has issued shares under these stock option plans and has aggressively repurchased shares to manage the resulting dilution of employee stock options. These transactions have greatly reduced book value per share in recent years. If this trend continues, DELL is not likely to see the increases in book value forecast in the model above, and the residual income model will likely overstate the value of DELL.

Example 5-6, Part 2, touched on the issue of violations of clean surplus accounting. The residual income model, as stated earlier, assumes clean surplus accounting. **Comprehensive income** is income under clean surplus accounting; as such, comprehensive income reflects all changes in equity other than contributions by, and distributions to, owners. Comprehensive income often includes several items that bypass the current income statement such as the impact of changes in the market value of certain securities.[14] Strictly speaking, in using residual income models we are concerned with comprehensive income (income under clean surplus accounting); analysts thus adjust net income for material differences from clean surplus accounting. Section 4.1 explores violations of the clean surplus accounting in more detail.

3.2. Fundamental Determinants of Residual Income

The residual income model in general makes no assumptions about future earnings and dividend growth. If we assume constant earnings and dividend growth (at g), we can derive a version of the residual income model that is useful for illustrating the fundamental drivers of residual income. In Chapter 4, we developed the following expression for justified P/B based on forecasted fundamentals, assuming the Gordon (constant growth) DDM and the sustainable growth rate equation, $g = b \times \text{ROE}$:[15]

$$\frac{P_0}{B_0} = \frac{\text{ROE} - g}{r - g}$$

which is mathematically equivalent to

$$\frac{P_0}{B_0} = 1 + \frac{\text{ROE} - r}{r - g}$$

The justified price is the stock's intrinsic value ($P_0 = V_0$). Therefore, using the previous equation, we can express a stock's intrinsic value under the residual income model, assuming constant growth, as

---

[14]In U.S. financial statements, items that bypass the income statement (**dirty surplus items**) are entered into **other comprehensive income**. The relationship is Comprehensive income = Net income + Other comprehensive income.

[15]Interestingly, the sustainable growth rate formula itself can be derived from the clean surplus relation.

$$V_0 = B_0 + \frac{\text{ROE} - r}{r - g} B_0 \qquad (5\text{-}5)$$

Under this model, the estimated value of a share is thus the book value per share (B_0) plus the present value of the expected level stream of residual income, $(\text{ROE} - r) \times B_0$. In the case of a company for which ROE exactly equals the cost of equity, the intrinsic value should equal the book value per share. We call Equation 5-5 the single-stage (or constant-growth) residual income model.

In an ideal world, where the book value of equity represents the fair value of net assets and clean surplus accounting prevails, the term B_0 reflects the value of assets owned by the company less its liabilities. The second term, $(\text{ROE} - r) \times B_0/(r - g)$, represents additional value expected because of the company's ability to generate returns in excess of its cost of equity; the second term is the present value of the company's expected economic profits. Unfortunately, both U.S. and international accounting rules enable companies to exclude some liabilities from their balance sheets, and neither set of rules reflects the fair value of many corporate assets. There is, however, a move internationally toward fair value accounting, particularly for financial assets. Controversies, such as the failure of Enron Corporation in the United States, have highlighted the importance of identifying off-balance-sheet financing techniques.

The single-stage residual income model also assumes that the company's positive residual income continues indefinitely and that book value grows at a constant rate. More likely, a company's ROE will revert to a mean value of ROE over time, and at some point, the company's residual income will be zero. In light of these considerations, the residual income model has been adapted in practice to handle declining residual income and deficiencies in the current accounting model. For example, Lee and Swaminathan (1999) and Lee, Myers, and Swaminathan (1999) used a residual income model to value the Dow 30 assuming that ROE fades (reverts) to the industry mean over time. Lee and Swaminathan found that the residual income model had more ability to predict future returns than traditional price multiples. Bauman (1999) demonstrated how accounting data could be useful in equity valuation using a residual income model.

3.3. Residual Income Valuation in Relation to Other Approaches

Before proceeding to the next section, which addresses both domestic and international issues in using accounting data in the residual income model, we should briefly summarize the relationships of the residual income model to other valuation models.

Valuation models based on discounting dividends or on discounting free cash flow to equity (FCFE) are theoretically sound models, as is the residual income model. Unlike the residual income model, however, DDM and FCFE models forecast future cash flows and find the value of stock by discounting them back to the present using the required return on equity. The RI model approaches this process differently. It starts with a value based on the balance sheet, the book value of equity, and adjusts this value by adding the present values of expected future residual income. Thus, the recognition of value is different, but the total present value, whether using expected dividends, expected free cash flow, or book value plus expected residual income, should be consistent, in theory.[16]

---

[16]See, for example, Shrieves and Wachowicz (2001).

In fact, because each model can be derived from the same underlying theoretical model, when fully consistent assumptions are used to forecast earnings, cash flow, dividends, book value, and residual income through a full set of pro forma (projected) financial statements, and the same required rate of return on equity is used as the discount rate, the same estimate of value should result using each model. Practically speaking, however, it may not be possible to forecast each of these items with the same degree of certainty.[17] For example, if a company has near-term negative free cash flow and forecasts for the terminal value are uncertain, a residual income model may be more appropriate. On the other hand, a company with positive, predictable cash flow that does not pay a dividend would be well suited for a discounted free cash flow valuation.

A residual income model can also be used in conjunction with other models to assess the consistency of results. If a wide variation of estimates is found and the models appear appropriate, the inconsistency may lie with the assumptions used in the models. The analyst would need to perform additional work to determine whether the assumptions are mutually consistent and which model is most appropriate for the subject company. Residual income models, just like the DDM and FCFE models, can also be used to establish justified market multiples, such as P/E or P/B. For example, the value can be determined using a residual income model and divided by earnings to arrive at a justified P/E in conjunction with a relative valuation approach. The residual income model is most closely related to the P/B ratio. A stock's justified P/B ratio is directly related to expected future residual income. Another closely related concept is **Tobin's q**, the ratio of the market value of debt and equity to the replacement cost of total assets:[18]

$$\text{Tobin's } q = \frac{\text{Market value of debt and equity}}{\text{Replacement cost of total assets}}$$

Although similar to P/B, Tobin's q also has some obvious differences: The numerator includes the market value of total capital (debt as well as equity). The denominator uses total assets rather than equity. Further, assets are valued at replacement cost rather than a historical accounting cost; replacement costs take account of the effects of inflation. All else equal, we expect Tobin's q to be higher, the greater the productivity of a company's assets.[19] One difficulty in computing Tobin's q is the lack of information on assets' replacement costs. If available, market values of assets or replacement costs can be more useful in a valuation than historical costs.

4. ACCOUNTING AND INTERNATIONAL CONSIDERATIONS

In practice, to most accurately apply the residual income model, the analyst needs to adjust book value of common equity for off-balance-sheet items and adjust reported net income to obtain comprehensive income. In this section, we will discuss issues relating to these tasks.

---

[17] For a lively debate on this issue, see Penman and Sougiannis (1998), Penman (2001), Lundholm and O'Keefe (2001a), and Lundholm and O'Keefe (2001b).

[18] See Tobin (1969) or more recent work such as Landsman and Shapiro (1995).

[19] Tobin theorized that q would average to 1 over all companies, as the economic rents or profits earned by assets would average to zero.

Bauman (1999) has noted that the strength of the residual income valuation model is that the two components (book value and future earnings) of the model have a balancing effect on each other, provided that the clean surplus relationship is followed:

All other things held constant, companies making aggressive (conservative) accounting choices will report higher (lower) book values and lower (higher) future earnings. In the model, the present value of differences in future income is exactly offset by the initial differences in book value. (Baumann 1999, p. 31)

Unfortunately, this argument has several problems in practice. The clean surplus relationship does not prevail, and analysts often use past earnings to predict future earnings. International Accounting Standards (IAS) and U.S. GAAP permit a variety of items to bypass the income statement and be reported directly in stockholders' equity. Further, companies have managed to keep some liabilities off the balance sheet and to obscure financial results with non-operating and nonrecurring items. The analyst must thus watch for such practices in evaluating the book value of equity and return on equity to be used as inputs into a residual income model.

With regard to the contention that aggressive accounting choices will lead to lower reported future earnings, take an example in which a company chooses to capitalize an expenditure in the current year rather than to expense it. Doing so overstates current-year earnings as well as current book value. If an analyst uses current earnings (or ROE) naively in predicting future residual earnings, the residual income model will overestimate the value of the company. Take, for example, a company with $1,000,000 of book value and $200,000 of earnings before taxes, after expensing an expenditure of $50,000. Ignoring taxes, this company has a ROE of 20 percent. If the company capitalized the expenditure rather than expensing it immediately, it would have a ROE of 23.81 percent ($250,000/$1,050,000).

Although at some time in the future this capitalized item will likely be amortized or written off, thus reducing realized future earnings, analysts' expectations often rely on historical data. If capitalization persists over time for a stable company, ROE can decline because net income will normalize over the long term, but book value will be overstated. For a growing company, for which the expenditure in question is increasing, ROE can continue at high levels over time. We suggest that because the residual income model uses primarily accounting data as inputs, the model can be sensitive to accounting choices and aggressive accounting methods (e.g., accelerating revenues or deferring expenses) can result in errors in valuation. The analyst must be particularly careful, therefore, in analyzing a company's reported data for use in a residual income model.

As we have seen, two principal drivers of residual earnings are ROE and book value. The analyst must understand how to use historical reported accounting data for these items to the extent he uses historical data in forecasting future ROE and book value. Chapter 2 explained the DuPont analysis of ROE, which can be used as a tool in forecasting. Chapter 4 discussed the calculation of book value. We extend these previous discussions below with specific application to residual income valuation, particularly in addressing the following accounting considerations:

- violations of the clean surplus relationship,
- balance sheet adjustments for fair value,
- intangible assets,
- nonrecurring items,
- aggressive accounting practices, and
- international considerations.

In any valuation, we must pay close attention to the accounting practices of the company being valued. In the following sections, we address the above issues as they particularly affect residual income valuation.

4.1. Violations of the Clean Surplus Relationship

One potential accounting issue in applying a residual income model is a violation of clean surplus accounting. Violations may occur when accounting standards permit charges directly to stockholders' equity, bypassing the income statement. An example is the case of changes in the market value of long-term investments. IAS provide that the change in market value can be reported in current profits or can bypass the income statement and be reported in shareholders' equity. Under U.S. GAAP, the balance sheet includes, at market value, investments considered to be "available for sale"; however, any change in their market value is reflected in stockholders' equity as other comprehensive income rather than as income on the income statement.

Earlier, we defined comprehensive income as all changes in equity other than contributions by and distributions to owners. Comprehensive income includes net income reported on the income statement. *Other comprehensive income* (also previously defined) is the result of other events and transactions that result in a change to equity but are not reported on the income statement. Items that commonly bypass the income statement include[20]

- foreign currency translation adjustments,
- certain pension adjustments, and
- fair value changes of some financial instruments.

In all of these cases, the book value of equity is stated accurately, but net income is not from the perspective of residual income valuation. The analyst should be most concerned with the impact of these items on forecasts of net income and ROE (which has net income in the numerator), and hence also residual income.[21] Because some items (including those listed above) bypass the income statement, they are excluded from historical ROE data. As noted by Frankel and Lee (1999), bias will be introduced into the valuation only if the present expected value of the clean surplus violations do not net to zero. In other words, reductions in income from some periods may be offset by increases from other periods. The analyst must examine the equity section of the balance sheet and the related statements of shareholders' equity and comprehensive income carefully for items that have bypassed the income statement; the analyst can then assess whether amounts are likely to be offsetting and can assess the impact on future ROE.

EXAMPLE 5-7   Evaluating Clean Surplus Violations

The statement of changes in stockholders' equity for Nokia Corporation (NYSE: NOK), prepared under IAS as of December 31, 1999, is partially replicated below:

---

[20] See Frankel and Lee (1999).

[21] The analyst should most precisely calculate historical ROE at the aggregate level (e.g., as net income divided by shareholders' equity) rather than as earnings per share divided by book value per share, because actions such as share issuance and share repurchases can distort ROE calculated on a per-share basis.

TABLE 5-6   Nokia Corporation Statement of Changes in Stockholders' Equity
(€ millions)

	Share Capital	Share Issue Premium	Treasury Share	Translation Differences	Retained Earnings	Total
Balance at December 31, 1998	255	909	(110)	182	3,873	5,109
Share issue	3	191				194
Bonus issue	36	(36)				0
Cancellation of Treasury shares	(15)	15	110		(110)	0
Acquisition of Treasury shares			(24)		24	0
Dividend					(586)	(586)
Dividend on Treasury shares					31	31
Translation differences				61		61
Other increase/decrease, net					(8)	(8)
Net profit					2,577	2,577
Balance at December 31, 1999	279	1,079	(24)	243	5,801	7,378

The column "Translation Differences" reflects the cumulative amount of translation adjustments on equity that have bypassed the income statement. Because there is a positive adjustment to stockholders' equity, this item would have increased income if it had been reported on the income statement. Because the balance is accumulating, it does not appear to be reversing (netting to zero) in the long term. If the analyst expects this trend to continue, an increase in expected ROE might be warranted. It is possible, however, that future exchange rates will reverse this impact. Additionally, the decision to forgo making an adjustment to ROE would result in a conservative valuation in this case.

4.2. Balance Sheet Adjustments for Fair Value

In order to have a reliable measure of book value of equity, an analyst must identify and scrutinize significant off-balance-sheet assets and liabilities. Additionally, reported assets and liabilities should be adjusted to fair value when possible. Off-balance-sheet assets and liabilities may become apparent by an examination of the financial statement footnotes. Examples include pension liabilities, the use of operating leases, and the use of special purpose entities to remove both debt and assets from the balance sheet. Some items such as the pension liability often result in an understatement of liabilities and overstatement of equity. Others, such as leases, may not affect the amount of equity (for example off-balance-sheet assets offset off-balance-sheet liabilities) but can impact an assessment of future earnings for the residual income component of value. Other assets and liabilities may be stated at other than fair value. For example, inventory may be stated at LIFO and require adjustment to restate to current value. Presented below are some common items to review for balance sheet adjustments. Note, however, that this list is not all-inclusive:[22]

- inventory,
- deferred tax assets and liabilities,
- pension plan assets and liabilities,
- operating leases,
- special-purpose entities,
- reserves and allowances (for example, bad debts), and
- intangible assets.

Additionally, the analyst should examine the financial statements and footnotes for items unique to the subject company.

4.3. Intangible Assets

Intangible assets can have a significant impact on book value. In the case of specifically identifiable intangibles that can be separated from the entity (e.g., sold), it is appropriate to include these in the determination of book value of equity. If these assets are wasting (declining in value over time), they will be amortized over time as an expense. Goodwill, on the other hand, requires special consideration, particularly in light of recent changes in accounting for goodwill. Goodwill represents the excess of the purchase price of an acquisition over the value of the net assets acquired. Goodwill is generally not recognized as an asset unless it results from an acquisition (most international accounting standards do not allow the recognition of internally generated goodwill on the balance sheet). To demonstrate this, consider two companies, Alpha and Beta, with the following summary financial information (all amounts in thousands, except per-share data):

	Alpha	Beta
Cash	€1,600	€100
Property, plant, and equipment	€3,400	€900
Total assets	€5,000	€1,000
Equity	€5,000	€1,000
Net income	€600	€150

Each company pays out all net income as dividends (no growth), and the clean surplus relation holds. Alpha has a 12 percent ROE and Beta has a 15 percent ROE, both expected to continue indefinitely. Each has a 10 percent required rate of return. The fair market value of each company's property, plant, and equipment is the same as its book value. What is the value of each company in a residual income framework?

Using total book value rather than per-share data, the value of Alpha would be €6,000, determined as follows:[23]

$$V_0 = B_0 + \frac{\text{ROE} - r}{r - g} B_0 = 5,000 + \frac{0.12 - 0.10}{0.10 - 0.00} 5,000 = 6,000$$

---

[22] See also Chapter 17 of White, Sondhi, and Fried (1998).
[23] Results would be the same if done on a per-share basis.

Similarly, the value of Beta would be €1,500:

$$V_0 = B_0 + \frac{\text{ROE} - r}{r - g}B_0 = 1{,}000 + \frac{0.15 - 0.10}{0.10 - 0.00}1{,}000 = 1{,}500$$

The value of the companies on a combined basis would be €7,500. Note that both companies are valued more highly than the book value of equity because they have ROEs in excess of the required rate of return. Absent an acquisition transaction, the financial statements of Alpha and Beta do not reflect this value. If either is acquired, however, goodwill would appear as an asset and result in higher book value of equity. For instance, suppose Alpha acquires Beta by paying Beta's former shareholders €1,500 in cash. Alpha has just paid €500 in excess of the value of Beta's total assets (€1,000), which is recorded as goodwill. The balance sheet of Alpha immediately after the acquisition would be[24]

	Alpha
Cash	€200
Property, plant, and equipment	€4,300
Goodwill	€500
Total assets	€5,000
Equity	€5,000

Note that the total book value of equity did not change, because cash was used in the transaction. Assuming that goodwill is amortized over a 10-year period, the combined company's expected net income would be €700 (€600 + €150 − €50 amortization). Expected ROE would be 14 percent. Under a residual income model with no adjustment for goodwill amortization, the value of the combined company would be

$$V_0 = B_0 + \frac{\text{ROE} - r}{r - g}B_0 = 5{,}000 + \frac{0.14 - 0.10}{0.10 - 0.00}5{,}000 = 7{,}000$$

Why should the combined company be worth less than the two separate companies? Assuming that a fair price was paid to the former shareholders, the combined value should not be lower. The lower value results from a reduction in ROE due to the amortization of goodwill. If goodwill were not amortized (or we added back the amortization expense before computing ROE), net income would be €750 and ROE would be 15 percent. The value of the combined entity would be

$$V_0 = B_0 + \frac{\text{ROE} - r}{r - g}B_0 = 5{,}000 + \frac{0.15 - 0.10}{0.10 - 0.00}5{,}000 = 7{,}500$$

This amount is the same as the sum of the values of the companies on a separate basis.

Recently, U.S. GAAP has altered the treatment of goodwill amortization. Goodwill is still listed as an asset when purchased but is no longer amortized.[25] Under IAS, goodwill is currently required to be amortized over a period not to exceed 20 years. To ensure international comparability and to avoid the adverse impact of amortization noted above, we recommend adjusting earnings to remove any amortization of goodwill.

---

[24] For example, cash at €200 is calculated as €1,600 (cash of Alpha) + €100 (cash of Beta) − €1,500 (purchase price of Beta).

[25] If goodwill is later deemed to be impaired, a write-off or loss is taken.

Would the answer be different if the acquiring company used newly issued stock rather than cash in the acquisition? The form of currency used to pay for the transaction should not impact the total value. If Alpha used €1,500 of newly issued stock to acquire Beta, its balance sheet would be

	Alpha
Cash	€1,700
Property, plant, and equipment	€4,300
Goodwill	€500
Total assets	€6,500
Equity	€6,500

Projected earnings, excluding the amortization of goodwill, would be €750, and projected ROE would be 11.538 percent. Value under the residual income model would be

$$V_0 = B_0 + \frac{\text{ROE} - r}{r - g} B_0 = 6,500 + \frac{0.11538 - 0.10}{0.10 - 0.00} 6,500 = 7,500$$

The overall value remains unchanged. The book value of equity is higher but offset by the impact on ROE. Once again, this assumes that the buyer paid a fair value for the acquisition. If an acquirer overpays for an acquisition, this should become evident in a reduction in future residual income and write-off of previously recorded goodwill.

Research and development costs provide another example of an intangible asset that must be given careful consideration. Under U.S. GAAP, R&D is expensed to the income statement directly. Under IAS, some R&D costs can be capitalized and amortized over time. R&D expenditures are reflected in a company's ROE, and hence residual income, over time. If a company engages in unproductive R&D expenditures, these will lower residual income through the expenditures made. If a company engages in productive R&D expenditures, these should result in higher revenues to offset the expenditures over time. In summary, on an ongoing basis for a mature company, ROE should reflect the productivity of R&D expenditures.

Bauman (1999) applied a residual income model to Cisco Systems, Inc., by capitalizing and amortizing purchased in-process R&D that was expensed under U.S. GAAP rather than becoming part of goodwill. He found that when purchased in-process R&D is capitalized and then amortized over a short period, there is no impact on overall value compared with immediate expensing of R&D in a residual income framework. White, Sondhi, and Fried (1998), however, noted that expensing of R&D in the long term results in higher ROEs over the long term. The analyst should carefully consider the company's R&D expenditures and their impact on long-term ROE.

4.4. Nonrecurring Items

In applying a residual income model, it is important to develop a forecast of future residual income based on recurring items. Often, companies report nonrecurring charges as part of earnings or classify nonoperating income (e.g., sale of assets) as part of operating income. These misclassifications can lead to overestimates and underestimates of future residual earnings if no adjustments are made. No adjustments to book value are necessary for these items, however, because nonrecurring gains and losses are reflected in the value of assets in place. Hirst and Hopkins (2000) noted that nonrecurring items sometimes result from accounting rules and at other times result from "strategic" management decisions. Regardless, they highlighted the importance of examining the financial statement notes and other sources for items that may warrant adjustment in determining recurring earnings, such as

- unusual items,
- extraordinary items,
- restructuring charges,
- discontinued operations, and
- accounting changes.

In some cases, management may record restructuring or unusual charges in every period. In these cases, the item may be considered an ordinary operating expense and may not require adjustment.

Companies sometimes inappropriately classify nonoperating gains as a reduction in operating expenses (such as selling, general, and administrative expenses). If material, this inappropriate classification can usually be uncovered by a careful reading of financial statement footnotes and press releases. Analysts should consider whether these items are likely to continue and contribute to residual income over time. More likely, they should be removed from operating earnings when forecasting residual income.

4.5. Other Aggressive Accounting Practices

Companies may engage in accounting practices that result in the overstatement of assets (book value) and/or overstatement of earnings. We discussed many of these practices in the preceding sections.[26] Other activities that a company may engage in include accelerating revenues to the current period or deferring expenses to a later period.[27] Both activities simultaneously increase earnings and book value. For example, a company might ship unordered goods to customers at year-end, recording revenues and a receivable. Conversely, a company could capitalize rather than expense a cash payment, resulting in lower expenses and an increase in assets. The analyst must evaluate a company's accounting policies carefully and consider the integrity of management in assessing the inputs in a residual income model. Companies have also been criticized recently for the use of "cookie jar" reserves (reserves saved for future use), in which excess losses or expenses are recorded in an earlier period (for example, in conjunction with an acquisition or restructuring) and then used to reduce expense and increase income in future periods. The analyst should carefully examine the use of reserves when assessing residual earnings.

4.6. International Considerations

Accounting standards differ internationally. These differences result in different measures of book value and earnings internationally and suggest that valuation models based on accrual accounting data might not perform as well as other present value models in international contexts. It is interesting to note, however, that Frankel and Lee (1999) found that the residual income model works well in valuing companies on an international basis. Using a simple residual income model without any of the adjustments discussed in this chapter, they found that their residual income valuation model accounted for 70 percent of the cross-sectional variation of stock prices across 20 countries. Table 5-7 shows the model's explanatory power by country.

---

[26]Also see Chapter 1.

[27]See, for example, Schilit (1993).

TABLE 5-7   International Application of Residual
Income Models

Explanatory Power	Country
40–50 percent	Germany
	Japan (Parent company reporting)
60–70 percent	Australia
	Canada
	Japan (Consolidated reporting)
	United Kingdom
More than 70 percent	France
	United States

Source: Frankel and Lee (1999).

Germany had the lowest explanatory power. Japan had low explanatory power for companies reporting only parent company results; the explanatory power for Japanese companies reporting on a consolidated basis was considerably higher. Explanatory power was highest in France, the United Kingdom, and the United States. Frankel and Lee concluded that there are three primary considerations in applying a residual income model internationally:

- the availability of reliable earnings forecasts,
- systematic violations of the clean surplus assumption, and
- "poor quality" accounting rules that result in delayed recognition of value changes.

Analysts should expect the model to work best in situations in which earnings forecasts are available, clean surplus violations are limited, and accounting rules do not result in delayed recognition. Because Frankel and Lee found good explanatory power for a residual income model using unadjusted accounting data, it should be expected that if adjustments are made to the reported data to correct for clean surplus and other violations, international comparisons should result in comparable valuations. For circumstances in which clean surplus violations exist, accounting choices result in delayed recognition, or accounting disclosures do not permit adjustment, the residual income model would not be appropriate and the analyst should consider a model less dependent on accounting data, such as a FCFE model.

5. SINGLE-STAGE RESIDUAL INCOME VALUATION

The single-stage (constant-growth) residual income model assumes that a company has a constant return on equity and constant earnings growth rate over time. This model was given in Equation 5-5, repeated below:

$$V_0 = B_0 + \frac{\text{ROE} - r}{r - g} B_0$$

EXAMPLE 5-8   Single-Stage Residual Income Model (1)

Joseph Yoh is evaluating a purchase of Canon, Inc. (NYSE: CAJ). Current book value per share is \$12.90, and the current price per share is \$32.41 (from Value Line, 8 February 2002). Yoh expects long-term ROE to be 10 percent and long-term growth to be 8 percent. Assuming a cost of equity of 9 percent, what is the intrinsic value of Canon stock using a residual income model?

$$V_0 = 12.90 + \frac{0.10 - 0.09}{0.09 - 0.08} 12.90 = \$25.80$$

Similar to the Gordon growth DDM, the single-stage residual income model can be used to assess the market expectations of residual income growth by inputting the current price into the model and solving for g.

EXAMPLE 5-9   Single-Stage Residual Income Model (2)

Joseph Yoh is curious about the market-perceived growth rate, given that he is comfortable with his other inputs. Using the current price per share of \$32.41 for Canon, Yoh solves for g:

$$\$32.41 = 12.90 + \frac{0.10 - 0.09}{0.09 - g} 12.90$$

He finds an implied growth rate of 8.34 percent.

In the above example, the company was valued at twice its book value because its ROE exceeded its cost of equity. If ROE were equal to the cost of equity, the company would be valued at book value. If ROE were lower than the cost of equity, the company would have negative residual income and be valued at less than book value. In the case in which a company cannot cover its cost of capital, a liquidation of the company and redeployment of assets may be appropriate. Assuming the market appropriately values the company below book value, this case may also be an opportunity for an acquisition or other restructuring in which new management may be able to improve residual income and add value to the company.

In many applications, a drawback to the single-stage model is that it assumes the excess ROE above the cost of equity will persist indefinitely. Evidence suggests that ROE is mean reverting over time, which should not be surprising. If a company or industry has an abnormally high ROE, other companies will enter the marketplace, increasing competition and lowering returns for all companies. Similarly, if an industry has a low ROE, companies will exit the industry (through bankruptcy or otherwise) and ROEs will tend to rise over time. As with the single-stage DDM, the single-stage residual income model assumes a constant growth rate over time. Fortunately, other models are available that enable us to relax these assumptions.

6. MULTISTAGE RESIDUAL INCOME VALUATION

As with the DDM and DCF approaches, a multistage approach can be used when residual income is forecast for a certain time horizon and a terminal value based on continuing residual income is estimated at the end of the time horizon. **Continuing residual income** is residual income after the forecast horizon. As with other valuation models, the forecast horizon for the initial stage should based on the ability to explicitly forecast inputs into the model. Unlike in other models, the terminal value is not a major driver of value in a residual income approach. Frequently, in DCF approaches, the value of early cash flows makes up a small portion of total value, whereas the present value of the terminal value is a significant portion of that value. In a residual income approach, the current book value often captures a large portion of total value. Because ROEs have been found to revert to mean levels over time and may decline to the cost of equity in a competitive environment, the terminal value may not be a large component of total value, particularly as ROE approaches the cost of equity. An ROE equal to the cost of equity would result in residual income of zero.

Analysts make a variety of assumptions concerning continuing residual income. Frequently, one of the following assumptions is made:

- Residual income continues indefinitely at a positive level;
- Residual income is zero from the terminal year forward;
- Residual income declines to zero as ROE reverts to the cost of equity over time; or
- Residual income reflects the reversion of ROE to some mean level.

We illustrate several of these approaches below.

One finite-horizon model of residual income valuation assumes that at the end of time horizon T, there is a certain premium over book value ($P_T - B_T$) for the company; in this case, current value equals the following:[28]

$$V_0 = B_0 + \sum_{t=1}^{T} \frac{(E_t - rB_{t-1})}{(1+r)^t} + \frac{P_T - B_T}{(1+r)^T} \tag{5-6}$$

Alternatively,

$$V_0 = B_0 + \sum_{t=1}^{T} \frac{(\text{ROE}_t - r) \times B_{t-1}}{(1+r)^t} + \frac{P_T - B_T}{(1+r)^T} \tag{5-7}$$

The last component in both specifications represents the premium over book value at the end of the forecast horizon. The longer the forecast period, the greater the chance that the company's residual income will converge to zero. For long forecast periods, this last term may thus be treated as zero. For shorter forecast periods, a forecast of the premium must be calculated.

---

[28] See Bauman (1999).

EXAMPLE 5-10   Multistage Residual Income Model (1)

Diana Rosato, CFA, is considering an investment in Taiwan Semiconductor Manufacturing Ltd., a manufacturer and marketer of integrated circuits. Listed on the Taiwan Stock Exchange (2330), the company's stock is also traded on the New York Stock Exchange (NYSE: TSM). Rosato obtained the following information from Bloomberg and Value Line as of February 21, 2002:

- Current price = TWD81.
- Cost of equity = 14.33 percent.
- Taiwan Semiconductor's ROEs have ranged from 18.3 percent to 26.2 percent over the last four years.
- Five-year forecast of growth in book value = 22 percent a year.
- TSM does not pay dividends.

Additionally, Rosato reviews annual financial statements for 2000 and quarterly financial statements for 2001. The fourth-quarter financial statements indicate a book value per share of TWD16.47. In 2001, ROE declined to 5.5 percent, but Rosato and other analysts expect a rebound in ROE for the years 2002 and 2003. Analyst EPS forecasts (from Multex Global Estimates) are 2.07 for 2002 and 4.81 for 2003.

Rosato expects Taiwan Semiconductor's ROE after 2003 to stabilize at 25 percent until 2011 and then decline to 20 percent until 2021. Rosato assumes that after that date, residual income will be zero and the terminal premium over book value would thus be zero. Rosato's residual income model is as follows:

TABLE 5-8   Taiwan Semiconductor

Year	Projected Income	Book Value	Forecast ROE (beg. equity, %)	Cost of Equity (%)	Cost of Equity (TWD)	Residual Income	PV of RI	Total PV of RI
		16.47					16.47	59.18
2002	2.07	18.54	12.57	14.33	2.36	−0.29	(0.25)	
2003	4.81	23.35	25.94	14.33	2.66	2.15	1.65	
2004	5.84	29.19	25.00	14.33	3.35	2.49	1.67	
2005	7.30	36.48	25.00	14.33	4.18	3.11	1.82	
2006	9.12	45.61	25.00	14.33	5.23	3.89	1.99	
2007	11.40	57.01	25.00	14.33	6.54	4.87	2.18	
2008	14.25	71.26	25.00	14.33	8.17	6.08	2.38	
2009	17.81	89.07	25.00	14.33	10.21	7.60	2.60	
2010	22.27	111.34	25.00	14.33	12.76	9.50	2.85	
2011	27.84	139.18	25.00	14.33	15.96	11.88	3.11	
2012	27.84	167.01	20.00	14.33	19.94	7.89	1.81	
2013	33.40	200.41	20.00	14.33	23.93	9.47	1.90	
2014	40.08	240.50	20.00	14.33	28.72	11.36	1.99	
2015	48.10	288.60	20.00	14.33	34.46	13.64	2.09	

TABLE 5-8   (*continued*)

Year	Projected Income	Book Value	Forecast ROE (beg. equity, %)	Cost of Equity (%)	Cost of Equity (TWD)	Residual Income	PV of RI	Total PV of RI
2016	57.72	346.32	20.00	14.33	41.36	16.36	2.20	
2017	69.26	415.58	20.00	14.33	49.63	19.64	2.30	
2018	83.12	498.70	20.00	14.33	59.55	23.56	2.42	
2019	99.74	598.43	20.00	14.33	71.46	28.28	2.54	
2020	119.69	718.12	20.00	14.33	85.76	33.93	2.66	
2021	143.62	861.75	20.00	14.33	102.91	40.72	2.80	
Terminal Premium = 0.00								

The market price of TWD81 exceeds the estimated value of TWD59.18. Rosato concludes that the company is overvalued in the current marketplace.

Lee and Swaminathan (1999) and Lee, Myers, and Swaminathan (1999) have presented a residual income model based on explicit forecasts of residual income for three years. Thereafter, ROE is forecast to fade to the industry mean value of ROE. The terminal value at the end of the forecast horizon (T) is estimated as the terminal-year residual income discounted as a perpetuity. Lee and Swaminathan stated that this assumes that any growth in earnings after T is value neutral. Table 5-9 presents some recent industry ROE data from Baseline. In forecasting a fading ROE, the analyst should also consider any trends in industry ROE.

EXAMPLE 5-11   Multistage Residual Income Model (2)

Rosato's supervisor questions her assumption that Taiwan Semiconductor will have no premium at the end of her forecast period. Rosato amends her model to use a terminal value based on a perpetuity of Year 2021 residual income. She computes the following terminal value:

$$TV = 40.72/0.1433 = 284.16$$

The present value of this terminal value is as follows:

$$PV = 284.16/(1.1433)^{20} = 19.51$$

Adding this number to the previous value of 58.91 (for which the terminal value was zero) yields a total value of TWD78.69. Because the current market price of TWD81 is greater than TWD78.69, Rosato concludes that market participants expect a positive continuing residual income after her forecast period.

TABLE 5-9   U.S. Industry ROEs, 2000

Industry	ROE	Industry	ROE
Advertising	32.00%	Insurance—Multiline	14.00%
Aerospace/Defense	18.00	Insurance—Prop/Casualty	10.00
Agricultural Product	5.00	IT Consulting & Svc	20.00
Air Freight & Couriers	14.00	Internet Software & Svc	4.00
Aluminum	18.00	Leisure Facilities	9.00
Apparel & Accessory	17.00	Leisure Products	9.00
Application Software	19.00	Machinery Industrial	19.00
Airlines	13.00	Meat Poultry & Fish	11.00
Auto Parts & Equip	20.00	Broadcasting & Cable	2.00
Automobile Mfrs	23.00	Diverse Metal/Mining	6.00
Banks	34.00	Motorcycle Mfrs	27.00
Soft Drinks	30.00	Multi—Utilities	12.00
Biotechnology	24.00	Networking Equipment	21.00
Building Products	18.00	Office Electronics	20.00
Brewers	37.00	Services—Office/Supp	37.00
Chemicals—Commodity	45.00	Oil & Gas—Drilling	6.00
Consumer Electronics	15.00	Oil & Gas—Equip/Svc	7.00
Computer Hardware	29.00	Oil & Gas—Explor/Prod	27.00
Industrial Conglomerates	28.00	Oil & Gas—Integrated	30.00
Construction Materials	16.00	Oil & Gas—Refng/Mktg	21.00
Contain Metal/Glass	9.00	Services—Environmental	18.00
Casinos & Gaming	12.00	Integrated Telecom Svc	24.00
Personal Products	53.00	Photographic Prods	38.00
Chemicals—Diverse	17.00	Packaged Foods	55.00
Services—Div/Comm'l	29.00	Paper Packaging	12.00
Computer Storage/Peripherals	27.00	Paper Products	7.00
Distributors	18.00	Precious Metal & Mineral	19.00
Diverse Financial Svc	24.00	Commercial Printing	22.00
Services—Data Proc	24.00	Publishing & Printing	18.00
Pharmaceuticals	34.00	Railroads	8.00
Distiller & Vintners	22.00	Reinsurance	8.00
Electrical Component	18.00	Restaurants	24.00
Electronic Equip/Inst	17.00	Retail—Apparel	36.00
Construction & Engineer	5.00	Retail—Catalog	18.00
Movies & Entertainment	11.00	Retail—Comp/Electronic	21.00
Electric Utilities	15.00	Department Stores	12.00
Chemicals—Agri/Fertilizer	11.00	Retail—Drugs	19.00
Consumer Finance	25.00	General Merchandise	23.00
Food Distributors	27.00	Retail—Home Improve	18.00
Retail—Food	23.00	Specialty Stores	19.00
Forest Products	11.00	Chemicals—Specialty	15.00
Gold	6.00	Semiconductors	27.00
Gas Utilities	14.00	Semiconductor Equip	32.00
Healthcare—Dist/Svc	14.00	Marine	12.00

TABLE 5-9   (*continued*)

Industry	ROE	Industry	ROE
Healthcare—Equipment	27.00	Footwear	18.00
Healthcare—Facility	6.00	Services—Employment	29.00
Healthcare—Managed Care	17.00	Steel	10.00
Healthcare—Supplies	7.00	Systems Software	37.00
Homebuilding	23.00	Tobacco	55.00
Home Furnishings	15.00	Telecom Equipment	11.00
Hotels	16.00	Tires & Rubber	3.00
Household Appliances	36.00	Wireless Telecom Svc	5.00
Household Products	36.00	Trade Cos & Distr	15.00
Housewares & Specs	16.00	Machinery Const/Farm	16.00
Industrial Gases	9.00	Trucking	9.00
Insurance—Brokers	21.00	Textiles	5.00
Insurance—Life/Health	12.00	Water Utilities	10.00

Source: Baseline.

Another multistage model assumes that ROE fades over time to the cost of equity. In this approach, ROE can be explicitly forecast each period until reaching the cost of equity. The forecast would then end and the terminal value would be zero. Example 5-6 presented such a model using Dell Computer Corporation.

Dechow, Hutton, and Sloan (1998) presented an analysis of a residual income model in which residual income fades over time:[29]

$$V_0 = B_0 + \sum_{t=1}^{T-1} \frac{(E_t - rB_{t-1})}{(1+r)^t} + \frac{E_T - rB_{T-1}}{(1+r-\omega)(1+r)^{T-1}} \tag{5-8}$$

This model adds a persistence factor, ω, which is between 0 and 1. A persistence factor of 1.0 implies that residual income will continue indefinitely (a perpetuity). A persistence factor of 0 implies that residual income will not continue after the initial forecast horizon. The higher the value of the persistence factor, the higher the valuation. Dechow et al. found that in a large sample of company data from 1976 to 1995, the persistence factor equaled 0.62. This persistence factor considers the long-run mean-reverting nature of ROE, assuming that over time ROE regresses toward r and that resulting residual income fades toward zero. Bauman (1999) noted that the above results imply that residual income decays at a rate of 38 percent a year on average. Bauman uses the Dechow et al. model to demonstrate residual income valuation for Cisco. Bauman uses a persistence factor of 0.80 for Cisco, stating that Cisco's market leadership implies a lower rate of decay (20 percent). Clearly, the persistence factor varies from company to company. Dechow et al. provided insight into some characteristics that can indicate a lower or higher level of persistence, listed in Table 5-10.

Example 5-12 illustrates the assumption that continuing residual income will decline to zero as ROE approaches the required rate of return on equity.

---

[29] See Dechow, Hutton, and Sloan (1998) and Bauman (1999).

TABLE 5-10   Final-Stage Residual Income Persistence

Lower Residual Income Persistence	Higher Residual Income Persistence
Extreme accounting rates of return (ROE)	Low dividend payout
Extreme levels of special items (e.g., nonrecurring items)	High historical persistence in the industry
Extreme levels of accounting accruals	

EXAMPLE 5-12   Multistage Residual Income Model (3)

Rosato extends her analysis to consider the possibility that ROE will slowly decay after 2022 toward r, rather than using a perpetuity of Year 2021 residual income. Rosato estimates a persistence parameter of 0.60. The present value of the terminal value is determined as

$$\frac{E_T - rB_{T-1}}{(1 + r - \omega)(1 + r)^{T-1}}$$

with $T = 21$ and 2022 residual income equal to $40.72 \times 1.20 = 48.86$.

$$\frac{48.86}{(1 + 0.1433 - 0.60)(1.1433)^{20}} = 6.18$$

Total value is TWD65.36 calculated by adding 6.18 to 59.18. Rosato concludes that if Taiwan Semiconductor's residual income does not persist at a stable level past 2022 and deteriorates over time, the shares are overvalued.

---

7. SUMMARY

This chapter has discussed the use of residual income models in valuation. Residual income is an appealing economic concept because it attempts to measure economic profit: profits after accounting for all opportunity costs of capital.

- Residual income is calculated as net income minus a deduction for the cost of equity capital. The deduction is called the equity charge, and is equal to equity capital multiplied by the required rate of return on equity (the cost of equity capital in percent).
- Economic value added (EVA) is a commercial implementation of the residual income concept. EVA = NOPAT − (C% × TC), where NOPAT is net operating profit after taxes, C% is the percent cost of equity capital, and TC equals total capital.
- Residual income models (including commercial implementations) are used not only for equity valuation but also to measure internal corporate performance and for determining executive compensation.
- We can forecast per-share residual income as forecasted earnings per share minus the required rate of return on equity multiplied by beginning book value per share. Alternatively, we can forecast per-share residual income as beginning book value per share multiplied by the difference between forecasted ROE and the required rate of return on equity.

- According to the residual income model, the intrinsic value of a share of common stock is the sum of book value per share and the present value of expected future per-share residual income. According to the residual income model, equivalent mathematical expressions for intrinsic value of a common stock are

$$V_0 = B_0 + \sum_{t=1}^{\infty} \frac{RI_t}{(1+r)^t} = B_0 + \sum_{t=1}^{\infty} \frac{E_t - rB_{t-1}}{(1+r)^t} = B_0 + \sum_{t=1}^{\infty} \frac{(ROE_t - r) \times B_{t-1}}{(1+r)^t}$$

where

V_0 = value of a share of stock today $(t = 0)$

B_0 = current per-share book value of equity

B_t = expected per-share book value of equity at any time t

r = required rate of return on equity (cost of equity)

E_t = expected earnings per share for period t

RI_t = expected per-share residual income, equal to $E_t - rB_{t-1}$ or to $(ROE - r) \times B_{t-1}$

- In most cases, value is recognized earlier in the residual income model compared with other present value models of stock value such as the dividend discount model.
- Strengths of the residual income model include the following:
  - Terminal values do not make up a large portion of the value relative to other models.
  - The models use readily available accounting data.
  - The models can be used in the absence of dividends and near-term positive free cash flows.
  - The models can be used when cash flows are unpredictable.
- Weaknesses of the residual income model include the following:
  - These models are based on accounting data that can be subject to manipulation by management.
  - Accounting data used as inputs may require significant adjustments.
  - The models require that the clean surplus relation holds, or that the analyst makes appropriate adjustments when the clean surplus relation does not hold.
- The residual income model is most appropriate in the following cases:
  - A company is not paying dividends or it exhibits an unpredictable dividend pattern.
  - A company has negative free cash flow many years out but is expected to generate positive cash flow at some point in the future.
  - There is a great deal of uncertainty in forecasting terminal values.
- The fundamental determinants or drivers of residual income are book value of equity and return on equity.
- Residual income valuation is most closely related to P/B. When the present value of expected future residual income is positive (negative), the justified P/B based on fundamentals is greater than (less than) 1.
- When fully consistent assumptions are used to forecast earnings, cash flow, dividends, book value, and residual income through a full set of pro forma (projected) financial statements, and the same required rate of return on equity is used as the discount rate, the same estimate of value should result from a residual income, dividend discount, or free cash flow valuation. In practice, however, analysts may find one model much easier to apply and possibly arrive at different valuations using the different models.

- The residual income model assumes the clean surplus relation $B_t = B_{t-1} + E_t - D_t$. In other terms, the ending book value of equity equals the beginning book value plus earnings less dividends, apart from ownership transactions.
- In practice, to apply the residual income model most accurately, the analyst needs to
  - adjust book value of common equity for off-balance-sheet items; and
  - adjust reported net income to reflect clean surplus accounting, where necessary.
- Continuing residual income is residual income after the forecast horizon. Frequently, one of the following assumptions concerning continuing residual income is made:
  - Residual income continues indefinitely at a positive level.
  - Residual income is zero from the terminal year forward.
  - Residual income declines to zero as ROE reverts to the cost of equity over time.
  - Residual income declines to some mean level.

PROBLEMS

1. Based on the following information, determine whether Vertically Integrated Manufacturing (VIM) earned any residual income for its shareholders in 2001:
   - VIM had total assets of $3,000,000, financed with twice as much debt capital as equity capital.
   - VIM's pretax cost of debt is 6 percent and cost of equity capital is 10 percent.
   - VIM had EBIT of $300,000 and was taxed at a rate of 40 percent.

2. Using the following information, estimate the intrinsic value of VIM's common stock using the residual income model:
   - VIM had total assets of $3,000,000, financed with twice as much debt capital as equity capital.
   - VIM's pretax cost of debt is 6 percent and cost of equity capital is 10 percent.
   - VIM had EBIT of $300,000 and was taxed at a rate of 40 percent. EBIT is expected to continue at $300,000 indefinitely.
   - VIM's book value per share is $20.
   - VIM has 50,000 shares of common stock outstanding.

3. Palmetto Steel, Inc. (PSI), maintains a dividend payout ratio of 80 percent because of its limited opportunities for expansion. Its return on equity is 15 percent. The required rate of return on PSI equity is 12 percent, and its long-term growth rate is 3 percent. Compute the justified P/B based on forecasted fundamentals, consistent with the residual income model and a constant growth rate assumption.

4. Because New Market Products (NMP) markets consumer staples, it is able to make use of considerable debt in its capital structure; specifically, 90 percent of the company's total assets of $450,000,000 are financed with debt capital. Its cost of debt is 8 percent before taxes, and its cost of equity capital is 12 percent. NMP achieved a pretax income of $5.1 million in 2001 and had a tax rate of 40 percent. What was NMP's residual income for 2001?

5. In 2002, Smithson-Williams Investments (SWI) achieved an operating profit after taxes of €10 million on total assets of €100 million. Half of its assets were financed with debt with a pretax cost of 9 percent. Its cost of equity capital is 12 percent, and its tax rate is 40 percent. Did SWI achieve a positive residual income?

6. Calculate the economic value added (EVA) or residual income, as requested, for each of the following:

   A.   NOPAT = $100
        Beginning book value of debt = $200
        Beginning book value of equity = $300
        WACC = 11 percent
        Calculate EVA.

   B.   Net income = €5.00
        Dividends = €1.00
        Beginning book value of equity = €30.00
        Required rate of return on equity = 11 percent
        Calculate residual income.

   C.   Return on equity = 18 percent
        Required rate of return on equity = 12 percent
        Beginning book value of equity = €30.00
        Calculate residual income.

7. (Adapted from 2000 CFA Level II exam) Jim Martin is using economic value added (EVA) and market value added (MVA) to measure the performance of Sundanci. Martin uses the fiscal 2000 information below for his analysis.

   • Adjusted net operating profit after tax (NOPAT) is $100 million.
   • Total capital is $700 million (no debt).
   • Closing stock price is $26.
   • Sundanci has 84 million shares outstanding.
   • The cost of equity is 14 percent.

   Calculate the following for Sundanci. Show your work.

   A.   EVA for fiscal 2000
   B.   MVA as of fiscal year-end 2000

8. Protected Steel Corporation (PSC) has a book value of $6 per share. PSC is expected to earn $0.60 per share forever and pays out all of its earnings as dividends. The required rate of return on PSC's equity is 12 percent. Calculate the value of the stock using the following:

   A.   Dividend discount model
   B.   Residual income model

9. Notable Books (NB) is a family-controlled company that dominates the retail book market. NB has book value of $10 per share, is expected to earn $2.00 forever, and pays out all of its earnings as dividends. Its required return on equity is 12.5 percent. Place a value on the stock of NB using the following:

   A.   Dividend discount model
   B.   Residual income model

10. Simonson Investment Trust International (SITI) is expected to earn $4.00, $5.00, and $8.00 for the next three years. SITI will pay annual dividends of $2.00, $2.50, and $20.50 in each of these years. The last dividend includes the liquidating payment to shareholders at the end of Year 3 when the trust terminates. SITI's book value is $8 per share and its required return on equity is 10 percent.

    A. What is the current value per share of SITI according to the dividend discount model?

    B. Calculate per-share book value and residual income for SITI for each of the next three years and use those results to find the stock's value using the residual income model.

    C. Calculate return on equity and use it as an input to the residual income model to calculate SITI's value.

11. Foodsco Incorporated (FI), a leading distributor of food products and materials to restaurants and other institutions, has a remarkably steady track record in terms of both return on equity and growth. At year-end 2000, FI had a book value of $30 per share. For the foreseeable future, you expect the company to achieve a ROE of 15 percent (on trailing book value) and to pay out one-third of its earnings in dividends. Your required return is 12 percent. Forecast FI's residual income for the year ending December 31, 2005.

12. Lendex Electronics (LE) has had a great deal of turnover of top management for several years and was not followed by analysts during this period of turmoil. Because the company's performance has been improving steadily for the past three years, technology analyst Steve Kent recently reinitiated coverage of LE. A meeting with management confirmed Kent's positive impression of LE's operations and strategic plan. Kent decides LE merits further analysis.

    Careful examination of LE's financial statements revealed that the company had negative other comprehensive income from changes in the value of available-for-sale securities in each of the past five years. How, if at all, should this observation about LE's other comprehensive income affect the figures that Kent uses for the company's ROE and book value for those years?

13. Retail fund manager Seymour Simms is considering the purchase of shares in upstart retailer Hot Topic Stores (HTS). The current book value of HTS is $20 per share, and its market price is $35. Simms expects long-term ROE to be 18 percent, long-term growth to be 10 percent, and cost of equity to be 14 percent. What conclusion would you expect Simms to arrive at if he uses a single-stage residual income model to value these shares?

14. Dayton Manufactured Homes (DMH) builds prefabricated homes and mobile homes. Both favorable demographics and the likelihood of slow, steady increases in market share should enable DMH to maintain its ROE of 15 percent and growth rate of 10 percent over time. DMH has a book value of $30 per share and the required rate of return on its equity is 12 percent. Compute the value of its equity using the single-stage residual income model.

15. Use the following inputs and the finite horizon form of the residual income model to compute the value of Southern Trust Bank (STB) shares as of December 31, 2001:

- ROE will continue at 15 percent for the next five years (and 10 percent thereafter) with all earnings reinvested (no dividends paid).
- Cost of Equity = 10 percent.
- B_0 =$10 per share (at year-end 2001).
- Premium over book value at the end of five years will be 20 percent.

For Problems 16 and 17, use the following data for Taiwan Semiconductor Manufacturing Ltd. (TSM). Refer to Equation 5-8 in the text.

- Current price = TWD81.
- Cost of equity = 14.33 percent.
- Five-year forecast of growth in book value = 22 percent.
- Book value per share = TWD16.47.
- Analyst EPS forecasts are TWD2.07 for 2002 and TWD4.81 for 2003.
- Analysts expect ROE to stabilize at 25 percent from 2002 through 2011, and then decline to 20 percent through 2022 in Problem 16 and 2023 in Problem 17.
- As of the beginning of 2002, an analyst estimates the intrinsic value using the residual income model as TWD59.18 with the zero premium shown in Example 5-10.

16. In the above analysis, the analyst uses the multistage residual income model and assumes that TSM's ROE will fade toward the cost of equity capital after 2022. How would her conclusion about TSM's valuation change if she believed that the persistence parameter for this company should be 0.90 (rather than 0.60) because of patent protection for some of TSM's technology?

17. Having completed the revised analysis, which gives TSM greater credit for its patented technology, the analyst realizes that the changes warrant an additional adjustment. Although she generally employs a 20-year time frame when implementing the multistage residual income model, she believes that TSM's ROE will remain at 20 percent through 2023 before fading toward the cost of equity capital. (Recall she is now using a persistence parameter of 0.90.) How does this extension of the period with above-normal ROE alter her valuation of TSM?

18. Shunichi Kobayashi is valuing United Parcel Service (NYSE: UPS). Kobayashi has made the following assumptions:

- Book value per share is estimated at $9.62 on December 31, 2001.
- EPS will be 22 percent of the beginning book value per share for the next eight years.
- Cash dividends paid will be 30 percent of EPS.
- At the end of the eight-year period, the market price per share will be three times the book value per share.
- The beta for UPS is 0.60, the risk-free rate is 5.00 percent, and the equity risk premium is 5.50 percent.

The current market price of UPS is $59.38, which indicates a current P/B of 6.2.

A. Prepare a table showing the beginning and ending book values, net income, and cash dividends annually for the eight-year period.

B. Estimate the residual income and the present value of residual income for the eight years.

C. Estimate the value per share of UPS stock using the residual income model.

D. Estimate the value per share of UPS stock using the dividend discount model. How does this value compare with the estimate from the residual income model?

19. Boeing Company (NYSE: BA) has a current stock price of $49.86. It also has a P/B of
3.57 and book value per share of $13.97. Assume that the single-stage growth model is
appropriate for valuing BA. Boeing's beta is 0.80, the risk-free rate is 5.00 percent, and
the equity risk premium is 5.50 percent.

   A. If the growth rate is 6 percent and the ROE is 20 percent, what is the justified P/B
      for Boeing?
   B. If the growth rate is 6 percent, what ROE is required to yield Boeing's current P/B?
   C. If the ROE is 20 percent, what growth rate is required for Boeing to have its current
      P/B?

REFERENCES

American Accounting Association Financial Accounting Standards Committee. 2001. "Equity Valuation Models and Measuring Goodwill Impairment." *Accounting Horizons*. Vol. 15, No. 2: 161–170.

American Institute of Certified Public Accountants. 2002. Exposure Draft: *Proposed Statement on Auditing Standard: Consideration of Fraud in a Financial Statement Audit*. 28 February 2002.

Amihud, Yakov, and Haim Mendelson. 1986. "Liquidity and Stock Returns." *Financial Analysts Journal*. Vol. 42, No. 3: 43–48.

Articles of Incorporation. 1959. The Institute of Chartered Financial Analysts.

Bauman, Mark P. 1999. "Importance of Reported Book Value in Equity Valuation." *Journal of Financial Statement Analysis*. Vol. 4, No. 2: 31–40.

Benninga, Simon Z., and Oded H. Sarig. 1997. *Corporate Finance: A Valuation Approach*. New York: McGraw-Hill.

Bernstein, Richard, and Carmen Pigler. 1997. "An Analysis of EVA® " *Quantitative Viewpoint*. Merrill Lynch. 19 December.

Bernstein, Richard, Kari Bayer, and Carmen Pigler. 1998. "An Analysis of EVA® Part II." *Quantitative Viewpoint*. Merrill Lynch. 3 February.

Block, Stanley B. 1999. "A Study of Financial Analysts: Practice and Theory." *Financial Analysts Journal*. Vol. 55, No. 4: 86–95.

Bodie, Zvi, Alex Kane, and Alan J. Marcus. 2001. *Investments*, 5th edition. New York: McGraw-Hill/Irwin.

Brealey, Richard A., and Stewart C. Myers. 2000. *Principles of Corporate Finance*, 6th edition. New York: McGraw-Hill/Irwin.

Burmeister, Edwin, Richard Roll, and Stephen A. Ross. 1994. "A Practitioner's Guide to Arbitrage Pricing Theory." *A Practitioner's Guide to Factor Models*. Charlottesville, VA: The Research Foundation of the Institute of Chartered Financial Analysts.

Chan, Louis K.C., Narasimhan Jegadeesh, and Josef Lakonishok. 1999. "The Profitability of Momentum Strategies." *Financial Analysts Journal*. Vol. 55, No. 6: 80–90.

Copeland, Tom, Tim Koller, and Jack Murrin. 1994. *Valuation: Measuring and Managing the Value of Companies*, 2nd edition. New York: John Wiley & Sons. pp. 374–407.

Copeland, Tom, Tim Koller, and Jack Murrin. 2000. *Valuation: Measuring and Managing the Value of Companies*, 3rd edition. New York: John Wiley & Sons.

Cornell, Bradford. 2001. "Is the Response of Analysts to Information Consistent with Fundamental Valuation? The Case of Intel." *Financial Management*. Vol. 30, No. 1: 113–136.

Dechow, Patricia M., Amy P. Hutton, and Richard G. Sloan. 1999. "An Empirical Assessment of the Residual Income Valuation Model." *Journal of Accounting and Economics*. Vol. 26, No. 1–3: 1–34.

DeFusco, Richard A., Dennis W. McLeavey, Jerald E. Pinto, and David E. Runkle. 2001. *Quantitative Methods for Investment Analysis*. Charlottesville, VA: AIMR.

Dimson, Elroy, Paul Marsh, and Mike Staunton. 2000. *The Millennium Book: A Century of Investment Returns*. London: ABN-AMRO and London Business School.

Edwards, Edgar O., and Philip W. Bell. 1961. *The Theory and Measurement of Business Income*. Berkeley, CA: University of California Press.

Ehrbar, Al. 1998. *EVA: The Real Key to Creating Wealth*. New York: John Wiley & Sons.

Ellis, Charles D., with James R. Vertin. 1991. *Classics II: Another Investor's Anthology*. Charlottesville, VA: Association for Investment Management and Research.

Fabozzi, Frank J. 2000. *Fixed Income Analysis for the Chartered Financial Analyst® Program*. New Hope, PA: Frank J. Fabozzi Associates.

Fairfield, Patricia M. 1994. "P/E, P/B and the Present Value of Future Dividends." *Financial Analysts Journal*. Vol. 50, No. 4: 23–31.

Fairfield, Patricia M., and J. Scott Whisenant. 2001. "Using Fundamental Analysis to Assess Earnings Quality: Evidence from the Center for Financial Research and Analysis." *Journal of Accounting, Auditing and Finance*. Vol. 16, No. 4: 273–299.

Fama, Eugene F., and Kenneth R. French. 1992. "The Cross-Section of Expected Stock Returns." *Journal of Finance*. Vol. 47, No. 2: 427–466.

Fama, Eugene F., and Kenneth R. French. 1993. "Common Risk Factors in the Returns on Stocks and Bonds." *Journal of Financial Economics*. Vol. 33, No. 1: 3–53.

Fama, Eugene F., and Kenneth R. French. 2001. "Disappearing Dividends: Changing Firm Characteristics or Lower Propensity to Pay?" *Journal of Financial Economics*. Vol. 60, No. 1: 3–43.

Fama, Eugene F., and Kenneth R. French. 2001. "The Equity Premium." CRSP Working Paper 552.

Feltham, Gerald A., and James A. Ohlson. 1995. "Valuation and Clean Surplus Accounting for Operating and Financial Activities." *Contemporary Accounting Research*. Vol. 11, No. 4: 689–731.

Fleck, Shelby A., Scott D. Craig, Michael Bodenstab, Trevor Harris, and Elmer Huh. 2001. *Technology: Electronics Manufacturing Services*. Industry Overview; Morgan Stanley Dean Witter. 28 March.

Frankel, Richard M., and Charles M.C. Lee. 1999. "Accounting Diversity and International Valuation." Working Paper, May.

Fuller, Russell J., and Chi-Cheng Hsia. 1984. "A Simplified Common Stock Valuation Model." *Financial Analysts Journal*. Vol. 40, No. 5: 49–56.

Gordon, Myron J. 1962. *The Investment, Financing, and Valuation of the Corporation*. Homewood, IL: Richard D. Irwin.

Gordon, Myron J., and Eli Shapiro. 1956. "Capital Equipment Analysis: The Required Rate of Profit." *Management Science*. Vol. 3, No. 1: 102–110.

Graham, Benjamin. 1963. "The Future of Financial Analysis." *Financial Analysts Journal*. Vol. 19, No. 3: 65–70.

Graham, Benjamin, and David L. Dodd. 1934. *Security Analysis*. New York: McGraw-Hill Professional Publishing.

Grant, Julia, and Larry Parker. 2001. "EBITDA!" *Research in Accounting Regulation*. Vol. 15: 205–211.

Grossman, Sanford, and Joseph E. Stiglitz. 1980. "On the Impossibility of Informationally Efficient Markets." *American Economic Review*. Vol. 70, No. 3: 393–408.

Hackel, Kenneth S., and Joshua Livnat. 1991. *Cash Flow and Security Analysis*. Business One-Irwin.

Hackel, Kenneth S., Joshua Livnat, and Atul Rai. 1994. "The Free Cash Flow/Small-Cap Anomaly." *Financial Analysts Journal*. Vol. 50, No. 5: 33–42.

Haley, Adele M. 1993. "Valuing the Securities of Pharmaceutical Companies." *Industry Analysis: The Health Care Industry*. Charlottesville, VA: AIMR.

Harris, Mary, and Karl A. Muller, III. 1999. "The Market Valuation of IAS versus U.S. GAAP Accounting Measures Using Form 20-F Reconciliations." *Journal of Accounting and Economics*. Vol. 26, No. 1–3: 285–312.

Harris, Robert S., and Felicia C. Marston, 1994. "Value versus Growth Stocks: Book-to-Market, Growth, and Beta." *Financial Analysts Journal*. Vol. 50, No. 5: 18–24.

Hawkins, David F. 1998. "Detecting Lower Earnings Quality." *Accounting Bulletin #69*. Merrill Lynch Global Securities Research & Economics Group.

Hawkins, George B., and Michael A. Paschall. 2000. *CCH Business Valuation Guide*. Chicago: CCH Incorporated.

Hayes, Douglas A. 1962. "Ethical Considerations in the Professional Stature of Analysts." *Financial Analysts Journal*. Vol. 18, No. 5: 53–56.

Higgins, Robert C. 2001. *Analysis for Financial Management*, 6th edition. Boston: McGraw-Hill/Irwin.

Hirst, D. Eric, and Patrick E. Hopkins. 2000. *Earnings: Measurement, Disclosure, and the Impact on Equity Valuation*. Charlottesville, VA: Research Foundation of AIMR and Blackwell Series in Finance.

Hooke, Jeffrey. 1998. *Security Analysis on Wall Street: A Comprehensive Guide to Today's Valuation Methods*. New York: John Wiley & Sons.

Internal Revenue Service Revenue Ruling 68-609, 1968-2 C.B. 327.

International Federation of Accountants. March 2001. International Standards on Auditing 240. *The Auditor's Responsibility to Consider Fraud and Error in an Audit of Financial Statements*.

Jagannathan, Ravi, Ellen R. McGrattan, and Anna Scherbina. 2000. "The Declining U.S. Equity Premium." *Quarterly Review*. Federal Reserve Bank of Minnesota. Vol. 24, No. 4: 3–19.

Jensen, Michael C., and William H. Meckling. 1976. "Theory of the Firm: Managerial Behavior, Agency Costs and Ownership Structure." *Journal of Financial Economics*. Vol. 3, No. 4: 305–360.

Kisor, Manown, Jr., and Volkert S. Whitbeck. 1963. "A New Tool in Investment Decision-Making." *Financial Analysts Journal*. Vol. 19, No. 3: 55–62.

Landsman, Wayne, and Alan C. Shapiro. 1995. "Tobin's q and the Relation Between Accounting ROI and Economic Return." *Journal of Accounting, Auditing and Finance*. Vol. 10: 103–121.

Latané, Henry A., and Charles P. Jones. 1979. "Standardized Unexpected Earnings—1971–77." *Journal of Finance*, Vol. 34, No. 3: 717–724.

Lee, Charles M.C., and Bhaskaran Swaminathan. 1999. "Valuing the Dow: A Bottom-Up Approach." *Financial Analysts Journal*. Vol. 55, No. 5: 4–23.

Lee, Charles M.C., and Bhaskaran Swaminathan. 2000. "Price Momentum and Trading Volume." *Journal of Finance*. Vol. 55, No. 5: 2017–2069.

Lee, Charles M.C., James Myers, and Bhaskaran Swaminathan. 1999. "What Is the Intrinsic Value of the Dow?" *Journal of Finance*. Vol. 54, No. 5: 1693–1741.

Levitt, Arthur. 28 September 1998. "The Numbers Game," a speech at the NYU Center for Law and Business, New York. http://www.sec.gov/news/speech/speecharchive/1998/spch220.txt

Lo, Kin, and Thomas Lys. 2000. "The Ohlson Model: Contributions to Valuation Theory, Limitations, and Empirical Applications." *Journal of Accounting, Auditing and Finance*. Vol. 15, No. 3: 337–367.

Lundholm, Russell J., and Terrence B. O'Keefe. 2001a. "Reconciling Value Estimates from the Discounted Cash Flow Model and the Residual Income Model." *Contemporary Accounting Research*. Vol. 18, No. 2: 311–335.

Lundholm, Russell J., and Terrence B. O'Keefe. 2001b. "On Comparing Residual Income and Discounted Cash Flow Models of Equity Valuation: A Response to Penman 2001." *Contemporary Accounting Research*. Vol. 18, No. 4: 693–696.

Malkiel, Burton G., and John G. Cragg. 1970. "Expectations and the Structure of Share Prices." *American Economic Review*. Vol. 60, No. 4: 601–617.

Martin, Thomas A., Jr. 1998. "Traditional Equity Valuation Methods." *Equity Research and Valuation Techniques*. Charlottesville, VA: AIMR.

Mehra, Rajnish, and Edward C. Prescott. 1985. "The Equity Premium: A Puzzle." *Journal of Monetary Economics*. Vol. 15, No. 2: 145–161.

Merrill Lynch & Co. 1989–2001. *Quantitative Viewpoint: Institutional Factor Surveys*. Global Securities Research & Economics Group.

Michaud, Richard O. 1999. *Investment Styles, Market Anomalies, and Global Stock Selection*. Research Foundation of the ICFA: AIMR.

Miller, Merton H., and Franco Modigliani. 1961. "Dividend Policy, Growth, and the Valuation of Shares." *Journal of Business*. Vol. 34, No. 4: 411–433.

Modigliani, Franco, and Merton H. Miller. 1958. "The Cost of Capital, Corporation Finance and the Theory of Investment." *American Economic Review*. Vol. 48, No. 3: 261–297.

Moody's. 2000. *Putting EBITDA in Perspective*. Moody's Investors Service Global Credit Research.

Nathan, Siva, Kumar Sivakumar, and Jayaraman Vijayakumar. 2001. "Returns to Trading Strategies Based on Price-to-Earnings and Price-to-Sales Ratios." *Journal of Investing*. Vol. 10, No. 2: 17–28.

Ohlson, James A. 1995. "Earnings, Book Values, and Dividends in Equity Valuation." *Contemporary Accounting Research*. Vol. 11, No. 4: 661–687.

O'Shaughnessy, James P. 1997. Ch. 8. *What Works on Wall Street: A Guide to the Best-Performing Investment Strategies of All Time.* New York: McGraw-Hill Professional Publishing.

Penman, Stephen H. 2001. "On Comparing Cash Flow and Accrual Accounting Models for Use in Equity Valuation: A Response to Lundholm and O'Keefe." *Contemporary Accounting Research.* Vol. 18, No. 4: 681–692.

Penman, Stephen H., and Theodore Sougiannis. 1998. "A Comparison of Dividend, Cash Flow and Earnings Approaches to Equity Valuation." *Contemporary Accounting Research.* Vol. 15, No. 3: 343–383.

Peterson, Pamela P., and David R. Peterson. 1996. *Company Performance and Measures of Value Added.* Charlottesville, VA: The Research Foundation of the ICFA.

Phillips, Lawrence, Paul Munter, and Thomas Robinson. 2002. "Employee Stock Option Plans—Tax Planning Considerations." *Ohio CPA Journal.* Vol. 61, No. 1: 12–17.

Porter, Michael E. 1998. *Competitive Advantage: Creating and Sustaining Superior Performance.* New York: The Free Press.

Rappaport, Alfred. 1997. *Creating Shareholder Value: A Guide For Managers and Investors*, Revised and Updated. New York: The Free Press.

Reilly, Frank K., and Keith C. Brown. 2000. *Investment Analysis and Portfolio Management*, 6th edition. Orlando, FL: Dryden Press.

Robinson, Thomas, Julia Grant, Robert Kauer, and Peter Woodlock. 1998. "Earnings Management and Bond Risk Premia in the Individual versus Institutional Bond Markets." *Research in Accounting Regulation.* Vol. 12: 77–92.

Robinson, Thomas R., and Julia Grant. 1997. "The Impact of Earnings Management on Bond Risk Premia." *Advances in Accounting.* Vol. 15: 169–192.

Ross, Stephen A., Randolph W. Westerfield, and Jeffrey F. Jaffe. 2002. *Corporate Finance*, 6th edition. New York: McGraw-Hill/Irwin.

Salsman, Richard M. 1997. "Using Market Prices to Guide Sector Rotation." *Economic Analysis for Investment Professionals.* Charlottesville, VA: AIMR. 48–55.

Schieneman, Gary S. 2000. "Cross-Border Financial Statement Analysis." *Practical Issues in Equity Analysis.* Charlottesville, VA: AIMR. 27–35.

Schilit, Howard. 2002. *Financial Shenanigans*, 2nd edition. New York: McGraw-Hill.

Schilit, Howard M. 1993. *Financial Shenanigans: How to Detect Accounting Gimmicks and Fraud in Financial Reports.* New York: McGraw-Hill.

Senchack, A.J., Jr., and John D. Martin. 1987. "The Relative Performance of the PSR and PER Investment Strategies." *Financial Analysts Journal.* Vol. 43, No. 2: 46–56.

Sharpe, William F., Gordon J. Alexander, and Jeffery V. Bailey. 1999. *Investments*, 6th edition. Upper Saddle River, NJ: Prentice Hall.

Shrieves, Ronald E., and John M. Wachowicz, Jr. 2001. "Free Cash Flow (FCF), Economic Value Added (EVA^{TM}), and Net Present Value (NPV): A Reconciliation of Variations of Discounted-Cash-Flow (DCF) Valuation." *The Engineering Economist.* Vol. 46, No. 1: 33–52.

Siegel, Jeremy J. 1998. *Stocks for the Long Run,* 2nd edition. New York: McGraw-Hill.

Stern, G. Bennett, III. 1991. *The Quest for Value.* New York: HarperCollins.

Stux, Ivan E. 1994. "Earnings Growth: The Driver of Equity Value." Morgan Stanley *Global Equity and Derivatives Markets.* 12 July 1994.

Tobin, James. 1969. "A General Equilibrium Approach to Monetary Theory." *Journal of Money, Credit and Banking.* Vol. 1, No. 1: pp. 15–29.

University of California, Regents Meeting. January 2001. *Summary of University of California Retirement Plan Asset/Liability Forecast Study.*

Value Line. 2001. *How to Invest in Common Stocks: The Complete Guide to Using the Value Line Investment Survey.* New York: Value Line Publishing.

White, Gerald I., Ashwinpaul C. Sondhi, and Dov Fried. 1998. *The Analysis and Use of Financial Statements*, 2nd edition. New York: John Wiley & Sons.

Wild, John J., Leopold A. Bernstein, and K.R. Subramanyam. 2001. *Financial Statement Analysis*, 7th edition. New York: McGraw-Hill/Irwin.

Williams, John Burr. 1938. *The Theory of Investment Value*. Cambridge, MA: Harvard University Press.

Yardeni, Edward. 2000. "How to Value Earnings Growth." *Topical Study #49*. Deutsche Banc Alex Brown.

Young, S. David. 1999. "Some Reflections on Accounting Adjustments and Economic Value Added." *Journal of Financial Statement Analysis*. Vol. 4, No. 2: 7–19.

GLOSSARY

Abnormal earnings   See "Residual income."

Absolute valuation model   A model that specifies an asset's intrinsic value.

Accounting estimates   Estimates of items such as the useful lives of assets, warranty costs, and the amount of uncollectible receivables.

Acquisition   A combination of two corporations, usually with the connotation that the combination is not one of equals.

Active investment managers   Managers who hold portfolios that differ from their benchmark portfolio in an attempt to produce positive risk-adjusted returns.

Adjusted present value (APV)   As an approach to valuing a company, the sum of the value of the company, assuming no use of debt, and the net present value of any effects of debt on company value.

Alpha (or abnormal return)   The return on an asset in excess of the asset's required rate of return; the risk-adjusted return.

Asset-based valuation   An approach to valuing natural resource companies that estimates company value on the basis of the market value of the natural resources the company controls.

Basic earnings per share   Total earnings divided by the weighted-average number of shares actually outstanding during the period.

Benchmark   The comparison portfolio used to evaluate performance.

Benchmark value of the multiple   In using the method of comparables, the value of a price multiple for the comparison asset; when we have comparison assets (a group), the mean or median value of the multiple for the group of assets.

Bill-and-hold basis   Sales on a bill-and-hold basis involve selling products but not delivering those products until a later date.

Bond indenture   A legal contract specifying the terms of a bond issue.

Bond yield plus risk premium method   A method of determining the required rate of return on equity (cost of equity) for a company as the sum of the yield to maturity on the company's long-term debt plus a risk premium.

Book value of equity (or book value)   Shareholders' equity (total assets minus total liabilities) minus the value of preferred stock; common shareholders' equity.

Book value per share   Book value of equity divided by the number of common shares outstanding.

Bottom-up forecasting approach   A forecasting approach that involves aggregating the individual company forecasts of analysts into industry forecasts, and finally into macroeconomic forecasts.

Bottom-up investing   An approach to investing that focuses on the individual characteristics of securities rather than on macroeconomic or overall market forecasts.

Breakup value (or private market value)   The value of a business calculated as the sum of the expected value of the business's parts if the parts were independent entities.

Brokerage   The business of acting as agents for buyers or sellers, usually in return for commissions.

Build-up method   A method for determining the required rate of return on equity as the sum of risk premiums, in which one or more of the risk premiums is typically subjective rather than grounded in a formal equilibrium model.

Buy-side analysts   Analysts who work for investment management firms, trusts, and bank trust departments, and similar institutions.

Capital charge   The company's total cost of capital in money terms.

Capitalization rate   The divisor in the expression for the value of a perpetuity.

Catalyst   An event or piece of information that causes the marketplace to re-evaluate the prospects of a company.

Clean surplus accounting   Accounting that satisfies the condition that all changes in the book value of equity other than transactions with owners are reflected in income.

Clean surplus relation   The relationship between earnings, dividends, and book value in which ending book value is equal to the beginning book value plus earnings less dividends, apart from ownership transactions.

Comprehensive income   All changes in equity other than contributions by, and distributions to, owners; income under clean surplus accounting.

Continuing residual income   Residual income after the forecast horizon.

Control premium   An increment or premium to value associated with a controlling ownership interest in a company.

Cost leadership   The competitive strategy of being the lowest-cost producer while offering products comparable to those of other firms, so that products can be priced at or near the industry average.

Cost of equity   The required rate of return on common stock.

Cyclical businesses   Businesses with high sensitivity to business- or industry-cycle influences.

Differential expectations   Expectations that differ from consensus expectations.

Differentiation   The competitive strategy of offering unique products or services along some dimensions that are widely valued by buyers so that the firm can command premium prices.

Diluted earnings per share   Total earnings divided by the number of shares that would be outstanding if holders of securities such as executive stock options and convertible bonds exercised their options to obtain common stock.

Dirty surplus items   Items that affect comprehensive income but that bypass the income statement.

Discount   To reduce the cash flow's value in allowance for how far away it is in time.

Discount rate   Any rate used in finding the present value of a future cash flow.

Divestiture   The action of selling some major component of a business.

Dividend discount model (DDM)   A present value model of stock value that views the intrinsic value of a stock as present value of the stock's expected future dividends.

Dividend displacement of earnings   The concept that dividends paid now displace earnings in all future periods.

Dividend rate   The most recent quarterly dividend multiplied by four.

Due diligence   Investigation and analysis in support of a recommendation; the failure to exercise due diligence may sometimes result in liability according to various securities laws.

Earnings yield   Earnings per share divided by price; the reciprocal of the P/E ratio.

Economic profit   See "Residual income."

Economic sectors   Large industry groupings.

Economic value added (EVA®)   A commercial implementation of the residual income concept; the computation of EVA® is the net operating profit after taxes minus the cost of capital, where these inputs are adjusted for a number of items.

Enterprise value (EV)   Total company value (the market value of debt, common equity, and preferred equity) minus the value of cash and investments.

Equilibrium   The condition in which supply equals demand.

Equity charge   The estimated cost of equity capital in money terms.

Equity risk premium   The expected return on equities minus the risk-free rate.

Expectational arbitrage   Investing on the basis of differential expectations.

Expected holding-period return   The expected total return on an asset over a stated holding period; for stocks, the sum of the expected dividend yield and the expected price appreciation over the holding period.

Factor risk premium   A factor's expected return in excess of the risk-free rate.

Factor sensitivity   An asset's sensitivity to a particular factor (holding all other factors constant).

Fair value   The price at which an asset or liability would change hands between a willing buyer and a willing seller when the former is not under any compulsion to buy and the latter is not under any compulsion to sell.

Fixed-rate perpetual preferred stock   Stock with a specified dividend rate that has a claim on earnings senior to the claim of common stock, and no maturity date.

Focus   The competitive strategy of seeking a competitive advantage within a target segment or segments of the industry, either on the basis of cost leadership (**cost focus**) or differentiation (**differentiation focus**).

Free cash flow to equity   The cash flow available to a company's common shareholders after all operating expenses, interest, and principal payments have been made, and necessary investments in working and fixed capital have been made.

Free cash flow to equity model   A model of stock valuation that views a stock's intrinsic value as the present value of expected future free cash flows to equity.

Free cash flow to the firm   The cash flow available to the company's suppliers of capital after all operating expenses (including taxes) have been paid and necessary investments in working and fixed capital have been made.

Free cash flow to the firm model   A model of stock valuation that views the value of a firm as the present value of expected future free cash flows to the firm.

Fundamentals   Economic characteristics of a business such as profitability, financial strength, and risk.

Going-concern assumption   The assumption that the business will maintain its business activities into the foreseeable future.

Going-concern value   A business's value under a going-concern assumption.

Goodwill   An intangible asset that represents the excess of the purchase price of an acquisition over the value of the net assets acquired.

Gross domestic product   A money measure of the goods and services produced within a country's borders over a stated time period.

Growth phase   A stage of growth in which a company typically enjoys rapidly expanding markets, high profit margins, and an abnormally high growth rate in earnings per share.

Human capital   The value of skills and knowledge possessed by the workforce.

Impairment   As used in accounting, a downward adjustment.

Industry structure   An industry's underlying economic and technical characteristics.

Initial public offering (IPO)   The initial issuance of common stock registered for public trading by a formerly private corporation.

Intrinsic value   The value of the asset given a hypothetically complete understanding of the asset's investment characteristics.

Investment constraints   Internal or external limitations on investments.

Investment objectives   Desired investment outcomes; includes risk objectives and return objectives.

Investment strategy   An approach to investment analysis and security selection.

Justified (fundamental) P/E   The price-to-earnings ratio that is fair, warranted, or justified on the basis of forecasted fundamentals.

Justified price multiple (or **warranted price multiple** or **intrinsic price multiple**)   The estimated fair value of the price multiple, usually based on forecasted fundamentals or comparables.

Leading dividend yield   Forecasted dividends per share over the next year divided by current stock price.

Leading P/E (or **forward P/E** or **prospective P/E**)   A stock's current price divided by next year's expected earnings.

Leveraged recapitalization   A corporate transaction involving the repurchase of common stock in which some stock remains in the hands of the public.

Liquidation value   The value of a company if the company were dissolved and its assets sold individually.

Liquidity discount   A reduction or discount to value that reflects the lack of depth of trading or liquidity in that asset's market.

Look-ahead bias   Bias that may result from the use of information that is not contemporaneously available.

Management buyout (MBO)   A corporate transaction in which management repurchases all outstanding common stock, usually using the proceeds of debt issuance.

Marketability discount   A reduction or discount to value for shares that are not publicly traded.

Market efficiency   A finance perspective on capital markets that deals with the relationship of price to intrinsic value. The **traditional efficient markets formulation** asserts that an asset's price is the best available estimate of its intrinsic value. The **rational efficient markets formulation** asserts that investors should expect to be rewarded for the costs of information gathering and analysis by higher gross returns.

Market risk premium   The expected return on the market minus the risk-free rate.

Mature growth rate   The earnings growth rate in a company's mature phase; an earnings growth rate that can be sustained long term.

Mature phase   A stage of growth in which the company reaches an equilibrium in which investment opportunities on average just earn their opportunity cost of capital.

Merger   The combination of two corporations.

Method based on forecasted fundamentals   An approach to using price multiples that relates a price multiple to forecasts of fundamentals through a discounted cash flow model.

Method of comparables   An approach to valuation that involves using a price multiple to evaluate whether an asset is relatively fairly valued, relatively undervalued, or relatively overvalued when compared to a benchmark value of the multiple.

Mispricing   Any departure of the market price of an asset from the asset's estimated intrinsic value.

Molodovsky effect   The observation that P/Es tend to be high on depressed EPS at the bottom of a business cycle, and tend to be low on unusually high EPS at the top of a business cycle.

Momentum indicators   Valuation indicators that relate either price or a fundamental (such as earnings) to the time series of their own past values (or in some cases to their expected value).

No-growth company   A company without positive expected net present value projects.

No-growth value per share   The value per share of a no-growth company, equal to the expected level amount of earnings divided by the stock's required rate of return.

Normalized earnings per share (or **normal earnings per share**)   The earnings per share that a business could achieve currently under mid-cyclical conditions.

Opportunity cost   The alternative return that investors forgo when they commit to an investment.

Other comprehensive income   Changes to equity that bypass (are not reported in) the income statement; the difference between comprehensive income and net income.

Pairs arbitrage   A trade in two closely related stocks that involves buying the relatively undervalued stock and selling short the relatively overvalued stock.

PEG   The P/E-to-growth ratio, calculated as the stock's P/E divided by the expected earnings growth rate.

Perpetuity   A stream of level payments extending to infinity.

Portfolio implementation problem   The part of the execution step of the portfolio management process that involves the implementation of portfolio decisions by trading desks.

Portfolio selection/composition problem   The part of the execution step of the portfolio management process in which investment strategies are integrated with expectations to select a portfolio of assets.

Present value model (or **discounted cash flow model**)   A model of intrinsic value that views the value of an asset as the present value of the asset's expected future cash flows.

Present value of growth opportunities (or **value of growth**)   The difference between the actual value per share and the no-growth value per share.

Price momentum   The compound rate of return on an asset over some specified time horizon.

Price multiple   The ratio of a stock's market price to some measure of value per share.

Purchased in-process research and development costs   Costs of research and development in progress at an acquired company; often, part of the purchase price of an acquired company is allocated to such costs.

Quality of earnings analysis   The investigation of issues relating to the accuracy of reported accounting results as reflections of economic performance; quality of earnings analysis is broadly understood to include not only earnings management, but also balance sheet management.

Rational efficient markets formulation   See "Market efficiency."

Relative strength (RSTR) indicators   Valuation indicators that compare a stock's performance during a period either to its own past performance or to the performance of some group of stocks.

Relative valuation models   A model that specifies an asset's value relative to the value of another asset.

Required rate of return   The minimum rate of return required by an investor to invest in an asset, given the asset's riskiness.

Residual income (or **economic profit** or **abnormal earnings**)   Earnings for a given time period, minus a deduction for common shareholders' opportunity cost in generating the earnings.

Residual income model (RIM) (also **discounted abnormal earnings model** or **Edwards-Bell-Ohlson model**)   A model of stock valuation that views intrinsic value of stock as the sum of book value per share plus the present value of the stock's expected future residual income per share.

Return on invested capital (ROIC)   The after-tax net operating profits as a percent of total assets or capital.

Risk premium   Compensation for risk, measured relative to the risk-free rate.

Scaled earnings surprise   Unexpected earnings divided by the standard deviation of analysts' earnings forecasts.

Screening   The application of a set of criteria to reduce an investment universe to a smaller set of investments.

Sector neutral   Said of a portfolio for which economic sectors are represented in the same proportions as in the benchmark, using market-value weights.

Sector rotation strategy   A type of top-down investing approach that involves emphasizing different economic sectors based on considerations such as macroeconomic forecasts.

Sell-side analysts   Analysts who work at brokerages.

Shareholders' equity   Total assets minus total liabilities.

Special purpose entity (SPE)   A non-operating entity created to carry out a specified purpose, such as leasing assets or securitizing receivables.

Spin-off   A transaction in which a corporation separates off and separately capitalizes a component business, which is then transferred to the corporation's common stockholders.

Spreadsheet modeling   As used in this book, the use of a spreadsheet in executing a dividend discount model valuation, or other present value model valuation.

Standardized unexpected earnings (SUE)   Unexpected earnings per share divided by the standard deviation of unexpected earnings per share over a specified prior time period.

Supernormal growth   Above average or abnormally high growth rate in earnings per share.

Survivorship bias   Bias that may result when failed or defunct companies are excluded from membership in a group.

Sustainable growth rate   The rate of dividend (and earnings) growth that can be sustained for a given level of return on equity, keeping the capital structure constant over time and without issuing additional common stock.

Tangible book value per share   Common shareholders' equity minus intangible assets from the balance sheet, divided by the number of shares outstanding.

Technical indicators   Momentum indicators based on price.

Terminal price multiple   The price multiple for a stock assumed to hold at a stated future time.

Terminal share price   The share price at a particular point in the future.

Terminal value of the stock (or **continuing value of the stock**)   The analyst's estimate of a stock's value at a particular point in the future.

Tobin's q   The ratio of the market value of debt and equity to the replacement cost of total assets.

Top-down forecasting approach   A forecasting approach that involves moving from international and national macroeconomic forecasts to industry forecasts and then to individual company and asset forecasts.

Top-down investing   An approach to investing that typically begins with macroeconomic forecasts.

Tracking risk   The standard deviation of the differences between a portfolio's and a benchmark's returns.

Traditional efficient markets formulation   See "Market efficiency."

Trailing dividend yield   Current market price divided by the most recent quarterly per-share dividend multiplied by four.

Trailing P/E (or current P/E)   A stock's current market price divided by the most recent four quarters of earnings per share.

Transition phase   The stage of growth between the growth phase and the mature phase of a company in which earnings growth typically slows.

Underlying earnings (or persistent earnings, continuing earnings, or core earnings)   Earnings excluding nonrecurring components.

Unexpected earnings (also earnings surprise)   The difference between reported earnings per share and expected earnings per share.

Valuation   The estimation of the value of an asset on the basis of variables perceived to be related to future investment returns, or on the basis of comparisons with closely similar assets.

Visibility   The extent to which a company's operations are predictable with substantial confidence.

Weighted-average cost of capital (WACC)   The weighted average of the required rate of return on equity, the after-tax required rate of return on debt, and required rate of return on preferred stock.

Write-down   A reduction in the value of an asset as stated in the balance sheet.

ABOUT THE
CFA PROGRAM

The Chartered Financial Analyst® designation (CFA®) is a globally recognized standard of excellence for measuring the competence and integrity of investment professionals. To earn the CFA charter, candidates must successfully pass through the CFA Program, a global graduate-level self-study program that combines a broad curriculum with professional conduct requirements as preparation for a wide range of investment specialties.

Anchored by a practice-based curriculum, the CFA Program is focused on the knowledge identified by professionals as essential to the investment decision-making process. This body of knowledge maintains current relevance through a regular, extensive survey of practicing CFA charterholders across the globe. The curriculum covers 10 general topic areas ranging from equity and fixed-income analysis to portfolio management to corporate finance, all with a heavy emphasis on the application of ethics in professional practice. Known for its rigor and breadth, the CFA Program curriculum highlights principles common to every market so that professionals who earn the CFA designation have a thoroughly global investment perspective and a profound understanding of the global marketplace.

www.cfainstitute.org

ABOUT THE AUTHORS

John D. Stowe, CFA, Ph.D., is Head of Curriculum Development at CFA Institute. Prior to joining CFA Institute, he was a professor of finance and associate dean at the University of Missouri-Columbia, where he taught investments and corporate finance. Stowe has won several teaching awards and has published frequently in academic and professional journals in finance. Stowe earned his BA from Centenary College and his Ph.D. in economics from the University of Houston. He obtained his CFA charter in 1995 and began grading CFA examinations in 1996.

Thomas R. Robinson, CFA, Ph.D., CPA, CFP, is an associate professor of accounting and director of the master of professional accounting program at the University of Miami. He is also managing director of Robinson, Desmond & Zwerner, a state registered investment advisory firm. Robinson has a BA in economics from the University of Pennsylvania and a masters and Ph.D. in accounting from Case Western Reserve University. He is a Certified Public Accountant (Ohio), Certified Financial Planner® (CFP®) certificant, and Chartered Financial Analyst® (CFA®) charterholder. Prior to joining the University of Miami, Robinson practiced public accounting and financial planning for ten years and served as a consultant in the areas of financial statement analysis and valuation.

Jerald E. Pinto, CFA, is Director in the CFA and CIPM Programs Division at CFA Institute. Before coming to CFA Institute in 2002, he was a consultant to corporations, foundations, and partnerships in investment planning, portfolio analysis, and quantitative analysis. He has also worked in the investment and banking industries in New York City and taught finance at New York University's Stern School of Business. He holds an MBA from Baruch College and a Ph.D. in finance from the Stern School. He obtained his CFA charter in 1992.

Dennis W. McLeavey, CFA, is Head of Professional Development Products at CFA Institute. During his twenty-five year academic career, he has taught at the University of Western Ontario, the University of Connecticut, the University of Rhode Island (where he founded a student-managed fund), and Babson College. McLeavey completed a doctorate in production management and industrial engineering at Indiana University in 1972, and obtained his CFA charter in 1990.

Index

Online Instructor Tools

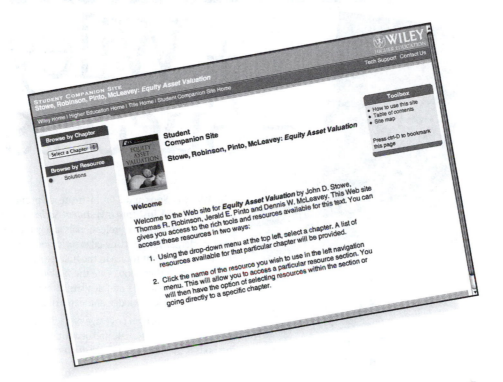

Make the best use of *Equity Asset Valuation* in the classroom with Wiley's robust online component for instructors. It includes an Instructor's Manual with teaching tips and solutions to the end-of-chapter problems as well as PowerPoint Slides. Go to www.wiley.com/college/stowe to register and access this material.

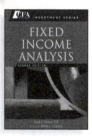

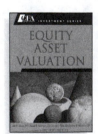